Emerging Security Challenges

Emerging Security Challenges

*American Jihad, Terrorism, Civil War,
and Human Rights*

SEUNG-WHAN CHOI

Praeger Security International

 PRAEGER™

An Imprint of ABC-CLIO, LLC
Santa Barbara, California • Denver, Colorado

Library of Congress Cataloging-in-Publication Data

Names: Choi, Seung-Whan, author.
Title: Emerging security challenges : American jihad, terrorism, civil war, and
    human rights / Seung-Whan Choi.
Description: Santa Barbara, California : Praeger, [2018] | Series: Praeger security
    international | Includes bibliographical references and index.
Identifiers: LCCN 2017056366 (print) | LCCN 2017059052 (ebook) |
    ISBN 9781440863059 (ebook) | ISBN 9781440863042 (alk. paper)
Subjects: LCSH: Terrorists—Recruiting—United States. | Terrorism—Religious
    aspects—Islam. | Terrorism—Prevention. | Civil war. | Human rights. |
    Security, International.
Classification: LCC HV6432 (ebook) | LCC HV6432 .C468 2018 (print) |
    DDC 363.3250973—dc23
LC record available at https://lccn.loc.gov/2017056366

ISBN: 978-1-4408-6304-2 (print)
      978-1-4408-6305-9 (ebook)

22 21 20 19 18   1 2 3 4 5

This book is also available as an eBook.

Praeger
An Imprint of ABC-CLIO, LLC

ABC-CLIO, LLC
130 Cremona Drive, P.O. Box 1911
Santa Barbara, California 93116-1911
www.abc-clio.com

This book is printed on acid-free paper ∞

Manufactured in the United States of America

To Shali Luo and William Yangyang Choi,
with much love and affection

Contents

Preface

Although the contemporary world creates various security challenges on both domestic and international fronts, surprisingly little scholarly work attempts to provide a comprehensive analysis of how domestic and international security concerns should be addressed. In this single volume, I delve into four new security dangers that have emerged since the collapse of the Cold War: America's homegrown terrorists, international terrorist activities, the outbreak of civil war, and human rights violations. The big questions that I examine in this book include the following: Why do some otherwise average Americans become terrorists on American soil or abroad? How should political leaders respond to these growing terrorist threats? What are the causes and effects of terrorist organizations? What factors precipitate the outbreak of civil war? How do political leaders prevent human rights violations and torture? As a way to tackle these questions effectively, I offer a single, coherent analysis of the four salient and interrelated security issues utilizing state-of-the art statistical techniques, which should help readers increase their scientific knowledge of contemporary security studies. Although a few edited volumes may deal with more than one security issue, they are written by several different authors who come from diverse perspectives and approach these questions with widely varying methodologies. Put differently, this single volume analyzes a broader range of imperative security challenges than most single- or multiauthored books, and it avoids the inconsistencies in coverage, quality, and style that are common in many edited volumes.

While writing 11 chapters for this book, I have received valuable comments and suggestions from many friends and colleagues. I wish to acknowledge my deep gratitude to Katherine Blachut, William Braun, Rebecca Clendenen, Tom Del Regno, Anahit Gomtsian, Patricia Hajek, Maria Hartas, Muhammad Jehangir, Christine Kim, Eric Kloczkowski, Dina Lupancu, Ryan Maness, Josh Pakter, Thomas A. Papanicolas, Matthew Powers, Saimithra Reddy, Mexhit Rexhepi, Dimitrios Simitsis, Keith Simonds, Cori Smith, and Nora Willy. I am especially indebted to Katharine M. Floros, Emilie M. Hafner-Burton, Patrick James, Dongwook Kim, Hunjoon Kim, Jin Man Lee, Chungshik Moon, Johann Park, Yiagadeesen (Teddy) Samy, Todd Sandler, Jae Hyeok Shin, Abraham Singer, Gary Uzonyi, and John Van Benthuysen, who challenged my ideas and thoughts and eventually helped me improve earlier versions of this book. Finally, I thank Padraic (Pat) Carlin at Praeger for his efficient work in helping publish this book.

Introduction

Given that contemporary security problems are not simple but rather multifaceted, complex, and interrelated, this book addresses four emerging and interconnected security issues. Put differently, just as solving a puzzle requires that all the pieces are appropriately placed in relation to one another, a scholarly book that aims to help us understand the complex phenomenon of contemporary security should cover multiple related security issues. A book that presents a single security issue while turning a blind eye to other closely related issues is akin to getting only one piece of a puzzle placed correctly. There are some collaborative volumes that attempt to deal with more than one issue by having the various issues addressed by several different contributors; however, the major recurring weakness of these collaborative volumes is that their theoretical perspectives are often too diverse, with inconsistent methodologies that all too often speak past each other. This solo-authored book overcomes this issue by applying a consistent theoretical and empirical approach to closely related security issues.

In order to further understand the multifaceted and interrelated nature of contemporary security problems, we need to look at the recent history of modern international relations. It is widely known that after the Cold War rivalry between the capitalist West and the Communist East ended following the collapse of the former Soviet Union, scholars and policy makers speculated that conventional approaches to military engagement would become obsolete in the world of foreign policy. The primary rationale for this assumption was the decreased likelihood of interstate wars due to the relatively peaceful and stable transition to the post–Cold War world. This expectation has rarely failed in the new security environment in which peace-loving democracies seem to triumph over bellicose autocracies, as noted in democratic peace studies (see Russett and Oneal 2001; Choi 2016a, 2016b). The 21st century has already witnessed political upheavals that further challenged old ways of thinking about security interests, including the attacks of September 11, the Boston Marathon bombing, and the San Bernardino massacre. These incidents created and reinforced a fear of the possibility of terrorist attacks occurring anywhere and at any moment with no warning, largely replacing the fear of traditional warfare. The threat and nature of terrorism requires an appropriately new and broader view of security studies; accordingly, scholars and policy makers must refocus their research agenda from the old conditions of interstate crisis to new conditions of internal crisis.

During the Cold War period, when interstate crisis was a dominant research theme, scholars and policy makers mainly understood world politics through the lens of superpower rivalry, resulting in the valuation of most other security issues as less relevant to world governments. The emergence of internal crisis in the post–Cold War world has, however, shifted the focus away from superpower rivalries and forced scholars and policy makers to broaden the perspective and scope of security studies. Any analytical frame that continues to center on interstate conflict is not suited for a world that is no longer understood in terms of a bipolar balance of power. The prevalence of internal crisis calls for a new manner of thinking about security research. By analyzing a series of pressing security problems emerging largely from internal crisis in the post–Cold War era, this book answers the call.

This book looks specifically into emerging issues and challenges that national governments must contend with in regard to four crucial security areas of internal crisis: the growing threat of America's homegrown jihadists, the continuing rise of terrorism, the pervasiveness of civil war, and the consequences of gross domestic violations of human rights. How might national governments best survive these four new challenges that make up the tangled landscape of the contemporary security environment? This question is important insofar as it will generate new dialogues on emerging security problems that confront national governments. Previous studies fail to provide such a comprehensive and cutting-edge examination of this pressing issue. This book tackles the question of the survivability of national governments in the midst of these four newly emerged and rapidly growing security challenges. In doing so, this book offers a dire warning to governments that remain largely unprepared for the new security environment and the new approaches it will require.

How closely are the four security issues presented connected to one another? While America's homegrown jihadists have engaged in attacks within the United States (e.g., the Boston Marathon bombings on April 15, 2013), they often instead go abroad to fight for their beliefs (e.g., a U.S.-born man named Abu Hurayra Al-Amriki blew himself up in a terrorist attack in Syria on May 25, 2014). When American jihadists join international terrorist organizations such as the Islamic State of Iraq and Syria and al-Qaeda, the danger to security and stability is often magnified at both global and domestic fronts. The rise of terrorism, in turn, causes a deterioration in the quality of human rights for politically disadvantaged people or minority groups within a national territory for reasons of security exigency. Also of concern—and controversy—is that national governments may ignore the legal rights of terrorist suspects and turn to torture in the name of national security and expediency. The internal crisis created by terrorist violence and human rights abuses may expedite the development of civil wars. The outbreak of civil wars is then likely to endanger domestic and international stability (see Piazza 2008). What are the best ways for national governments to deter such danger? Institutionalizing the rule of law may serve as a preventive measure to internal crisis and prevent potentially destabilizing human rights violations. The establishment of military laws related to soldier recruitment may be another answer. Each of these issues has the potential for perpetuating the conditions that give rise to the others. Hence, this book operates from the observation that national governments suffer from these four multifaceted and interrelated security problems that together develop into a formidable threat to the stability of national governance and which demands new approaches to these emerging problems.

To date, much scholarship looks at security issues in isolation from each other in a manner that approximates a vacuum. This approach limits the ability of previously published books to successfully cater to students of contemporary security studies who wish to grasp quickly, efficiently, and effectively—within a single book—how such important security issues are evolving, what policy initiatives should be drawn, and what security topics should be identified for future research. As briefly mentioned earlier, though a few edited volumes may include more than one topic, they are written by several authors, and so they come from multiple perspectives and employ different research methods. This solo-authored book offers a coherent perspective, accompanied with state-of-the-art empirical analyses on the crucial security concerns in the four research areas identified. It examines a broader range of security issues than most single- or multi-authored books, while avoiding the inconsistency of coverage and quality that is a problem with many edited volumes.

A majority of traditional security studies in book format take a qualitative approach, drawing heavily on a small number of case studies (e.g., James 2012; Hayes 2015).[1] Although qualitative research is useful for pointing out the particular characteristics of a few cases, it is far less effective at uncovering general patterns across all nation-states and over time, as can be achieved with the use of advanced statistical techniques. Researchers have grown increasingly open to primarily quantitative research, but very few security books have been published with an emphasis on statistical analysis. Each chapter of this book relies on the most current statistical approach to find systematic, empirical evidence of security trends for more than 100 sample countries. Given that security studies should provide useful policy recommendations, this book also offers potentially effective policy suggestions at the end of each chapter. In sum, this book is unique to the extent that it deals with multiple pressing security issues; employs a systematic, empirical approach; and strives to make feasible policy recommendations pertaining to growing security threats coming mostly from inside a national territory.

The main themes of each chapter of this book are presented in the following chapter-by-chapter outline. A recent series of terrorist plots originating on American soil prompted the Obama administration to include homegrown terrorism as a key component of its National Security Strategy in May 2010 (Benson 2010). Despite this, more deadly terrorist attacks carried out by homegrown terrorists, such as the San Bernardino massacre on December 2, 2015, and the Boston Marathon bombings on April 15, 2013, continue to shock Washington in spite of this shift in focus toward this new emerging threat. These incidents are directly associated with a growing number of American citizens and residents who are radicalized with jihadist ideology online while not necessarily being directly connected or affiliated with international terrorist organizations. These days, the growth of homegrown terrorism alarms not only politicians but the general public as well; however, to date there is little scientific political research that offers a way of understanding where America's homegrown terrorists come from and how their threats should be most effectively countered. Chapter 1 aims to answer these imperative security questions and to draw possible policy suggestions on how to confront the growing threats of American jihad.

Chapter 2 offers another component of analysis on America's homegrown terrorism. Although the news media frequently report on American-born citizens who fight abroad for their jihadist Islamic beliefs, the public is less informed about *why* these American jihadists choose to fight abroad rather than to attack seemingly more easily accessible targets at home. To examine this pressing but largely understudied issue, Chapter 2 considers 11 alternative explanations: ethnic ties to the target country, eight personal characteristics of the perpetrator, counterterrorism capabilities of the target country, and the perceived legitimacy of foreign fighting over domestic fighting. Based on an original dataset of 235 American jihadists collected since the terrorist attacks of September 11, 2001, this chapter conducts a series of logistic regression analyses to find an answer.

Chapters 3–5 present stimulating perspectives on terrorist activities that have caught Washington's attention since 9/11. Edward Snowden's public disclosure of several top-secret U.S. and British government mass surveillance programs has sparked intense debates over the proper balance between Internet privacy and national security. These debates are also related to the broader discussion on whether democratic countries should restrict civil liberties in their attempts to deter acts of terrorism. In the spirit of this debate, Chapter 3 investigates an empirical question of whether countries with large winning coalitions (i.e., democracies) are likely to decrease the protections afforded by civil liberties when confronted with the threat of terrorism.

The theoretical literature on terrorist outbidding has long argued that domestic competition among terrorist organizations leads to an increase in political violence as a result of each organization's effort to distinguish itself and stand out from the crowd. However, there is very little supporting evidence for this theory in recent empirical literature. Why does such a discrepancy between theory and empirical findings exist? Unfortunately, existing studies neglect to reconcile the gap between the two research activities. Chapter 4 seeks to resolve this failure by reanalyzing an empirical model of terrorist outbidding.

A central component to our understanding of the root causes of terrorism is the question of how economic performance is associated with acts of terrorism. For example, academic and policy circles often raise a question of whether a strong national economy is beneficial to the war on terrorism. Unlike previous research, Chapter 5 conceptualizes economic growth into two important sectors (i.e., agricultural and industrial) and categorizes terrorism into three different forms (i.e., domestic, international, and suicide). Chapter 5 then evaluates whether this revised conceptualization and categorization provide a better understanding of the relationship between different types of economic growth and types of terrorist activities.

The security exigency during the West and East rivalry stifled the promotion of human rights. But the post–Cold War environment has encouraged national leaders to reconsider the foundational tenet of human rights: each person in any nation-state is a moral and rational being who deserves to be treated with dignity. Accordingly, researchers have gained momentum in producing a plethora of research projects on the subject, while recognizing some key limitations of their data on human rights conditions. This means that the empirical findings reported in existing studies may not be as credible as they should be, which hampers the ability for these studies to inform policy makers and other researchers. By relying on inaccurate human rights data, researchers may have drawn their inferences and conclusions too hastily in the past three decades. If so, reexamining

previous findings with more accurate measures of human rights violations should be the first step to facilitating further research and improving
our understanding of this important issue. As an attempt to remedy the
potential bias of the previously reported empirical patterns, Chapter 6 reevaluates 18 existing studies utilizing new human rights data and offers
novel findings on the causes and effects of human rights violations.

The topic of naming and shaming political regimes for their offenses
has been a popular subject for study, and several studies have examined
its effect on political and economic outcomes, as well as its potential conditional effect on targeted-state repression during the past decade (e.g.,
Hafner-Burton 2008; Murdie and Peksen 2014). However, because the literature introduces inconsistent arguments and findings pertaining to the
impact of naming and shaming, Chapter 7 takes a closer look at the question of whether shaming really triggers humanitarian military intervention intended to ameliorate the conditions created by abuses of human
rights.

Whether human rights treaties provide the international community
with an enforceable mechanism for penalizing human rights abusers is
another controversial and widely discussed issue. A particular point of
contention is that some studies claim that preferential trade agreements
that contain clauses which enforce a reduction of economic benefits to
human rights abusers can, in some important instances, help to improve
human rights conditions in beneficiary countries. Chapter 8 examines the
dampening effect of human rights laws on the conditions of human rights.

Chapter 9 delves into the causes of a particular aspect of human rights
abuse—torture. Why does the cessation of political torture differ so widely
across countries? Under what conditions are countries willing to terminate their use of torture? To answer these questions, Chapter 9 puts forward and tests the hypothesis that leaders with higher levels of education
are more effective in stopping the use of torture by their government than
those with less education. The relationship between states' use of repressive acts like torture has important ramifications for the preservation and
advancement of security for individuals and the conditioning of their relationship to the state as either conflictive or collaborative.

Chapters 10 and 11 discuss two important but unexplored institutional
factors that influence the outbreak of civil wars. Chapter 10 argues that
when a minority group (defined in terms of ethnicity, religion, and/or
political ideology) has the opportunity to resolve its grievances nonviolently by way of an impartial justice system, members of the group are
less likely to develop feelings of hopelessness and bitterness, which, ultimately, cause some individuals to resort to political violence as the only
conceivable avenue through which they can hope to challenge the government. Therefore, a rule of law system that is perceived as legitimate by

those it serves may help prevent minority groups from turning to violent rebellion; presumably, such a state is less likely to experience civil war.

Chapter 11 contends that a state's choice between two opposing military manpower systems affects its vulnerability to civil violence. The postulation is that, compared to conscripted soldiers, volunteer soldiers are more likely to regard themselves as guardians of a sacred nation and are, therefore, more inclined to perceive episodes of social unrest as opportunities which call on them to defend certain moral positions in defiance of sitting governments. Consider, for example, the 1999 military intervention laid out by Pakistani general Pervez Musharraf: he reasoned that the nation was in a state of political turmoil and economic collapse so that "[the military intervened] with all sincerity, loyalty and selfless devotion to the country" (quoted in Dugger October 13, 1999). From this perspective, the volunteer military sees itself as acting extra-politically, if you will, in order to safeguard the unity and security of the nation that it has volunteered to defend.

NOTE

1. Notable exceptions to case-oriented studies are Russett and Oneal (2001), Choi and James (2005), Enders and Sandler (2006), and Choi (2016a, 2016b).

REFERENCES

Benson, Pam. May 27, 2010. "Homegrown Terrorist Threat to Be Part of National Security Strategy." CNN. http://www.cnn.com/2010/POLITICS/05/27/homegrown.terror/index.html

Choi, Seung-Whan. 2016a. "A Menace to the Democratic Peace? Dyadic and Systemic Difference." *International Studies Quarterly* 60(3): 573–577.

Choi, Seung-Whan. 2016b. *New Explorations into International Relations: Democracy, Foreign Investment, Terrorism and Conflict.* Athens: University of Georgia Press.

Choi, Seung-Whan and Patrick James. 2005. *Civil-Military Dynamics, Democracy, and International Conflict: A New Quest for International Peace.* New York: Palgrave.

Dugger, Celia W. October 13, 1999. "Coup in Pakistan." *New York Times.* http://www.nytimes.com/1999/10/13/world/coup-pakistan-overview-pakistan-army-seizes-power-hours-after-prime-minister.html

Enders, Walter and Todd Sandler. 2006. *The Political Economy of Terrorism.* New York: Cambridge University Press.

Hafner-Burton, Emilie. 2008. "Sticks and Stones." *International Organization* 62(4): 689–716.

Hayes, Jarrod. 2015. *Constructing National Security.* New York: Cambridge University Press.

James, Patrick. 2012. *Canada and Conflict.* Oxford: Oxford University Press.

Murdie, Amanda and Dursun Peksen. 2014. "The Impact of Human Rights INGO Shaming on Humanitarian Interventions." *Journal of Politics* 76(1): 215–228.

Piazza, James. 2008. "Incubators of Terror." *International Studies Quarterly* 52(3): 469–488.

Russett, Bruce and John Oneal. 2001. *Triangulating Peace*. New York: W.W. Norton & Company.

CHAPTER 1

American Jihad, Muslim Americans, and the General Public

The terrorist attacks of September 11, 2001, focused Washington's attention on international threats; however, a recent series of terror-related plots on American soil prompted the Obama administration to include homegrown terrorism as an additional key part of its National Security Strategy in May 2010 (Benson 2010). Several deadly terrorist incidents, such as the Boston Marathon bombings on April 15, 2013, and the Fort Hood shooting on November 5, 2009, also pressured Attorney General Eric Holder to take decisive action against homegrown terrorism by creating the Domestic Terrorism Executive Committee that includes officials from the Justice Department, the FBI, and U.S. Attorneys' offices (Barrett 2014). Despite a growing awareness, homegrown terrorism still has the capacity to shock and surprise. For example, Douglas McCain, 33, a one-time aspiring rapper and basketball fan from California, was the first American killed while fighting for the Islamic State in Iraq and Syria (ISIS), prompting disbelief and shock in the media. Consequently, by 2014 the Obama administration was tracking as many as 300 Americans supposedly fighting with ISIS (Healy 2014; Schmidt and Schmitt 2014). In addition, there have been a growing number of American citizens and residents radicalized with jihadist ideology online, who are not necessarily connected to international terrorist organizations outside the United States. This new trend of homegrown terrorism has become a major security concern for politicians, policy makers, and the public; however, there is little scientific political research that could offer an understanding of where America's homegrown terrorists come from and how their threats should be countered.

While political empiricists have not yet tackled the topic of American ji-hadists, there have been numerous stimulating works in other disciplines and by numerous think tanks. For instance, in his seminal article "What Makes a Homegrown Terrorist?" economist Krueger (2008) compares the demographic backgrounds of 63 homegrown terrorists with a sample of approximately 1,000 Muslim Americans,[1] and his data analysis indi-cates that homegrown terrorists tend to be better educated, younger, and non-U.S. citizens. While several existing studies have advanced this area of research, they were unable to analyze more recent incidents of home-grown terrorism such as the Boston Marathon bombings and the first sui-cide attack in Syria by American citizen Abu Hurayra Al-Amriki, which may offer more relevant information to the homeland security community today.[2] Concerns about homegrown terrorism have also spurred a variety of think tank reports. Of these policy-oriented works, Bjelopera's (2013, 2) Congressional Research Service Report for Congress offers a timely quali-tative analysis on American jihadist terrorism but importantly concludes that "no workable general profile of domestic violent jihadists exists." Bergen et al.'s (2013, 13) report provides another useful threat assessment about jihadist terrorism but similarly asserts "there is no single ethnic pro-file for homegrown jihadist extremists." Simcox and Dyer's (2013, 86) re-port performs a thorough frequency table analysis on the characteristics of al-Qaeda in the United States, showing an important finding that "the majority of individuals who committed al-Qaeda related offenses were young, educated men." Although these policy reports are informative for politicians, anti-terrorism authorities, policy makers, and the public, their findings may be less instrumental for scholars to draw inferences about general behavioral patterns of individual American jihadists because they are based on descriptive and anecdotal episodes rather than systematic statistical analysis.

In this study, I look into the personal characteristics of America's home-grown jihadists by compiling a list of 235 terrorists active since 9/11, and then employing a set of weighted logistic regression models, I compare this list with Pew survey data on other Muslim Americans and with the broader American population. My statistical analysis is performed under the premise that terrorists do not fall from the sky; rather, their radicaliza-tion is strongly related to their personal experiences and backgrounds as underlined by Hambrick and Mason's (1984) study, which views demo-graphic characteristics to be acceptable proxies to capture differences in the thinking of individuals. My statistical analysis, supplemented by six cases of homegrown terrorism, shows three distinctive characteristics of American jihadists: (1) they are likely to be young, male, and economi-cally disadvantaged; (2) when compared to other Muslim Americans, they are more likely to have citizenship status; and (3) they possess a better education than the Muslim Americans who expressed a favorable view of al-Qaeda in a 2011 survey interview. These findings attest that the personal attributes of America's homegrown terrorists during the past 13 years have changed in some important respects from those found in previous studies. Accordingly, these findings may help identify the mechanisms and motives of radicalization, thus providing updated information for the counterterrorism community so that it can develop new optimal strategies for preventing the proliferation of homegrown terrorism on American soil. For example, a significant counterterrorism measure may be to establish a special hotline program within local communities, as the German and British governments are currently experimenting with. Through such a program, young people who are troubled with radical ideas can ask questions without having to resort to the police. A hotline is also of value to local people who may wish to report something innocuous but are fearful of involving law enforcement (Pantucci 2014).

The rest of this study is organized as follows: the first section describes data collection, survey data, hypotheses of interest, and statistical estimation strategy; the second section presents a discussion of empirical results; the third section introduces six case studies of America's homegrown jihadists as a supplementary analysis to the statistical examination; and the fourth section summarizes the main findings of this study and puts forward several important policy implications.

AMERICA'S HOMEGROWN JIHADISTS, MUSLIM AMERICANS, AND THE GENERAL PUBLIC

This section explains my data collection on American jihadists, Bjelopera's (2013) list of jihadist attacks and plots, and the Pew survey data. This explanation leads to an introduction of 12 hypotheses of interest that will be used in the following statistical analysis.

America's homegrown jihadists: Relying on various open sources,[3] I collected individual information on America's homegrown jihadists, compiling a database of 235 terrorists. The data collection started immediately after September 11, 2001—a critical historical juncture of America's global War on Terror—and ended on June 30, 2014. America's homegrown jihadists are defined as American citizens, legal permanent residents, or temporary visitors who were radicalized largely within the United States, who were either indicted or convicted for involvement in terrorist activities, or who were killed before they could be indicted (see Bjelopera 2013). When arrested individuals were acquitted of terrorism charges or charged with lesser crimes such as immigration violations, they were not included in the database. A majority of jihadists living in the United States are American citizens, indicating that the terrorist threat starts in America's own backyard. Of the 235 jihadists, 102 are U.S.-born citizens, 56 are naturalized citizens, 40 are legal permanent residents, and 37 are temporary visitors. The data collection is comprehensive, including American jihadists who supported, plotted, or committed terrorist violence, regardless of their success in carrying out their plans. Such data is advantageous in comparison to other collections, which are confined to only those individuals who successfully carried out terrorist acts.

In an effort to verify the reliability and validity of my data collection as well as estimated results, I also consulted Bjelopera's (2013) jihadist list and made use of it as part of the robustness check in the next section. As a specialist in Organized Crime and Terrorism at the Congressional Research Service, Bjelopera prepared a report for members and committees of Congress on January 23, 2013. In the report, he identifies 63 homegrown violent jihadist plots or attacks in the United States since 9/11 and discusses those plots involving persons indicted at either the federal or state level. I garnered a list of his jihadist names from Table B-2 of the report. Of the 235 jihadists in my database, 141 jihadists overlap with Bjelopera's jihadist list. Of these 141 jihadists, 69 are U.S.-born citizens, 37 are naturalized citizens, 17 are legal residents, and 18 are visitors.

Muslim Americans: In order to assess the demographics, attitudes, and experience of Muslims in America, the Pew Research Center has conducted two national probability surveys of Muslims living in the United States. The first phone interview was conducted with 1,050 adult Muslims from January 24 to April 30, 2007, and the second one with 1,033 adult Muslim respondents ran from April 14 to July 22, 2011. Because identifying a representative sample of a minority religious group that is both highly diverse and highly dispersed was quite a daunting task, the Pew Research Center employed a complex sampling design to obtain a probability sample of Muslims in America. More important, in order to make the sample selection representative of the true Muslim population, the Pew Research Center constructed sample weights to be used for any point estimates.[4] Otherwise, statistical estimates based on unweighted data are likely to be unreliable and thus unrepresentative of the true Muslim population living in the United States (for more technical details, see Pew Research Center May 2007, August 2011).[5] I combine the 2011 survey data with my database of 235 American jihadists and use the pooled data as the baseline statistical analysis of this study; the 2007 survey data is then employed as part of a robustness test. As will be shown shortly, both baseline and robustness tests yield quite similar results.

General public: In addition to the Muslim population in America, it is relevant to look at the broader public in relation to the list of American jihadists, since they are also a subgroup of the entire population that includes Muslims, and we therefore cannot assume that they are distinct solely by virtue of their Muslim faith. Every year, the Pew Research Center conducts interviews on various issues with a sample of the general public. In addition to thematic questions, these surveys ask for basic demographic information such as income and education. Because they also include a survey item about religious affiliation, respondents can be identified as Protestant, Roman Catholic, Muslim, and so on. Of different general public surveys, I choose the General Public Survey on Veterans & Generational Change conducted from September 1–15, 2011 (see Pew Research Center September 2011). The total number of respondents is 2,003, and English and Spanish are used for phone interview. Because the survey year is the same as the 2011 Muslim Americans survey, the concern about the comparability between surveys should be minimal. For the purposes of this study, I gather individual demographic information from the general public survey and compare it with that of my American jihadist database.

Twelve variables of interest: By pooling together my jihadist data and the Pew survey data, I created 12 variables of interest for use in my statistical analysis: *American jihadist, education, income, age, male, married, citizen,* and *five regions of birth place* (*USA, Middle East and North Africa, sub-Saharan Africa, South Asia,* and *other*). The selection of these variables largely depends on their availability in both datasets. The dependent variable, *American jihadist,* is a dichotomous measure, recoded as "1" when an American jihadist is observed in the pooled dataset and as "0" otherwise. Naturally, 235 American jihadists are recorded based on my data collection, and 1,033 non-jihadist Muslim Americans are identified from the 2011 Pew survey on Muslim Americans. For estimation, I employ a logistic regression model[6] adjusted for Huber-White robust standard errors because the nature of the dependent variable is binary. I rely on two-tailed significance tests because presumed relationships between predictors and the outcome variable can be either positive or negative as explained.

As the focus of this study is American jihadists, the discussion of causal relationships is confined to previous studies that examine American cases. Krueger's (2008) study is the first devoted to the examination of the personal backgrounds of American jihadists. After comparing the characteristics of 63 indicted or convicted homegrown Islamic terrorists with those of a sample of 1,050 Muslim Americans from the 2007 Pew phone survey, he finds a positive correlation between education and terrorism: American jihadists are on average better educated than average Muslims living in the United States. Gartenstein-Ross and Grossman (2009) examine 117 homegrown Islamic terrorists in the United States and United Kingdom and conclude that the causal relationship between education and terrorism is negative, as compared to internationally known terrorists. After analyzing 171 individuals who were convicted for al-Qaeda–related offenses or committed suicide attacks between 1997 and 2011 in the United States, Simcox and Dyer (2013) contend that the majority of jihadists were well educated. Collectively, these studies showcase an inconclusive relationship between education and terrorism. Thus, in an attempt to address the question of how the level of education that an American jihadist possessed at the time of the attack or planned attack is related to America's homegrown terrorism, *education* is the first independent variable in my statistical model. The educational category is coded as "1" for high school graduate or less, "2" for some college, "3" for college degree, and "4" for postgraduate degree.

The significance of poverty as a predictor of terrorism is controversial among scholars, politicians, policy makers, and journalists; however, there are few scholarly studies on this issue with a particular focus on American jihadists. Gartenstein-Ross and Grossman's (2009) study finds that the job prospects of homegrown Islamic terrorists in the United States and United Kingdom were dismal. Yet Krueger's (2008) statistical models predict no significant effect of poverty on being charged as an American homegrown terrorist. Simcox and Dyer's (2013) recent study also indicates no correlation between a lack of employment prospects and committing al-Qaeda–related offenses or having committed suicide attacks in the United States. Accordingly, I created *income* as the second independent variable and evaluated how well an American jihadist lived (low, middle, or high level).

Moreover, it appears that young Americans are the most likely to be radicalized by jihadist ideology and then to follow through and engage in terrorist activities (see Krueger 2007, 2008; Roy 2008). After identifying 139 Muslim Americans who were linked to terrorist violence during the period from September 11, 2001, to December 31, 2009, Schanzer, Kurzman, and Moosa (2010) present a bar graph, depicting two-thirds of homegrown jihadists as being less than 30 years old. Young jihadists, passionate and impulsive, may be more prone to an extreme view that characterizes Muslims as oppressed and marginalized all over the world and are more likely to act in response (Krueger 2008). Temple-Raston (2010) states that "intelligence officials say there is a wave of young people who are attracted to the adventure of jihad but would like to skip all the rigors of Islam, such as reading the Quran and fasting." Perhaps, young Muslims join jihadist rebels for the adventure and excitement of holy war rather than for religion itself. Hence, the third variable, *age,* examines how old an American jihadist was at the time of arrest or attack.

Despite the fact that American jihadists are overwhelmingly male, gender is another potential predictor. My jihadist database includes 9 females and 226 males. When they examine 221 homegrown extremists since 9/11, Bergen et al. (2013) find that regardless of ethnic backgrounds, most homegrown jihadists are male—only eight women are involved in homegrown terrorism. Simcox and Dyer's (2013) report indicates that 163 out of 171 terrorist offenses were committed by men. Thus, the fourth variable, *male,* looks into the effect of gender on the probability of being charged or identified as an American jihadist.

The fifth variable, *married,* assesses how marital status is associated with homegrown terrorism given that the presence (or lack) of a family may affect the radicalization of American jihadists. Although some religions such as Roman Catholicism and Buddhism generally require celibacy for certain positions, Islam is a strong advocate of marriage. Marriage is considered to be a religious duty among Muslims, and thus, it is a moral safeguard as well as a social necessity to establish a family-based society (Adeney 2002; Tucker 2008).[7]

Butcher and Piehl's (2007) study notes an interesting crime statistic: in general, the incarceration rate of immigrants is only one-fifth of that of native-born Americans. Yet when Krueger's (2008) study looks into America's homegrown jihadists, his finding points in the opposite direction: citizens are less likely to commit jihadist terrorism. Recent studies, however, concur with Butcher and Piehl's (2007) finding. For example, Schanzer, Kurzman, and Moosa (2010) show that almost two-thirds of the homegrown jihadists were U.S.-born or naturalized citizens. Simcox and Dyer's (2013) study also reports that the majority (54%) of individuals in their dataset were U.S. citizens. Accordingly, the sixth variable, *citizen*, examines the status of citizenship. In the dataset, American citizenship is recorded by either birth or naturalization.

The remaining variables are related to the region of birth and divided into five categories: *USA, Middle East and North Africa, sub-Saharan Africa, South Asia,* and *other.* These subdivisions are introduced to control for region fixed effects because each region may exert a unique impact on homegrown jihadist terrorism. *USA* is used as the comparison variable.

Table 1.1 provides descriptive statistics of the personal attributes of American jihadists from my data collection and the 2011 Pew survey.[8] It appears that the average years of schooling, income, age, and marital status of Muslims living in the United States are greater than those of the homegrown jihadists, while the latter includes more males than females and more U.S. citizens than residents and visitors.

EMPIRICAL FINDINGS

As shown in Table 1.2, I fit nine logistic regression models to a pooled data of American jihadists and Muslim Americans.[9] The first column shows a list of independent variables.[10] Models 1–3 pool together my American jihadist list and "all" Muslim Americans who were interviewed in the 2011 Pew phone survey. A majority of Muslims in America are uninterested in al-Qaeda's mission, so they are presumed to be much less likely to take up arms for jihadist causes. However, those Muslims who possess radical political views may be more predisposed to engage in homegrown terrorism. Simply put, the impact of a split opinion about al-Qaeda among Muslims in America on the activities of homegrown jihadists warrants empirical scrutiny. Models 4–6 focus on those Muslim Americans who expressed a very favorable or somewhat favorable opinion of al-Qaeda in

Table 1.1
Descriptive Statistics

Variable	Muslim Americans in the 2011 Pew Survey					America's Homegrown Jihadists since 9/11				
	Observations	Mean	Standard Deviation	Minimum	Maximum	Observations	Mean	Standard Deviation	Minimum	Maximum
Education	1,028	2.446	1.138	1	4	235	1.860	0.984	1	4
Income	1,017	2.030	0.502	1	3	235	1.557	0.654	1	3
Age	1,019	2.477	1.079	1	4	235	1.553	0.811	1	4
Male	1,033	0.554	0.497	0	1	235	0.962	0.192	0	1
Married	1,024	0.751	0.433	0	1	235	0.460	0.499	0	1
Citizen	1,025	0.552	0.498	0	1	235	0.672	0.470	0	1
Born in										
USA	1,033	0.280	0.449	0	1	235	0.434	0.497	0	1
Middle East and North Africa	1,033	0.268	0.443	0	1	235	0.128	0.334	0	1
Sub-Saharan Africa	1,033	0.068	0.251	0	1	235	0.145	0.353	0	1
South Asia	1,033	0.274	0.446	0	1	235	0.149	0.357	0	1
Other	1,033	0.092	0.289	0	1	235	0.145	0.353	0	1

Table 1.2
Where Do America's Homegrown Jihadists Come From?

Variable	All Muslim Americans			Pro-al-Qaeda Muslim Americans			Anti-al-Qaeda Muslim Americans		
	Unweighted	Weighted		Unweighted	Weighted		Unweighted	Weighted	
	Model 1	Model 2	Model 3	Model 4	Model 5	Model 6	Model 7	Model 8	Model 9
Education	-0.359***	-0.022	-0.0084	0.254	0.526**	0.101	-0.412***	-0.068	-0.028
	(0.094)	(0.146)		(0.184)	(0.259)		(0.097)	(0.150)	
Income	-1.258***	-1.714***	-0.3139	-1.288***	-3.976***	-0.525	-1.202***	-1.619***	-0.305
	(0.199)	(0.365)		(0.269)	(0.623)		(0.205)	(0.394)	
Age	-0.794***	-0.763***	-0.283	-0.723***	-1.687***	-0.444	-0.817***	-0.761***	-0.291
	(0.121)	(0.213)		(0.203)	(0.364)		(0.129)	(0.235)	
Male	2.955***	3.149***	0.5558	3.734***	6.492***	0.730	2.781***	2.597***	0.484
	(0.343)	(0.488)		(0.403)	(0.915)		(0.345)	(0.404)	
Married	-0.080	-0.066	-0.0112	0.130	1.124*	0.125	-0.067	-0.051	-0.009
	(0.240)	(0.454)		(0.391)	(0.646)		(0.249)	(0.480)	
Citizen	1.278***	2.442***	0.4292	0.953***	2.014***	0.224	1.286***	2.463***	0.460
	(0.233)	(0.514)		(0.356)	(0.736)		(0.237)	(0.528)	
Birth region									
Middle East and North Africa	-1.022***	-2.356***	-0.3786	-1.247***	-3.931***	-0.388	-0.855***	-2.284***	-0.393
	(0.292)	(0.584)		(0.384)	(0.847)		(0.292)	(0.633)	
South Asia	-0.998***	-1.501***	-0.1952	-0.800*	-2.053**	-0.163	-0.954***	-1.436***	-0.200
	(0.280)	(0.477)		(0.418)	(0.837)		(0.280)	(0.480)	
Other	0.125	-1.655**	-0.1819	0.549	-1.254	-0.075	0.141	-1.638*	-0.197
	(0.335)	(0.832)		(0.574)	(1.060)		(0.345)	(0.854)	

(Continued)

Table 1.2
(Continued)

| Variable | All Muslim Americans | | | Pro-al-Qaeda Muslim Americans | | | Anti-al-Qaeda Muslim Americans | | |
| | Unweighted | Weighted | | Unweighted | Weighted | | Unweighted | Weighted | |
	Model 1	Model 2	Model 3	Model 4	Model 5	Model 6	Model 7	Model 8	Model 9
Constant	0.516	−7.274***		0.566	−3.700***		0.823	−6.729***	
	(0.568)	(0.881)		(0.594)	(1.319)		(0.588)	(1.012)	
Wald chi^2	210.68	87.16		128.04	123.13		200.08	102.48	
Probability > chi^2	0.001	0.001		0.001	0.001		0.001	0.001	
Log pseudolikelihood	−365.09	−1,949.63		−138.30	−1,284.48		−344.91	−1,920.45	
Pseudo R^2	0.39	0.16		0.49	0.33		0.39	0.15	
Observations	1,240	1,240		399	399		1,076	1,076	

Notes: Robust standard errors are in parentheses. Models 2, 4, and 6 display standardized coefficients.

* 0.10 two-tailed

** 0.05 two-tailed

*** 0.01 two-tailed

the survey, while Models 7–9 look at those respondents who expressed a somewhat unfavorable or very unfavorable opinion of al-Qaeda. Columns 1, 4, and 7 report coefficients and standard errors that were obtained without weights, while the remaining columns employ weighted logistic regression models. As will be detailed further, the comparison of logit estimates with and without the use of weights uncovers an intriguing finding pertaining to the significance of educational attainment. Because the pseudo-R^2 statistics for all the statistical models assume a moderate value that ranges from 0.15 to 0.49, it is fair to say that they are instrumental in providing a valid description of American homegrown jihadists.

Model 1 shows that Muslim Americans are at greater risk of becoming homegrown jihadists when they are younger, male, and less educated; live under poor economic conditions; and have citizenship, but their birth origin is not necessarily the Middle East, North Africa, or South Asia. Yet, because these estimated results do not take sample weights into account, they should be interpreted with caution because they may not be representative of all Muslims living in the United States. Model 2 displays weighted coefficients and standard errors. At first glance, the results may look similar to those from Model 1 because poverty, age, gender, and citizenship still remain as significant predictors. Nevertheless, there is a notable difference between the two models. The implementation of sample weights in Model 2 causes *education* to be insignificant though the coefficient still assumes a positive sign. It appears that *education* alone is not a sufficient predictor for homegrown jihadists.

It would be interesting to evaluate the relative importance of variables; however, because the coefficients in Model 2 are unstandardized—they are measured in their natural units—they cannot be compared with one another directly to determine which is a more important or influential predictor in the statistical model. Model 3 addresses this issue by reporting standardized coefficients. When the relative effects of variables are evaluated in absolute terms, *male* emerges as the most influential predictor of American homegrown terrorism, *citizen* comes out as the second, *Middle East and North Africa* is ranked as the third, *income* exerts the fourth strongest influence, and so on.

Models 4, 5, and 6 replicate Models 1, 2, and 3 after selecting exclusively Muslim Americans who are sympathetic to the causes of al-Qaeda. When the results in weighted Models 2 and 5 are compared, an interesting finding emerges with regard to the statistical significance and causal relationship of *education*. When looking at both American jihadists and Muslim Americans who have a positive political opinion of al-Qaeda, I find that Muslims with a higher level of education are more likely to become American jihadists. However, when American jihadists are examined against those Muslim Americans who do not have a favorable opinion of al-Qaeda in Model 8, the significant and positive effect of *education* disappears. The comparison of weighted Models 2, 5, and 8 provides some useful clues to the question of why better-educated Muslims may turn into jihadists in the first place. In short, further education appears to embolden political ideology only for those Muslim Americans who already possess a positive viewpoint of terrorist activities abroad.

When looking across models in Table 1.2, we can find some fairly consistent patterns of American homegrown terrorism. American jihadists tend to be young, male, economically deprived, and citizens. It is unlikely that they were originally born in regions of the Middle East, North Africa, or South Asia. These findings somewhat deviate from common beliefs as exemplified by Jenkins's (2010, 7) argument that "there is no easily identifiable terrorist-prone personality, no single path to radicalization and terrorism." Instead, the empirical findings of this study indicate that law enforcement authorities would do well to consider how they could discourage poverty-stricken, young, and male Muslims under 30 with U.S. citizenship away from radicalization. While these indicators do not provide a fully concrete or precise profile to predict exactly who will radicalize and terrorize, they are useful in creating a broad profile of America's homegrown jihadists.

To visualize the effects of the variables that achieve statistical significance in Model 5 in Table 1.2,[11] Figure 1.1 depicts the predicted probabilities of becoming an American jihadist. Dashed lines indicate the 95 percent confidence intervals. The figure shows that the reduction in America's homegrown terrorism is pronounced when he or she becomes more affluent and older and the place of birth is the Middle East, North Africa, or South Asia. But when the perpetrator is better educated as well

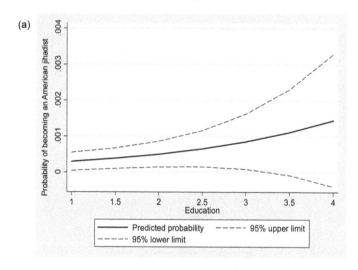

Figure 1.1 Probability of becoming an American jihadist.

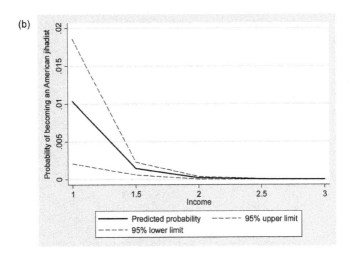

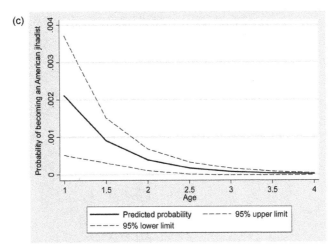

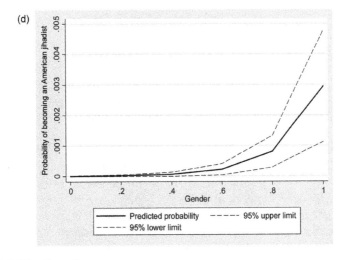

Figure 1.1 (Continued)

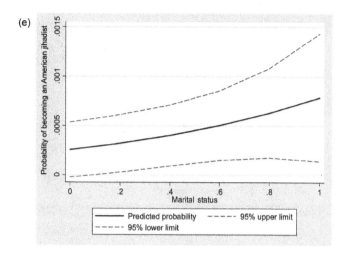

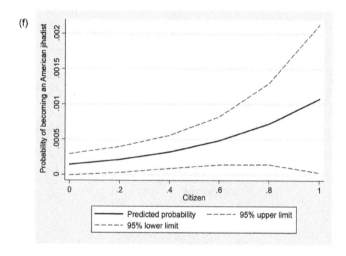

Figure 1.1 (Continued)

as when he or she is male, married, and an American citizen, there is a substantial increase in the probability of becoming an American jihadist. Simply put, Figure 1.1 confirms the general pattern of homegrown terrorism reported in Table 1.2.

In order to verify the findings reported thus far, Table 1.3 performs three sets of robustness tests in terms of the differences in sampling and measurement of the dependent variable. Models 1–3 make use of a pooled dataset of my American jihadist list and the 2007 Pew survey data on Muslim Americans, Model 4 looks into American jihadists versus the general

Table 1.3
Where Do America's Homegrown Jihadists Come From? Robustness Tests

Variable	Muslim Americans in 2007			General Public	Bjelopera's (2013) Jihadist List		
	Model 1	Model 2	Model 3	Model 4	Model 5	Model 6	Model 7
Education	-0.094	0.272	-0.242	0.025	-0.068	0.606*	-0.116
	(0.146)	(0.243)	(0.167)	(0.097)	(0.183)	(0.333)	(0.186)
Income	-2.124***	-2.687***	-2.111***	-0.964***	-1.952***	-4.910***	-1.842***
	(0.301)	(0.437)	(0.346)	(0.173)	(0.460)	(0.731)	(0.493)
Age	-1.197***	-1.648***	-1.025***	-1.014***	-0.935***	-2.275***	-0.920***
	(0.259)	(0.396)	(0.264)	(0.113)	(0.295)	(0.537)	(0.313)
Male	3.400***	3.510***	3.513***	3.141***	3.480***	7.574***	2.758***
	(0.443)	(0.496)	(0.506)	(0.361)	(0.690)	(1.065)	(0.589)
Married	0.352	-0.431	0.433	0.159	-0.109	1.380*	-0.092
	(0.454)	(0.590)	(0.512)	(0.220)	(0.600)	(0.762)	(0.621)
Citizen	2.232***	2.047***	2.454***	-1.701***	3.060***	2.908***	3.061***
	(0.540)	(0.526)	(0.635)	(0.227)	(0.678)	(0.860)	(0.676)
Birth region							
Middle East	-1.606***	-1.277**	-1.814***		-2.745***	-5.169***	-2.650***
	(0.494)	(0.636)	(0.589)		(0.763)	(1.071)	(0.820)
South Asia	-1.444***	-0.907	-1.822***		-1.840***	-2.744**	-1.744***

(Continued)

Table 1.3
(Continued)

Variable	Muslim Americans in 2007			General Public	Bjelopera's (2013) Jihadist List		
	Model 1	Model 2	Model 3	Model 4	Model 5	Model 6	Model 7
	(0.539)	(0.600)	(0.630)		(0.612)	(1.078)	(0.603)
Other	−1.391**	−2.923***	−1.163		−1.857*	−1.415	−1.807*
	(0.653)	(0.838)	(0.752)		(0.981)	(1.148)	(0.992)
Constant	−5.750***	−2.603**	−5.725***	−0.700	−7.692***	−3.440**	−7.018***
	(0.726)	(1.193)	(0.748)	(0.562)	(1.089)	(1.644)	(1.273)
Wald chi²	118.29	120.22	92.65	238.70	62.88	114.04	75.51
Probability > chi²	0.001	0.001	0.001	0.001	0.001	0.001	0.001
Log pseudolikelihood	−1,828.66	−1,415.42	−1,762.55	−687.74	−1,181.40	−740.71	−1,165.24
Pseudo R²	0.18	0.27	0.18	0.31	0.19	0.40	0.19
Observations	1,232	465	1,002	2,144	1,146	305	982

Note: Robust standard errors are in parentheses.

* 0.10 two-tailed

** 0.05 two-tailed

*** 0.01 two-tailed

public survey conducted in 2011,[12] and Models 5–7 replace my compilation of American jihadists with Bjelopera's (2013) list as the dependent variable. The robustness tests uphold the significance of three personal characteristics of America's homegrown jihadists: young, male, and poor. Note that U.S. citizenship is negatively associated with homegrown terrorism when my jihadist data is analyzed in comparison with the general public in Model 4, as opposed to the remaining models where a positive relationship is the norm.[13] The results demonstrate that average Americans with citizenship are *less* likely to participate in terrorist acts, while average Muslim Americans with citizenship are *more* likely. These mixed findings preclude me from claiming *citizen* to be a consistent and significant predictor of homegrown terrorism.

SIX ILLUSTRATIONS OF AMERICA'S HOMEGROWN JIHADISTS

One of the main purposes of this study is to conduct a more current assessment of the danger of America's homegrown terrorism, offering the counterterrorism community a more accurate picture of the magnitude of the threat that Americans are facing from homegrown jihadists. The statistical analysis reveals that the threat comes more likely from those Muslim Americans who are young, male, and economically deprived. These findings are not in agreement with recent cross-national economics literature concerning terrorism, in which terrorists are depicted as largely from well-educated or high-income families (e.g., Sageman 2004; Berrebi 2007; Altunbas and Thornton 2011; for a dissenting view, see Bakker 2008; Gartenstein-Ross and Grossman 2009). However, because my study focuses specifically on *America's* homegrown jihadists, the discrepancy is not so surprising. What make the American case unique? I speculate that the housing bubble and the ensuing financial crisis may be directly responsible for the new trend of America's homegrown terrorism.[14] The economic crisis had a definite impact on Muslim communities, most of which are comprised of first-generation immigrants whose economic situations are yet to be improved. As a result, the economic crisis may have crippled the economic welfare of many Muslims in America, especially young Muslims who were at a point in their life where they were looking for a job (Holt 2009). The frustration and anger of economically deprived, young, male Muslims, caused by the financial debacle, may have encouraged acts of terrorism.

To further examine why and how America's jihadist terrorism has been growing during the past decade, I introduce six individual cases: (1) Michael Finton, (2) Antonio Martinez, (3) Jose Pimentel, (4) Sidi Mohamed Amine El Khalifi, (5) Tamerlan Tsarnaev, and (6) Faisal Shahzad. To diversify the selection of cases, I choose them from a pool of American-born converts to Islam, foreign-born converts, and Muslims from birth.

Michael Finton is a redheaded, Caucasian-American citizen born in 1980 and raised in foster care. He did not finish high school and had a criminal record, so he struggled to find a steady job, eventually landing a position as a part-time fry cook for the local Seals Fish & Chicken in Decatur, Illinois. In his early 20s, he converted to Islam in prison while serving a sentence for aggravated robbery and assault (Rushton 2007; Johnson 2009; Greenberg 2010). After his conversion, he self-radicalized, having no connection to known terrorist organizations. The economic difficulty that the young, part-time worker had to face was particularly harsh during the housing bubble and the financial crisis, leading to feelings of anger and frustration which consequently led to more extreme ideas about his life, religion, and the government. Further, the economic suffering drove the young Muslim to misperceive the intended goals of the presence of American troops in Iraq and Afghanistan where his adopted religion was often transgressed. Put differently, given that he is young, economically distressed, and religiously biased, he was prone to hostility toward the government. Such hostility was aggravated by his anger and frustration at America's antagonistic foreign policy toward Islamic countries, and his aggression was further cultivated against the U.S. government and its employees. Fortunately, his attempt to destroy the Paul Findley Federal Building and Courthouse with a truck bomb on September 24, 2009, was thwarted by the FBI Anti-Terrorism Task Force. He was then 29 years old (Mueller 2014).

Antonio Martinez is a naturalized U.S. citizen born in Nicaragua, who dropped out of high school and got married to Maimah Ismail-Hussain. He was arrested for attempting to bomb an armed forces recruiting station in Cantonsville, Maryland, in December 2010. At that time he was only 21 years old and working as a part-time construction worker (Glod, Markon, and Brahmpour 2010; Dominguez 2012). Note that because the housing bubble and the ensuing economic crisis drastically dampened job growth in both construction and housing-related industries, construction workers like Antonio Martinez likely faced a limited job market. When the young Muslim became angered by his poor economic conditions as well as American military interventions in the Middle East, he turned to Facebook to express his interest in recruiting Afghani jihadists to help him terrorize a military recruiting station in retaliation for what he perceived as an American war against Islam (Drogin and Serrano 2010; Savage and Gately 2010). When his foiled attempt to kill members of the American military came to light, he appeared to have no direct connections to al-Qaeda or its affiliated organizations (Glod, Markon, and Brahmpour 2010).

When Jose Pimentel was arrested by the New York Police Department on November 19, 2011, he was 27 years old. He was born in the Dominican

Republic and moved to the United States at the age of five. The naturalized Muslim American was trying to make pipe bombs that were intended
to blow up American soldiers returning from Afghanistan and Iraq (Jules
2014). He was resentful when he heard of the death of a radical Muslim
cleric and American citizen, Anwar al-Awlaki, in the U.S. drone attack in
Yemen. This incident led to a negative perception of American military
operations in the Middle East. Married and a father, he did not have a
stable job but temporarily worked in a store (Karoliszyn, Blain, and Connor 2011). In their *New York Times* article, Rashbaum and Goldstein (2011)
indeed report that "the suspect had little money to speak of, was unable
to pay his cell phone bill and scrounged for money to buy the drill bits
that . . . required to make his pipe bombs."

The case of Sidi Mohamed Amine El Khalifi is unique on the grounds
that he attempted to carry out suicide bombings against the whole dome
of the Capitol Building in Washington, D.C. Originally from Morocco, he
had lived in the United States illegally for over 12 years after the expiration
of his tourist visa. He was 29 years old at the time he was arrested for the
terrorism charge on February 17, 2012. He was a high school dropout who
had never married. His economic situation never improved, despite holding various jobs such as a cook, busboy, and salesman (Wilber 2012). He
taught himself the Quran and became radicalized by embracing extreme
interpretations of Islam. As is the case with many other young Muslims,
the online access to American-born cleric Anwar al-Awlaki's sermons so-
lidified his extreme views. Furthermore, his belief that the War on Terror
was actually a war on Muslims led him to engaging in various terrorist
plots, including the unsuccessful suicide attack at the Capitol Building. It
appears that he was not connected to any larger terrorist network or any
overseas group (Associated Press 2012; Barakat 2012; Miller 2012).

While the previous four cases were successfully foiled by security authorities, Tamerlan Tsarnaev—one of the two young Chechen American
brothers in the Boston Marathon bombings—was actually able to carry out
his plan on April 15, 2013. He was a 26-year-old permanent resident with
some community college education in the United States. His Muslim parents came to America by applying for asylum, citing fears of deadly perse-
cution due to their ties to Chechnya. Their new life with four children was
not an easy one, as they had to rely on welfare benefits for an extended
period of time (Allen 2013; Schmitt, Schmidt, and Barry 2013). According
to Chris Cassidy's (2013) report in the *Boston Herald*, Tamerlan Tsarnaev,
his wife, and their three-year-old daughter also lived on welfare up until
2012. Tamerlan Tsarnaev was unemployed prior to the bombings but was
financially supported by his wife, who worked over 70 hours a week as
a home health-care aide (*Sacchetti* et al. 2013). While the young Chechen
American was experiencing economic hardship, he was outraged by what
he perceived to be the unfair treatment of his Muslim brethren around the

globe. The bombings were his expression of seeking to protect coreligionists (Mueller 2014).

A failed attempt of homegrown terrorism is also an interesting case. Faisal Shahzad, a 30-year-old male of Pakistani descent, was unable to set off a car bomb in Times Square on May 1, 2010. He was raised in an affluent Muslim family in his homeland, moved to the United States for his undergraduate degree in computer science and an MBA, worked in the financial sector, and became a U.S. citizen 13 months before the Times Square terrorist incident. While living with his wife and two children in a newly bought house in the Connecticut suburbs of New York City, he appeared to be well adjusted to an American life. However, everything changed during the housing bubble and the ensuing financial crisis when he lost his house through foreclosure. He became more religious and keen to talk about politics, especially drone attacks in his homeland. Simply put, the economic difficulties seem to have catalyzed the radicalization of the young Muslim. In anger, bitterness, and frustration, he traveled to his homeland in 2009 where he met with the Pakistani Taliban and trained in bomb-making. On his return to the United States he drove his Nissan Pathfinder packed with explosives and detonators and left it in Times Square to kill civilians (Barron and Schmidt 2000; Elliott, Tavernise, and Barnard 2010; Kleinmann 2012).

All in all, these six cases illustrate that the origins of America's homegrown jihadists can be traced back to those Muslim Americans who are young, male, and economically disadvantaged.

CONCLUSION

In his press conference related to the Boston Marathon bombings, President Obama stated that "one of the dangers that we now face are self-radicalized individuals who are already here in the United States," also mentioning that homegrown terrorist plots "are in some ways more difficult to prevent" (quoted in Shane and Barry 2013). President Obama's evaluation of America's homegrown terrorists is on target. Yet the important question is how best to identify and deter this growing threat. A counterterrorism strategy would be impossible without understanding exactly what makes an American homegrown jihadist.

I collected a dataset of 235 American jihadists during the past 13 years and contrasted them with Pew's survey data of Muslim Americans as well as the general public. The data analysis revealed a unique and consistent pattern of American jihadists, regardless of the model specification, sample selection, and measurement choice of the dependent variable. American jihadists appear to be male, younger, and economically poorer than their counterparts in the samples. These statistical findings are also confirmed with the six case studies of homegrown jihadists. Accordingly, I contend that the personal characteristics of America's homegrown terrorists have changed in some important respects from those described in previous studies.

Relying on a sample of 63 American jihadists who were indicted or convicted for involvement in terrorist activities for the years 1993–2005, Krueger's (2008) seminal work, for example, showed that better education increases the risk of homegrown terrorism, poverty and birth regions have no bearing on homegrown terrorism, and citizens are less likely to become homegrown jihadists. However, my quantitative and qualitative analysis uncovers a new trend in America's homegrown terrorism: education attainment is not necessarily a significant cause of terrorism; rather, poverty is a strong predictor of acts of homegrown terrorism, and U.S. citizens are more likely to commit homegrown terrorism. My logistic regression analysis is also different from what Simcox and Dyer's (2013) frequency table analysis of 171 American jihadists for the years 1997–2011 indicates. Their findings are that "the majority of individuals who committed [homegrown terrorism] were young, educated men. . . . There was little correlation between a lack of employment prospects and committing [homegrown terrorism]" (86). However, my statistical estimates indicate that education may matter only among Muslim Americans who already have radical ideas about jihadist causes and that poverty emerges as an important predictor of homegrown terrorism on American soil.

NOTES

1. In this study, I use the term "Muslim Americans" rather than "American Muslims" because it is an official term that is used by the Pew Research Center without having a negative connotation of otherness and because previous studies rely on the same term (e.g., Krueger 2008).

2. Altunbas and Thornton (2011) from Bangor Business School provide another excellent analysis on homegrown Islamic terrorists, but their work focuses on U.K. cases.

3. Though not exhaustive, the sources include the Citizens Crime Commission of New York City, CNN, the Congressional Research Service Report for Congress, court documents, FBI press releases, Google, the Homeland Security Digital Library, local newspapers, the New America Foundation, the *New York Times*, and the Terrorist Trial Report Card. Note that due to a lack of personal information on American jihadists, I did not consult widely used terrorism datasets such as the International Terrorism: Attributes of Terrorist Events (ITERATE) and the Global Terrorism Database.

4. The sum of the weights approximately equals the total number of Muslims aged 18 and older in the U.S. population.

5. Because my data on American jihadists is the population of homegrown terrorists in the period under study, each observation is assigned a weight of 1 as implemented in Krueger's (2008, 294) study.

6. In order to address potential estimation problems associated with many zero observations in the outcome data, I used a rare events logistical modeling technique. Because the results were substantively similar to those from logit, they are not reported in this study to save space.

7. See also http://www.islamawareness.net/Marriage/marriage_article001.html.

8. Note that the levels of education, income, and age are ordinal in order to make the measurements from the two sample datasets comparable.

9. When multicollinearity diagnostics such as variance inflation factors, eigenvalues, and R^2 statistics are performed, I find no severe multicollinearity among predictors.

10. Sub-Saharan Africa was not included in the Stata command line after I found that some weighted logistic regression models failed to converge.

11. The other two weighted models yield similar results.

12. The general public survey does not identify respondents' region of birth place, so the model includes no region controls.

13. The general public survey includes 11 Muslims out of 2,003 respondents.

14. Housing prices peaked in early 2006, started to decline in 2006 and 2007, and reached new lows in 2012.

REFERENCES

Adeney, Miriam. 2002. *Daughters of Islam: Building Bridges with Muslim Women.* Downers Grove, IL: InterVarsity Press.

Allen, Evan. April 26, 2013. "Family of Suspected Bombers Received Welfare, Food Stamps." *Boston Globe.* https://www.bostonglobe.com/2013/04/26/bombbenefits/VNPB285wfdHTQ0biFWJnLM/story.html

Altunbas, Yener and John Thornton. 2011. "Are Homegrown Islamic Terrorist Different? Some UK Evidence." *Southern Economic Journal* 78(2): 262–272.

Associated Press. September 14, 2012. "Amine El-Khalifi Sentenced to 30 Years in Capitol Bomb Plot." *Daily News.* http://www.nydailynews.com/news/national/amine-el-khalifi-sentenced-30-years-capitol-bomb-plot-article-1.1159847.

Bakker, Edwin. 2008. "Jihadi Terrorists in Europe and Global Salalfi Jihadis." In Rik Coolsaet, ed., *Jihad Terrorism and the Radicalization Challenge in Europe.* Aldershot: Ashgate Publishers. 69–84.

Barakat, Matthew. September 10, 2012. "Capitol Bomb Plot Suspect Amine El-Khalifi Promised 'Martyrdom Payments,' Court Papers Say." *Huffington Post.* http://www.huffingtonpost.com/2012/09/10/amine-el-khalifi-bomb_n_1871971.html.

Barrett, Devlin. June 3, 2014. "Justice Department Relaunches Domestic Terror Task Force." *Wall Street Journal.* http://online.wsj.com/articles/justice-department-relaunches-domestic-terror-task-force-1401820635.

Barron, James and Michael S. Schmidt. May 4, 2000. "From Suburban Father to a Terrorism Suspect." *New York Times.* http://www.nytimes.com/2010/05/05/nyregion/05profile.html?pagewanted=all&_r=0.

Benson, Pam. May 27, 2010. "Homegrown Terrorist Threat to Be Part of National Security Strategy." CNN. http://www.cnn.com/2010/POLITICS/05/27/homegrown.terror/.

Bergen, Peter, Bruce Hoffman, Michael Hurley, and Erroll Southers. September 2013. "Jihadist Terrorism: A Threat Assessment." Bipartisan Policy Center's Homeland Security Project. http://bipartisanpolicy.org/sites/default/files/Jihadist%20Terrorism-A%20Threat%20Assesment_0.pdf.

Berrebi, Claude. 2007. "Evidence about the Link between Education, Poverty and Terrorism among Palestinians." *Peace Economics, Peace Science and Public Policy* 13(1): 1–36.

Bjelopera, Jerome P. January 23, 2013. "American Jihadist Terrorism: Combating a Complex Threat." Congressional Research Service Report for Congress. https://fas.org/sgp/crs/terror/R41416.pdf

Butcher, Kristin F. and Anne Morrison Piehl. 2007. "Why Are Immigrants' Incarceration Rates So Low? Evidence of Selective Immigration, Deterrence, and Deportation." NBER Working Paper No. 13229. http://www.nber.org/papers/w13229.pdf.

Cassidy, Chris. April 24, 2013. "Tamerlan Tsarnaev Got Mass. Welfare Benefits." *Boston Herald*. http://bostonherald.com/news_opinion/local_coverage/2013/04/tamerlan_tsarnaev_got_mass_welfare_benefits.

Dominguez, Alex. April 6, 2012. "Antonio Martinez, Maryland Man in Recruiting Center Bomb Plot, Sentenced to 25 Years in Prison." *Huffington Post*. http://www.huffingtonpost.com/2012/04/06/antonio-martinez-terror_n_1408078.html.

Drogin, Bob and Richard Serrano. December 9, 2010. "Baltimore Man Arrested in Foiled Terrorism Plot." *Los Angeles Times*. http://articles.latimes.com/2010/dec/09/nation/la-na-bomb-plot-arrest-20101209.

Elliott, Andrea, Sabrina Tavernise, and Anne Barnard. May 15, 2010. "For Times Sq. Suspect, Long Roots of Discontent." *New York Times*. http://www.nytimes.com/2010/05/16/nyregion/16suspect.html?pagewanted=all.

Gartenstein-Ross, Daveed and Laura Grossman. 2009. "Homegrown Terrorists in the US and UK: An Empirical Examination of the Radicalization Process." Washington, DC: Foundation for Defense of Democracies Press. http://www.defenddemocracy.org/stuff/uploads/documents/HomegrownTerrorists_USandUK.pdf.

Glod, Maria, Jerry Markon, and Tara Brahmpour. December 9, 2010. "MD. Man Accused of Attempted Bombing." *Washington Post*. http://www.washingtonpost.com/wp-dyn/content/article/2010/12/08/AR2010120807273.html.

Greenberg, Karen J. May 21, 2010. "Homegrown." *New Republic*. http://www.newrepublic.com/article/75075/homegrown.

Hambrick, Donald C. and Phyllis A. Mason. 1984. "Upper Echelons." *Academy of Management Review* 9(2): 193–206.

Healy, Jack. September 6, 2014. "For Jihad Recruits, a Pipeline from Minnesota to Militancy." *New York Times*. http://www.nytimes.com/2014/09/07/us/for-Jihad-recruits-a-pipeline-from-Minnesota-to-militancy.html?_r=0.

Holt, Jeff. 2009. "A Summary of the Primary Causes of the Housing Bubble and the Resulting Credit Crisis: A Non-Technical Paper." *Journal of Business Inquiry: Research, Education & Application* 8(1): 120–129.

Jenkins, Brian Michael. 2010. *Would-Be Warriors: Incidents of Jihadist Terrorist Radicalization in the United States since September 11, 2001.* Santa Monica, CA: RAND Corporation. https://www.rand.org/pubs/occasional_papers/OP292.html.

Johnson, Dirk. September 27, 2009. "Suspect in Illinois Bomb Plot 'Didn't Like America Very Much.'" *New York Times.* http://www.nytimes.com/2009/09/28/us/28springfield.html?pagewanted=all.

Jules, Anny. March 26, 2014. "Dominican-Born Muslim Terrorist Jose Pimentel Sentenced to 16 Years in Prison." *Latin Post.* http://www.latinpost.com/articles/9567/20140326/dominican-born-muslim-terrorist-jose-pimentel-sentenced-16-years-prison.htm.

Karoliszyn, Hendrick, Glenn Blain, and Tracy Connor. November 21, 2011. "Terror Suspect Jose Pimentel's Mom Says Sorry to City: I Feel Very Bad . . . I Thank the Police." *New York Daily News.* http://www.nydailynews.com/news/crime/terror-suspect-jose-pimentel-mom-city-police-article-1.980715.

Kleinmann, Scott Matthew. 2012. "Radicalization of Homegrown Sunni Militants in the United States: Comparing Converts and Non-Converts." *Studies in Conflict & Terrorism* 35(4): 278–297.

Krueger, Alan B. 2007. *What Makes a Terrorist.* Princeton, NJ: Princeton University Press.

Krueger, Alan B. 2008. "What Makes a Homegrown Terrorist? Human Capital and Participation in Domestic Islamic Terrorist Groups in the U.S.A." *Economic Letters* 101(3): 293–296.

Miller, John. February 18, 2012. "Inside the Plans of Capitol Bomb Suspect." *CBS.* http://www.cbsnews.com/news/inside-the-plans-of-capitol-bomb-suspect/.

Mueller, John. 2014. "Terrorism since 9/11: The American Cases." https://politicalscience.osu.edu/faculty/jmueller/since.html

Pantucci, Raffaello. August 28, 2014. "There Are Ways to Address Radicalism Early." *New York Times.* http://www.nytimes.com/roomfordebate/2014/08/28/how-to-stop-radicalization-in-the-west/there-are-ways-to-address-radicalism-early.

Pew Research Center. May 2007. "Muslim Americans: Middle Class and Mostly Mainstream." http://pewresearch.org/files/old-assets/pdf/muslim-americans.pdf.

Pew Research Center. August 2011. "Muslim Americans: No Signs of Growth in Alienation or Support for Extremism." http://www.people-press.org/files/legacy-pdf/Muslim%20American%20Report%2010-02-12%20fix.pdf.

Pew Research Center. September 2011. "General Public Survey on Veterans & Generational Change." http://www.pewsocialtrends.org/2012/11/27/general-public-survey-on-veterans-generational-change/.

Rashbaum, William K. and Joseph Goldstein. November 21, 2011. "Informer's Role in Terror Case Is Said to Have Deterred F.B.I." *New York Times.* http://www.nytimes.com/2011/11/22/nyregion/for-jose-pimentel-bomb-plot-suspect-an-online-trail.html?pagewanted=all&_r=0.

Roy, Olivier. 2008. *Al Qaeda in the West as a Youth Movement: The Power of a Narrative.* MICROCON Policy Working Paper 2, Brighton: MICROCON. http://aei.pitt.edu/9378/2/9378.pdf.

Rushton, Bruce. September 24, 2007. "Man Accused in Bombing Plot Known for Strong Stance on Islam." *Journal Star.* http://www.pjstar.com/article/20090925/NEWS/309259924/0/SEARCH.

Russel, Jenna, Jenn Abelson, Patricia Wen, Michael Rezendes, and David Fili-
pov. April 19, 2013. "Brothers Veered Violently Off Track." *Boston Globe.*
http://www.bostonglobe.com/metro/2013/04/19/relatives-marathon-
bombing-suspects-worried-that-older-brother-was-corrupting-sweet-
younger-sibling/UCYHkiP9nfsjAtMjJPWJJL/story.html.

Sageman, Marc. 2004. *Understanding Terror Networks.* Philadelphia: University of
Pennsylvania Press.

Savage, Charlie and Gary Gately. December 8, 2010. "Maryland Bomb Plot Foiled,
Authorities Say." *New York Times.* http://www.nytimes.com/2010/12/09/
us/09bomb.html?_r=0.

Schanzer, David, Charles Kurzman, and Ebrahim Moosa. 2010. "Anti-Terror Les-
sons of Muslim Americans." https://fds.duke.edu/db/attachment/1255.

Schmidt, Michael S. and Eric Schmitt. August 28, 2014. "U.S. Identifies Citizens
Joining Rebels in Syria, Including ISIS." *New York Times.* http://www.
nytimes.com/2014/08/29/world/middleeast/us-identifies-citizens-
joining-rebels-in-syria.html.

Schmitt, Eric, Michael S. Schmidt, and Ellen Barry. April 20, 2013. "Bombing Inquiry Turns to Motive and Russian Trip." *New York Times.* http://
www.nytimes.com/2013/04/21/us/boston-marathon-bombings.
html?pagewanted=all&_r=0.

Shane, Scott and Ellen Barry. April 30, 2013. "As Bombing Inquiry Proceeds, Obama
Offers Measured Praise for F.B.I." *New York Times.* http://www.nytimes.
com/2013/05/01/us/politics/obama-hints-bomb-suspects-were-self-rad-
icalized.html?pagewanted=all&_r=0.

Simcox, Robin and Emily Dyer. 2013. *Al-Qaeda in the United States: A Complete
Analysis of Terrorism Offenses.* London: Henry Jackson Society. http://hen-
ryjacksonsociety.org/wp-content/uploads/2013/02/Al-Qaeda-in-the-
USAbridged-version-LOWRES-Final.pdf.

Temple-Raston, Dina. March 26, 2010. "Jihadi Cool: Terrorist Recruiters' Latest
Weapon." *NPR.* http://www.npr.org/templates/story/story.php?storyId=12
5186382.

Tucker, Judith E. 2008. *Women, Family, and Gender in Islamic Law.* New York: Cambridge University Press.

Wilber, Del Quentin. November 25, 2012. "Inside an FBI Anti-Terrorist Sting Operation." *Washington Post.* http://www.washingtonpost.com/local/crime/
inside-an-fbi-anti-terrorist-sting-operation/2012/11/25/0838eee0-2f55-
11e2-a30e-5ca76eeec857_story.html.

CHAPTER 2

America's Homegrown Jihadists and Foreign Fighting

The 2013 Boston Marathon bombing that resulted in five casualties and the injury of 280 participants and bystanders drew attention to the dangers of America's homegrown terrorism. The perpetrators—Dzhokhar Tsarnaev, a naturalized U.S. citizen, and Tamerlan Tsarnaev, a permanent U.S. resident—were self-radicalized and unconnected to any outside terrorist groups (Almasy 2013). This bombing was only one in a string of incidents of homegrown terrorism since September 11, 2001. On May 25, 2014, when a man named Abu Hurayra Al-Amriki blew himself up in an attack in Syria, the American public was shocked by the fact that Al-Amriki was in his early 20s and grew up in Florida (Mazzetti, Schmitt, and Schmidt 2014). Several years prior, on October 21, 2009, a community in Massachusetts was caught seriously off guard with news that two U.S.-born citizens—Tarek Mehanna, a graduate of the Massachusetts College of Pharmacy, and Ahmad Abousamra, who attended Northeastern University and was on the Dean's List—were charged in a 10-count indictment with, among other terrorism-related charges, joining a terrorist camp overseas and conspiracy to attack U.S. soldiers in Iraq and Afghanistan (Clayton 2009; Murphy and Valencia 2009).

These three acts of terrorism share an obvious commonality—the perpetrators were radicalized on American soil and subscribed to jihadist ideology. This kind of terrorism is commonly known as America's homegrown terrorism,[1] reflecting the notion that the terrorist threat comes from within America's own borders. In recent years, homegrown terrorism has emerged as a major security concern due to the increasingly "prominent role in planning and operations that U.S. citizens and residents have played in the leadership of al-Qaida and aligned groups" (Bergen and

Hoffman 2010). Despite a growth of research interests in the subject, existing studies fail to identify those who are at risk of becoming American jihadists, as indicated by Bjelopera's (2013, 2) conclusion in his Congressional Research Service Report for Congress: "No workable general profile of domestic violent jihadists exists."

While all three terrorist incidents mentioned thus far showcase homegrown terrorism, there exists dissimilarity between the Boston Marathon bombings and the other two incidents. While the Boston Marathon bombings occurred domestically, the Syrian suicide bomber and the Massachusetts plotters targeted civilians and military personnel abroad. When examining my collected data of 193 American jihadists over the past 13 years, I find that more American jihadists fight on foreign rather than domestic soil—the former outnumbering the latter by about three to one. This raises an important question—why do most of America's homegrown jihadists conduct terrorist operations abroad when it is more costly in terms of time, energy, finances, and distance traveled, rather than engage in the same activities at home?

The existing literature says little about the *individual* behavior of American jihadists in the sense that their underlying motivations and behavioral patterns have not yet been examined through statistical modeling. The current scholarly research instead relies on a rough distribution of Western Muslims terrorizing Western targets versus non-Western targets. This is in large part due to the difficulty of gathering data on individual terrorists. For example, Hegghammer (2013) does his best to speculate on the total number of domestic and foreign Islamic fighters,[2] without performing advanced statistical analysis on individual data, and concludes that Western jihadists prefer foreign to domestic fighting because they see it as more legitimate (see also Hewitt and Kelley-Moore 2009; Hegghammer 2010/11). Likewise, before addressing the question of how international insurgents affect a domestic insurgent movement's strength, especially in the context of the Chechen wars, Bakke (2014) lists several potential determinants of foreign fighting without going into detail. Simply put, much of what is known about Western jihadists is in terms of crude estimates rather than in detail. Considering the domestic, regional, and international security risks involved, the dearth of cumulative knowledge about determinants of American jihadists going abroad is, from a U.S. policy perspective, a serious deficit in terrorism research (Simcox and Dyer 2013). What if American jihadists were to return to the United States and decide to terrorize at home? What if their foreign fighting further endangers global political stability and economic prosperity, as exemplified in the case of the Islamic State in Iraq and Syria (Schmidt and Schmitt 2014)? Though rhetorical, these are critical questions that underscore the urgency of examining why American jihadists decide to become foreign fighters.[3]

Given that no empirical research offers a formal model on the behavior of America's homegrown jihadists, I develop theoretical explanations of two kinds: (1) demographic characteristics—ethnic ties to the target country and 10 individual traits of the perpetrator (Vidino, Pantucci, and Kohlmann 2010; Mendelsohn 2011; Vidino 2011)—and (2) benefit-risk assessments—counterterrorism capabilities of the target country and perceived legitimacy of foreign fighting (Hegghammer 2013). Categories (1) and (2) together can be considered comprehensive because they combine material and ideational explanations as to why America's homegrown jihadists decide to fight abroad rather than at home. While another possible explanation is the presence of U.S. military occupation in the target country (Hewitt and Kelley-Moore 2009), it is not included in this statistical analysis because of a lack of variation.[4] The explanation that looks to whether or not a conflict abroad has been widely declared to be a jihad cannot serve as a valid variable, again, due to a lack of statistical variation. Other potential explanations, such as whether the perpetrator has family connections in the target country, are not explored because the collection of such detailed information from open sources that are consulted for this study is not feasible.

After compiling an original dataset of homegrown terrorists in the post 9/11 era, I convert the data to a dyadic format, in which each American jihadist is matched with his or her target country, and then perform a set of logistic regression analyses. I find evidence that American jihadists are more likely to engage in foreign fighting, especially when they are ethnically tied to the target countries, when they are young, and when the counterterrorism capacities of target countries are weak. In the face of the common belief that American society is characterized by, among other things, a rich ethnic and cultural diversity,[5] my analysis reveals the potential tension and conflict that diversity can inspire, as a large part of America's homegrown jihadists of the past decade have come from first- or second-generation immigrants. Accordingly, given that ethnic terrorism emerges as a real and growing threat to national and international security, politicians and policy makers should perhaps consider reforming the American immigration process. Because many American jihadists include immigrants, a possible policy option is to more carefully scrutinize immigration applications from terrorism-prone countries. The findings also indicate that Washington should look to develop counterterrorism capacities in terrorism-vulnerable countries. It would also be beneficial to focus anti-terrorism efforts on American jihadists who are relatively young by developing civic education programs at the community level.

The remainder of this study is divided into four sections: the first section offers 13 motives and conditions that may drive America's homegrown jihadists to join terrorist activities abroad; the second section explains the statistical model construction, operationalization of variables, and data

sources; the third section presents a discussion of empirical results; and
the fourth and final section summarizes the main findings of this study
and discusses some important policy implications.

WHY AMERICA'S HOMEGROWN JIHADISTS
FIGHT ABROAD

Given that existing literature offers no causal theory directly related to
American jihadists' decisions to fight abroad rather than attack at home,[6]
I put forward two possible sets of my own explanations—demographic
characteristics and benefit-risk assessments. Demographic characteristics should be useful proxies to capture differences in the thinking of individuals (e.g., Hambrick and Mason 1984; Wiersema and Bantel 1992),
so I discuss 11 demographic factors including ethnicity, whether they are
converts to Islam, and their education status. Benefit-risk assessments
are also key determinants of an individual's participation in an organization (e.g., Axelrod 1976; Markóczy 1997); thus, counterterrorism capacity
and legitimacy of foreign fighting over domestic fighting are included in
the theoretical discussion. On explaining the demographic characteristics
and benefit-risk assessments, I draw 13 comprehensive hypotheses that
allow for testing of the nature of America's homegrown terrorism. That
the pseudo-R^2 statistics of statistical models in the empirical section are
as high as 0.64 enforces my belief that the causal explanations are well
grounded in this section.

Demographic Characteristics

I argue that ethnic ties should influence the individual behavior of
American jihadists.[7] The United States is a land of immigrants, so it is
likely that "migrants [brought] with them sets of rules and norms unique
to their Homeland" (LaFree and Bersani 2014, 459). The unique rules and
norms are interrelated with the ethnic origins of American jihadists. Accordingly, I consider a Somali immigrant in the United States as having an ethnic tie to Somalia; a U.S.-born person with Albanian parents
is counted as having an ethnic tie to Kosovo and not to the United States
because he or she likely has strong emotional connections to his or her
homeland. I argue that when American jihadists are grouped by ethnic
origin, we should find that they share similar distinctive culture and traditions as well as a common sense of identity. It is not surprising to see
that immigrants on American soil have a tendency to move to and live in
areas populated by people with similar ethnic backgrounds (National Research Council 1997). In fact, ethnic identity is important because it creates
feelings of loyalty, interest, and fears of extinction (Horowitz 1985). We
can expect immigrants from Arab, Middle Eastern, and/or South Asian

countries to have political attitudes different from those who come from European countries. For instance, political upheavals in the Middle East are likely to matter to people of Middle Eastern origin more than those of East Asian origins (Carment and James 1997; Saideman 2001, 2002).

As compared to American jihadists who have no ethnic ties outside the United States, those with ethnic ties are more likely to fight abroad than domestically for two reasons. First, American jihadists born or raised in the United States are able to acquire a good understanding of the culture, the area, and language of their national origins through family members, close ethnic friends, and neighbors. This understanding provides a natural advantage for fighting abroad, as American jihadists possess multicultural familiarity, knowledge of the target area, and language skills necessary to conduct terrorist operations in the country of their ethnic background or neighboring countries (Kenney 2010; Pregulman and Burke 2012; Bjelopera 2013). Second, American jihadists are likely to fight outside the United States because of patriotic sentiments. Often, when American jihadists hear of political troubles in their home country, they are motivated to go abroad and join the fight due to patriotic fervor, as exemplified by a group of young Somali immigrants who traveled to Somalia after the 2006 Ethiopian invasion (Vidino, Pantucci, and Kohlmann 2010; Mendelsohn 2011; Vidino 2011). Indeed, Bergen and Sterman (2013) maintain that 23 individuals from a Somali community in Minneapolis, who were radicalized and recruited in the United States, then traveled to Somalia to fight for the al-Qaeda-affiliated al-Shabaab between 2007 and 2008. This Somali case is not unique—there are a plethora of similar instances of American jihadists fighting abroad. For example, Anwar al-Awlaki, an American-born citizen of Yemeni ancestry, had served as a notorious Yemeni imam and Islamist militant until he was killed in a joint CIA-U.S. military air strike on his convoy in Yemen (Mazzetti, Schmitt, and Worth 2011).[8] Jude Kenan Mohammad, *a U.S.-born* son of South Asian immigrants, was part of an eight-member group based in North Carolina accused of planning terrorist attacks. He left the United States to join Islamist militants in Pakistan's tribal region but was killed in a drone strike there in November 2011 (Shane and Schmitt 2013).

However, when American jihadists have no ethnic ties to an overseas target, they are more likely to fight domestically because of a familiarity with the political and security environment on American soil as well as easy access to financing, weapons, and explosives. In particular, American jihadists without ethnic ties abroad are more likely to engage in domestic attacks, with influence from al-Qaeda's propaganda media. For example, in a video message, American-born al-Qaeda spokesman Adam Gadahn urges American Muslims to carry out deadly one-man terrorist attacks using fully automatic weapons purchased at gun shows and to target major facilities and public figures. From Yemen, the imam Anwar al-Awlaki regularly released sermons and messages for American Muslims to attack targets inside the United States (Cole 2011). With this in mind, I offer the following hypothesis about ethnic ties:

Hypothesis of ethnic ties: American jihadists are more likely to engage in foreign fighting in those countries where they have an ethnic tie.

I discuss 10 personal characteristics that may make American jihadists predisposed to fight abroad: preference of American jihadists for acting alone; how old, wealthy, or educated they are; whether they are married, are convicted felons, or served in the military; whether they are converts to Islam; and whether they are second-generation Americans or ringleaders. As a personal preference, some individuals would rather act alone than with partners (Pierce and Cheney 2013). As such, some American jihadists may choose to engage in terrorist acts by themselves. Those terrorists who are radicalized online and choose to become lone wolves[9] are likely to seek excitement and adventure by joining the fight overseas, making them more likely to fight abroad rather than to stay at home (Sageman 2004). Although recent propaganda disseminated by terrorist organizations (e.g., al-Shabaab) over the Internet urges Muslims living abroad to either undertake a lone wolf mission in their home countries or go abroad to join terrorist groups,[10] I argue that American lone wolves prefer going abroad to attacking at home for two reasons. First, they are proud of fighting in one of the popular jihadist destinations of choice (e.g., Iraq and Syria) and are likely to have a sensationalized notion of training camps (Pantucci 2014). Second, they are attracted by more tangible rewards such as money and the lure of companionship such as the promise of wives for young militants (Bates 2012; Borum, Fein, and Vossekuil 2012; Spaaij 2012; Spaaij and Hamm 2015).

Young people are more likely to be inspired by jihadist ideology or become involved in terrorist activities than old people (Krueger 2007, 2008; Roy 2008). Because young American jihadists tend to perceive Muslims to be oppressed all over the world, they are more willing to go and fight with jihadists overseas. In her "Jihadi Cool" article, Temple-Raston (2010) contends that young Muslims may join jihadist rebels for the adventure of holy war rather than religious reasons: "Intelligence officials say there is a wave of young people who are attracted to the adventure of jihad but would like to skip all the rigors of Islam, such as reading the Quran and fasting." In today's globalized world, educated people are more likely to travel abroad (Richards 1996). For example, Kastenholz, Carneiro, and Eusébio (2005, 15) show that "the relatively older, wealthier and more educated respondents tended to be mostly foreign tourists." In particular, in order for American jihadists to conceive terrorist plots abroad, they should be better educated because overseas operations require knowledge about local people and facilities (Benmelech and Berrebi 2007; Krueger 2007, 2008; Altunbas and Thornton 2011). American Muslims are more up-wardly mobile and socially integrated compared to many of their Euro-pean counterparts (Elliott 2010). For instance, Vigdor (2011) observes that recent immigrants to the United States assimilate more successfully than those in Europe given that U.S. immigrants are better able to reach stan-dards of economic well-being compared to native-born Americans. Ac-cordingly, American jihadists are more likely to fight abroad rather than stay home as their economic conditions improve to the extent that they can afford the high cost of airfare for international traveling. According to defensive jihad, fighting becomes obligatory, and therefore, even men with families are expected to depart and join the jihad. However, I argue that American jihadists are less likely to fight abroad when they are mar-ried, compared to when they have no family members to support. The obvious reason is that married jihadists are likely to feel more responsible for family matters than unmarried ones. Thus, family responsibilities may preclude married jihadists from having the mobility, flexibility, and initia-tive to a jihadist cause (Russell and Miller 1977; Hudson 1999).

There are many American jihadists who are converts to Islam (Vidino 2009). Because converts often find going abroad challenging due to en-hanced homeland security measures and because they have greater famil-iarity with local areas and possess knowledge of the cultural and linguistic dimensions of their operating environment, they may choose to strike at home rather than risk traveling outside the United States (Cilluffo, Coz-zens, and Ranstorp 2010). For instance, Antonio Martinez, a Maryland man, attempted to remotely detonate a bomb placed in a vehicle at the armed forces recruiting station in Catonsville, Maryland (Cratty 2012). When second-generation Americans fail to integrate in the society, they often experience discrimination based on their identities and are unable to find a mainstream Western identity that merges easily with their heri-tage identity. To take revenge for discrimination, humiliation, and frus-tration, second-generation jihadists may prefer to attack domestic rather than overseas targets (Stroink 2007; King and Taylor 2011).

If American jihadists acquired military skills by serving in the armed forces, they may be better prepared for foreign adventures rather than fighting at home (Sageman 2004). In 2013, Eric Harroun, a former U.S. Army private from Arizona, carried out his terrorist acts abroad and was charged for firing a rocket-propelled grenade while fighting along-side al-Nusra, al-Qaeda's official affiliate in Syria (Shane and Zemansky 2013; Tepper and Zion 2013). On the other hand, when potential terrorists are radicalized in prisons, their activities are more likely to be confined within the United States and they are less likely to fight abroad because their criminal record may restrict international travel. Travel restrictions may lead aspiring jihadists to stay at home and do nothing or just rant online. In general, it is not easy to travel to a foreign country if a jihad-ist has violent or repeated criminal convictions, as legal authorities may prohibit them from leaving the country (Martin 2004). In particular, if a jihadist is on probation or parole, he or she must follow the travel poli-cies set by his or her probation officer, and leaving the country without permission will result in a violation.[11] Conversely, when American jihad-ists have not previously engaged in criminal activity, it is relatively easy to escape detection and surveillance by law enforcement and thus fight abroad (Bjelopera 2013). Therefore, I draw the following 10 hypotheses about personal characteristics:[12]

Ten hypotheses on personal characteristics: American jihadists are more likely to engage in foreign fighting than domestic fighting when they (1) act alone, (2) are ringleaders, (3) are young, (4) are wealthy, (5) are unmarried, (6) are well educated, (7) are converts to Islam, (8) are second-generation immigrants, (9) have military experience, and (10) have no prison record.

Benefit-Risk Assessments

In the wake of the 9/11 attacks, the United States drastically bolstered counterterrorism efforts. New anti-terrorism measures, including the 2001 USA PATRIOT Act, were implemented to enhance the federal govern-ment's ability to collect and analyze private information related to U.S. citizens and residents, indicating that Washington has become more ac-tive in its efforts to uncover and neutralize terrorist plots as early as possi-ble. Local counterterrorism efforts are also visibly active. For example, the New York City Police Department (NYPD) created a specialized Counter-terrorism Bureau after 9/11 and runs the NYPD Shield program, which was introduced for the NYPD to send and receive information from pri-vate sector security. The NYPD also has developed successful federal–local partnerships with government agencies, particularly through a Joint Ter-rorism Task Force, which enables the exchange of intelligence between local and federal law enforcement authorities (Deflem 2011).

Perhaps the adage "once burned, twice cautious" best explains Wash-ington's post-9/11 efforts to deter future terrorist attacks on American soil (Campbell 1998). The American efforts are recognized in Patrick and Ker-ra's (2013) assessment that "the United States stands out as the leader of counterterrorism efforts worldwide." Also noteworthy are Brooks's (2012) remarks that "the United States presents a difficult security environment in which to be a modern-day terrorist; those who initiate plotting are apt to be detected and foiled by arrests before they can act on their plans" (see also Brooks 2011). Indeed, as far as effective international counter-terrorism operations are concerned, the United States is a leader in the field. It is true that other countries have revamped their counterterrorism efforts in recent years, but their skills and proactive strategies, like planning, prevention, and resolution, are less developed than those in the United States. This disparity is largely due to insufficient funds, technologies, and political will. The superiority of anti-terrorism measures and strategies in the United States is likely to drive American jihadists to plan and operate abroad rather than on their home turf (Enders and Sandler 2006). That is, the United States' enhanced homeland security shifts terrorist attacks to other countries where American jihadists may aim at U.S. or local targets. An example can be found in the Toledo terror plot. In June 2008, Mohammad Amawi, Marwan El-Hindi, and Wassim Mazloum were convicted of conspiring to commit acts of terrorism against Americans overseas, including U.S. military personnel in Iraq, and other terrorism-related violations (Bjelopera 2013). The relatively limited reach of American counterterrorism capabilities abroad makes it much more convenient for American jihadists to carry out terrorist plots on foreign soil. Therefore, we can draw the following hypothesis about counterterrorism capacity:

Hypothesis of counterterrorism capacity: American jihadists are more likely to use terrorist violence in those countries whose counterterrorism capacity is weak.

American jihadists may perceive that foreign fighting is more legitimate than domestic fighting because they are radicalized with the idea cultivated by Islamic religious leaders that "fighting in established conflict zones is more legitimate than attacks in the West" (Hegghammer 2013, 7). In their NYPD report "Radicalization in the West: The Homegrown Threat," Silber and Bhatt (2007) term Islamic religious leaders as "spiritual sanctioners" because they provide the justification for jihad. Not surprisingly, if American jihadists are indoctrinated with Osama bin Laden's teaching that the United States is at war with Islam, they should perceive American soldiers who are fighting wars in Muslim countries to be more compelling targets than those inside the United States (Bjelopera 2013). These kinds of moral indignations or perceptions of increased legitimacy are plausible reasons for why American jihadists fight abroad. Yet it is difficult to verify these concepts because different religious figures have often advocated different ways of fighting throughout Islamic history; the quantification of these concepts is another challenging task as religious summons are hard to trace to the indoctrination of each American jihadist individually.

Another way to explain how American jihadists are radicalized and inspired by foreign fighting is to analyze what political events triggered them to pursue terrorism. Elliott's (2010) report may be useful in understanding how potential American terrorists are provoked to anger and frustration and decided to engage in foreign fighting.

The presence of Western troops in Afghanistan and Iraq has brought those conflicts closer for many Muslims in America. . . . For Omar Hammami [a U.S.-born citizen who publicly disclosed jihadist activity in Somalia in an interview with Al Jazeera in October 2007], the war in Iraq provided a critical spark as he turned toward militancy.

Because, in the eyes of many radicalized individuals, U.S. military interventions in Afghanistan and Iraq were perceived as an unjust attack on Muslims, it can be construed that Omar Hammami was pushed toward terrorist violence primarily by his perceptions of U.S. military activity abroad. Another specific example can be found in the testimony of Sulejah Hadzovic, who testified against U.S.-born citizen Betim Kaziu who traveled to the Middle East to join al-Qaeda (quoted in Hays 2012):

We were upset at what was happening in places like Abu Ghraib prison and Guantanamo Bay, how they were humiliating and torturing Muslims there. . . . It's what ultimately made us want to go and fight in jihad.

Although there is a possibility that these jihadists might not be truthful, they have less incentive to lie about their radicalization and motivations for fighting internationally when they were being prosecuted with the possibility of a less-severe sentencing. In fact, Berger's (2011) case studies provide a similar observation that the radicalization of American jihadists starts with their conviction that Muslims are a victim class. Therefore, I draw the following hypothesis about the perceived legitimacy of foreign fighting:

Hypothesis of legitimacy of foreign fighting: American jihadists who see foreign fighting as more legitimate will be more likely to fight abroad than attack at home.

BUILDING A STATISTICAL MODEL, OPERATIONALIZATION, AND DATA SOURCES

The following is a statistical model built to test the aforementioned 13 hypotheses:

$$
\begin{aligned}
\textit{Fighting abroad} = {}& \alpha + \beta_1 {}^* \textit{ethnic ties} + \beta_2 {}^* \textit{lone wolf} + \beta_3 {}^* \textit{ringleader} + \beta_4 {}^* \textit{age} \\
& + \beta_5 {}^* \textit{education} + \beta_6 {}^* \textit{income} + \beta_7 {}^* \textit{married} + \beta_8 {}^* \textit{convert} \\
& + \beta_9 {}^* \textit{second generation} + \beta_{10} {}^* \textit{military experience} \\
& + \beta_{11} {}^* \textit{ex-convict} + \beta_{12} {}^* \textit{counterterrorism capacity} \\
& + \beta_{13} {}^* \textit{legitimacy of foreign fighting} + \varepsilon
\end{aligned}
$$

where *fighting abroad* is the dependent variable, α is a constant term, β_1 through β_{13} are coefficients for independent variables, and ε is an error term.

Based on individual information concerning America's homegrown jihadists from various open sources,[13] I compiled a database of 193 terrorists during the period from 2001 to 2014.[14] The sample jihadists include American citizens and residents who were radicalized largely within the United States according to court documents and who were either indicted or convicted for involvement in terrorist activities, or who were killed before they could be indicted. Those individuals who were acquitted of terrorism charges or charged with lesser crimes, such as immigration violations, are excluded in the sample. By definition, the militant environmentalists or the antiabortion activists are excluded in my data collection. Note that the data is advantageous in comparison to other datasets, such as the global terrorism database, that are confined to individuals who were successful in carrying out terrorist acts. This dataset is comprehensive in the sense that it includes American jihadists who supported, plotted, or committed terrorist violence whether they were successful or not. Put differently, the dataset is the population of America's homegrown jihadists in the period under study. Of the 193 jihadists, 91 are born in the United States, 46 are naturalized citizens, and 56 are residents, indicating the terrorist threat starts in America's own backyard.

Using descriptions of the activities of American terrorists from open sources, each jihadist is identified and then matched with his or her target country, making the unit of analysis dyadic. When an individual jihadist planned to terrorize or terrorized civilian or military targets on American soil, his or her act is classified as domestic fighting. For example, Dzhokhar Tsarnaev and Tamerlan Tsarnaev, the two perpetrators of the Boston Marathon bombings, are recorded as domestic fighters. When an American terrorist's targets are located outside the United States,[15] a jihadist act is coded as foreign fighting. The May 25, 2014, attack by the U.S.-born terrorist Abu Hurayra Al-Amriki in Syria is a case in point.

The dependent variable, *fighting abroad,* is a dichotomous measure, recoded as "1" for an American jihadist aiming at targets outside American soil at the time of arrest or death and "0" otherwise. Of 193 American jihadists, 139 are recorded as foreign fighters and 54 as domestic fighters. Because the nature of the dependent variable is binary (i.e., the issue is whether a jihadist went abroad), I employed a logistic regression model adjusted for Huber-White robust standard errors.

Table 2.1 provides descriptive statistics of the dependent and independent variables. The first independent variable, *ethnic ties,* measures whether there is an ethnic tie between each American jihadist and his or her target country. I categorized the ethnicity or race of each of 193 American jihadists into 16 subgroups:[16] Arab/Middle Eastern (44 jihadists), South Asian (35 jihadists), Somali (26 jihadists), Caucasian (21 jihadists), African American (20 jihadists), Caribbean (12 jihadists), Hispanic (10 jihadists), Albanian (7 jihadists), Mixed/Other (7 jihadists), Uzbek

Table 2.1
Descriptive Statistics

Variable	Observations	Mean	Standard Deviation	Minimum	Maximum
Fighting abroad	193	0.720	0.450	0	1
Demographic characteristics					
Ethnic ties	193	0.363	0.482	0	1
Lone wolf	193	0.238	0.427	0	1
Ringleader	193	0.192	0.395	0	1
Age	193	29	9	17	68
Education	193	3.617	1.361	1	7
Income	193	1.534	0.662	1	3
Married	193	0.456	0.499	0	1
Convert	193	0.394	0.490	0	1
Second generation	193	0.171	0.377	0	1
Military experience	193	0.109	0.312	0	1
Ex-convict	193	0.145	0.353	0	1
Benefit-risk assessments					
Counterterrorism capacity	193	8.202	2.447	5.231	10.733
Legitimacy of foreign fighting					
Conflict index	193	2,479	2,636	0	9,125
Human rights abuses	193	356	393	0	1,280

(1 jihadist), Ethiopian (3 jihadists), Bosnian (2 jihadists), Chechen (2 jihadists), Turkish (1 jihadist), East Asian (1 jihadist), and Uighur (1 jihadist). The *ethnic ties* variable is dichotomous, coded as either "1" for the presence of an ethnic tie or "0" otherwise. For example, because Betim Kaziu is a U.S.-born son of Albanian Muslim immigrants from the former Yugoslavia and traveled to Kosovo in an effort to target U.S. troops stationed there (Hays 2012), he is recorded as "1" for *ethnic ties*. In contrast, John Walker Lindh is recorded "0" for *ethnic ties*, because he was a Caucasian-American who provided his services to the Taliban in Afghanistan and was captured during the U.S. invasion of Afghanistan in November 2001 (Lewis 2002).

The 2nd to 11th independent variables look at 10 attributes of each individual jihadist. They capture whether he or she acted alone (i.e., a lone wolf), as a ringleader of a terrorist group, or as a terrorist group member; how old he or she was at the time of arrest or attack; what level of education he or she had received (primary education or less, high school dropout, high school graduate, some college, college degree, some graduate education, and postgraduate degree) at the time of the attack/planned attack; how well he or she lived (lower, middle, and upper class); whether he or she was married; whether he or she converted to Islam; whether he or she is second generation; whether he or she served in the military; and whether he or she had past convictions.[17] As noted, these personal characteristics are collected from numerous open sources.

The 12th independent variable, *counterterrorism capacity*, assesses the ability of a targeted country to employ counterterrorism activities. This independent variable is measured by the logged gross domestic product (GDP), per capita, in constant 2005 U.S. dollars, collected from the World Bank's 2013 World Development Indicator. The literature on civil war and terrorism commonly employs the measure as an effort to gauge the level of state counterterrorism capacity (e.g., Fearon and Laitin 2003; Walsh and Piazza 2010).[18] Note that after closely examining 15 different indicators of state capacity, Hendrix (2010) suggests total taxes/GDP and bureaucratic quality as two best measures. When total taxes/GDP is used in place of the GDP per capita, it is negatively associated with American jihadist fighting abroad, as expected. But when the GDP per capita is replaced with bureaucratic quality, it is dropped out of estimation because of a lack of variation.[19]

The 13th independent variable, *legitimacy of foreign fighting*, is measured in two ways: by a weighted conflict index and by the presence of human rights abuses.[20] I introduce two measures as part of robustness checks rather than relying on one measure given that Hegghammer's (2013) study underlines the significant role of legitimacy in the decision-making of Western fighters. The two measures are introduced as proxies to assess whether American jihadists perceive foreign fighting as a legitimate cause, as the concept is difficult to quantify. The weighted conflict index captures the notion that it is more legitimate for an American jihadist to fight in a war-prone foreign country than to start terrorizing in relatively peaceful Western territories (Hegghammer 2013). The index is a continuous measure, garnered from Banks and Wilson's (2014) dataset of political events that include guerrilla warfare, government crises, revolutions, anti-government demonstrations, assassinations, purges, riots, and general strikes. The second measure purports to assess the degree of possible frustration and anger when jihadists hear of human rights violations in other countries, which might provide sufficient justification for their violent action abroad. Because American jihadists could have learned of human rights abuses through mass media (Hegghammer 2010/11; Walsh and Piazza 2010), I compiled a dataset based on the *New York Times'* coverage of countries related to human rights. The *New York Times* article archive at http://query.nytimes.com/search/sitesearch/ provides the number of articles the *New York Times* prints in a given year, starting from 1851. I calculated the number of articles that include two key words: "country name" (e.g., Afghanistan) and "human rights." The variable is constructed by counting the total number of articles. Online jihad forums are not used for the collection of this data because they are relatively new and because U.S. counterterrorism authorities frequently shut them down.

EMPIRICAL RESULTS

Table 2.2 presents statistical results of the logistic regression models. The first column lists independent variables. While Models 1, 2, 3, 4, and 6 show estimated coefficients and standard errors, Models 5 and 7 display standardized coefficients for comparison purposes. Eleven demographic characteristics are evaluated in Model 1, while two factors of benefit-risk assessments are examined in Models 2 and 3. Models 4 and 6 expand the previous three models by combining demographic characteristics with benefit-risk assessments.[21] Note that given the high pseudo-R^2 statistics that range from 0.30 to 0.64, it is fair to say that these models are well built to predict the likelihood of American jihadists fighting abroad.

Among 11 demographic characteristics shown in Model 1, *ethnic ties, age,* and *income* are significantly different from zero. This implicates that, as expected, America's homegrown jihadists are more likely to leave the country to fight for al-Qaeda or its affiliates rather than to attack at home when they have ethnic ties to the target country, when they are younger, and when their economic status is better. Model 2 tests the effects of two benefit-risk assessments: counterterrorism capabilities of the target country and legitimacy of foreign fighting over domestic fighting. *Counterterrorism capacity* turns out to be significant and in the hypothesized direction; the *legitimacy of foreign fighting* measured by conflict index achieves significance but not in the expected way. It appears that when anti-terrorism measures of the target country are relatively weak, American jihadists are more likely to engage in terrorist activities abroad. Yet the perception that American jihadists hold about the deteriorating conflict environment of the target country does not necessarily motivate American jihadists to fight abroad. In Model 3, the conflict index is replaced with human rights abuses as an alternative measure for the *legitimacy of foreign fighting. Counterterrorism capacity* achieves significance, while human rights abuses do not. Concerning the effect of the latter, it appears that reports of human rights abuses abroad are not associated with the behavior of American jihadists going after the perceived abusers.

By combining Models 1 and 2, Model 4 brings together demographic characteristics and benefit-risk assessments, helping to assess the complete picture of the individual behavior of America's homegrown jihadists. *Ethnic ties, lone wolf, age, convert,* and *counterterrorism capacity* are significant

Table 2.2
Why Do America's Homegrown Jihadists Fight Abroad?

Variable	Model 1	Model 2	Model 3	Model 4	Model 5	Model 6	Model 7
Demographic characteristics							
Ethnic ties	3.874***			4.365***	0.150	4.538***	0.117
	(0.857)			(1.217)		(1.189)	
Lone wolf	0.336			1.679*	0.051	1.604*	0.037
	(0.513)			(0.677)		(0.728)	
Ringleader	-0.619			-0.473	-0.013	-0.582	-0.012
	(0.484)			(0.723)		(0.700)	
Age	-0.065**			-0.102*	-0.069	-0.096*	-0.049
	(0.023)			(0.045)		(0.046)	
Education	-0.180			-0.390	-0.038	-0.435	-0.032
	(0.185)			(0.303)		(0.279)	
Income	0.907*			0.690	0.033	0.822	0.029
	(0.412)			(0.795)		(0.676)	
Married	0.503			1.011	0.036	0.956	0.026
	(0.389)			(0.711)		(0.708)	
Convert	0.065			-1.968*	-0.069	-1.887*	-0.050
	(0.478)			(0.944)		(0.888)	
Second generation	0.818			-1.687	-0.045	-1.810	-0.037
	(0.688)			(1.308)		(1.161)	

(Continued)

Table 2.2
(Continued)

Variable	Model 1	Model 2	Model 3	Model 4	Model 5	Model 6	Model 7
Military experience	1.338			2.135	0.048	2.423*	0.041
	(0.751)			(1.186)		(1.142)	
Ex-convict	−0.485			0.828	0.021	0.690	0.013
	(0.539)			(0.885)		(0.859)	
Benefit-risk assessments							
Counterterrorism capacity		−8.226**	−7.400**	−7.054*	−1.233	−7.298*	−0.958
		(2.613)	(2.654)	(3.005)		(3.613)	
Legitimacy of foreign fighting							
Conflict index		−0.002*		−0.002	−0.395		
		(0.001)		(0.001)			
Human rights abuses			0.001			0.001	0.018
			(0.001)			(0.001)	
Constant	0.990	88.052**	78.054**	77.753*		79.093*	
	(0.795)	(28.147)	(28.238)	(32.350)		(38.588)	
Wald chi²	38.55	37.33	8.51	48.29	33.77		
Probability > chi²	0.001	0.001	0.001	0.001	0.001		
Log pseudolikelihood	−79.98	−56.71	−56.84	−41.19	−41.19		
Pseudo R²	0.30	0.50	0.50	0.64	0.64		
Observations	193	193	193	193	193		

Note: Robust standard errors are in parentheses. Models 5 and 7 display standardized coefficients.

* 0.05 two-tailed

** 0.01 two-tailed

*** 0.001 two-tailed

predictors of American jihadist terrorism abroad, while conflict index and seven other demographic characteristic variables remain insignificant. Although the overall results in the combined model are similar to those in the separate models, they also indicate that America's homegrown jihadists are likely to engage in foreign fighting more than domestic fighting when they act alone but not necessarily when they are relatively affluent.

The coefficients in Model 4 are unstandardized, because they are measured in their natural units. As such, the coefficients cannot be compared with one another to determine which one is more important or influential in the statistical model. Model 5 addresses this concern by reporting standardized coefficients. When the relative effects of the 13 factors are evaluated in absolute terms, *counterterrorism capacity* emerges as the most influential determinant of the individual behavior of American jihadists, followed in descending order by *ethnic ties, age, convert,* and *lone wolf.*

Model 6 is an alternative version of Model 4, utilizing human rights abuses instead of the conflict index as a proxy measure of the *legitimacy of foreign fighting.* Although the main findings of Models 4 and 6 closely resemble each other, *military experience* in Model 6 turns out to be significantly different from zero. As displayed in Model 7, the rank order of the relative importance among the variables is *counterterrorism capacity, ethnic ties, convert, age, military experience,* and then *lone wolf.*

The overall results in Table 2.2 beg for a discussion of a necessary policy-related question—how to best deter an American jihadist planning on going abroad? Although it is true that "there is no easily identifiable terrorist-prone personality, no single path to radicalization and terrorism" (Jenkins 2010, 7), my research indicates that counterterrorism and law enforcement authorities should seek to identify individuals under 30 who are descended from terrorism-prone countries with an underdeveloped counterterrorism capacity and those individuals who are not particularly involved in social activities within their Muslim immigrant communities but instead spend most of their time online on terrorism-related websites.[22] Of course, these indicators do not provide a concrete and specific profile to predict exactly who will become American jihadists, but it offers a broad profile and a starting point for identification.

Although reporting statistical significance is an important step in any data analysis, a calculation of the substantive effects of the variables is another crucial step for empirical verification. If the analysis of substantive effects is consistent with the statistical significance, then the estimated coefficients and standard errors reported in Table 2.2 can rightly be called meaningful. As an example, I estimate the substantive effects of the three variables that achieve statistical significance in Model 4 in Table 2.2.

Table 2.3 displays the substantive effects. It demonstrates that *ethnic ties, age,* and *counterterrorism capacity* exert significant effects on the individual behavior of America's homegrown jihadists. The percentage change

Table 2.3
Substantive Effects

Variable	Model 4 in Table 2.2
Demographic characteristics	
Ethnic ties	
Changed from 0 to 1	5%
Age	
Increased by one standard deviation	–13%
Benefit-risk assessments	
Counterterrorism capacity	
Increased by one standard deviation	–100%

in the likelihood of American jihadist terrorism going abroad increases by 5 when there is an ethnic connection between an American jihadist and the target country; the predicted probability of going abroad decreases by 13 percentage points when *age* increases by one standard deviation, or nine years; and the probability decreases 100 percentage points when *counterterrorism capacity* increases by one standard deviation. The analysis of substantive effects shows no deviation from the reported statistical significance in Table 2.3.

It is important to note that, given the high human and financial costs associated with terrorism, even small changes in the predicted probability of a terrorist attack should not be dismissed. Reducing the probability of America's homegrown terrorism by 5 percentage points is hardly trivial when we recognize that a single successful attack can cost dozens or hundreds of human lives, result in millions of dollars of damage, and cause considerable socioeconomic disruption. A good example is David Coleman Headley, a U.S. citizen of Pakistani descent, whose involvement in Lashkar-e-Taiba's 2008 attacks on the Taj Mahal hotel and other targets in Mumbai, India, killed 172 people, including 6 Americans. His surveillance on targets for the terrorist group played a key role in the raids (Yaccino 2013).

CONCLUSION

The question of why American homegrown terrorists decide to fight abroad rather than at home is of mounting concern; however, little empirical research has addressed this question to date. Instances of American jihadists attacking abroad, such as the al-Shabaab-related cases in which young Somali immigrants left the United States to fight in Somalia, continue to alarm the American public and law enforcement authorities. My empirical analysis offers a first cut at modeling the determinants of the *individual* behavior of American jihadists at the dyadic level and, consequently, suggests important policy recommendations. By including 13 causal factors based on demographic characteristics and benefit-risk assessments, I built a statistical model that is comprehensive but which still features some degree of economy of explanation. My data analysis of 193 American jihadists demonstrates that *ethnic ties, age,* and *counterterrorism capabilities* provide substantial and consistent predictive power with regard to where an American jihadist ends up fighting. That is, when an American jihadist is ethnically linked to a potential overseas target and when he or she is young, he or she is inclined to engage in foreign fighting more than domestic fighting. In addition, when counterterrorism measures of the target country are weak, he or she is more likely to fight abroad.

My findings show several advanced signs of terrorism prevention programs. Given the fact that one of my main findings indicates the emerging danger related to ethnic terrorism, politicians and policy makers should approach the generally lauded description of America as a melting pot with some caution. Although several studies claim that the American melting pot provides a firewall against the radicalization of Americans because they are better integrated, better educated, and wealthier than their peers abroad (see Elliott 2010; Vigdor 2011), cultural diversity may not be the best policy approach if the public policy goal is to create a terrorism-free environment by eradicating terrorism altogether from American soil. Perhaps, Loza's (2007) study provides a relevant observation that the West's immigration policies allow terrorism to flourish and to spread, especially when immigrants are radicalizing in their host states. Loza's observation appears to urge Washington to more carefully scrutinize immigration applicants from terrorism-prone countries such as Afghanistan, Iraq, and Syria.

An instrumental counterterrorism measure at the community level may be to provide young Muslims with civic education courses about the danger of jihadist terrorism and an American way of life related to the American Dream—the idea that upward mobility is achievable by any American through hard work. Such civic engagement efforts may be helpful at countering radicalism given the fact that many of them often come from the Muslim community itself (Bergen and Hoffman 2010; Bergen et al. 2013). Another important counterterrorism effort is to establish a special hotline program within local communities—such a program is introduced in Germany and the United Kingdom. Such a program would allow local people to report seemingly innocuous activity to security authorities rather than taking the more severe measure of contacting the police (Pantucci 2014).

The findings also underline the importance of strengthening counter-terrorism capacities in terrorism-vulnerable places such as Iraq, Pakistan, and Afghanistan. If this policy implication is correct, former president Barack Obama's initiative to set up a $5 billion fund to "train, build capacity and facilitate partner countries on the front lines"[23] of fighting terrorism was welcome news. The significant role that lone wolves played in recent years is alarming, especially considering that terrorist plots committed by individuals and pairs who lack ties to known foreign groups are rapidly growing and are much more difficult to detect than those by groups of terrorists. The positive correlation between age and going abroad also suggests that there is a greater supply of potential terrorists among younger jihadists. Thus, it is necessary to focus anti-terrorism efforts on American jihadists who are likely to act individually and who are relatively young.

NOTES

1. Note that many different definitions of American homegrown terrorism have been employed in both the policy and academic world. Yet, for the purpose of parsimony, I rely on a slightly modified definition of Bjelopera (2013, 7)—jihadist terrorist activity or plots perpetuated within the United States or abroad by American citizens and residents who are radicalized largely within the United States. In this study, I do not discuss right- and left-wing terrorism such as the militant environmentalists or the antiabortion activists (see Piazza [2014] for details on right and left-wing terrorism).

2. For more descriptive information on the differences between domestic and foreign fighters, see Bjelopera and Randol (2010), Bjelopera (2013), Cilluffo, Cozzens, and Ranstorp (2010), Kurzman, Schanzer, and Moosa (2011), and Kurzman (2011).

3. I focus on American jihadist terrorism because it has emerged as one of the most important security issues among American scholars and policy makers. Yet Americans appear to have engaged in overseas terrorist activities at lower per capita rates than other Westerners. This implies that America may be less vulnerable to homegrown terrorism than other Western countries.

4. The Stata error message is that "[the occupation variable] predicts success perfectly."

5. George H. W. Bush once said that "we are a nation of communities . . . a brilliant diversity spread like stars, like a thousand points of light in a broad and peaceful sky"; and Gary Locke points out that "ethnic diversity adds richness to a society" (Wong 2012).

6. Though not related specifically to American jihadists, several studies introduce religious duty, response to threat, opportunity to influence failed states, or role expectations as a potential cause of radicalization (see Roy 2004; Hafez 2007; Moore and Tumelty 2008; Hegghammer 2010/11; Malet 2013).

7. One may infer from existing literature that ethnic diasporas or people with similar ideological beliefs enable recruitment and decisions to fight abroad (Clutterbuck and Warnes 2011; LaFree and Bersani 2014). However, because many

American jihadists are self-radicalized and have no real connection to international terrorist groups, the inference on recruitment by other terrorists is less useful.

8. The al-Awlaki case was seen as a targeted killing (a.k.a. selective assassination) because it was the premeditated killing of an individual by the U.S. government. Kamal Derwish, a U.S.-born son of Yemeni parents, was the first public instance of an American citizen killed by the CIA as part of a covert targeted killing mission in Yemen on November 5, 2002 (Sandler 2003). These cases indicate that *ethnic ties*, whether due to local familiarity or patriotic fervor, affect the decisions of American jihadists when choosing target countries.

9. A lone wolf is one who is inspired to engage in terrorist attacks on one's own and not part of a formal terrorist group.

10. However, other terrorist groups, such as al-Qaeda in the Arabian Peninsula, advocate Muslims to undertake lone wolf attacks against domestic targets rather than travel abroad (Bergen et al. 2013).

11. See also http://wikitravel.org/en/Traveling_with_a_criminal_history.

12. Ten hypotheses are put together in a sentence to save space.

13. Though not exhaustive, the sources include the Citizens Crime Commission of New York City, CNN, the Congressional Research Service Report for Congress, court documents, FBI press releases, Google, the Homeland Security Digital Library, local newspapers, the New America Foundation, the *New York Times*, and the Terrorist Trial Report Card. Note that due to a lack of individual information of American jihadists, I did not consult widely used terrorism datasets such as the International *Terrorism*: Attributes of *Terrorist* Events (ITERATE) and the Global Terrorism Database.

14. More precisely, the study period starts right after 9/11 because it is a critical historical juncture of America's global War on Terror and ends on June 30, 2014.

15. The targets, by definition, also include U.S. targets such as soldiers operating in a foreign theater of war.

16. When the Pew Research Center's definition of geographic categories for birth places is used instead (see http://www.people-press.org/2011/08/30/survey-methodology-9/), the main findings of this study do not change.

17. Although sex is another potential predictor, it is not included in the model specification due to a lack of variation. Of 193 jihadists, males are 185 and females are 8.

18. One may assert that logged GDP per capita is not a good indicator of *counterterrorism capacity* because some poor countries may invest heavily in internal security and because they may get infusion of real money from the United States for counterterrorism efforts (e.g., Yemen). Yet, as the old saying goes, there is no rule without an exception. Yemen is an exception. Furthermore, a majority of poor countries are unable to afford costly counterterrorism operations.

19. The Stata error message is that "[the highest score] predicts success perfectly."

20. Alternative measures such as the Uppsala and PRIO Armed Conflict Dataset, the Cingranelli-Richards index of physical integrity rights, and the Political Terror Scale lead to results that are similar to those reported in the next section.

21. When three sets of multicollinearity diagnostics (i.e., R^2 statistics, variance inflation factors, eigenvalues) are performed for the independent variables, no severe multicollinearity is found.

22. These findings may provide justification for the National Security Agency's domestic spying program. Through the program, law enforcement authorities utilize the use of computer software programs that enable them to crawl social media and open-source Internet and thus to look for keywords to terrorist activities.

23. https://www.whitehouse.gov/the-press-office/2014/05/28/remarks-president-united-states-military-academy-commencement-ceremony.

REFERENCES

Almasy, Steve. 2013. "What We Know about the Boston Marathon Bombing and Its Aftermath." http://www.cnn.com/2013/04/17/us/boston-marathon-things-we-know/.

Altunbas, Yener and John Thornton. 2011. "Are Homegrown Islamic Terrorist Different?" *Southern Economic Journal* 78(2): 262–272.

Axelrod, Robert, ed. 1976. *Structure of Decision.* Princeton, NJ: Princeton University Press.

Bakke, Kristin. 2014. "Help Wanted?" *International Security* 38(4): 150–187.

Banks, Arthur and Kenneth Wilson. 2014. "Cross-National Time-Series Data Archive." Databanks International, Jerusalem, Israel.

Bates, Rodger. 2012. "Dancing with Wolves." *Journal of Public and Professional Sociology* 4(1): 1–14.

Benmelech, Effraim and Claude Berrebi. 2007. "Human Capital and the Productivity of Suicide Bombers." *Journal of Economic Perspectives* 21(3): 223–238.

Bergen, Peter and Bruce Hoffman. 2010. "Assessing the Terrorist Threat." http://bipartisanpolicy.org/sites/default/files/NSPG%20Final%20Threat%20Assessment.pdf.

Bergen, Peter, Bruce Hoffman, Michael Hurley, and Erroll Southers. 2013. "Jihadist Terrorism." http://bipartisanpolicy.org/sites/default/files/Jihadist%20Terrorism-A%20Threat%20Assesment_0.pdf.

Bergen, Peter and David Sterman. 2013. "Al-Shabaab's American Allies." http://www.cnn.com/2013/09/23/opinion/bergen-al-shabaab-american-ties/.

Berger, J. M. 2011. *Jihad Joe.* Washington, DC: Potomac Books.

Bjelopera, Jerome. 2013. "American Jihadist Terrorism." https://fas.org/sgp/crs/terror/R41416.pdf

Bjelopera, Jerome and Mark Randol. 2010. "American Jihadist Terrorism." http://www.dtic.mil/cgi-bin/GetTRDoc?Location=U2&doc=GetTRDoc.pdf&AD=ADA536056.

Borum, Randy, Robert Fein, and Bryan Vossekuil. 2012. "A Dimensional Approach to Analyzing Lone Offender Terrorism." *Aggression and Violent Behavior* 17(5): 389–396.

Brooks, Lisa. 2011. "Muslim 'Homegrown' Terrorism in the United States." *International Security* 36(2): 7–47.

Brooks, Lisa. 2012. "An Exaggerated Threat." http://www.cato-unbound.org/print-issue/147.

Campbell, Kenneth. 1998. "Once Burned, Twice Cautious." *Armed Forces & Society* 24(3): 357–374.

Carment, David and Patrick James, eds. 1997. *Wars in the Midst of Peace*. Pittsburg, PA: University of Pittsburgh Press.

Cilluffo, Frank, Jeffrey Cozzens, and Magnus Ranstorp. 2010. "Foreign Fighters." http://www.diva-portal.org/smash/get/diva2:380558/FULLTEXT01.pdf.

Clayton, Mark. 2009. "How FBI Traced Tarek Mehanna in His Quest to Become a Jihadi." http://www.csmonitor.com/USA/Justice/2009/1022/p02s10-usju.html.

Clutterbuck, Lindsay and Richard Warnes. 2011. "Exploring Patterns of Behaviour in Violent Jihadist Terrorists." http://www.jstor.org/stable/10.7249/tr923ant.

Cole, Matthew. 2011. "New Al Qaeda Video." http://abcnews.go.com/Blotter/al-qaeda-video-buy-automatic-weapons-start-shooting/story?id=13704264.

Cratty, Carol. 2012. "Maryland Man Sentenced to 25 Years for Plot to Bomb Military Recruiting Center." http://www.cnn.com/2012/04/06/justice/maryland-bomb-plot-sentence/.

Deflem, Mathieu. 2011. "Policing the Modern City." In Siddik Ekici, ed., *Counter Terrorism in Diverse Communities*. Amsterdam: IOS Press. 261–267.

Elliott, Andrea. 2010. "The Jihadist Next Door." http://www.nytimes.com/2010/01/31/magazine/31Jihadist-t.html?pagewanted=all&_r=0.

Enders, Walter and Todd Sandler. 2006. *The Political Economy of Terrorism*. New York: Cambridge University Press.

Fearon, James and David Laitin. 2003. "Ethnicity, Insurgency, and Civil War." *American Political Science Review* 97(1): 75–90.

Hafez, Mohammed. 2007. *Suicide Bombers in Iraq*. Washington, DC: United States Institute of Peace.

Hambrick, Donald and Phyllis Mason. 1984. "Upper Echelons." *Academy of Management Review* 9(2): 193–206.

Hays, Tom. 2012. "Betim Kaziu Gets 27 Years in Homegrown Terror Case." http://www.huffingtonpost.com/2012/03/03/betim-kaziu-gets-27-years_n_1318288.html.

Hegghammer, Thomas. 2010/11. "The Rise of Muslim Foreign Fighters." *International Security* 35(3): 53–94.

Hegghammer, Thomas. 2013. "Should I Stay or Should I Go?" *American Political Science Review* 107(1): 1–15.

Hendrix, Cullen. 2010. "Measuring State Capacity." *Journal of Peace Research* 47(3): 273–285.

Hewitt, Christopher and Jessica Kelley-Moore. 2009. "Foreign Fighters in Iraq." *Terrorism and Political Violence* 21(2): 211–220.

Horowitz, Donald. 1985. *Ethnic Groups in Conflict*. Berkeley: University of California Press.

Hudson, Rex. 1999. "The Sociology and Psychology of Terrorism." http://www.loc.gov/rr/frd/pdf-files/Soc_Psych_of_Terrorism.pdf.

Jenkins, Brian Michael. 2010. *Would-Be Warriors*. Santa Monica, CA: RAND Corporation. https://www.rand.org/pubs/occasional_papers/OP292.html

Kastenholz, Elisabeth, Maria João Carneiro, and Celeste Eusébio. 2005. "The Impact of Socio-Demographics on Tourist Behavior—Analyzing Segments of Cultural Tourists Visiting Coimbra." http://www.tram-research.com/atlas/Aveiro.pdf.

Kenney, Michael. 2010. "Organizational Learning and Islamic Militancy." http://www.nij.gov/journals/265/Pages/militancy.aspx.

King, Michael and Donald Taylor. 2011. "The Radicalization of Homegrown Jihadists." *Terrorism and Political Violence* 23(4): 602–622.

Krueger, Alan. 2007. *What Makes a Terrorist*. Princeton, NJ: Princeton University Press.

Krueger, Alan. 2008. "What Makes a Homegrown Terrorist?" *Economic Letters* 101(3): 293–296.

Kurzman, Charles. 2011. *The Missing Martyrs: Why There Are So Few Muslim Terrorists*. New York: Oxford University Press.

Kurzman, Charles, David Schanzer, and Ebrahim Moosa. 2011. "Muslim American Terrorism since 9/11." *Muslim World* 101(3): 464–483.

LaFree, Gary and Bianca Bersani. 2014. "County-Level Correlates of Terrorist Attacks in the United States." *Criminology & Public Policy* 13(3): 455–481.

Lewis, Neil. 2002. "American Who Joined Taliban Pleads Guilty." http://www.nytimes.com/2002/07/15/national/15CND-LINDH.html.

Loza, Wagdy. 2007. "The Psychology of Extremism and Terrorism." *Aggression and Violent Behavior* 12(2): 141–155.

Malet, David. 2013. *Foreign Fighters*. New York: Oxford University Press.

Markóczy, Lívia. 1997. "Measuring Beliefs." *Academy of Management Journal* 40(5): 1228–1242.

Martin, Kate. 2004. "Domestic Intelligence and Civil Liberties." *SAIS Review of International Affairs* 24(1): 7–21.

Mazzetti, Mark, Eric Schmitt, and Michael Schmidt. 2014. "Suicide Bomber Is identified as a Florida Man." http://www.nytimes.com/2014/05/31/world/middleeast/american-suicide-bomber-in-syria.html?_r=0.

Mazzetti, Mark, Eric Schmitt, and Robert Worth. 2011. "Two-Year Manhunt Led to Killing of Awlaki in Yemen." http://www.nytimes.com/2011/10/01/world/middleeast/anwar-al-awlaki-is-killed-in-yemen.html?pagewanted=all&_r=0.

Mendelsohn, Barak. 2011. "Foreign Fighters." *Orbis* 55(2): 189–202.

Moore, Cerwyn and Paul Tumelty. 2008. "Foreign Fighters and the Case of Chechnya." *Studies in Conflict and Terrorism* 31(5): 412–433.

Murphy, Shelley and Milton Valencia. 2009. "Details Emerge on Plot Suspects." http://www.boston.com/news/local/massachusetts/articles/2009/10/23/details_emerge_on_plot_suspects/.

National Research Council. 1997. *The New Americans*. Washington, DC: National Academies Press.

Pantucci, Raffaello. 2014. "There Are Ways to Address Radicalism Early." http://www.nytimes.com/roomfordebate/2014/08/28/how-to-stop-radicalization-in-the-west/there-are-ways-to-address-radicalism-early.

Patrick, Stewart and Alexandra Kerra. 2013. "Why America Gets a B+ in Counterterrorism." http://www.theatlantic.com/international/archive/2013/05/why-america-gets-a-b-in-counterterrorism/275504/.

Piazza, James. 2014. "The Determinants of Domestic Right-Wing Terrorism in the United States." http://www.utdallas.edu/epps/cgca/Papers.html.

Pierce, W. and Carl Cheney. 2013. *Behavior Analysis and Learning*. New York: Psychology Press.

Pregulman, Ally and Emily Burke. 2012. "Homegrown Terrorism." https://www.csis.org/analysis/homegrown-terrorism

Richards, Greg. 1996. "Cultural Tourism in Context." In Greg Richards, ed., *Cultural Tourism in Europe*. Wallingford: Cab International.

Roy, Olivier. 2004. *Globalized Islam*. New York: Columbia University Press.

Roy, Olivier. 2008. "Al Qaeda in the West as a Youth Movement." https://papers.ssrn.com/sol3/papers.cfm?abstract_id=1333550

Russell, Charles and Bowman Miller. 1977. "Profile of a Terrorist." *Studies in Conflict & Terrorism* 1(1): 17–34.

Sageman, Marc. 2004. *Understanding Terror Networks*. Philadelphia: University of Pennsylvania Press.

Saideman, Stephen. 2001. *The Ties That Divide*. New York: Columbia University Press.

Saideman, Stephen. 2002. "Discrimination in International Relations." *Journal of Peace Research* 39(1): 27–50.

Sandler, James. 2003. "*Kamal Derwish*." http://www.pbs.org/wgbh/pages/frontline/shows/sleeper/inside/derwish.html.

Schmidt, Michael and Eric Schmitt. 2014. "U.S. identifies Citizens Joining Rebels in Syria, Including ISIS." http://www.nytimes.com/2014/08/29/world/middleeast/us-identifies-citizens-joining-rebels-in-syria.html.

Shane, Scott and Eric Schmitt. 2013. "One Drone Victim's Trail from Raleigh to Pakistan." http://www.nytimes.com/2013/05/23/us/one-drone-victims-trail-from-raleigh-to-pakistan.html.

Shane, Scott and Rebekah Zemansky. 2013. "Judge Rules against Veteran Who Fought alongside Syrian Rebels." http://www.nytimes.com/2013/04/09/world/eric-harroun-who-fought-with-syrian-rebels-loses-a-court-fight.html?pagewanted=all.

Silber, Mitchell and Arvin Bhatt. 2007. "Radicalization in the West: The Homegrown Threat." https://www.brennancenter.org/sites/default/files/legacy/Justice/20070816.NYPD.Radicalization.in.the.West.pdf

Simcox, Robin and Emily Dyer. 2013. "Al-Qaeda in the United States." http://henryjacksonsociety.org/wp-content/uploads/2013/02/Al-Qaeda-in-the-USAbridged-version-LOWRES-Final.pdf.

Spaaij, Ramón. 2012. *Understanding Lone Wolf Terrorism*. New York: Springer.

Spaaij, Ramón and Mark Hamm. 2015. "Key Issues and Research Agendas in Lone Wolf Terrorism." *Studies in Conflict & Terrorism* 38(3): 167–178.

Stroink, Mirella. 2007. "Processes and Preconditions Underlying Terrorism in Second-Generation Immigrants." *Peace and Conflict* 13(3): 293–312.

Temple-Raston, Dina. 2010. "Jihadi Cool." http://www.npr.org/templates/story/story.php?storyId=125186382.

Tepper, Greg and Ilan Zion. 2013. "The Jihadist from Phoenix." http://foreignpolicy.com/2013/03/22/the-jihadist-from-phoenix/

Vidino, Lorenzo. 2009. "Homegrown Jihadist Terrorism in the United States." *Studies in Conflict & Terrorism* 32(1): 1–17.

Vidino, Lorenzo. 2011. "Radicalization, Linkage, and Diversity." http://www.dtic.mil/dtic/tr/fulltext/u2/a545352.pdf.

Vidino, Lorenzo, Raffaello Pantucci, and Evan Kohlmann. 2010. "Bringing Global Jihad to the Horn of Africa: Al Shabaab, Western Fighters, and the Sacralization of the Somali Conflict." *African Security* 3 (4): 216–238

Vigdor, Jacob. 2011. "Comparing Immigrant Assimilation in North America and Europe." Manhattan Institute. Civic Report 64

Walsh, James and James Piazza. 2010. "Why Respecting Physical Integrity Rights Reduces Terrorism." *Comparative Political Studies* 43(5): 551–577.

Wiersema, Margarethe and Karen Bantel. 1992. "Top Management Team Demography and Corporate Strategic Change." *Academy of Management Journal* 35(1): 91–121.

Wong, Edward. October 17, 2012. "U.S. Ambassador Confirms Meeting with Tibetans in Western China." http://www.nytimes.com/2012/10/18/world/asia/ambassador-gary-locke-met-with-tibetans-last-month.html.

Yaccino, Steven. 2013. "Planner of Mumbai Attacks Is Given a 35-Year Sentence." http://www.nytimes.com/2013/01/25/us/david-c-headley-gets-35-years-for-mumbai-attack.html.

CHAPTER 3

Democracy, Civil Liberties, and Terrorism

After having disclosed the classified details of several top-secret U.S. and British government mass surveillance programs to the international press, Edward Snowden explained his motivation for this momentous act, saying, "I don't want to live in a society that does these sort of things. . . . I do not want to live in a world where everything I do and say is recorded. . . . My sole motive is to inform the public as to that which is done in their name and that which is done against them" (*The Guardian* [London] June 9, 2013). Snowden's actions have rekindled debates inside the United States and across the world over the appropriate balance between national security and Internet privacy. Accordingly, academics, politicians, and policy makers alike ponder how best to reconfigure national policies in response to the growing terrorist threat.[1] Perhaps, the most important debate has revolved around the question of whether or not democratic countries are justified in restricting civil liberties and the rule of law in the attempt to enhance national security (e.g., by the practice of warrantless wiretapping; by denying suspects access to lawyers and detaining them indefinitely without formal charges being laid or interning them without trial—see Chalk 1995; Matthew and Shambaugh 2005; Hinnen April 28, 2009). Although this debate has played out quite visibly across popular media, as of yet there has been no scientific analysis conducted by scholars of national and international security.[2] Accordingly, this study will systematically examine the democracy-terrorism-public policy link from a scientific standpoint while expanding on the main tenets of the selectorate theory and its empirical model.

Bueno de Mesquita et al.'s 2004 study (364) states that "we use the phrase large coalition and the term democracy interchangeable to improve readability"; this study follows them by deeming countries with large winning coalitions democratic countries. In *The Logic of Political Survival,* Bueno de Mesquita et al. (2003) draw a simple but intuitive hypothesis regarding the policy behavior of political leaders. It states that, all other things being equal, leaders with large winning coalitions tend to shift the focus of public policy away from the acquisition of private benefits and toward the provision of public goods. Bueno de Mesquita et al. then point out that "the rule of law and national security are possibly the most important public goods leaders can provide to encourage peace and prosperity" (31).[3] Although the authors report a statistical analysis on national security, their study neglects to provide theoretical elaboration and empirical evidence related to the rule of law. More important, the selectorate theory and the works that have grown out of it remain silent regarding whether or not democratic leaders limit the provision of the rule of law and civil liberties in the effort to fight terrorism more effectively.

This study attempts to fill the gaps by offering an empirical analysis of the determinants of the maintenance or lessening of civil liberties and the rule of law in the context of the threat of terrorism. In its effort to probe the proposed connection, this study also improves the selectorate theory and statistical model on four fronts. First, it offers a substantive discussion of the selectorate theory of the rule of law and civil liberties; second, it presents an empirical assessment of the rule of law and civil liberties in the context of terrorism; third, it introduces a new estimation method; and fourth, it adds to the analysis several key control variables that may attenuate the effect of the winning coalition. As a whole, this study offers a theoretical explanation of why democracies might restrict civil liberties and the rule of law under the threat of terrorism; it also provides several improvements in research design, including a new estimator and more controls. However, the findings of this study are counterintuitive because they indicate that when faced with terrorist threats, democratic countries are still more likely than nondemocratic countries to protect the rule of law and civil liberties.

THE SELECTORATE THEORY OF THE RULE OF LAW AND CIVIL LIBERTIES

The selectorate theory refers to the rule of law as one of the two "pure" public goods of universal importance to citizens of a country (Bueno de Mesquita et al. 2003, 31). However, it neither offers a definition of the concept nor develops a theoretical argument. At the same time, it considers civil liberties to be a "core" public good on the grounds that they protect citizens against potential domestic tyranny (179–180). This study provides an understanding of the concepts of civil liberties and the rule of law as they pertain to the policy decisions of democratic leaders under the threat of terrorism; it will then move on to develop the theoretical link between terrorism and the provision of public goods.

Defining Civil Liberties and the Rule of Law

The concept of civil liberties is straightforward. The term generally refers to the fundamental individual rights that protect citizens from the unregulated coercive power or arbitrary actions of a government. Examples include freedom from arbitrary arrest or detention, as well as the guarantee of habeas corpus, freedom of speech, freedom of lawful assembly, freedom of association and movement, and the right to refrain from incriminating oneself; some, such as the right to a fair trial, are also taken as indicators of respect for the rule of law, as it is the tendency of a truly law-abiding society not only to protect but also to glorify these civil liberties (Carothers 1998; O'Donnell 2004; Reeve 2010). However, because the empirical correlation between the rule of law and civil liberties is only 0.48 during the study period from 1984 to 1999, one can accurately claim that each measure for these variables is distinct.

Compared to civil liberties, the concept of the rule of law "is subject to various definitional and normative disputes" (O'Donnell 2004, 34; Carothers 2009). For the purposes of analytical clarity, this study focuses on two fundamental components of the rule of law. The first component is the presence of an independent judiciary and legal system that ensures the fair and just treatment of individuals within a society (Andrews and Montinola 2004, 65). As legal scholar Joseph Raz (1977, 198–201) aptly points out, fair and impartial judicial systems require, at the very least, an independent judicial branch with fair-minded judges, prosecutors, and lawyers, as well as a strong and stable capacity for consistent law enforcement (for a similar view, see Fuller 1969). The establishment of an independent judicial system reflects a strong commitment on the part of a government to the basic principle that all people should be treated equally before the law and deserve the opportunity to have their grievances heard and settled in court. The second component of the rule of law centers on a recognition, by a majority of citizens, of the legitimacy of the concomitant and legal institutions. This affects not only the way citizens relate to judicial authority but also how they relate to one another. When fair and independent judicial bodies are well established, citizens develop a level of trust in their norms and procedures, as well as in the courts and police. When this is the case, citizens are more likely to consult established laws and legal procedures as they seek to reconcile political and personal differences instead of resorting to physical violence as the primary means of conflict resolution (Hardin 2001; Pious 2006; Carothers 2009; Choi 2010).[4]

Overview of the Selectorate Theory

Before conceptualizing the selectorate theory of the rule of law and civil liberties, a brief review of Morrow et al.'s (2008) selectorate theory is in order.[5] Morrow et al. assume that any political leader's ultimate goal is to maintain power; thus, political leaders are strongly incentivized to satisfy the interests of their domestic constituencies to protect their position. The selectorate theorists purport to facilitate cross-national generalization on the basis of three institutional characteristics of political systems which, they claim, determine the retention and selection of leaders: the selectorate, the winning coalition, and the support coalitions. The selectorate is comprised of individuals within the state who have a say in policy outcomes insofar as they select the leader; the winning coalition is the portion of the selectorate sufficient to return a leader to office; and the support coalition is a subset of those selectors who support the current leader. Consistent with Morrow et al., this study focuses only on variations in winning coalition size in relation to terrorism, the rule of law, and civil liberties.

The logic of selectorate theory produces a straightforward hypothesis: as winning coalitions become larger, distributing private goods becomes increasingly difficult as they inevitably suffer limitations on their revenue resources. For this reason, the political survival of these leaders is dependent on the distribution of public goods (e.g., the rule of law). This is especially true in democratic countries where political leaders are expected to make an effort to deliver public goods to all members of the winning coalition, which is often as large as 51 percent of the voting population. However, leaders who preside over small winning coalitions, such as those in autocracies, have less incentive to implement policies delivering public goods because they are able to maintain power by efficiently targeting private benefits to key supporters in their ruling coalitions. Thus, these leaders are more likely to retain their offices despite failing national policies such as ongoing economic crises or military defeats.

Winning Coalition Size, Terrorism, the Rule of Law, and Civil Liberties

This study will now discuss how leaders with large winning coalitions (i.e., democratic leaders) handle the provision of two important public goods (i.e., the rule of law and civil liberties) when faced with the threat of terrorism. This discussion revolves around four different factors: winning coalition (W), terrorism, the rule of law, and civil liberties. Part one explains the effect of W on the rule of law and civil liberties; part two shows the terrorism-rule of law and civil liberties connection; and part three presents the causal explanation of how W and terrorism interact to influence the provision of the rule of law and civil liberties.

In applying the logic of the selectorate theory, Morrow et al. expect that democratic countries will work harder than nondemocratic countries to improve the quality of the rule of law and civil liberties. This is a reasonable expectation insofar as leaders with large winning coalitions are more likely than those with smaller coalitions to lose political power when they fail to provide the public with these basic goods. The popularity of political leaders will decline when a majority of citizens become disillusioned by gang rule or lawlessness or are angered by rampant violations of their civil liberties; supporters turn their backs on leaders who are lenient with illegal strikes and high crime rates or those who abuse their authority to arrest citizens without probable cause. Furthermore, when a justice system is corrupt—that is, when the law is routinely ignored without effective sanction—many people may choose to take justice into their own hands, resorting to resolving grievances through physical violence and rendering a leader's capacity to govern ineffective. A regime that frequently infringes on the civil liberties of its citizens for political purposes will lose their trust, ultimately putting their own political careers at risk (see Hogg and Brown 1998; Hardin 2001; O'Donnell 2004; Smith August 11, 2007; Choi 2010). It follows then that as the size of the winning coalition increases, so does the incentive for democratic leaders to enhance the quality of the rule of law and civil liberties in order to protect their own political survival.

H_{1a}: As the size of the winning coalition increases, the quality of the rule of law is likely to improve.

H_{1b}: As the size of the winning coalition increases, the protection of civil liberties is likely to be enhanced.

Because the main research question of this study concerns democratic leadership in relation to the threat of terrorism, a more complete theoretical discussion is in order. However, before investigating the interaction of W and terrorism and its influence on policy outcomes, it is necessary to provide a theoretical prediction about the relationship between terrorism and the rule of law and civil liberties. Existing studies present evidence that a country with a well-established rule of law and a respect for civil liberties is more vulnerable to terrorist attacks than is a country lacking the same because, they suppose, these institutions provide a favorable environment for terrorist operations (e.g., Enders and Sandler 2006). The flip side of this coin is that political leaders in such countries are likely to introduce legislative and security measures limiting the rule of law or curtailing civil liberties in the attempt to stifle terrorist activity and curb the frequency of terrorist attacks; as the old saying goes, "desperate times call for desperate measures." In this context, the present study asserts that an eruption of terrorist activity is likely to disturb the institutionalization of

the rule of law and to encroach on the protection of civil liberties, specifically if it prompts the state, in response to the terrorist threat, to abandon
the principles of its constitution by imposing martial law or waiving basic
individual rights; some examples of such behavior include the United
States after September 11, the United Kingdom in the 1970s, and Russia in
the mid-1990s (see Ramraj, Hor, and Roach 2005; Smith August 11, 2007).

H_{2a}: As the number of terrorist attacks increases, the quality of the rule of law is
likely to deteriorate.

H_{2b}: As the number of terrorist attacks increases, the protection of civil liberties is
likely to be abandoned.

The selectorate theory makes predictions regarding the incentives for
democratic leaders to respond to national security threats, in general, but
not to terrorist threats, in particular. Because a national security failure
may jeopardize the political survival of democratic leadership, such leaders are likely to put serious effort into protecting the lives and property
of citizens from both internal and external threats. Existing studies of terrorism argue that because democratic countries maintain a respect for the
rule of law and individual civil liberties not only for law-abiding citizens
but also for those accused of crimes and even for foreign nationals, they
become, essentially, safe havens for budding terrorists. For example, Eubank and Weinberg (1994) provide evidence that liberal democratic countries, due to their structural mandate to preserve entrenched liberties, host
more terrorist organizations than do authoritarian countries. Presumably,
then, as a result of this institutionalized governmental restraint, which
allows terrorist groups the opportunity to recruit, train, and mobilize in
such societies with relative freedom, democracies experience more terrorist attacks than do nondemocracies.

However, existing studies of selectorate theory and terrorism have
overlooked "the pendulum effect," which defines the successful modern
democratic response to terrorist threats. Matthew and Shambaugh (2005,
223) argue that "when faced with external threats such as global terrorism, democracies respond in a pendulum fashion—acting initially by
giving security precedence over other values and then swinging back towards moderation [and] the pursuit of tolerance." In fact, with little ado,
many governments and regional and international organizations have introduced anti-terrorism laws and policies that cross boundaries between
states as well as between domestic, regional, and international law (see
Ramraj, Hor, and Roach 2005). Democratic countries are better equipped
than nondemocratic countries to fight terrorism because (1) they are capable of the timely implementation of anti-terrorist measures, and (2)
they exhibit a flexibility of legal interpretation and enforcement measures.
That is, since frequent terrorist attacks such as assassinations, bombings,

kidnappings, and hijackings undermine national security and kill inno-
cent people, leaders are able to use democratic institutions to bolster their
national security capabilities in response to the vulnerabilities created by
those very same institutions.

Of course, democratic citizens appreciate the fact that "without a vigor-
ous rule of law, defended by an independent judiciary, [civil] rights [such
as secret ballots and freedom of expression] are not safe and the equality
and dignity of all citizens are at risk" (O'Donnell 2004, 32). Nonetheless, in
response to growing terrorist threats, a majority of citizens in democratic
countries are willing to follow policy initiatives that limit the rule of law
and depress their civil liberties. According to the last six Gallup Polls that
asked about the PATRIOT Act and civil liberties during the period 2002–
2006, "more than half of Americans say the Bush administration has been
about right or has not gone far enough in restricting people's civil liberties
in order to combat terrorism" (http://news.gallup.com/poll/5263/civil-
liberties.aspx); Table 3.1 shows the precise wording and opinion trend:

Table 3.1
Gallup Polls

Do you think the Bush administration has gone too far, has been about right,
or has not gone far enough in restricting people's civil liberties in order to
fight terrorism?

	Too Far (%)	About Right (%)	Not Far Enough (%)	No Opinion (%)
May 12–13, 2006	41	34	19	6
January 6–8, 2006	38	40	19	3
November 10–12, 2003[a]	28	48	21	3
August 25–26, 2003[a]	21	55	19	5
September 2–4, 2002[a]	15	55	26	4
June 21–23, 2002[a]	11	60	25	4

[a]Asked of a half sample.

It is understandable that a government might enjoy this kind of majority support as long as its citizens have a general trust in the overriding
democratic values of their fair and impartial legal system and are willing
to abide by (even somewhat arbitrary) laws and procedures in support of
the public good. In other words, the general consensus surrounding the
spirit of the rule of law and the protection of civil liberties inclines democratic citizens to tolerate some inconvenient changes of legal rules and/or
some infringements of civil liberties in the wake of a terrorist threat in the

name of national security (Chalk 1995). Accordingly, in response to growing terrorist threats, countries with large winning coalitions (i.e., democracies) can more easily adjust the level of the rule of law and civil liberties.
From this discussion, we can glean the following hypotheses:

H_{3a}: Leaders with large winning coalitions are more likely to restrict the rule of law
  when confronted with terrorist threats.

H_{3b}: Leaders with large winning coalitions are more likely to restrict civil liberties
  when confronted with terrorist threats.

RESEARCH DESIGN

For the purposes of empirical testing, cross-sectional, time-series data is
collected on a sample of 126 countries during the period 1984–1999. The
number of sample countries and the length of the study period are limited
by the availability of data on the rule of law (which is compiled by Political Risk Services [PRS] Group only for the years following 1984) and the
data on winning coalitions (which, in the publicly available selectorate
dataset, ends in 1999).[6]

Dependent Variables

Consistent with the theoretical discussion in the previous section, this
study employs two dependent variables. The first is the rule of law variable, which measures the coexistence of two features: (1) the strength and
impartiality of the legal system and (2) the degree of popular observance
of law as a legitimate and fair way to settle claims. The source of this variable is the International Country Risk Guide (ICRG) compiled by the PRS
Group.[7] The ICRG first assesses each of these features on a scale from 0 to
3. A country may enjoy a high rating of 3 in terms of its judicial system,
while being assigned a low rating of 1 if, for example, laws are routinely
ignored by the public without effective sanction or if the crime rate is very
high. The ICRG then combines the two scores from each feature to produce a seven-point scale. A "0" indicates a weak law and order tradition
where citizens depend on physical force or illegal means to resolve grievances, and a "6" denotes a strong law and order tradition where established law enforcement and judicial channels are seen as legitimate and
are effectively used by citizens to settle disputes.[8] Since the first ordinal
level, '0,' has only 5 out of 1,716 observations in total, it is combined with
the second ordinal level, '1,' for a more meaningful estimation.

The second dependent variable, civil liberties, comes from the Freedom
House website. Freedom House (2009) compiles a measure of the quality
of civil liberties and is considered to be the best dataset available for this
variable due to its scope and quality (Keech 2009, 9). Freedom House's

civil liberties measure taps into qualities of democracy such as the freedoms of expression and belief, associational and organizational rights,
and rule of law and personal autonomy; in particular, it assesses the degree of individual freedom to develop views, institutions, and personal
autonomy apart from government on a seven-point scale, with low scores
indicating a high degree of freedom and high scores indicating a low degree of freedom. Then, for ease of interpretation, the civil liberties variable
is rerecorded as "7" for the highest level of civil liberties and as "1" for the
lowest.[9]

Independent Variables

This study includes seven independent variables: W, *terrorism*, $W * ter-
rorism$, *executive constraints, economic development, political instability,* and
international conflict. The first three are related to the interaction effect between W and *terrorism*, while the next four control variables are included
to avoid omitted variable bias. Because the main purpose of this study
is not to explain as much variance of the rule of law and civil liberties as
possible but to test the predictions of the "elaborated" selectorate theory,
other possible control factors are not included. (This same approach was
adopted in Bueno de Mesquita et al.'s 2004, 378, study on war.) Since testing the interaction effect requires a multiplicative interaction model, and
since the estimated results from a multiplicative interaction model are
not easy to interpret, this study centers all independent variables—except
for the dichotomous measure of *international conflict*—at their means for
ease of interpretation. To save space, this study does not explain the cen-
tering procedures in the operationalization discussion. All independent
variables are lagged one year to ensure that they cause changes in the dependent variable instead of the other way around.

W: Morrow et al.'s study[10] operationalizes the key concept of W based
on three individual components of the Polity indicator (i.e., competitiveness of executive recruitment, openness of executive recruitment, and
competitiveness of political competition [for a detailed discussion on Polity, see Marshall and Jaggers 2007]), as well as on an indicator of the nature
of the regime which comes from Arthur Banks (1996). W is a normalized
ordinal measure ranging from 0 to 1 (i.e., 0, 0.25, 0.50, 0.75, and 1).

Terrorism: The *terrorism* variable is a log transformation of the annual
total number of domestic and international terrorist events that occurred
in a country, collected from the Global Terrorism Database (GTD) Explorer (Lee 2008).[11] Although there are other widely used datasets on terrorism (e.g., Mickolus et al.'s 2006 data on transnational terrorism), the
GTD is the most comprehensive dataset as it includes incidents of both
domestic and international terrorism. Although the GTD provides comprehensive terrorism data dating back to 1970, the data for 1993 is missing

due to an office move (LaFree and Dugan 2007). In order to complete the cross-sectional, time-series data analysis, the missing data is interpolated by averaging the preceding and following years.

Interaction variable between W and terrorism: The *W * terrorism* variable, which tests the interaction effect hypothesis, is created by multiplying the *W* variable by the *terrorism* variable; this formulation is consistent with the earlier discussion, which theorized that the joint effect of *W* and *terrorism* determines the level of the rule of law or civil liberties within a country.

Executive constraints: Morrow et al.'s study makes clear that the theoretical predictions of *W* and other aspects of democratic regimes should be in the same direction. Accordingly, this study argues that because legislative constraints put checks and balances on the arbitrary power of the executive (Tsebelis 2002), it is expected that democratic countries generally maintain a strong tradition of the rule of law and are concerned with the protection of individual civil liberties. The *executive constraints* variable is a normalized ordinal measure with "0" for its smallest value and "1" for its greatest.

Economic development: Less economically developed countries are unlikely to enjoy a high-quality rule of law or to provide many civil liberties due to their underdeveloped political and judicial systems (Barro 1997; Piazza 2006). Accordingly, this variable controls for the effect of *economic development* on the rule of law and civil liberties. It is measured by the logged real GDP per capita, adjusted for purchasing power parity; data is derived from Gleditsch (2002).

Political instability: *Political instability* is likely to hinder the development of the rule of law and the establishment of civil liberties insofar as institutions require time without major disturbance to take root (Feng 1997). To measure *political instability*, this study uses Banks's (1996) event counts of assassinations, strikes, guerilla wars, government crises, purges, riots, revolts, and anti-government demonstrations. These counts are summed into an index of *political instability*, which is then log transformed to address a skewed distribution.

International conflict: Involvement in *international conflict* is another predictor of the restriction of the rule of law and civil liberties because it breeds instability and makes regimes vulnerable to lawlessness and disorder (e.g., Iraq and Afghanistan; see Jones et al. 2005). Based on data from Gleditsch et al. (2002), the *international conflict* variable is coded as "1" for militarized interstate disputes or war involvement and as "0" otherwise.

Consistent with Morrow et al.'s research design, this study implements fixed effects to control for the interaction of geographic region and year, which should alleviate the potential for problems caused by spurious temporal or spatial effects in the pooled panel data. The cross-sectional, time-series data analysis of fixed effects is likely to report biased estimates if the error term is heteroskedastic and/or serially correlated. This study performs a likelihood-ratio test for heteroskedasticity and the Wooldridge test for autocorrelation (Wooldridge 2002; Drukker 2003). These two test results indicate that correction for both panel heteroskedasticity and temporally correlated errors is required for this study. The empirical results reported in the next section are obtained after accounting for both heteroskedasticity and autocorrelation.

Estimation Methods

This study fits the multiplicative interactive model with two estimation methods: OLS (ordinary least squares) and ordered logit. Morrow et al.'s study relies exclusively on OLS regression even though its dependent variables are collected at ordinal levels. For instance, the empirical assessment of the effect of W on civil liberties, an ordinal variable on a scale of 1 to 7, is performed with OLS regression; however, because OLS regression forces the variable to be treated as though it were continuous, the estimates it produces are likely to be biased and inefficient. In the next section, this study reports OLS and ordered logit results; the latter is introduced to correct the biased estimates of the former.[12]

EMPIRICAL RESULTS

Table 3.2 reports the results from two different statistical estimators in order to assess the interaction effect between W and *terrorism* on the rule

Table 3.2
The Effects of W and *Terrorism* on the Rule of Law and Civil Liberties, 1984–1999

	OLS Regression		Ordered Logit Regression	
	Rule of Law	Civil Liberties	Rule of Law	Civil Liberties
Variable	Model 1	Model 2	Model 3	Model 4
W	0.501**	0.334*	1.416***	1.111**
	(0.171)	(0.198)	(0.394)	(0.434)
Terrorism	−0.198***	−0.106***	−0.325***	−0.242***
	(0.020)	(0.022)	(0.052)	(0.039)
W * *terrorism*	−0.135	−0.145**	−0.335**	−0.336**
	(0.083)	(0.059)	(0.129)	(0.141)

(Continued)

Table 3.2
(Continued)

Variable	OLS Regression		Ordered Logit Regression	
	Rule of Law	Civil Liberties	Rule of Law	Civil Liberties
	Model 1	Model 2	Model 3	Model 4
Executive constraints	0.357** (0.133)	3.013*** (0.130)	0.729*** (0.226)	5.871*** (0.283)
Economic development	0.683*** (0.055)	0.560*** (0.035)	1.078*** (0.106)	0.720*** (0.084)
Political instability	−0.035*** (0.007)	−0.002 (0.007)	−0.073*** (0.014)	−0.022* (0.013)
International conflict	0.028 (0.127)	−0.108 (0.099)	−0.197 (0.334)	−0.482 (0.321)
Constant	3.654*** (0.009)	4.187*** (0.007)	n/a	n/a
R^2				
Within	0.43	0.66		
Between	0.52	0.82		
Overall	0.49	0.73		
Pseudo R^2			0.19	0.32
Log pseudolikelihood			−2,457.01	−2,242.66
Observations	1,716	1,716	1,716	1,716

Notes: Robust standard errors, adjusted over countries, in parentheses. n/a: not applicable.
*$p < .05$ one-tailed tests
**$p < .01$ one-tailed tests
***$p < .001$ one-tailed tests

of law and civil liberties while controlling for four other compounding factors. While Models 1 and 2 use OLS regression, Models 3 and 4 employ ordered logit regression to correct the potentially biased estimates of the OLS regression; while the odd models are built to predict the rule of law variable, the even are used to predict the civil liberties variable. A one-tailed significance test is employed at the 0.05, 0.01 and 0.001 levels because the theoretical expectations are directional.

The results in Model 1, where OLS regression is used for estimation, indicate no interaction effect between W and *terrorism*: with a p value of 0.107, the $W * terrorism$ variable fails to achieve significance even at the 0.05 level. However, as shown in Model 3, where ordered logit regression is employed for a more precise estimation, the $W * terrorism$ variable becomes significant at the 0.01 level.[13] Before interpreting the interaction term of $W * terrorism$, this study discusses the effects of the two constitutive terms in Model 3. As hypothesized, W is significant at the 0.001 level, indicating that leaders with large winning coalitions work harder to produce a high-quality rule of law. The coefficient (i.e., 1.416) of W indicates its considerable influence on the rule of law when both *terrorism* and $W * terrorism$ are set at zero. This interpretation is possible because these variables are mean centered; in other words, the coefficient for *terrorism* shows the effect of *terrorism* at the mean of W because both variables have been centered at their means. Because the coefficient (i.e., –0.325) of *terrorism* is significant and in the hypothesized direction, it is fair to speculate that as the number of terrorist incidents experienced by a democracy increases, the rule of law tradition is likely to weaken.

Note that the absolute magnitude of W is much larger than that of *terrorism*. This means that the effect of the interaction term $W * terrorism$ is likely to be influenced by the positive effect of the former. With this in mind, let us examine the interaction term which turns out to be significantly different from zero. It appears that W and *terrorism* interact to influence the policy behavior of democratic leaders. The important question is whether or not democratic leaders limit the rule of law in the effort to better protect the security of their citizens, thereby helping to ensure their own political survival. That is, does the coefficient of –0.335 for the $W * terrorism$ variable imply that democratic countries are prone to sacrifice aspects of their rule of law foundations in order to fight terrorism more effectively? Given the fact that it is inefficient to interpret coefficients of interaction variables in terms of standard significance, this study calculates the marginal effects of the interactions and reports them in a formal way. Figure 3.1 shows counterintuitive results—that is, an increase in Pr (civil liberties) over a range of the $W * terrorism$ variable—as the predicted probability line is moving upward along the X axis. It appears that democratic countries are more likely than nondemocracies to preserve the rule of law tradition when under threat from terrorist violence.

The hypothesis regarding *executive constraints* is supported. Where there exist checks and balances between the executive and the legislature, the quality of the rule of law is enhanced. Although it is hypothesized that both W and *executive constraints* correspond to an increasingly stable rule of law, it is essential to note that the effect of the former is expected to be stronger than that of the latter. As alluded to in Morrow et al.'s study, *executive constraints* not contained in the selectorate theory are expected

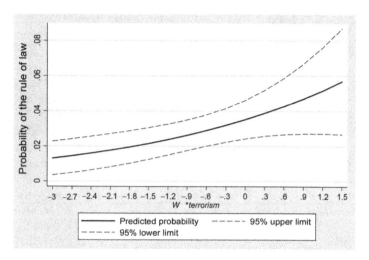

Figure 3.1 Probability of the rule of law by *W * terrorism*.

to explain less of the variance in the rule of law than is the theory's core factor, winning coalition size. The fact that the absolute size (i.e., 1,416) of *W* is larger than that of *executive constraints* (i.e., 0.729) confirms this expectation.

The *economic development* variable achieves significance, indicating that the institutionalization of the rule of law is likely to increase as countries become industrialized. It also appears that *political instability* exerts a dampening effect on the rule of law. On the other hand, the hypothesis regarding *international conflict* is not supported, perhaps because its effect is washed out by the other predictors in the model.

Models 2 and 4 are built to examine the determinants of civil liberties. In both models, the interaction variable of *W* and *terrorism* is significant in the hypothesized direction. Not surprisingly, these results are similar to those reported in Model 3, indicating that even when democratic countries experience terrorist attacks, they do not necessarily attempt to undermine the quality of civil liberties (see the predicted probability line in Figure 3.2). However, as indicated by the significance of the constitutive term, *W*, democratic countries do try harder than nondemocratic countries to improve the overall quality of civil liberties in the absence of an imminent terrorist threat. In the meantime, the significance of the *terrorism* variable indicates that frequent terrorist incidents will generally put strain on the quality of civil liberties. The significance of the other control variables—with the exception of *political instability*—is similar to that in Models 2 and 4. While the *political instability* variable is not significant with OLS estimation in Model 2, it is with ordered logit estimation in Model 4. This result should not be surprising given the fact that the latter generates less-biased and inconsistent estimates than the former.

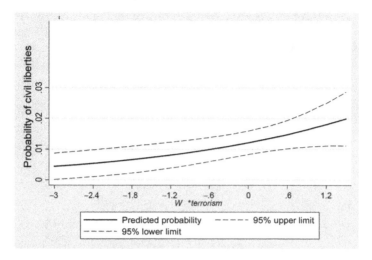

Figure 3.2 Probability of civil liberties by $W * terrorism$.

CONCLUSION

While the restriction of civil liberties and the rule of law in the wake of
terrorist attacks has emerged as a topic of heated debate among and between political conservatives and liberals alike, it has remained relatively
unexplored by students and scientists of national and international security. This study has drawn on and elaborated the selectorate theory and
model to examine how, in relation to terrorist threats, democratic leaders
determine their level of commitment to respecting for the rule of law and
civil liberties, which are two important public goods in the contemporary
era. In doing so, this study has made two contributions to the literature of
democracy and terrorism. It is the first study to explore the theoretical and
empirical implications of the selectorate theory of the rule of law and civil
liberties in the context of terrorism. In addition, this study has developed
theoretical arguments regarding why terrorist threats correspond to en-
croachments on the rule of law and civil liberties in democratic countries.
It also offers several improvements in research design, including a better
statistical model and more rigorous empirical tests.

The empirical results seem to indicate that democratic leaders will exert
greater effort to enhance the rule of law and civil liberties; still, frequent terrorist attacks appear to undermine the quality of the rule of law and the protection of civil liberties. However, the results show no supporting evidence
for the interaction effect between democracy and terrorism. Although the
significant effect of $W * terrorism$ on the rule of law and civil liberties remains
consistent across models, it is a counterintuitive result. This finding implies
that democratic leaders do not consider limiting the rule of law and civil liberties to be an essential step toward combating terrorism. (Note that because

the results indicate the general pattern of *average* democratic leaders over the world, they do not adequately explain the peculiar case of the U.S. leadership's response to the Edward Snowden scandal.) By and large though, the results indicate that nondemocratic leaders may be more skillful or cold-blooded in dealing with terrorism than democratic leaders. The national security maneuver initiated by nondemocratic leaders is probably politically expedient insofar as it is intended to better protect the lives and property of citizens. Flexible or ruthless policy responses from top leadership in contemporary nondemocratic nations appear to help fend off the menace presented by terrorist organizations.

Table 3.A1
Average Scores of the Rule of Law and Civil Liberties by Country, 1984–1999

	Rule of Law	Civil Liberties		Rule of Law	Civil Liberties
Albania	3.7	2.7	Kuwait	4.1	3.3
Algeria	2.2	2.4	Latvia	4.0	6.0
Angola	2.1	1.2	Liberia	2.0	3.0
Argentina	3.8	5.6	Libya	3.0	1.3
Armenia	3.0	4.0	Lithuania	4.0	6.0
Australia	6.0	7.0	Madagascar	3.3	3.6
Austria	6.0	7.0	Malawi	2.7	2.8
Azerbaijan	4.0	4.0	Malaysia	4.2	3.3
Bahrain	4.6	2.6	Mali	2.5	3.6
Bangladesh	1.8	3.8	Mexico	2.9	4.2
Belgium	5.8	6.8	Moldova	5.0	4.0
Bolivia	1.8	4.9	Morocco	3.9	3.2
Botswana	4.7	5.6	Mozambique	2.5	2.7
Brazil	3.5	4.8	Myanmar	2.8	1.1
Bulgaria	4.8	3.6	Namibia	5.5	5.1
Burkina Faso	3.4	3.2	Netherlands	6.0	7.0
Cameroon	2.8	2.3	New Zealand	6.0	7.0
Canada	6.0	7.0	Nicaragua	2.7	4.0
Chile	4.4	5.1	Niger	2.8	2.7
China	3.9	1.4	Nigeria	1.9	2.8
Colombia	1.4	4.3	Norway	6.0	7.0
Democratic Republic of the Congo	1.9	2.9	Pakistan	2.3	3.3
Costa Rica	4.0	6.6	Panama	2.4	4.8
Cuba	4.9	1.3	Papua New Guinea	3.4	5.0
Cyprus	4.0	6.7	Paraguay	2.9	4.2

	Rule of Law	Civil Liberties		Rule of Law	Civil Liberties
Czechoslovakia	5.0	3.3	Peru	1.8	4.2
Denmark	6.0	7.0	Philippines	2.5	4.7
Dominican Republic	3.4	5.0	Poland	4.8	5.0
Ecuador	3.9	5.2	Portugal	5.1	6.6
Egypt	3.1	3.0	Qatar	4.3	2.5
El Salvador	1.9	4.6	Romania	3.6	3.5
Ethiopia	4.0	6.0	Russia	3.4	3.9
Estonia	3.7	1.9	Saudi Arabia	4.4	1.1
Finland	6.0	6.7	Senegal	2.3	4.1
France	5.3	6.0	Sierra Leone	2.7	2.7
Gabon	2.6	3.2	Singapore	5.4	3.2
Gambia	4.1	4.1	Slovak Republic	5.4	4.8
Germany East	5.0	2.0	Slovenia	5.0	6.0
Germany West	5.3	6.2	Somalia	2.8	1.0
Ghana	2.3	3.3	South Africa	2.4	3.9
Greece	4.1	5.6	Spain	4.7	6.3
Guatemala	1.9	3.7	Sri Lanka	2.0	3.5
Guinea	3.0	2.8	Sudan	2.0	1.4
Guinea-Bissau	1.0	2.8	Sweden	6.0	7.0
Guyana	2.1	4.6	Switzerland	6.0	7.0
Haiti	1.8	2.4	Syria	3.3	1.0
Honduras	2.3	5.0	Taiwan	4.8	4.6
Hungary	5.4	5.1	Tanzania	4.0	2.7
India	2.9	4.6	Thailand	4.2	4.4
Indonesia	2.9	2.7	Togo	2.4	2.5
Iran	3.1	1.9	Trinidad and Tobago	4.0	6.4
Iraq	1.6	1.1	Tunisia	3.3	3.2
Ireland	5.0	6.9	Turkey	3.3	3.6
Israel	3.6	5.6	Uganda	2.4	3.4
Italy	5.3	6.4	Ukraine	4.0	4.0
Ivory Coast	3.4	3.3	United Kingdom	5.3	6.4
Jamaica	2.4	5.5	United States	6.0	7.0
Japan	5.5	6.4	Uruguay	3.0	5.9
Jordan	3.3	3.6	Venezuela	4.0	5.3
Kazakhstan	4.0	3.0	Yemen South	1.0	1.0
Kenya	3.4	2.4	Yugoslavia	2.6	2.8
Korea North	3.3	1.0	Zambia	2.8	3.7
Korea South	3.7	5.2	Zimbabwe	2.9	3.1

Note: Correlation between the rule of law and civil liberties is 0.48.

NOTES

1. In this study, terrorism is referred to as "the threatened or actual use of illegal force, directed against civilian targets, by non-state actors, in order to attain a political goal, through fear, coercion or intimidation" (LaFree and Ackerman 2009, 348).

2. An exception is Piazza and Walsh's (2009) study, which examines individual human rights indicators and counts of terrorist attacks but finds mostly null results, concluding that experience of terrorism produces little consistent effect on the rights enjoyed by citizens.

3. Other scholars have also equated the rule of law with a public good. For example, Andrews and Montinola (2004, 65) argue that "the rule of law is a set of stable political rules and rights applied impartially to all citizens. . . . As such, it is a public good." O'Donnell (2004, 35) reasons that "achieving [the] situation [in which 'the government shall be ruled by law and subject to it'] . . . is a great public good."

4. Even though the concept of democracy should, in theory, include the rule of law and civil liberties as its key features, each of these three concepts is constructed and measured differently, as will be discussed in the section Research Design.

5. Morrow et al.'s (2008) selectorate theory is a "refined" version of Bueno de Mesquita et al.'s. Morrow et al. redefine the concept of *winning coalition* into two subgroups: (1) the leader's support coalition and (2) the minimum size that the coalition must be for the leader to remain in office (see footnote 2 on p. 393).

6. See http://www.nyu.edu/gsas/dept/politics/data/bdm2s2/Logic.htm.

7. Many existing studies rely on the ICRG measure. When Ivanova and Sandler (2007, 280) explore the democracy-terrorism connection, they state that "the ICRG index of law and order (i.e., rule of law) is based on two subcomponents." Barro (2000, 215) similarly refers to the law and order variable as the rule of law: "The index for overall maintenance of the rule of law (also referred to as 'law and order tradition') turns out to have the most explanatory power for investment and economic growth." For Knack (1996, 226), the rule of law is also the same as the law and order tradition: "This [rule of law] variable 'reflects the degree to which the citizens of a country are willing to accept the established institutions to make and implement laws and adjudicate disputes.' . . . Original variable name in ICRG is 'law and order tradition.'" Moreover, Andrews and Montinola (2004, 72) use the PRS measure of law and order as their concept of rule of law: "The data that we use, an index of perceived levels of the rule of law, are collected by Political Risk Services (PRS). . . . In particular, we use PRS's index on Law and Order."

Although the World Bank's (2008) Worldwide Governance Indicators provide another source of a rule of law measure, its data range is limited, as it begins only in 1996.

8. It should be noted that the ICRG releases only the aggregate measure for public use. For more detailed information, see the PRS Group website at http://www.prsgroup.com/

9. Table 3.A1 shows the average scores of the rule of law and civil liberties by country during the period 1984–1999.

10. Morrow et al.'s (2008) selectorate model is slightly different from that of Bueno de Mesquita et al. (2003). To underscore the importance of controlling for aspects of democracy that fall outside of the selectorate theory, they refine the

measure of democracy (or, more accurately, cut out part of the democracy variable) in order to achieve the same effect for which they were criticized in Clarke and Stone's (2008) study. Morrow et al. introduce institutional constraints on executive power in place of the cut-out democracy variable.

11. The website can be found at http://www.start.umd.edu/gtd/features/ GTD-Data-Rivers.aspx. It should be noted that the GTD does not distinguish between threats and actual incidents.

12. One may contend that an ordered variable with five or more categories sufficiently mimics a continuous variable for the purposes of statistical analysis; it would be likely, in this case, that estimated coefficients have no changes of sign when switching from OLS to ordered logit. A similar contention could be made regarding the relationship between OLS and standard logit. It is well known that, for a dichotomous dependent variable, OLS and standard logit may produce similar estimates (e.g., no sign changes). Accordingly, one might assert that OLS can be employed for a dichotomous variable even though it produces biased estimates. However, this assertion has not been well received among researchers who strive for the most precise statistical analysis. The same logic applies when choosing between OLS and ordered logit for an ordered dependent variable. The researcher should keep in mind that OLS estimates are not as unbiased and efficient as those of ordered logit, despite the fact that OLS "mimics" ordered logit. For this reason, Bueno de Mesquita, Downs, Smith, and Cherif (2005, 446 and 448) employ ordered logit, not OLS, when dealing with measurements on the five-point political terror scale.

13. Standard interpretation of the ordered logit coefficient is that for a one unit increase in the predictor, the response variable level is expected to change by its respective regression coefficient in the ordered log-odds scale, while the other variables in the model are held constant.

The issue of endogeneity is not discussed in this study because simultaneous equation models are used only for two continuous, endogenous variables and because ordered and count variables (i.e., the rule of law, civil liberties, and *terrorism*) in this study are not suitable for simultaneous equation models. However, as noted, lagging the predictors one year behind the outcome variable should assuage the endogeneity concern to some degree.

REFERENCES

Andrews, Josephine T. and Gabriella R. Montinola. 2004. "Veto Players and the Rule of Law in Emerging Democracies." *Comparative Political Studies* 37(1): 55–87.

Banks, Arthur S. 1996. *Political Handbook of the World*. New York: CSA Publications.

Barro, Robert J. 1997. *Determinants of Economic Growth: A Cross-Country Empirical Study*. Cambridge, MA: MIT Press.

Barro, Robert J. 2000. "Democracy and the Rule of Law." In Bruce Bueno de Mesquita and Hilton Root, eds., *Governing for Prosperity*. New Haven, CT: Yale University Press. 209–231.

Bueno de Mesquita, Bruce, James D. Morrow, Randolph M. Siverson, and Alastair Smith. 2004. "Testing Novel Implications from the Selectorate Theory of War." *World Politics* 56(3): 363–388.

Bueno de Mesquita, Bruce, Alastair Smith, Randolph M. Siverson, and James D. Morrow. 2003. *The Logic of Political Survival*. Cambridge, MA: MIT Press.

Carothers, Thomas. 1998. "The Rule of Law Revival." *Foreign Affairs* 77(2): 95–106.

Carothers, Thomas. 2009. "Rule of Law Temptations." *Fletcher Forum of World Affairs* 33(1): 49–61.

Chalk, Peter. 1995. "The Liberal Democratic Response to Terrorism." *Terrorism and Political Violence* 7(4): 10–44.

Choi, Seung-Whan. 2010. "Fighting Terrorism through the Rule of Law?" *Journal of Conflict Resolution* 54(6): 940–966.

Clarke, Kevin A. and Randall Stone. 2008. "Democracy and the Logic of Political Survival." *American Political Science Review* 102(3): 387–392.

Drukker, David M. 2003. "Testing for Serial Correlation in Linear Panel-Data Models." *Stata Journal* 3(2): 168–177.

Enders, Walter and Todd Sandler. 2006. *The Political Economy of Terrorism*. Cambridge and New York: Cambridge University Press.

Eubank, William and Leonard Weinberg. 1994. "Does Democracy Encourage Terrorism?" *Terrorism and Political Violence* 6(4): 417–443.

Feng, Yi. 1997. "Democracy, Political Stability, and Economic Growth." *British Journal of Political Science* 27(3): 391–418.

Freedom House. 2009. *Freedom in the World 2009: Setbacks and Resilience*. Washington, DC: Freedom House.

Fuller, Lon L. 1969. *The Morality of Law*. New Haven, CT: Yale University Press.

Gleditsch, Kristian. 2002. "Expanded Trade and GDP Data." *Journal of Conflict Resolution* 46(5): 712–724. http://privatewww.essex.ac.uk/~ksg/exptradegdp.html.

Gleditsch, Nils, Peter Wallensteen, Mikael Eriksson, Margareta Sollenberg, and Harvard Strand. 2002. "Armed Conflict 1946–2001: A New Dataset." *Journal of Peace Research* 39(5): 615–637.

The Guardian (London). June 9, 2013. "NSA Whistleblower Edward Snowden: 'I Don't Want to Live in a Society That Does These Sort of Things'— Video." http://www.theguardian.com/world/video/2013/jun/09/nsa-whistleblower-edward-snowden-interview-video.

Hardin, Russell. 2001. "Law and Social Order." *Philosophical Issues* 11: 61–85.

Hinnen, Todd. April 28, 2009. "Prepared Remarks to the Washington Institute for Near East Policy." http://www.washingtoninstitute.org/html/pdf/hinnen.pdf.

Hogg, Russell and David Brown. 1998. *Rethinking Law & Order*. Annandale, NSW: Pluto Press.

Ivanova, Kate and Todd Sandler. 2007. "CBRN Attack Perpetrators: An Empirical Study." *Foreign Policy Analysis* 3(4): 273–294.

Jones, Seth G., Jeremy M. Wilson, Andrew Rathmell, and K. Jack Riley. 2005. *Establishing Law and Order after Conflict*. Santa Monica, CA: RAND Corporation.

Keech, William. 2009. "A Scientifically Superior Conception of Democracy." Presented at the Midwest Political Science Association Conference, Chicago, Illinois, April 16–19.

Knack, Steve. 1996. "Institutions and the Convergence Hypothesis: The Cross-National Evidence." *Public Choice* 87(3–4): 207–228.

LaFree, Gary and Gary Ackerman. 2009. "The Empirical Study of Terrorism: Social and Legal Research." *Annual Review of Law and Social Science* 5: 347–374.

LaFree, Gary and Laura Dugan. 2007. "Introducing the Global Terrorism Database." *Terrorism and Political Violence* 19(2): 181–204.

Lee, Joonghoon. 2008. "Exploring Global Terrorism Data: A Web-Based Visualization of Temporal Data." *ACM Crossroads* 15(2): 7–16.

Marshall, Monty and Keith Jaggers. 2007. "POLITY IV Project: Political Regime Characteristics and Transitions, 1800–2006 Dataset Users' Manual." http://www.systemicpeace.org/inscrdata.html.

Matthew, Richard and George Shambaugh. 2005. "The Pendulum Effect: Explaining Shifts in the Democratic Response to Terrorism." *Analyses of Social Issues and Public Policy* 5(1): 223–233.

Mesquita, Bruce Bueno, George W. Downs, Alastair Smith, and Feryal Marie Cherif. 2005. "Thinking Inside the Box: A Closer Look at Democracy and Human Rights." *International Studies Quarterly.* 49 (3): 439-57

Mickolus, Edward F., Todd Sandler, Jean M. Murdock, and Peter Flemming. 2006. "International Terrorism: Attributes of Terrorist Events, 1968–2005 (ITERATE 5)." Vinyard Software, Dunn Loring, VA.

Morrow, James D., Bruce Bueno de Mesquita, Randolph M. Siverson, and Alastair Smith. 2008. "Retesting Selectorate Theory: Separating the Effects of *W* from Other Elements of Democracy." *American Political Science Review* 102(3): 393–400.

O'Donnell, Guillermo. 2004. "Why the Rule of Law Matters." *Journal of Democracy* 15(4): 32–46.

Piazza, James A. 2006. "Rooted in Poverty?" *Terrorism and Political Violence* 18(1): 159–177.

Piazza, James A. and James I. Walsh. 2009. "Transnational Terror and Human Rights." *International Studies Quarterly* 53(1): 125–148.

Pious, Richard M. 2006. *The War on Terrorism and the Rule of Law.* Los Angeles, CA: Roxbury.

Ramraj, Victor V., Michael Hor, and Kent Roach, eds. 2005. *Global Anti-Terrorism Law and Policy.* New York: Cambridge University Press.

Raz, Joseph. 1977. "The Rule of Law and Its Virtue." *Law Quarterly Review* 93: 195–211.

Reeve, Andrew. 2010. "Civil Liberties." http://www.answers.com/topic/civil-liberties.

Smith, Andreas Whittam. August 11, 2007. "I'd Rather Risk Terrorism Than Destroy the Rule of Law." *The Independent.* http://www.independent.co.uk/voices/commentators/andreas-whittam-smith/id-rather-risk-terrorism-than-destroy-the-rule-of-law-488957.html

Tsebelis, George. 2002. *Veto Players: How Political Institutions Work.* New York: Russell Sage Foundation and Princeton, NJ: Princeton University Press.

Wooldridge, Jeffrey M. 2002. *Econometric Analysis of Cross Section and Panel Data.* Cambridge, MA: MIT Press.

World Bank. 2008. "Worldwide Governance Indicators, 1996–2007." http://info.worldbank.org/governance/wgi/#reports.

CHAPTER 4

Theory of Terrorist Outbidding and Its Empirical Evidence

The literature on the theory of outbidding is based on the long-standing assumption that outbidding is one of the primary strategies employed by terrorist organizations. Domestic competition for attention and support among terrorist groups leads to an increase in political violence as they each make an effort to distinguish themselves or to stand out from the crowd (see Crenshaw 1985, 1987; Oots 1989; Bloom 2005; Kydd and Walter 2006). The essence of the theory of outbidding is epitomized in Bloom's (2005, 95) statement that "where there are multiple groups, violence is a technique to gain credibility and win the public relations competition." Kydd and Walter (2006) later elaborate that, despite the costs, terrorist groups are likely to be rewarded for becoming more militant in demonstrating their determination to continue the armed struggle at any cost. However, a series of recent empirical studies using cross-national, time-series data produced limited or no supporting evidence for the outbidding theory.

Findley and Young (2012) provide the first statistical analysis that tests the effect of outbidding on (suicide) terrorism.[1] In their study, outbidding is measured as the total number of terrorist organizations drawn from the Global Terrorism Database. The overall results of Findley and Young show scant evidence for the causal connection between the two factors. Independent of the Findley and Young investigation, Nemeth (2014) poses the same research question but tests it with an alternative measure of outbidding—the organization's market share relative to other organizations. He finds "nationalist and religious terrorist groups responding to competition with more [domestic] terrorism and left-wing organizations responding with less" (336).

By and large, Findley and Young (2012) appear to have set the standard for the subsequent *empirical* research that often borrows their outbidding measure to capture the behavior of multiple terrorist groups. Subsequent related studies usually begin their inquiry by taking the null finding on outbidding and suicide terrorism reported by Findley and Young for granted rather than challenging the analysis. These studies then probe into a question about how outbidding is related to different political outcomes. For instance, Young and Dugan (2014) use a measure of outbidding that is fairly similar to Findley and Young's in order to explore how strategic competition among terrorist groups is associated with group duration. Conrad and Greene (2015) offer another example, analyzing whether an increase in the competitiveness of a political market leads to more severe or shocking types of terrorist attacks. There are also ongoing studies that ask slightly different questions—whether context or group identity matters. Indisputably, these studies have advanced our scientific knowledge of the behavior of terrorist organizations. However, they do not directly address the original tenet of the theory of outbidding put forward by qualitative researchers such as Bloom (2005) and Kydd and Walter (2006). More important, although the new developments of research are welcome, investigating the gap between the original theory of terrorist outbidding and empirical findings remains a very important task, as it provides the foundation for subsequent studies.

This study asserts that just as we cannot build our conceptualizations as a house of sand, we cannot build a research program on a flawed finding. As the outgrowths of the Findley and Young study increase, it grows increasingly critical for the foundations to be solid. This study finds a serious flaw with the statistical models within existing studies, though not with their underlying theoretical arguments. In particular, this study argues that when a causal time order is properly applied to statistical analysis—ensuring that cause precedes effect,[2] the original theory of outbidding garners robust empirical evidence across countries and times. To test this argument, a new statistical model is proposed in which the dependent variable is measured in three different ways: domestic, international, and suicide. The results corroborate the prediction of the theory of outbidding: terrorist group competition is positively associated with increased activities of political violence, regardless of the domain or type of terrorism.

Before presenting the empirical analysis, this study expands the scope of the outbidding theory in the next section. The theoretical elaboration revolves around the new argument that terrorist organizations rely on all types of tactics rather than a single expression to signal their political determination and rationale for existence.

EXPANDING THE SCOPE OF THE OUTBIDDING ARGUMENT

The literature on terrorist outbidding focuses on suicide attacks,[3] both theoretically and empirically (e.g., Bloom 2005; Findley and Young 2012). This emphasis is justified by the fact that suicide attacks are the deadliest, most extreme tactic available to these groups and therefore allows us to gauge the fierceness of the competition among terrorist organizations and to understand the outcome. Suicide attacks are a crucial tactical choice for terrorist organizations to use to distinguish themselves; however, it comes at a high price. The reliance on suicide tactics is likely to run the risk of depleting the groups' limited human resources by expending cadres that cannot be used again and by alienating supporters who may object to such an extreme tactic (Piazza 2008a). Accordingly, a terrorist organization will employ alternative methods in order to rationalize its distinct existence as well as to demonstrate its greater commitment and capability relative to other competing organizations. In fact, it is impractical to assume that a terrorist organization relies exclusively on suicide tactics to outbid others when less costly and controversial alternatives are available. Therefore, this study expands the scope of the inquiry into alternative tactics in both the domestic and international domains.

Militant organizations rarely commit exclusively to a single terrorist tactic when competing for the attention of recruits and public support. As a result, there is typically a range of tactical options available to these organizations, rather than a simple choice between suicide attacks and inactivity. Different tactical options such as hostage taking, airline hijacking, car bombings, shootings, and suicide attacks can all be used individually or as a series of mixed tools to win the hearts and minds of local populations. The Tamil Tigers in Sri Lanka, for example, were notorious for their suicide bombing campaigns; however, they simultaneously utilized other tactics against both domestic and international targets to demonstrate their resolve for armed resistance as well as to achieve their political goals. Indeed, the Tamil Tigers did not hesitate to terrorize the Sinhalese, moderate Tamils, and other groups to come out on top over their rivals (Bloom 2005; Nemeth 2014). In the literature of outbidding, Hamas is a classic example of this phenomenon; it has been historically known to vie for the support of the Palestinian citizens in rivalry with Fatah (Kydd and Walter 2006). For some time, Hamas expanded its political influence through suicide attacks against Israeli military and civilian targets, but it also focused its attacks on international interests in an effort to signal its capability to protect the interests of Palestinians while attracting media attention required for the advancement of its domestic and international reputation. Inarguably, foreigners and foreign facilities are high-value targets for Hamas in its effort to distinguish itself from other terrorist groups.

For example, on September 3, 1998, Hamas fighters attacked an outpost belonging to the Lahdist 20th Artillery Regiment of the South Lebanon Army in the al-Ahmadiyah hills with machine guns, rockets, and mortars. On April 5, 2004, in retaliation for the assassination of Sheik Ahmed Yassin, the founder of Hamas, Hamas members threw a firebomb into the library of a Jewish elementary school in Montreal, Canada.[4]

It is worth noting that media attention is critical to the success of terrorist organizations, who must secure constant attention from the mass media if they desire to succeed in differentiating themselves from their competitors and ultimately come out on top in the competitive market (Levitt 2006). Nemeth (2014, 338) makes a similar observation that "groups will not remain relevant without the use of action and people will not join an organization that does not appear to be either active or effective." In order to continuously and successfully convey their message to the public and thus gain a significant advantage over their competition, terrorist organizations are likely to rely on any and all tactics available to them that they believe will successfully capture the media's attention (Hoffman 2006; Conrad and Greene 2015). Because the exclusive use of constant suicide bombings is impractical due to the limited supply of human resources and the inhumane nature of the tactic, a terrorist organization may also employ other means to terrorize domestic and international targets in an effort to maintain its competitive edge over other organizations. This is why the Tamil Tigers and Hamas have, in order to "keep the ball rolling," used both non-suicide and suicide attacks as part of their outbidding strategies. Both domestic and international tactics, and particularly suicide attacks, are all desirable venues for terrorist organizations when they wish to ensure widespread media coverage. This study thus proposes the following hypothesis:

H_1: As the degree of outbidding increases, activities of political violence should increase, regardless of the type of tactics.

Previous research typically examines a single type of terrorist activity and thus fails to account for the bigger picture. By examining the two domains of terrorism—international and domestic—and then with a closer look at suicide attacks, this study maintains that when a terrorist organization tries to outbid its competition in order to garner public support, it should provoke an increase in all three measures. Thus, the empirical investigation of this study broadens the scope of inquiry, marking an important departure from previous studies in its attempt to reconcile the incongruence between theoretical and empirical studies.

BUILDING A NEW TERRORISM MODEL

In order to examine the relationship between outbidding and terrorist violence, a statistical model is proposed as follows:

$$Terrorist\ attacks_{it} = a_1 + a_2 outbidding_{it-1} + a_3 democracy_{it-1} + a_4 political\ stability_{it-1}$$
$$+ a_5 economic\ development_{it-1} + a_6 population_{it-1}$$
$$+ a_7 failed\ state_{it-1} + a_8 internal\ conflict_{it-1}$$
$$+ a_9 international\ conflict_{it-1} + \varepsilon_1$$

As indicated in the t subscripts of the model, the independent variables at time $t-1$ are assumed to predict the dependent variable at time t—the time interval between the cause and effect variables is one year. The fact that all explanatory variables are lagged one year behind the outcome variable mitigates the possibility that the latter serves as a cause of the former. For empirical testing, this study collects a pooled panel dataset of 140 countries[5] during the period 1970–2004.

The unit of analysis is the country-year mainly because the outbidding hypothesis predicts the overall increase of any type of terrorism in proportion to an increased level of competition among terrorist groups. This unit is also consistent with the majority of studies on terrorist outbidding mentioned earlier. The use of group-year as the unit of analysis suffers from a lack of precision since perpetrators of terrorist attacks are known for only about 50 percent of the cases due to the lack of informational resources. As Laura Dugan (2012, 182)—one of the main compilers of the Global Terrorism Database—points out, "Nearly half of the attacks in the GTD are unattributed to any terrorist organization." If one's statistical analysis relies only on those attacks that are verifiably attributed to a specific terrorist organization, it would be subject to selection bias that would distort the estimated results and thus any inferences gleaned from them. The bottom line is that the group-year unit of analysis remains inadequate for the purposes of this study as a result of the limitations in collecting and documenting data that would make it possible to assign attacks to specific organizations.

The dependent variable is measured in seven different but related ways. These are all count measures capturing the total number of incidents related to domestic, international, and suicide terrorism that occurred in a country in a given year. The data came from LaFree and Dugan's (2007) Global Terrorism Database that is systematically separated into domestic and international terrorist incidents by Enders, Sandler, and Gaibulloev (2011). Note that "no other [researchers provide] such a complete partitioning of domestic and transnational incidents" (Enders, Sandler, and Gaibulloev 2011, 3).

One drawback of the total count measures of domestic and international terrorism is that they indiscriminately amalgamate terrorist events of differing magnitudes (in terms of resulting numbers of deaths and injuries). Accordingly, the "shocking" behavior of terrorist organizations that escalate and turn to severe types of attacks in recent years may not be fully captured (Conrad and Greene 2015). Indeed, a "new terrorism" that is characterized by a drop in the number of incidents but an increase in lethality has replaced the "old terrorism" of the 1970s and 1980s. Frey and Luechinger (2005) attempt to capture the unequal degree of severity in each terrorist incident by operationalizing the number of persons killed and the number of persons injured in terrorist attacks—alternative measures to total incident counts. Following Frey and Luechinger's step, this study creates variables for the total number of individuals either wounded or killed from the total number of domestic and international terrorist incidents. In light of the failure of counts to capture the magnitude of attacks, measuring the variation in the number of suicide attacks—the most extreme tactic of terrorist organizations—is useful in addition to the variables for numbers of individuals wounded and killed.

In addition to *domestic terrorism, domestic terrorism-killed, domestic terrorism-wounded, international terrorism, international terrorism-killed,* and *international terrorism-wounded,* this study creates *suicide terrorism* as another dependent variable. Using the Global Terrorism Database, this study identifies suicide attacks as instances where the terrorists themselves did not intend to escape the attack alive. Domestic and international terrorist incidents are mutually exclusive and collectively exhaustive, but suicide terrorist incidents are not because suicide bombers may choose either domestic or international targets.

To ensure the robustness of the main findings, this study creates four alternative measures for the dependent variable on the basis of another widely used dataset—the International Terrorism: Attributes of Terrorist Events (ITERATE). They are (1) terrorist events categorized by place of attack, (2) total number of people killed by place of attack, (3) total number of people wounded by place of attack, and (4) suicide attacks categorized by place of attack. Table 4.A2 displays estimated results that do not deviate from the main results reported in the next section: the strategy of outbidding matters.

The main independent variable, *outbidding,* is measured as the total number of terrorist organizations. This measure is obtained from Findley and Young (2012) and Young and Dugan (2014), who took the lead on designing a measure for terrorist outbidding drawn from the Global Terrorism Database.[6] Note that previous studies also rely on the same outbidding measure. For example, Conrad and Greene's (2015) study uses Young and Dugan's measure.

By acknowledging that "rapid increases in the number of organizations is likely to represent a more competitive environment than one in which multiple organizations have existed for some time," Conrad and Greene (2015, 554) suggest the annual change in the total number of terrorist organizations as an alternative measure for Young and Dugan's outbidding variable. This study slightly modifies the measure of the annual change to accommodate for more precise empirical testing.[7] However, because the results from the annual change measure and the original values of Young and Dugan are similar, they are not reported in the next section in an effort to save space.

To avoid obtaining spurious statistical results, seven control variables that have commonly appeared in previous research are incorporated into the model: *democracy, political stability, economic development, population, failed state, internal conflict,* and *international conflict.*[8] Previous studies on terrorism show mixed effects that result from democratic institutions (Eyerman 1998; Li 2005; Choi 2010). Because democracy is not the main variable of interest in this study, its causal influence is left agnostic. Collected from the Polity dataset (Marshall and Jaggers 2007), the democracy variable ranges from –10 (least democratic) to +10 (most democratic). Given that politically stable countries provide militant groups with fewer opportunities to terrorize (Eubank and Weinberg 2001), this study includes political stability as another control. This control factor is operationalized as the number of years elapsed since a country underwent a regime change, measured as a three-point shift in a country's Polity score for a given year.

As national economy prospers, countries should encounter fewer terrorist incidents stemming from economic grievances (Li 2005; Choi 2015). Economic development is measured as GDP per capita, garnered from the World Bank's Economic Development Indicator. More populous countries are likely to experience high levels of terrorist activities, in that they harbor more terrorist groups and provide more target opportunities (Krieger and Meierrieks 2011). The total population count is obtained from the U.S. Census Bureau. Because a failed state is too weak to exercise legal authority over much of its territory, it should induce more terrorist events (Piazza 2008b; Choi and James 2016). The failed state variable is measured on a scale of 0 to 12, gathered from the Political Instability Task Force. This study also includes two conflict-related measures, which is "1" if a country experiences an internal conflict or an international conflict in a given year, and "0" otherwise, using the Uppsala Conflict Data Program (UCDP) dataset (Nemeth 2014).

The dependent variable is the count of terrorist incidents per country-year, and thus the baseline model of this study is considered a Poisson regression model. However, the Pearson goodness-of-fit chi-squared test is found to be statistically significant ($chi^2 = 244,540.2, p < 0.001$), resulting in a Poisson regression approach that does not to fit the data well. Negative binomial maximum-likelihood regression with Huber-White robust standard errors clustered by country is instead proposed as an alternative estimation method. Because negative binomial regression adds a dispersion parameter to model the unobserved heterogeneity among observations, it is able to correct for the overdispersion found in a Poisson regression model (Hilbe 2007).

EMPIRICAL RESULTS

Table 4.1 presents estimated results of the model for terrorist attacks in the context of domestic, international, and suicide terrorism. Findley and Young's outbidding measure, denoted as *number of terror groups*, is used in Models 1–7, while Young and Dugan's measure appears in Models 8–14. The outbidding variable is significantly different from zero across all models except for Model 13. This implies that a terrorist group is, in general, likely to resort to political violence to distinguish itself from other competing groups. Given that the outbidding variable achieves significance irrespective of the domain or tactic, a terrorist group seems to employ any and all available options rather than relying on a particular method of attack. This is consistent with the theoretical speculation noted earlier. Among seven control variables, *population* and *international conflict* emerge as consistent predictors of increased terrorist activities, as they are found to be statistically significant across all models.

As a sample size increases, statistical significance may not be meaningful in a practical sense. For this reason, the substantive effects of variables should also be discussed. Because *number of terror groups* is the most theoretically interesting and significant variable among the eight predictors in Table 4.1, its substantive effect is calculated by setting the continuous variables in the estimations at their means and the dichotomized variables at 1. This study then adjusts *number of terror groups* one at a time to examine the change in the predicted probability of terrorism. This study finds that the likelihood of terrorism increases when *number of terror groups* changes from the mean to the mean plus one or two standard deviations, holding all other factors constant. Thus, this substantive effect analysis confirms the positive relationship between outbidding and terrorist violence.

The important question is how it is that this study finds a significant relationship between outbidding and terrorism, whereas previous empirical studies do not. For example, this study reports the significance of the outbidding variable in Suicide Models 7 and 14 in Table 4.1, while the outbidding variable—*number of terror groups*—in Table 1 of Findley and Young's (2012, 711) piece does not pass the significance test. Given the fact that the outbidding measure in Model 7 of this study comes from Findley and Young's data collection, the different finding warrants further investigation.

The investigation begins with reviewing the way Findley and Young built their negative binomial model. It turns out that the causal time order between the predictors and the outcome variable is set at the same point t in the model as follows:

$$
\begin{aligned}
Suicide\ attacks_{it} = {} & \beta_1 + \beta_2 number\ of\ terror\ groups_{it} + \beta_3 partly\ free_{it} + \beta_4 not\ free_{it} \\
& + \beta_5 energy/capita_{it} + \beta_6 population_{it} + \beta_7 Islam_{it} \\
& + \beta_8 past\ attracts\ (country)_{it} + \beta_9 past\ attracts\ (global\ count)_{it} \\
& + \beta_{10} partly\ free^*minorities_{it} + \beta_{11} not\ free^*minorities_{it} \\
& + \beta_{12} minorities_{it} + \beta_{13} regime\ durability_{it} + \varepsilon_2
\end{aligned}
$$

Table 4.1
The Effect of Outbidding on Terrorism

	Findley and Young							Young and Dugan						
	Domestic			International				Domestic			International			
Variable	All	Killed	Wounded	All	Killed	Wounded	Suicide	All	Killed	Wounded	All	Killed	Wounded	Suicide
	Model 1	Model 2	Model 3	Model 4	Model 5	Model 6	Model 7	Model 8	Model 9	Model 10	Model 11	Model 12	Model 13	Model 14
Number of terror groups	0.365***	0.278***	0.293***	0.220***	0.163**	0.353*	0.181**	0.379***	0.336***	0.249***	0.202***	0.161*	0.234	0.203*
	(0.064)	(0.057)	(0.051)	(0.037)	(0.050)	(0.145)	(0.058)	(0.101)	(0.084)	(0.069)	(0.052)	(0.075)	(0.171)	(0.082)
Democracy	0.025	-0.014	-0.017	0.028**	-0.035	0.001	-0.079**	0.020	-0.015	-0.017	0.031**	-0.035	0.004	-0.074*
	(0.017)	(0.016)	(0.014)	(0.010)	(0.021)	(0.021)	(0.029)	(0.020)	(0.015)	(0.015)	(0.010)	(0.021)	(0.021)	(0.029)
Political stability	-0.012***	0.008	-0.005	-0.010***	0.001	-0.008	0.019	-0.015***	-0.000	-0.005	-0.011**	0.001	-0.011	0.019
	(0.003)	(0.005)	(0.003)	(0.003)	(0.007)	(0.007)	(0.011)	(0.003)	(0.005)	(0.004)	(0.004)	(0.007)	(0.007)	(0.011)
Economic development	0.370**	-0.366**	0.181	0.463***	0.334	0.429**	0.761***	0.390**	-0.393*	0.190	0.473***	0.323	0.377*	0.658**
	(0.121)	(0.133)	(0.122)	(0.084)	(0.198)	(0.149)	(0.221)	(0.136)	(0.135)	(0.131)	(0.085)	(0.201)	(0.165)	(0.243)
Population	0.488***	0.658***	0.773***	0.374***	0.638***	0.967***	0.703***	0.521***	0.645***	0.821***	0.389***	0.662***	1.138***	0.722***
	(0.071)	(0.103)	(0.107)	(0.065)	(0.114)	(0.142)	(0.157)	(0.078)	(0.101)	(0.111)	(0.065)	(0.118)	(0.151)	(0.165)
Failed state	0.214***	0.504***	0.311***	0.117**	0.219*	0.070	-0.093	0.225***	0.592***	0.378***	0.124**	0.237*	0.072	-0.072
	(0.050)	(0.134)	(0.082)	(0.042)	(0.086)	(0.077)	(0.147)	(0.059)	(0.177)	(0.103)	(0.044)	(0.095)	(0.090)	(0.156)
Internal conflict	0.529***	0.741***	0.819***	0.395***	0.391*	0.703**	1.484***	0.662***	0.782***	0.889***	0.462**	0.421**	0.776**	1.400***
	(0.078)	(0.142)	(0.150)	(0.078)	(0.159)	(0.267)	(0.274)	(0.092)	(0.169)	(0.162)	(0.087)	(0.163)	(0.280)	(0.326)
International conflict	-0.133	-0.031	-0.027	0.026	-0.390*	0.024	0.417	-0.109	-0.023	-0.015	0.046	-0.429*	-0.100	0.367
	(0.124)	(0.193)	(0.173)	(0.071)	(0.190)	(0.220)	(0.370)	(0.124)	(0.174)	(0.161)	(0.080)	(0.178)	(0.204)	(0.338)

(Continued)

Table 4.1
(Continued)

Variable	Findley and Young							Young and Dugan						
	Domestic			International				Domestic			International			
	All	Killed	Wounded	All	Killed	Wounded	Suicide	All	Killed	Wounded	All	Killed	Wounded	Suicide
	Model 1	Model 2	Model 3	Model 4	Model 5	Model 6	Model 7	Model 8	Model 9	Model 10	Model 11	Model 12	Model 13	Model 14
Constant	−7.422***	−3.178*	−8.155***	−7.855***	−9.271***	−12.686***	−18.716***	−7.727***	−2.717	−8.530***	−7.982***	−9.346***	−13.391***	−17.959***
	(1.244)	(1.537)	(1.325)	(0.967)	(2.028)	(1.876)	(1.970)	(1.403)	(1.546)	(1.428)	(0.932)	(2.086)	(1.876)	(1.956)
Wald chi²	324.73	289.03	228.90	311.72	111.14	107.87	124.92	272.47	263.32	198.22	302.63	110.50	102.92	126.14
Probability > chi²	0.001	0.001	0.001	0.001	0.001	0.001	0.001	0.001	0.001	0.001	0.001	0.001	0.001	0.001
Log pseudo-likelihood	−6,835.55	−5,751.55	−6,242.29	−4,980.38	−3,539.22	−3,567.45	−471.83	−6,899.40	−5,755.39	−6,266.14	−5,015.58	−3,545.68	−3,592.94	−471.47
Dispersion = 1	4.47	10.45	11.86	2.67	12.86	19.39	27.92	4.82	10.55	12.30	2.80	13.05	20.49	27.6
Observations	3,961	3,961	3,961	3,961	3,961	3,961	3,961	3,961	3,961	3,961	3,961	3,961	3,961	3,961

Note: Robust standard errors are in parentheses.

*p < .05 two-tailed tests

**p < .01 two-tailed tests

***p < .001 two-tailed tests

This model construction guarantees that the *number of terror groups* at time *t* have the potential to cause the incidence of suicide terrorism at the same time point *t*.

Since Findley and Young state that "the unit of analysis for these tests is the country-year" (709), their model assumes that the number of terror groups in year 2000, for instance, likely leads to an increase of suicide attacks in that country in the same year. This causal timeline between the explanatory and dependent variables is not ideal when one considers cases in which some terrorist groups are formed in November 2000 while suicide attacks are carried out in January 2000. In such cases, the hypothesized effect of the theory of outbidding (suicide attacks in January) could precede the hypothesized cause (birth of new terrorist groups in November) up to 11 months, which is implausible in the real world. The same logic applies to control variables. Imagine that a country experiences suicide attacks in February 2000, but it becomes partly free in December 2000. Again, this causal timeline for a relationship where democratization leads to suicide attacks is not reasonable because the democratic transition did not start until the last month of the year. Furthermore, while one can easily identify the month and year of any terrorist incident recorded in the Global Terrorism Database, the exact date of the founding of a terrorist organization is unknown to researchers. Given this lack of information, establishing the causal time order between the number of organizations and terrorist activity requires careful consideration. This poses the question of how best to correct the potential problem of causal time order in the Findley and Young model. A quick, easy, and simple solution is to set all predictors at time *t*–1 instead of time *t* to ensure that outbidding serves as a potential cause of suicide attacks, not the other way around. For example, in his attempt to evaluate the effect of outbidding on domestic terrorism, Nemeth (2014, 349) "lagged the independent variables to account for endogeneity."

After having corrected the causal time order in the Findley and Young model, I replicated the results reported in their Table 1 on page 711. Model 1 in Table 4.2 displays the replicated results that closely resemble those reported in the work of Findley and Young.[9] Not surprisingly, as Findley and Young put it, "The measure of the number of groups is not statistically significant at standard levels" (711). When the causal timeline is corrected in Model 2, the same variable becomes significant with a positive sign, indicating that outbidding contributes to an increase in the likelihood of suicide attacks. This result is indeed consistent with the theoretical logic of outbidding. In Model 3, Findley and Young's measure of the *number of terror groups* is replaced with Young and Dugan's as a means to check for further robustness. The *number of terror groups* variable still emerges as a significant predictor of suicide attacks. The overall results in Table 4.2 are not in line with the main finding of the Findley and Young study in which the cause and effect variables are erroneously set at the same time point *t* but corroborate those displayed in Table 4.1 of this study in which a more appropriate causal time order is specified.

Table 4.2
Replication of Findley and Young 2012, "More Combatant Groups, More Terror?"

	Suicide Terrorism		
		Independent Variables at time $t–1$	Young and Dugan at time $t–1$
Variable	Model 1	Model 2	Model 3
Number of terror groups	0.086	0.229***	0.215***
	(0.053)	(0.037)	(0.056)
Partly free	2.031**	0.933	1.045
	(0.714)	(0.698)	(0.735)
Not free	1.239	0.150	0.264
	(0.786)	(0.798)	(0.837)
Energy / capita	0.235	0.337*	0.303*
	(0.173)	(0.167)	(0.153)
Population	0.500**	0.286	0.302
	(0.157)	(0.179)	(0.161)
Islam	0.816	0.992*	1.080*
	(0.465)	(0.500)	(0.462)
Past attracts (country)	2.552**	3.921**	4.261***
	(0.890)	(1.234)	(1.207)
Past attracts (global count)	0.004*	0.005*	0.004
	(0.002)	(0.002)	(0.003)
*Partly free * minorities*	–0.020	0.139	–0.002
	(0.137)	(0.150)	(0.179)
*Not free * minorities*	–0.422*	–0.233	–0.366
	(0.185)	(0.193)	(0.230)
Minorities	0.176	0.121	0.254
	(0.112)	(0.182)	(0.209)
Regime durability	0.014*	0.013*	0.008
	(0.007)	(0.005)	(0.006)
Intercept	–12.007***	–9.634***	–9.503***
	(1.756)	(2.359)	(2.234)
Wald chi^2	387.80	275.76	174.97
Probability > chi^2	0.001	0.001	0.001
Log pseudolikelihood	–343.53	–370.88	–377.24
Dispersion = 1	4.25	10.20	10.99
Observations	3,605	3,444	3,444

Note: Robust standard errors are in parentheses.

*$p < .05$ two-tailed tests

**$p < .01$ two-tailed tests

***$p < .001$ two-tailed tests

DID A DIFFERENT SET OF CONTROL VARIABLES
PRODUCE DIFFERENT RESULTS?

One might argue that there is a notable difference in the model building of this study compared to that of Findley and Young, which could explain the contrasting results. The use of control variables that should filter intervening effects between the main predictor and the outcome variable is not the same, so comparing the two studies might be like comparing apples and oranges. To address the concern, this study performs additional robustness tests that employ Findley and Young's model specifications in the context of domestic, international, and suicide terrorism. This strategy follows Dafoe, Oneal, and Russett's (2013, 204) suggestion that "absent justification, statistical critiques of robust empirical associations should change as little as possible from standard analyses. . . . Otherwise, it is hard to know what novel aspect of the specification accounts for the different results." The results from additional robustness tests are reported in Table 4.3. It appears that no matter how the outbidding prediction is tested, there is strong, consistent evidence for the positive effect of the *number of terror groups* across all models. Again, the results confirm the main finding of this empirical study.

CONCLUSION

The qualitative literature of outbidding has long made an important contribution in explaining and understanding the behavior of terrorist organizations; however, the theory of outbidding has failed to garner quantitative evidence from recent cross-sectional, time-series data analyses. The previously irreconcilable disparity between the theory and the empirical findings has left many scholars and policy makers uncertain of the theoretical utility or unsure of how best to approach resolving this disparity. This study has addressed the described concern by designing a new statistical model after providing a refined causal mechanism in which the phenomenon of terrorist violence is expanded into both domestic and international domains, and with a particular focus on suicide terrorism. In addition, this study provides a critical examination of the pioneering empirical research on the theory of outbidding conducted by Findley and Young (2012). The conclusion is clear and simple: when a causal timeline is properly set in statistical models, the theory of outbidding is supported by empirical analysis across countries and across time. This unambiguously suggests that terrorist organizations are inclined to employ political violence to distinguish themselves, adopting whichever tactic suits their political agenda.

This study also illustrates a critical component of the advancement of scientific knowledge on terrorism. It is well known and accepted that data-driven research progresses scientific knowledge by demonstrating the existence of previously unknown phenomena. This demonstration is

Table 4.3 Does Outbidding Really Matter?

	Findley and Young							Young and Dugan						
	Domestic			International				Domestic			International			
	All	Killed	Wounded	All	Killed	Wounded	Suicide	All	Killed	Wounded	All	Killed	Wounded	Suicide
Variable	Model 1	Model 2	Model 3	Model 4	Model 5	Model 6	Model 7	Model 8	Model 9	Model 10	Model 11	Model 12	Model 13	Model 14
Number of terror groups	0.351***	0.399***	0.339***	0.220***	0.232***	0.356***	0.129***	0.357***	0.416***	0.313***	0.206***	0.284***	0.253***	0.155*
	(0.053)	(0.066)	(0.050)	(0.034)	(0.048)	(0.090)	(0.039)	(0.086)	(0.084)	(0.073)	(0.056)	(0.076)	(0.095)	(0.062)
Partly free	0.446*	1.281***	0.626*	-0.160	0.847*	0.634	0.902	0.441	1.118***	0.791**	-0.107	1.000**	0.577	1.074
	(0.192)	(0.288)	(0.253)	(0.137)	(0.346)	(0.391)	(0.583)	(0.247)	(0.272)	(0.268)	(0.148)	(0.323)	(0.440)	(0.645)
Not free	0.494	2.234***	1.317***	-0.028	1.354***	0.550	0.583	0.400	2.224***	1.508***	-0.059	1.570***	0.713	0.736
	(0.269)	(0.361)	(0.376)	(0.248)	(0.399)	(0.484)	(0.679)	(0.309)	(0.411)	(0.396)	(0.250)	(0.415)	(0.543)	(0.765)
Energy/capita	0.142*	-0.204*	0.033	0.092*	0.198*	0.296**	0.122	0.117	-0.193*	0.025	0.087	0.189*	0.336**	0.125
	(0.059)	(0.086)	(0.088)	(0.047)	(0.080)	(0.101)	(0.117)	(0.069)	(0.088)	(0.088)	(0.047)	(0.079)	(0.106)	(0.114)
Population	0.472***	0.767***	0.698***	0.322***	0.518***	0.992***	0.354*	0.486***	0.736***	0.743***	0.347***	0.509***	1.113***	0.339*
	(0.078)	(0.126)	(0.113)	(0.067)	(0.109)	(0.118)	(0.139)	(0.089)	(0.137)	(0.112)	(0.069)	(0.107)	(0.141)	(0.137)
Islam	-0.339	0.022	0.083	0.016	0.326	-0.293	1.239***	-0.348	-0.051	0.001	0.011	0.312	-0.556	1.293***
	(0.181)	(0.273)	(0.337)	(0.168)	(0.317)	(0.336)	(0.333)	(0.206)	(0.265)	(0.328)	(0.174)	(0.313)	(0.356)	(0.338)
Past attracts (country)	0.032***	0.020***	0.025***	0.114***	0.107*	-0.000	6.092***	0.035***	0.029***	0.031***	0.123***	0.105*	0.000	6.510***
	(0.006)	(0.005)	(0.006)	(0.026)	(0.047)	(0.001)	(1.476)	(0.006)	(0.005)	(0.008)	(0.030)	(0.052)	(0.001)	(1.650)
Past attracts (global)	0.000***	-0.000***	-0.000	0.001***	-0.000	-0.000	0.027***	0.000***	-0.000*	-0.000	0.002***	-0.000	-0.000	0.026***
	(0.000)	(0.000)	(0.000)	(0.000)	(0.001)	(0.000)	(0.006)	(0.000)	(0.000)	(0.000)	(0.000)	(0.001)	(0.000)	(0.006)
Partly free * minorities	-0.203	-0.343	-0.105	0.096	-0.787*	-1.738**	-0.174	-0.121	-0.314	-0.121	0.029	-0.813*	-1.823*	-0.293
	(0.188)	(0.361)	(0.147)	(0.094)	(0.331)	(0.666)	(0.908)	(0.204)	(0.418)	(0.175)	(0.089)	(0.336)	(0.816)	(0.906)

Not free * minorities	-0.239	-0.504	-0.241	0.114	-0.725	-0.914	-0.463	-0.221	-0.575	-0.348	0.049	-0.781*	-1.132	-0.560
	(0.220)	(0.403)	(0.256)	(0.150)	(0.373)	(0.677)	(0.965)	(0.202)	(0.447)	(0.245)	(0.139)	(0.375)	(0.807)	(0.963)
Minorities	0.278	0.364	0.081	-0.056	0.772*	1.554*	0.562	0.227	0.362	0.112	-0.003	0.802*	1.766*	0.690
	(0.185)	(0.365)	(0.140)	(0.096)	(0.332)	(0.642)	(0.969)	(0.159)	(0.411)	(0.152)	(0.087)	(0.333)	(0.782)	(0.954)
Regime durability	-0.009**	0.001	-0.004	-0.006	-0.009	-0.017**	0.010	-0.009*	-0.008	-0.004	-0.006	-0.008	-0.020**	0.008
	(0.003)	(0.005)	(0.004)	(0.003)	(0.005)	(0.006)	(0.006)	(0.004)	(0.005)	(0.005)	(0.004)	(0.006)	(0.006)	(0.007)
Intercept	-4.545***	-7.130***	-6.018***	-3.714***	-5.853***	-9.296***	-9.691***	-4.671***	-6.635***	-6.350***	-4.052***	-5.888***	-10.035***	-9.654***
	(0.700)	(1.134)	(1.154)	(0.611)	(0.905)	(1.011)	(1.695)	(0.823)	(1.241)	(1.116)	(0.641)	(0.911)	(1.204)	(1.694)
Wald chi²	348.71	286.08	268.97	198.23	137.44	297.49	358.51	277.22	274.76	220.76	173.57	141.88	395.95	306.27
Probability > chi²	0.001	0.001	0.001	0.001	0.001	0.001	0.001	0.001	0.001	0.001	0.001	0.001	0.001	0.001
Log pseudo-likelihood	-7,332.23	-6,383.94	-6,803.83	-5,456.22	-3,851.34	-3,892.42	-474.11	-7,410.78	-6,411.82	-6,835.09	-5,499.65	-3,854.22	-3,921.68	-474.39
Dispersion = 1	4.54	11.35	12.52	2.92	12.19	18.95	10.02	4.93	11.78	13.08	3.10	12.29	20.07	11.14
Observations	4,156	4,156	4,156	4,156	4,156	4,156	4,156	4,156	4,156	4,156	4,156	4,156	4,156	4,156

Note: Robust standard errors are in parentheses.

*p < .05 two-tailed tests

**p < .01 two-tailed tests

***p < .001 two-tailed tests

achieved by illuminating new relationships between existing phenomena, or often by discovering that some widely shared understanding is either incomplete or entirely wrong. In the 16th century, for example, scholars such as Galileo Galilei would have been prosecuted, had they spoken the scientific truth about heliocentrism versus the well-established theory of geocentrism. Or consider the supersession of Newton's 200-year-old theory of mechanics by Albert Einstein's theory of relativity at the beginning of the 20th century. In general, we ought to remind ourselves of Karl Popper's (1965, 216) insight in *Conjectures and Refutations: The Growth of Scientific Knowledge* that "science is . . . perhaps the only [human activity]—in which errors are systematically criticized and, in time, corrected. This is why we can say that, in science, we often learn from our mistakes." This study appreciates the spirit of Karl Popper's philosophy and thus scrutinizes the previous empirical findings related to the logic of outbidding. It is in this spirit that this study presents these empirical findings as a contribution to the advancement of our scientific knowledge on the behavior of terrorist organizations.

Table 4.A1
A List of Sample Countries

Afghanistan	Costa Rica	Hungary	Mauritius	Singapore
Albania	Croatia	India	Mexico	Slovakia
Algeria	Cuba	Indonesia	Mongolia	Somalia
Angola	Cyprus	Iran	Morocco	South Africa
Argentina	Czech Republic	Iraq	Mozambique	Spain
Armenia	Denmark	Ireland	Nepal	Sri Lanka
Australia	Djibouti	Israel	Netherlands	Sudan
Austria	Dominican Republic	Italy	New Zealand	Swaziland
Azerbaijan	Ecuador	Ivory Coast	Nicaragua	Sweden
Bahrain	Egypt	Jamaica	Niger	Switzerland
Belgium	El Salvador	Japan	Nigeria	Syria
Benin	Eritrea	Jordan	Norway	Tajikistan
Bhutan	Ethiopia	Kazakhstan	Oman	Tanzania
Bolivia	Fiji	Kenya	Pakistan	Thailand
Botswana	Finland	Korea, South	Panama	Togo
Brazil	France	Kuwait	Papua New Guinea	Trinidad and Tobago
Burkina Faso	Gabon	Kyrgyzstan	Paraguay	Tunisia
Burundi	Gambia	Laos	Peru	Turkey
Cambodia	Georgia	Lebanon	Philippines	Turkmenistan
Cameroon	Germany	Lesotho	Poland	Uganda
Canada	Ghana	Liberia	Portugal	United Kingdom
Central African Republic	Greece	Libya	Qatar	Ukraine
Chad	Guatemala	Macedonia	Romania	Uruguay
Chile	Guinea	Madagascar	Russia	United States
China	Guinea Bissau	Malawi	Rwanda	Uzbekistan
Colombia	Guyana	Malaysia	Saudi Arabia	Venezuela
Comoros	Haiti	Mali	Senegal	Zambia
Congo	Honduras	Mauritania	Sierra Leone	Zimbabwe

Table 4.A2 The Effect of Outbidding on Terrorism: ITERATE

	Findley and Young				Young and Dugan			
	International				International			
	All	Killed	Wounded	Suicide	All	Killed	Wounded	Suicide
Variable	Model 1	Model 2	Model 3	Model 4	Model 5	Model 6	Model 7	Model 8
Number of terror groups	0.145***	0.109**	0.163***	0.278***	0.121***	0.115*	0.160**	0.248**
	(0.030)	(0.041)	(0.040)	(0.070)	(0.028)	(0.053)	(0.060)	(0.083)
Democracy	0.016	-0.011	-0.027	-0.182**	0.019	-0.010	-0.027	-0.155**
	(0.012)	(0.020)	(0.023)	(0.064)	(0.012)	(0.020)	(0.022)	(0.057)
Political stability	-0.008**	-0.003	-0.001	0.001	-0.009**	-0.005	-0.002	-0.007
	(0.003)	(0.004)	(0.006)	(0.015)	(0.003)	(0.005)	(0.007)	(0.015)
Economic development	0.659***	0.388*	0.618***	0.965**	0.675***	0.383*	0.624***	0.935**
	(0.088)	(0.173)	(0.182)	(0.294)	(0.087)	(0.169)	(0.183)	(0.306)
Population	0.388***	0.533***	0.495***	0.737*	0.409***	0.548***	0.539***	0.871**
	(0.076)	(0.097)	(0.117)	(0.299)	(0.078)	(0.101)	(0.119)	(0.310)
Failed state	0.117**	0.236**	0.038	-0.806**	0.120***	0.235**	0.045	-0.652**
	(0.037)	(0.072)	(0.071)	(0.271)	(0.035)	(0.072)	(0.071)	(0.235)
Internal conflict	0.319***	0.615***	0.738***	1.322***	0.366***	0.633***	0.745***	1.157**
	(0.073)	(0.171)	(0.215)	(0.376)	(0.076)	(0.170)	(0.209)	(0.440)

International conflict							
0.102	0.018	0.214	-0.151	0.072	-0.010	0.144	-0.291
(0.072)	(0.144)	(0.136)	(0.580)	(0.068)	(0.145)	(0.124)	(0.527)
Constant							
-9.196***	-8.475***	-9.494***	-21.602***	-9.433***	-8.520***	-9.882***	-22.154***
(1.018)	(1.858)	(1.964)	(4.229)	(1.026)	(1.834)	(1.963)	(4.068)
Wald chi²							
383.10	115.96	111.13	59.66	378.05	115.28	81.16	98.09
Probability > chi²							
0.001	0.001	0.001	0.001	0.001	0.001	0.001	0.001
Log pseudolikelihood							
-5,462.43	-3,567.21	-3,912.61	-100.42	-5,475.95	-3,568.57	-3,915.06	-101.38
Dispersion = 1							
2.42	13.13	18.64	134.42	2.45	13.17	18.75	146.46
Observations							
3,696	3,696	3,696	3,696	3,696	3,696	3,696	3,696

Note: Robust standard errors are in parentheses.

*p < .05 two-tailed tests

**p < .01 two-tailed tests

***p < .001 two-tailed tests

NOTES

1. Chenoweth's (2010) work may be considered the one that also performs empirical analysis on the concept of outbidding. Yet, as Nemeth (2014, 340) points out, her examination is closely related to political outbidding among democratic actors rather than terrorist organizations because the outbidding measure relies on Polity's concept variable—political competition.

2. To paraphrase it, whatever causes the outcome actually has to occur before the outcome because the connection between cause and effect takes place in time (Davis 1985).

3. For the purposes of this study, suicide terrorism and attacks are used interchangeably.

4. See http://www.start.umd.edu/gtd/.

5. Table 4.A1 lists 140 sample countries.

6. The measures from Findley and Young (2012) and Young and Dugan (2014) are highly correlated (0.87).

7. Conrad and Greene calculate the annual change by deducting the number of active organizations at time t–1 from the number of organizations at time t. This measure is incomplete, in that it does not account for the number of organizations at time t–1 as the base of the formula. A more accurate statistic should be (number of organizations$_t$–number of organizations$_{t-1}$) divided by number of organizations$_{t-1}$, which enables researchers to better assess the impact of dynamic changes from the previous number of organizations.

8. An inclusion of a lagged term for the dependent variable on the right-hand side of the equation is controversial because it may take up too much variation in the dependent variable and thus wash out the significance of variables of interest (Achen 2000). When included in the model, it does not soak up much of the variation in the *terrorism* variable because the *outbidding* variable remains significant across most models.

9. The minor difference occurs due to the deletion of duplicated observations in Findley and Young's replication data that are available at http://nw18.american.edu/~jyoung/publication.html.

REFERENCES

Achen, Christopher. 2000. "Why Lagged Dependent Variables Can Suppress the Explanatory Power of Other Independent Variables." Working paper, Society for Political Methodology, St. Louis, WA.

Bloom, Mia. 2005. *Dying to Kill*. New York: Columbia University Press.

Chenoweth, Erica. 2010. "Democratic Competition and Terrorist Activity." *Journal of Politics* 72(1): 16–30.

Choi, Seung-Whan. 2010. "Fighting Terrorism through the Rule of Law?" *Journal of Conflict Resolution* 54(6): 940-966.

Choi, Seung-Whan. 2015. "Economic Growth and Terrorism: Domestic, International, and Suicide." *Oxford Economic Papers* 67(1): 157–181.

Choi, Seung-Whan and James Piazza. 2016. "Internally-Displaced Populations and Suicide Terrorism." *Journal of Conflict Resolution* 60(6): 1008–1040.

Conrad, Justin and Kevin Greene. 2015. "Differentiation and the Severity of Terrorist Attacks." *Journal of Politics* 77(2): 546–561.

Crenshaw, Martha. 1985. "An Organizational Approach to the Analysis of Political Terrorism." *Orbis* 29(3): 465–489.

Dafoe, Allan, John R. Oneal, and Bruce Russet. 2013. "The Democratic Peace." *International Studies Quarterly* 57(1): 201–214.

Davis, James A. 1985. *The Logic of Causal Order*. Thousand Oaks, CA: Sage.

Dugan, Laura. 2012. "The Making of the Global Terrorism Database and Its Applicability to Studying the Lifecycles of Terrorist Organizations." In David Gadd, Susanne Karstedt, and Steven Messner, eds., *The Sage Handbook of Criminological Research Methods*. Los Angeles, CA: Sage. 175–199.

Enders, Walter, Todd Sandler, and Khusrav Gaibulloev. 2011. "Domestic versus Transnational Terrorism." *Journal of Peace Research* 48(3): 319–337.

Eubank, William and Leonard Weinberg. 2001. "Terrorism and Democracy." *Terrorism and Political Violence* 13(1): 155–164.

Eyerman, Joe. 1998. "Terrorism and Democratic States." *International Interactions* 24(2): 151–170.

Findley, Michael and Joseph Young. 2012. "More Combatant Groups, More Terror?" *Terrorism and Political Violence* 24(5): 706–721.

Frey, Bruno and Simon Luechinger. 2005. "Measuring Terrorism." In Alain Marciano and Jean-Michel Josselin, eds., *Law and the State*. Cheltenham: Edward Elgar. 142–181.

Hilbe, Joseph. 2007. *Negative Binomial Regression*. Cambridge: Cambridge University Press.

Hoffman, Bruce. 2006. *Inside Terrorism*. New York: Columbia University Press.

Krieger, Tim and Daniel Meierrieks. 2011. "What Causes Terrorism?" *Public Choice* 147(1–2): 3–27.

Kydd, Andrew and Barbara Walter. 2006. "The Strategies of Terrorism." *International Security* 31(1): 49–80.

LaFree, Gary and Laura Dugan. 2007. "Introducing the Global Terrorism Database." *Terrorism and Political Violence* 19(2): 181–204.

Levitt, Matthew. 2006. *Hamas*. New Haven, CT: Yale University Press.

Li, Quan. 2005. "Does Democracy Promote or Reduce Transnational Terrorist Incidents?" *Journal of Conflict Resolution* 49(2): 278–297.

Marshall, Monty and Keith Jaggers. 2007. POLITY IV Project. http://www.systemicpeace.org/inscrdata.html.

Nemeth, Stephen. 2014. "The Effect of Competition on Terrorist Group Operations." *Journal of Conflict Resolution* 58(2): 336–362.

Oots, Kent. 1989. "Organizational Perspectives on the Formation and Disintegration of Terrorist Groups." *Studies in Conflict & Terrorism* 12(3): 139–152.

Piazza, James. 2008a. "A Supply-Side View of Suicide Terrorism." *Journal of Politics* 70(1): 28–39.

Piazza, James. 2008b. "Incubators of Terror." *International Studies Quarterly* 52(3): 469–488.

Popper, Karl R. 1965. *Conjectures and Refutations: The Growth of Scientific Knowledge*. 2nd. ed. New York: Basic Books.

Young, Joseph and Laura Dugan. 2014. "Survival of the Fittest." *Perspectives on Terrorism* 8(2): 2–23.

CHAPTER 5

The Effect of Economic Growth on Terrorism[1]

Although the September 11 terrorist attacks prompted academics and policy makers to scrutinize more closely the effect of terrorism on economic growth (e.g., Gaibulloev and Sandler 2011; Gaibulloev, Sandler, and Sul 2014), the inverse relationship has received little attention and the findings are inconclusive. In this study, I examine the inverse relationship by noting that the inconclusive findings reported in previous studies neglect to consider the fact that not all sectors of economic growth are uniformly associated with terrorist activity. By arguing that some sectors of growth are capable of inducing or reducing particular forms of terrorist activity while others may not give cause for concern, this study marks a significant departure from previous studies. In particular, I contend that while growth in the agricultural sector has no bearing on terrorist events, industrial growth has a significant effect. Furthermore, I assert that industrial growth affects different forms of terrorism in different ways. For example, it may exert a dampening effect on domestic and international terrorism while simultaneously encouraging more suicide terrorism. Put differently, I argue that only some forms of economic growth are associated with terrorist activity and that even then, they correlate only with particular forms of terrorist attacks. I explain these different correlations by offering three modified theories of economic growth and terrorism, which emphasize economic opportunities, social cleavages, and hard targets, respectively.

For empirical testing, I collect a cross-national, time-series dataset for 127 countries from 1970 to 2007. A battery of negative binomial regression and rare events logit models are built to evaluate the different possible effects that agricultural and industrial growth have on three forms of terrorist activity. The estimated results show evidence that industrial growth, rather than agricultural growth, is related to a decrease in domestic and international terrorism, while it is associated with an increase in suicide bombings. These findings are consistent with the prediction made by the modified theory of hard targets but not with those made by the theories of economic opportunities or social cleavages. Overall, the results of this study demonstrate that economic growth is not a cure for terrorism because it may, in some instances, breed more terrorism. Nevertheless, healthy economic conditions are, without doubt, beneficial to the war on terrorism because the majority of suicide attacks occur in only a few countries.

The present study is divided into five sections: the first section reviews the relevant extant literature; the second section presents three modified theoretical perspectives on the connection between economic growth and terrorism (i.e., economic opportunities, social cleavages, and hard targets); the third section explains the research design with respect to statistical model building, operationalization, and data sources; the fourth section discusses the empirical results; finally, the fifth section summarizes this study's main findings and discusses some policy implications.

LITERATURE REVIEW

There are not many empirical studies that examine how economic growth affects terrorism. Interestingly, even among these few studies, there is no consensus on the relationship between economic growth and terrorism, which may have dissuaded researchers from further investigating this relationship. By reviewing existing recent studies in three groups, I highlight their arguments and findings and then discuss what is deficient in the current literature.

The first group maintains that economic growth is likely to reduce terrorist activity. For example, Blomberg, Hess, and Weerapana (2004) theorize that countries with low growth rates, high government tax rates, and higher political unrest will experience more terrorist incidents. Based on a pooled panel data for 130 countries from 1968 to 1991, Blomberg, Hess, and Weerapana show evidence that lower economic growth correlates with higher incidents of international terrorism. Relying on a sample dataset for 110 countries from 1971 to 2007, Freytag et al. (2011) run a series of negative binomial regression models and find the benefits of economic growth in terms of a reduction in terrorist incidents. On examining the effects of several socioeconomic determinants of terrorism and political violence with a sample of 12 countries in Western Europe, Caruso and Schneider (2011) uncover that high economic growth, inflation, and unemployment are associated with a decrease in terrorist activities.

The second group positions itself in opposition to the first group, asserting that economic growth actually leads to more terrorism. For example, after collecting time-series data for seven Western European countries, Gries, Krieger, and Meierrieks (2011) perform statistical tests for economic growth-domestic terrorism Granger causality. Gries, Krieger, and Meierrieks demonstrate with cases in Germany, Portugal, and Spain that economic growth Granger-causes domestic terrorist incidents. In order to investigate the impact of economic growth and inflation on terrorism in Pakistan, Shahbaz (2013) collects time-series data of terrorist activities for the years 1971–2010. After finding that economic growth and inflation are significant and positive predictors of terrorism, Shahbaz expresses a concern that although sustainable economic growth is desirable for Pakistan's pursuit of an increased national well-being, it also coincides with an increase of terrorist activities on Pakistani soil.

The third group reveals no causal relationship between economic growth and terrorism. Piazza (2006) evaluates the question of whether poor economic conditions are underlying factors of terrorism. Piazza gathers a cross-sectional, time-series dataset for 96 countries for the years 1986–2002 and performs a battery of multivariate regression analyses. Piazza finds no statistically meaningful connection between economic measures, including economic growth and terrorism. After developing a statistical model for international terrorism for a pooled panel data consisting of 139 countries from 1985 to 1998, Drakos and Gofas (2006) show no empirical evidence that economic growth is associated with international terrorism. When Kurrild-Klitgaard, Justesen, and Klemmensen (2006) conduct a statistical analysis of the relationship between economic and political freedom and the occurrence of transnational terrorism from 1996 to 2002, they also report no causal linkage between economic growth and terrorism.

Although these three research groups have advanced our scientific knowledge of terrorism, the inconclusive findings leave many researchers puzzled about the real impact of economic growth on terrorist activity. To solve the puzzle, I delve into two different sectors of economic growth. I assert that the aggregate measure of economic growth used in all of the existing studies is directly responsible for the mixed results because not all sectors of economic growth are uniformly relevant with the occurrence of terrorist activity. The aggregate growth measure may have distorted the estimated results because it misrepresents the *true* effects of some crucial or irrelevant sectors of economic growth on terrorism. In the next section, I make a theoretical argument that when the aggregate growth concept is separated into agricultural growth and industrial growth, we can have a better understanding of the causal relationship between growth and terrorism.

In addition, although the existing studies have attempted to explain terrorist incidents as causally related to certain economic conditions, their empirical research tends to focus on only one type of terrorist activity at a time. For example, when researchers investigate domestic terrorism, most of them neglect to compare determinants of domestic terrorism versus other forms of terrorism such as international (or suicide) terrorism. Regrettably, this means that researchers must remain uncertain whether their theoretical perspective will similarly account for the different types of terrorist events. This is another serious drawback in the literature given the fact that terrorists and terrorist organizations are rarely committed exclusively to a single tactic. The Tamil Tigers in Sri Lanka, for example, are notorious for their suicide bombings, but they also employ other tactics against both domestic and international targets to obtain their political goals. Thus, by focusing on only a single type of terrorist activity, previous studies have failed to perceive the entire picture. In this study, I attempt to explore the relationship between economic growth and three different forms of terrorist activity: international, domestic, and suicide.

THEORETICAL CONSIDERATIONS

The main focus of this study is the role of economic growth, understood as the change in income per capita over time. Other economic conditions such as economic development, poverty, and unemployment are beyond the purview of this study. Among the various economic conditions, I have chosen growth because it provides a foundation for the economic future of any society (see Ferrara 2014). I argue that not all areas of economic growth have an identical effect on terrorist activity. The productive power of an industrial economy in terms of financial and material surpluses has a much stronger impact on the well-being of the working and middle classes relative to an agricultural economy. Following La Free and Dugan's (2007) definition, I refer to terrorism as an intentional threat or act of violence by a non-state actor to attain a political, economic, religious, or social goal. To achieve their goals, terrorists or terrorist groups may choose to engage in domestic, international, and/or suicide terrorism, depending on their strategic and material advantages.

When the victims and perpetrators are from the venue country, an act of violence is defined as domestic terrorism (e.g., the nerve gas attack on the Tokyo subway in March 1995); international terrorism involves at least two different nationals (e.g., the destruction of the Al Khobar Towers that housed U.S. airmen in June 1996 near Dhahran, Saudi Arabia);[2] and suicide terrorism typically occurs when a terrorist purposefully dies in the process of carrying out his or her mission (e.g., the 1983 suicide car bombings of the U.S. Marine barracks and the French Paratroopers sleeping quarters in Beiruit, Lebanon) (see Enders and Sandler 2006). Note that because suicide terrorism is the most virulent form of the phenomenon, it has drawn special attention among scholars, policy makers, and journalists. For example, Pape and Feldman (2010, 5) point out that "this type of terrorism is responsible for more deaths than any other form of the phenomenon—from 1980 to 2001, over 70 percent of all deaths due to terrorism were the result of suicide terrorism even though this tactic amounted to only 3 percent of all terrorist attacks." Following this research trend, I also include suicide bombings as another critical terrorist phenomenon.

The theoretical foundation of this study relies on three perspectives prevalent in the political science and economics literature (i.e., economic opportunities, social cleavages, and hard targets). As explained in Sandler and Enders's (2004) work, a theory of economic opportunities predicts that as economic growth advances, a country's economy generates more job opportunities. As these opportunities extend to disadvantaged populations, the pursuit of economic interests is incentivized over the temptation to engage in risky terrorist violence (Blomberg, Hess, and Weerapana 2004; Enders and Sandler 2006; Freytag et al. 2011). When growth is both steady and fast, the overall level of terrorist activity will decrease because rather than resorting to political violence, potential terrorists and their would-be sympathizers have greater opportunity to participate in the economy by producing, buying, and selling products or services. On the other hand, slow growth rates will lessen economic incentives, thus lowering the opportunity costs for engaging in violence. This way, poor economic growth facilitates recruitment for domestic terrorist groups and leads to an increase in the rate of domestic terrorism. Likewise, foreign terrorist groups are then more likely to carry out plots to further destabilize an already-suffering domestic economy, thereby leading to a corresponding increase in international terrorism (Meierrieks and Gries 2013). The fundamental assumption of the theory of economic opportunities, then, is that economic growth stimulates economic activity among a potentially disadvantaged population, thereby reducing the incentive to engage in terrorist activity as a means of addressing their grievances.

I argue that the theory of economic opportunities must be modified on the assumption that growth in different sectors of the economy produces different effects on terrorist activity. That is, financial and material growth in the agricultural sector is quite limited compared to that represented by an increase in industrial capital stock; as a result, the latter is more likely to foster a favorable economic environment in which would-be terrorists can seek better opportunities and upward mobility. In general, a population that earns its livelihood primarily through agriculture remains poor, rural, and unlikely to reap the benefits of agricultural growth. This is why we find many workers attempting to switch from the agricultural sector to the industrial sector as a national economy grows (Kuznets 1973). Accordingly, the driving force of economic growth, and thus national well-being, is industrial output. Overall, industrialized economies allow people to consume more food, obtain better clothing and shelter, and gain access to more job opportunities, a social safety net, and better health care. These kinds of improvements in living standards tend to mitigate the political grievances of affected populations. Therefore, the economic opportunity theory must account for the fact that it is the economic growth which takes place specifically in the industrial sector, not the agricultural sector, that offers opportunities for social advancement that dissuade terrorist activity. With this in mind, I have constructed the following hypothesis about economic opportunities:

H_1: All other things being equal, as industrial economic growth progresses, more economic opportunities become available to potential terrorists, thereby reducing the risk of terrorism, whether domestic, international, or suicide.

Originally formulated in the 1950s, a theory of social cleavages notes that society is historically divided into groups based on specific demographic or socioeconomic factors, including economic wealth, class, vocation, ethnic group, and religious affiliation (see Berelson, Lazarsfeld, and McPhee 1954; Lijphart 1971). For example, Lipset and Rokkan (1967) consider industrial or economic cleavages to be interest based (e.g., workers vs. employers or owners). A theory of social cleavages explains that because members of a population will always benefit unequally from economic growth, there will inevitably be those who reap its greatest advantages (i.e., winners) and others who endure its disadvantages (i.e., losers); thus, any shift in the distribution of wealth which results from economic growth will cause some social groups to gain and others to suffer losses (Lijphart 1971). The "losers," according to this theory, may resort to terrorism in their effort to settle political and economic grievances. Therefore, we would expect to see terrorism rise along with economic growth because, as Caruso and Schneider (2011) demonstrate, terrorists and terrorist groups are likely to capitalize on an expanding gap between the rich and the poor by exploiting the grievances of economic losers.

However, the theory of social cleavages also offers an incomplete explanation of terrorist behavior because it fails to recognize that not all kinds of economic growth similarly result in an expansion of class inequality. Though economic growth in the industrial sector does indicate that an industrial economy is getting bigger, it does not necessarily indicate that it is getting better. Indeed, the process of growth may be uneven and unbalanced, thus aggravating social cleavages and favoring the emergence of terrorism. Compared to agricultural surpluses, a large industrial surplus encourages economic disparity and, in turn, social grievances. For example, when industrial growth increases the gap between the wages of urban and rural people, a good portion of the population is left without access to the benefits offered by the surplus; at this point, the demand for a redistribution of wealth becomes politically powerful (Piazza 2006). Therefore, we can draw the following hypothesis about social cleavages:

H$_2$: All other things being equal, as industrial economic growth progresses, social cleavages intensify between haves and have-nots, thereby favoring the emergence of terrorist activity in all its forms.

A theory of hard targets predicts that "as states become richer and better able to defend targets, suicide attacks are used more often" (Berman and Laitin 2008, 1944; see also Jain and Mukand 2004; Hastings and Chan 2013). However, this prediction is made without considering how countries acquire financial and material resources to provide additional protection for potential terrorist targets. These resources are often generated through quick-paced and steady economic growth, and these growth revenues are set aside for counterterrorism-related activities in anticipation of growing threats. A stagnant or slow growth economy is unlikely to produce sufficient funds to manufacture the security resources necessary to enhance defense. Although enhanced counterterrorism efforts typically succeed in decreasing the overall terrorist activity, they may, ironically, incite the use of more extreme measures such as suicide bombing against hardened targets. As Berman and Laitin find in their formal modeling article (2008, 1966), the "further hardening of targets may reduce overall violence but will increase suicide attacks and may lead to proliferation of radical clubs."

Though elegant, this theoretical prediction must once again be amended on the assumption that not all sectors of a national economy are equally capable of producing the surpluses necessary to acquire materials to harden potential targets. I assert that while agricultural growth is unlikely to produce adequate means to implement better security measures, industrial growth is likely to generate enough revenues to harden targets. Because agricultural growth is unrelated with either the development of innovative security technology or the production of counterterrorism devices, it makes no significant contribution to hardening potential terrorist targets. In addition, agricultural growth is unlikely to generate extra surplus to purchase and implement enhanced security devices. Even though some revenue from agricultural growth may be converted to protect a country's critical infrastructure from a terrorist attack, the conversion cannot last long because it is likely a temporary allocation. Fighting a War on Terror is expensive, requiring continuous enhancements and newly developed security resources over a sustained period of time. A country that relies on limited revenues from agricultural growth will face great difficulty as it attempts to respond to high security demands.

Industrial growth is likely to lead toward the development of new security measures and accumulation of counterterrorism funds. Because installing reinforced doors in aircraft cockpits and placing Jersey barriers outside tall or politically sensitive facilities are incredibly costly operations, governments depend primarily on industrial businesses to generate corporate tax revenue to fund these expenditures. Fast and steady industrial growth offers a government ample financial and material resources to set aside for counterterrorism measures, thus helping deter domestic and international terrorist events (Fearon and Laitin 2003; Meierrieks and Gries 2013). Even so, enhanced security measures may backfire by encouraging terrorists and terrorist groups to resort to suicide terrorism as the only means to overcome hardened targets (Berman and Laitin 2008). For example, enhanced security measures for the aviation industry, diplomatic compounds, and military facilities have helped produce some amount of deterrence against terrorist attacks; however, they have also encouraged terrorist groups to turn to suicide tactics because hardening targets raise the target's value to the terrorist group (Stewart 2012; Hastings and Chan 2013). Suicide bombings tend to draw more international headlines than other types of attacks and enable the terrorist group to have more bargaining power vis-à-vis the target government (Pape and Feldman 2010). Simply put, shifting tactics from general terrorist attacks to suicide bombings is a result of hardening targets that is accompanied with a steady growth of industrial businesses. As a result, I draw the following hypothesis about hard targets:

H_3: All other things being equal, as industrial economic growth progresses, more targets become hardened, making them more difficult for domestic and international terrorists to attack but prompting an increase in suicide attacks.

Among the three theoretical perspectives described, I argue that the modified theory of hard targets more accurately links economic growth to all three forms of terrorism. This is because the other two theories fail to account for the adaptability of terrorist groups in their explanations (Stewart 2012). When previous studies apply concepts of economic opportunities and social cleavages to terrorists or terrorist groups' activities, their focus is usually one type of terrorism, such as international terrorism, under the implicit assumption that terrorist groups will use the same conventional attack tactics despite the continuously enhanced security environment. Yet terrorist groups are unlikely to rely on the same attack methods when security is drastically tightened in airports, government facilities, and military installments. In the meantime, terrorist groups will not forgo attacking hardened targets until their political goals are achieved. One must recognize that terrorist groups adapt to enhanced anti-terrorism measures by changing their attack methods. Terrorist groups know that conventional attack methods will not be effective against newly hardened targets. Such groups understand that a new method of attack is required once targets are hardened, and they frequently turn to suicide bombings as a viable alternative tactic. I believe that this phenomenon of terrorist adaptability is consistent with the prediction of the hard targets theory but not the other two theories: conventional terrorism is likely to decrease, while suicide terrorism is likely to increase.

RESEARCH DESIGN

Two statistical models are built to test the aforementioned three hypotheses along with five others:

$$Terrorism_{it} = \beta_0 + \beta_1{}^*econ\ growth_{it-1} + \beta_2{}^*income\ inequality_{it-1}$$
$$+ \beta_3{}^*democracy_{it-1} + \beta_4{}^*state\ failure_{it-1} + \beta_5{}^*population_{it-1}$$
$$+ \beta_6{}^*post–Cold\ War_i + \varepsilon_{1it}$$
$$Terrorism_{it} = \gamma_0 + \gamma_1{}^*econ\ growth\ in\ agriculture_{it-1}$$
$$+ \gamma_2{}^*econ\ growth\ in\ industry_{it-1} + \gamma_3{}^*income\ inequality_{it-1}$$
$$+ \gamma_4{}^*democracy_{it-1} + \gamma_5{}^*state\ failure_{it-1} + \gamma_6{}^*population_{it-1}$$
$$+ \gamma_7{}^*post–Cold\ War_i + \varepsilon_{2it}$$

where subscript $i = 1, \ldots, N$ indicates the country and subscript $t = 1, \ldots,$ T indexes the time period. Terrorism is the dependent variable; β_0 and γ_0 are constant terms; β_1 through β_6 and γ_1 through γ_7 are coefficients for independent variables; and ε_{1it} and ε_{2it} are error terms.

I collect pooled panel data for 127 countries during the period 1970–2007, using the country-year as the unit of analysis.[3] I employ four different but related dependent variables. The first variable is a count measure capturing the total number of terrorist incidents, regardless of type, occurring in a country in a given year. The second through fourth variables recategorize the first measure into domestic, international, and suicide terrorist incidents, respectively. The data comes from the worldwide terrorism dataset of Enders, Sandler, and Gaibulloev (2011), who systematically separated La Free and Dugan's (2007) Global Terrorism Database (GTD)[4] into domestic and international terrorist incidents. Enders, Sandler, and Gaibulloev underscore that "no other article provides such a complete partitioning of domestic and transnational incidents" (3). Suicide terrorism is identified based on the GTD which records suicide attacks when the terrorist did not intend to escape from the attack alive.[5] Domestic and international terrorist incidents are mutually exclusive and collectively exhaustive, but suicide terrorist incidents are not because suicide bombers may choose either domestic or international targets.

The main independent variable, *economic growth*, captures an increase in the capacity of an economy to produce goods and services, compared from one period of time to another. Consistent with existing studies, it is measured as the annual percentage growth rate of GDP per capita in 2005. As explained in the data source—World Banks' World Development Indicator 2013—the partitioning of the agricultural and industrial sectors is determined by the International Standard Industrial Classification. The agricultural sector includes forestry, hunting, and fishing, as well as cultivation of crops and livestock production; the industrial sector is comprised of the value added through mining, manufacturing, and construction, as well as electricity, water, and gas services. Economic growth in the agricultural sector is represented by the annual percentage growth rate of GDP per capita in agricultural value-added; likewise, economic growth in the industrial sector is industrial value-added. The average agricultural growth is 2.58 percent during the study period, while the average industrial growth is 4.32 percent.[6]

To ensure the estimated results are not subject to omitted variable bias, I include five control variables: *income inequality, democracy, state failure, population,* and a *post–Cold War* indicator. Other control variables such as *foreign occupation* and *terrorist group competition* are not included because they have been well documented in previous studies (e.g., Santifort-Jordan and Sandler 2014) and because too many controls may complicate the estimation results (see Achen 2002).[7]

A majority of previous studies find no relationship between income inequality and terrorist attacks. For example, Abadie's (2006) empirical research reports no effect of several economic variables, including income inequality on terrorism. Yet a small number of recent studies point in the opposite direction. Derin-Güre (2009) finds some evidence that countries with high income inequality are associated with increased terrorism. Similarly, Lai (2007) reports that countries with higher levels of economic inequality are more likely to experience higher levels of terrorism. Consistent with the findings of recent studies, I expect that income inequality fuels terrorism. Income inequality is operationalized by the Gini index that measures net income inequality within each country, ranging from 0 to 100. Data is collected from Solt's (2009) newly collected data on Standardized World Income Inequality. Note that when the Gini index is included in the model, about 30 percent of terrorism data is dropped out of the estimation due to its missing observations.

Some studies show that because democracy provides peaceful channels of conflict resolution, it is inversely related to terrorist activity (e.g., Eyerman 1998; Li 2005; Choi 2010). Yet other studies find that democracies actually foster terrorist activity as a result of their commitment to individual freedoms, which, they argue, facilitates the opportunity to assemble and strategize (e.g., Eubank and Weinberg 2001). Because it is not my main variable of interest, I remain agnostic about the influence of democracy in this study. The democracy variable is a 21-point indicator ranging from least democracy (–10) to most democracy (+10), and its data is collected from the Polity dataset (Marshall and Jaggers 2007).

When the political leadership of a failed state is too weak to exercise legal authority over much of its territory, more terrorist activities are likely to occur (Rotberg 2002). In fact, there are several studies which find supporting evidence for the significant and positive effect of failed states on terrorism (e.g., Piazza 2008). Accordingly, I expect state failure to lead to increased terrorism. Gathered from the Political Instability Task Force

(2007), the *failed state* variable is set on a scale of 0 to 17 after combining the following four features: the severity of ethnic wars (0–4), revolutionary wars (0–4), adverse regime changes (1–4), and genocides and politicides (0–5).[8]

Since highly populated countries have a harder time providing adequate security for their large populations, they run a greater risk of experiencing terrorist attacks (Eyerman 1998). This positive correlation may also be due to a scale effect. That is, more populous countries simply tend to experience more terrorism (in absolute numbers) because they harbor more terrorists and provide more targets than small countries do. Choi and Luo's (2013) work, for example, shows evidence that highly populated countries experience more terrorist incidents than do less-populated ones (see also Krieger and Meierrieks 2011; Choi and Salehyan 2013; Choi 2014; Choi and Piazza 2016). With this in mind, the *population* variable—measured by the logged total population—is expected to correspond to an increase in terrorism. Data for this variable is taken from the U.S. Census Bureau (2008).[9]

Enders and Sandler (1999) provide evidence that the total number of terrorist attacks has decreased with the end of the Soviet funding of left-wing groups (see also Choi 2010, 2011). To account for the systemic decrease in terrorist activity since the end of the Cold War, a *post–Cold War* variable is included. The *post–Cold War* variable is coded as "1" since 1991 and as "0" prior to that year.

Because the total number of terrorist events per year is compiled for the operationalization of the dependent variable, I considered Poisson regression as my baseline model. However, because the Pearson goodness-of-fit chi-squared test is statistically significant (chi^2 = 93,490.82, $p < 0.001$), it does not indicate that the model fits reasonably well. As an alternative model, negative binomial maximum-likelihood regression with Huber-White robust standard errors clustered by country is introduced because the variance, 2,593.99, of the terrorism data is much larger than its mean, 15.40 (i.e., the presence of overdispersion). Negative binomial regression adds a dispersion parameter to model the unobserved heterogeneity among observations; this allows the variance to exceed the mean, thus correcting for the overdispersion found in Poisson regression models (Hilbe 2007). All predictors except for *post–Cold War* are lagged one year to ensure that they cause the outcome variable rather than the other way around.

EMPIRICAL RESULTS

This section consists of basic analysis and robustness checks. The former shows that among the three hypotheses, the hard targets hypothesis is statistically supported and the latter provides a series of robustness tests on the industrial growth and terrorism connection.

Basic Analysis

Following Santifort-Jordan and Sandler (2014) and Gaibulloev and Sandler (2011), I perform two-sided hypothesis tests. Table 5.1 includes negative binomial regression models built to examine the effect of economic growth on terrorism. The first column lists independent variables, including three economic growth-related variables: *econ growth, econ growth in agriculture,* and *econ growth in industry.* The next eight columns are arranged by types of terrorism: Models 1 and 2 for all terrorism, Models 3 and 4 for domestic terrorism, Models 5 and 6 for international terrorism, and Models 7 and 8 for suicide terrorism.[10] In an attempt to reduce a potential bias in data collection (because suicide incidents in the GTD become frequent only after 1988), the analysis of Models 7 and 8 limits the time period to after 1988, which causes them to be 18 years shorter than Models 1–6.[11] Because Israel and Sri Lanka experience unusually high volumes of suicide attacks, they are considered outliers, which may cause the estimated results to be distorted. For this reason, both countries are excluded from the statistical runs in Models 7 and 8. Furthermore, the *post–Cold War* dummy used in Models 1–6 may not be as relevant a factor in Models 7 and 8 because the start of the sample period is 1988—that is, only two years before the Cold War; therefore, Models 7 and 8 exclude the dummy.[12]

The *econ growth* variable in Models 1, 3, 5, and 7 does not differentiate economic growth in the agricultural sector from that in the industrial sector; therefore, it explores the possibility that undifferentiated economic growth is causally related to the rate of terrorist activity. Models 1, 3, and 5 show that the *econ growth* variable is negatively associated with terrorism, while Model 7 fails to show any evidence for a connection between economic growth and suicide terrorism. These mixed findings are consistent with those of previous studies, which have demonstrated the ambiguous relationship between growth and terrorism. Of course, the drawback of using the *econ growth* variable is that we cannot be certain about the driving force *behind* economic growth. Is it growth in the agricultural sector or in the industrial sector that affects the occurrence of terrorism? The *econ growth in agriculture* and the *econ growth in industry* variables were created precisely to explore this issue. As it turns out, *econ growth in agriculture* fails to achieve statistical significance in Models 2, 4, 6, and 8, while *econ growth in industry* emerges as a significant predictor of terrorism across all models. The insignificance of the *econ growth in agriculture* variable indicates that this sector of the national economy has no bearing on terrorist behavior. On the other hand, the significance of the *econ growth in industry* variable tells us that while industrializing economies are less vulnerable to terrorism, in general, they become, ironically, somewhat of a lightning rod for suicide attacks.[13]

Table 5.1
Growth and Terrorism: Negative Binomial Regression

| | 1970–2007 | | | | 1988–2007 | | | |
| | Terrorism | | Domestic Terrorism | | International Terrorism | Suicide Terrorism | | |
	Model 1	Model 2	Model 3	Model 4	Model 5	Model 6	Model 7	Model 8
Econ growth$_{it-1}$	-0.015**		-0.015*		-0.014*		0.035	-0.003
	(0.007)		(0.008)		(0.008)		(0.026)	(0.015)
Econ growth in agriculture$_{it-1}$		0.003		0.001		0.003		
		(0.002)		(0.003)		(0.003)		
Econ growth in industry$_{it-1}$		-0.010***		-0.010**		-0.010**		0.019***
		(0.004)		(0.004)		(0.005)		(0.007)
Income inequality$_{it-1}$	0.019***	0.019***	0.023***	0.023***	0.015*	0.015*	0.004	0.005
	(0.007)	(0.007)	(0.007)	(0.007)	(0.008)	(0.008)	(0.021)	(0.021)
Democracy$_{it-1}$	0.058***	0.057***	0.063***	0.062***	0.054***	0.053***	0.024	0.024
	(0.013)	(0.013)	(0.013)	(0.013)	(0.014)	(0.014)	(0.037)	(0.036)
State failure$_{it-1}$	0.230***	0.231***	0.243***	0.244***	0.213***	0.214***	0.271***	0.271***
	(0.031)	(0.031)	(0.035)	(0.035)	(0.032)	(0.032)	(0.067)	(0.065)
Population$_{it-1}$	0.349***	0.347***	0.383***	0.381***	0.326***	0.324***	0.734***	0.749***
	(0.046)	(0.046)	(0.047)	(0.047)	(0.051)	(0.051)	(0.084)	(0.081)
Post–Cold War$_i$	-0.305**	-0.306**	-0.196	-0.198	-0.532***	-0.532***		
	(0.133)	(0.133)	(0.146)	(0.146)	(0.137)	(0.138)		

(Continued)

Table 5.1
(Continued)

| | 1970–2007 | | | | 1988–2007 | | | |
| | Terrorism | | Domestic Terrorism | | International Terrorism | Suicide Terrorism | | | |
	Model 1	Model 2	Model 3	Model 4	Model 5	Model 6	Model 7	Model 8
Constant	-1.700***	-1.691***	-2.506***	-2.498***	-2.981***	-2.969***	-10.759***	-10.872***
	(0.552)	(0.552)	(0.606)	(0.604)	(0.613)	(0.612)	(1.392)	(1.411)
Wald chi^2	177.11	177.50	177.12	179.05	124.21	124.45	168.75	184.17
Probability > chi^2	0.001	0.001	0.001	0.001	0.001	0.001	0.001	0.001
Log pseudolikelihood	-6,666.27	-6,664.68	-5,816.61	-5,815.76	-4,029.75	-4,029.20	-314.11	-314.01
Dispersion = 1	76.28	76.22	82.05	82.02	11.85	11.84	3.31	3.31
Observations	2,665	2,665	2,665	2,665	2,665	2,665	1,787	1,787

Note: Robust standard errors are in parentheses.

* 0.10

** 0.05

*** 0.01

Interpreting the main findings in terms of incidence rate ratios should help assess the quantitative importance of the industrial growth variable on terrorism. It appears that if industrial growth increases by 1 percent, the percentage change in the incidence rate of domestic terrorism is a 1 percent decrease while holding the other variables constant; for the incidence rate of international terrorism, there is a 1 percent decrease. By contrast, if a country were to increase its industrial growth by 1 percent, its relative change in the expected number of suicide terrorism would be expected to increase by 2 percent, while holding all other variables in the model constant. It also would be interesting to look at some individual countries whose industrial growth performed well. Jordan is a good example, as its average growth rate in the industrial sector was 9.43 percent during the study period, which was much higher than 4.23 percent for the entire sample countries. If Jordan were to increase its industrial growth by 1 percent, the changes in the predicted rate would be –0.0082 for domestic terrorism, –0.0030 for international terrorism, and 0.0002 for suicide terrorism. Another example is South Korea whose industrial growth rate was 9.54 percent on average. For a 1 percent increase in its industrial growth, the changes in the predicted rate in South Korea would be –0.0591 for domestic terrorism, –0.0202 for international terrorism, and 0.0021 for suicide terrorism. These quantitative comparisons confirm that growth in the industrial sector appears to be a double-edged sword, producing both favorable and unfavorable consequences in terrorist activity.

Moving on to evaluate the validity of the three hypotheses of growth and terrorism put forward earlier, I find that the estimated results are consistent with the prediction of the hard targets hypothesis but not with either economic opportunities or social cleavages. *Econ growth in industry* is significantly different from zero across all models; it also produces a change in the coefficient sign relative to forms of terrorism. As hypothesized, the results show evidence for the negative connection between growth and domestic and international terrorism; likewise, it indicates a positive link between growth and suicide terrorism. Neither the economic opportunities hypothesis nor the social cleavages hypothesis garners statistical support in a consistent manner. For example, the coefficient sign on the *econ growth in industry* variable changes in its relationship with suicide terrorism even though both theories predict that there would be no such change. While the theory of economic opportunities can explain why *econ growth in industry* is negatively associated with domestic and international terrorist activity, it fails to account for the positive relationship between growth and suicide terrorism. Similarly, while the theory of social cleavages sheds light on why growth increases the likelihood of suicide attacks, it does not explain why it may lead to a lower rate of domestic and international terrorist events.

Use of several examples may further elucidate the predictive power of the hard targets theory. For comparison purposes, four countries are selected from the top 10 percentile of the industrial growth group (Turkey and Pakistan) and the bottom 10 percentile (El Salvador and Peru). In the dataset, El Salvador and Peru recorded 2.04 percent and 2.92 percent, which is much lower than the average industrial growth rate of 4.23 percent for the entire sample countries, while Turkey and Pakistan enjoyed a relatively high growth rate, 5.47 percent and 6.29 percent, respectively. According to the prediction of the hard targets theory, high growth performance should lead to less domestic and international terrorism but more suicide terrorism. This means that Turkey and Pakistan should experience less domestic and international terrorism than El Salvador and Peru, but the first two countries should encounter more suicide terrorism than the other two. The empirical data is consistent with this prediction because the frequency of the two high-growth countries was 46.47 and 39.35 for domestic terrorism, 6.91 and 6.50 for international terrorism, and 0.84 and 0.82 for suicide terrorism,[14] while that of the two low-growth countries was 84.11 and 171.19, 7.31 and 13.15, and 0 and 0. It appears that high growth performance in industrial sectors is the main driving force in reducing a great deal of domestic terrorism and a good size of international terrorism, while it fuels increased suicide terrorism.

The effects of the five control variables are also interesting. While the coefficients of *state failure* and *population* achieve significance with a positive sign regardless of the type of terrorism, those of *income inequality, democracy*, and *post–Cold War* do not receive consistent support across models. When countries are on the verge of state failure or have relatively large populations, they, as hypothesized, are more likely to fall victim to a variety of terrorist plots. We also see from the results that both domestic and international terrorism become more prevalent with a higher level of income inequality and democratic governance and that international terrorism has become less frequent since the end of the Cold War.

Robustness Checks

To further confirm the robustness of the results reported so far, I employ two alternative estimation methods used in previous studies: rare events logit and negative binomial regression with fixed effects. It may be the case that the terrorism data is prone to the problem of excessive zero observations, as terrorist incidents are rare across countries and time. To assuage such a problem, I turn to the rare events logit model which was developed by Tomz, King, and Zeng (1999). The rare events logit effectively addresses the issue of excessive zeros in the data.[15] To run this technique, the event count dependent variable is converted into a binary measure, coded as "1" if any attacks are recorded and as "0" otherwise. Table 5.2 shows the

Table 5.2
Growth and Terrorism: Rare Events Logit

| | 1970–2007 | | | | | | 1988–2007 | |
| | Terrorism | | Domestic Terrorism | | International Terrorism | | Suicide Terrorism | |
	Model 1	Model 2	Model 3	Model 4	Model 5	Model 6	Model 7	Model 8
Econ growth$_{it-1}$	-0.037***		-0.035***		-0.029***		0.049*	
	(0.010)		(0.010)		(0.010)		(0.026)	
Econ growth in agriculture$_{it-1}$		0.005		-0.000		0.005		-0.006
		(0.006)		(0.005)		(0.006)		(0.017)
Econ growth in industry$_{it-1}$		-0.023***		-0.022***		-0.017**		0.027***
		(0.007)		(0.008)		(0.008)		(0.007)
Income inequality$_{it-1}$	0.015***	0.015***	0.022***	0.022***	0.013***	0.012***	0.000	0.001
	(0.004)	(0.004)	(0.004)	(0.004)	(0.004)	(0.004)	(0.014)	(0.014)
Democracy$_{it-1}$	0.060***	0.060***	0.065***	0.064***	0.057***	0.057***	0.023	0.022
	(0.007)	(0.007)	(0.007)	(0.007)	(0.007)	(0.007)	(0.025)	(0.025)
State failure$_{it-1}$	0.491***	0.497***	0.422***	0.426***	0.407***	0.412***	0.327***	0.325***
	(0.066)	(0.066)	(0.058)	(0.057)	(0.053)	(0.053)	(0.065)	(0.063)
Population$_{it-1}$	0.535***	0.532***	0.540***	0.537***	0.499***	0.495***	0.821***	0.837***
	(0.037)	(0.038)	(0.037)	(0.037)	(0.035)	(0.036)	(0.088)	(0.087)
Post–Cold War$_i$	-0.321***	-0.320***	-0.078	-0.076	-0.598***	-0.595***		
	(0.090)	(0.090)	(0.090)	(0.090)	(0.094)	(0.094)		
Constant	-5.645***	-5.669***	-6.553***	-6.567***	-5.772***	-5.783***	-12.343***	-12.443***
	(0.418)	(0.416)	(0.428)	(0.427)	(0.403)	(0.403)	(1.259)	(1.255)
Observations	2,665	2,665	2,665	2,665	2,665	2,665	1,787	1,787

Note: Robust standard errors are in parentheses.

* 0.10

** 0.05

*** 0.01

estimated results of the rare events logit model, which, as it turns out, do not differ significantly from the main results in Table 5.1.[16]

In their "Dirty Pool" article, Green, Kim, and Yoon (2001, 442) speak critically of a pooled panel data analysis, saying that "analyses of [cross-sectional, time-series] data that make no allowance for fixed unobserved differences between [countries] often produce biased results." This is an important criticism to bear in mind because use of country fixed effects enables us to take into account the unique political and economic environments of each country in terms of its attractiveness to terrorists. While examining the relationship between economic growth and general terrorism, Meierrieks and Gries (2013, 93) similarly caution that "country-specific factors may influence whether growth exerts a causal effect on terrorism by governing the responsiveness to socio-economic progress." Taking advantage of these methodological insights, I employ conditional fixed-effects negative binomial regression models. As shown in Table 5.3, conditional fixed-effects negative binomial regression models reveal that *econ growth in industry* is related to all forms of terrorist activities except for international terrorism in Model 6. The insignificant effect of industrial growth on international terrorism has something to do with the loss of many observations, after the *income inequality* variable is included in the model. Models 7 and 8 display additional test results by replicating Models 5 and 6 after excluding the *income inequality* variable. The coefficient of *econ growth in industry* becomes significant and the sign is negative, as predicted by the modified theory of hard targets. By and large, the main findings of this study appear to be robust across a number of estimation techniques.

CONCLUSION

The impact of economic growth on terrorist activity is an understudied area, and the previous empirical results are mixed and inconsistent. This study sheds new light on the literature of economic growth and terrorism by reconceptualizing the former into two separate sectors (i.e., agriculture and industry) as well as by recategorizing the latter into three forms (i.e., domestic, international, and suicide). Given its potentially enormous impact on terrorist activity, the role of industrial growth is brought to the fore. This is in contrast to previous studies that lump together all the growth sectors. While previous studies focus on one type of terrorism at a time, I investigate the three different forms of terrorist activities together. In addition, three modified theoretical perspectives are offered to explain the industry growth and terrorism connection: economic opportunities, social cleavages, and hard targets.

Table 5.3
Growth and Terrorism: Fixed Effects

	1970–2007								1988–2007	
	Terrorism		Domestic Terrorism		International Terrorism				Suicide Terrorism	
	Model 1	Model 2	Model 3	Model 4	Model 5	Model 6	Model 7	Model 8	Model 9	Model 10
Econ growth$_{it-1}$	-0.018***		-0.020***		-0.010		-0.009*		0.067**	
	(0.005)		(0.005)		(0.006)		(0.005)		(0.031)	
Econ growth in agriculture$_{it-1}$		0.004		0.002		0.003		0.002		0.002
		(0.003)		(0.004)		(0.004)		(0.003)		(0.014)
Econ growth in industry$_{it-1}$		-0.013***		-0.014***		-0.006		-0.006*		0.026*
		(0.003)		(0.003)		(0.004)		(0.003)		(0.014)
Income inequality$_{it-1}$	-0.007*	-0.007*	-0.005	-0.005	-0.005	-0.005			0.047	0.049
	(0.004)	(0.004)	(0.004)	(0.004)	(0.005)	(0.005)			(0.049)	(0.048)
Democracy$_{it-1}$	0.039***	0.039***	0.045***	0.045***	0.026***	0.026***	0.034***	0.034***	-0.002	0.001
	(0.006)	(0.006)	(0.006)	(0.006)	(0.007)	(0.007)	(0.006)	(0.006)	(0.035)	(0.035)
State failure$_{it-1}$	0.169***	0.175***	0.184***	0.190***	0.151***	0.155***	0.148***	0.151***	0.170	0.166
	(0.016)	(0.016)	(0.017)	(0.017)	(0.019)	(0.019)	(0.016)	(0.015)	(0.124)	(0.122)
Population$_{it-1}$	0.082***	0.082***	0.126***	0.125***	0.069*	0.068	0.124***	0.124***	1.049**	1.067**
	(0.028)	(0.028)	(0.031)	(0.031)	(0.041)	(0.041)	(0.035)	(0.035)	(0.473)	(0.451)
Post–Cold War$_i$	-0.192***	-0.195***	-0.069	-0.073	-0.392***	-0.391***	-0.350***	-0.347***		
	(0.061)	(0.061)	(0.067)	(0.067)	(0.071)	(0.071)	(0.063)	(0.063)		

(Continued)

Table 5.3
(Continued)

	1970–2007								1988–2007	
	Terrorism		Domestic Terrorism		International Terrorism				Suicide Terrorism	
	Model 1	Model 2	Model 3	Model 4	Model 5	Model 6	Model 7	Model 8	Model 9	Model 10
Constant	−1.492***	−1.517***	−2.336***	−2.363***	−1.183**	−1.183**	−2.067***	−2.082***	−15.915***	−16.080***
	(0.358)	(0.358)	(0.404)	(0.403)	(0.522)	(0.522)	(0.360)	(0.360)	(5.795)	(5.667)
Observations	2,596	2,596	2,573	2,573	2,369	2,369	3,298	3,298	412	412

Note: Robust standard errors are in parentheses.

* 0.10

** 0.05

*** 0.01

A cross-national, time-series data analysis of 127 countries for the years 1970–2007 offers supporting evidence for the hypothesis of hard targets: when countries sustain higher levels of industrial growth rather than agricultural growth, they are less likely to experience domestic and international terrorism but are more likely to experience suicide attacks. What can a government learn from these findings? Unfortunately, the findings are not all optimistic because a well-functioning market economy based on quick-paced but steady economic growth is not necessarily a cure-all solution for growing terrorist threats. If a government seeks to benefit from industrial growth, it should take into consideration what forms of terrorism it needs to counter. If the goal is to deter domestic and international terrorism, it should not hesitate to harden potential targets; however, if it has suffered from a series of suicide attacks, it should be aware that an enhancement of its security measures may have the opposite of its intended effect. Simply put, politicians and policy makers in suicide terrorism-prone countries such as Iraq, Turkey, Pakistan, and Afghanistan should think hard about how to balance between economic growth and deterrence of different types of terrorism.

Table 5.A1
List of Sample Countries

Albania	Congo Brazzaville	Hungary	Mexico	Slovenia
Algeria	Costa Rica	India	Moldova	South Africa
Angola	Croatia	Indonesia	Mongolia	Spain
Argentina	Cuba	Iran	Morocco	Sri Lanka
Armenia	Cyprus	Israel	Mozambique	Switzerland
Australia	Czech Republic	Italy	Nepal	Sweden
Austria	Denmark	Ivory Coast	Netherlands	Tajikistan
Azerbaijan	Djibouti	Jamaica	New Zealand	Tanzania
Bangladesh	Dominican Republic	Japan	Nicaragua	Thailand
Belarus	Ecuador	Jordan	Nigeria	Togo
Benin	Egypt	Kazakhstan	Norway	Trinidad and Tobago
Bhutan	El Salvador	Kenya	Pakistan	Tunisia
Bolivia	Estonia	Korea South	Panama	Turkey
Botswana	Ethiopia	Kyrgyzstan	Papua New Guinea	Turkmenistan
Brazil	Fiji	Laos	Paraguay	Uganda
Burkina Faso	Finland	Latvia	Peru	Ukraine
Burundi	France	Lebanon	Philippines	United States
Cambodia	Gabon	Lesotho	Poland	Uruguay
Cameroon	Gambia	Liberia	Portugal	Uzbekistan
Canada	Georgia	Lithuania	Romania	Venezuela
Central African Republic	Germany	Madagascar	Russia	Yemen
Chad	Guatemala	Malawi	Rwanda	Zambia
Chile	Guinea	Malaysia	Senegal	Zimbabwe
China	Guyana	Mali	Sierra Leone	
Colombia	Haiti	Mauritania	Singapore	
Comoros	Honduras	Mauritius	Slovak Republic	

Table 5.A2
Growth and Terrorism: More Control Variables

	Negative Binomial Regression							
	1970–2007						1988–2007	
	Terrorism		Domestic Terrorism		International Terrorism		Suicide Terrorism	
	Model 1	Model 2	Model 3	Model 4	Model 5	Model 6	Model 7	Model 8
Econ growth$_{it-1}$	-0.024***		-0.024***		-0.023***		0.037	
	(0.007)		(0.007)		(0.008)		(0.030)	
Econ growth in agriculture$_{it-1}$		0.001		-0.001		0.000		-0.003
		(0.002)		(0.003)		(0.004)		(0.017)
Econ growth in industry$_{it-1}$		-0.014***		-0.014***		-0.012**		0.017**
		(0.004)		(0.005)		(0.005)		(0.007)
Income inequality$_{it-1}$	0.015**	0.015**	0.020***	0.019***	0.009	0.009	-0.010	-0.009
	(0.006)	(0.006)	(0.007)	(0.007)	(0.008)	(0.008)	(0.021)	(0.021)
Democracy$_{it-1}$	0.049***	0.049***	0.055***	0.055***	0.043***	0.043***	0.016	0.015
	(0.012)	(0.012)	(0.013)	(0.013)	(0.013)	(0.014)	(0.037)	(0.036)
State failure$_{it-1}$	0.225***	0.228***	0.241***	0.244***	0.206***	0.210***	0.263***	0.262***
	(0.033)	(0.033)	(0.037)	(0.037)	(0.034)	(0.034)	(0.068)	(0.067)
Population$_{it-1}$	0.249***	0.247***	0.295***	0.293***	0.211***	0.207***	0.601***	0.620***
	(0.048)	(0.048)	(0.052)	(0.052)	(0.046)	(0.047)	(0.087)	(0.084)
Post-Cold War$_i$	-0.258**	-0.256**	-0.159	-0.158	-0.443***	-0.442***		

(Continued)

119

Table 5.A2
(Continued)

	Negative Binomial Regression							
	1970–2007						1988–2007	
	Terrorism		Domestic Terrorism		International Terrorism		Suicide Terrorism	
	Model 1	Model 2	Model 3	Model 4	Model 5	Model 6	Model 7	Model 8
	(0.125)	(0.125)	(0.140)	(0.139)	(0.128)	(0.129)		
Foreign occupation$_{it-1}$	-0.500	-0.501	-0.532	-0.538	-0.716***	-0.712***	-0.569	-0.505
	(0.330)	(0.322)	(0.406)	(0.398)	(0.270)	(0.262)	(0.724)	(0.737)
Terrorist group competition$_{it-1}$	0.878***	0.864***	0.770***	0.757***	1.155***	1.141***	2.707***	2.698***
	(0.135)	(0.133)	(0.161)	(0.160)	(0.161)	(0.162)	(1.033)	(1.036)
Constant	-1.151**	-1.153**	-2.004***	-2.004***	-2.444***	-2.439***	-11.149***	-11.292***
	(0.540)	(0.539)	(0.617)	(0.615)	(0.561)	(0.561)	(1.649)	(1.671)
Observations	2,618	2,618	2,618	2,618	2,618	2,618	1,767	1,767

Note: Robust standard errors are in parentheses.

* 0.10

** 0.05

*** 0.01

Table 5.A3
Multicollinearity Diagnostics[a]

	R^2	Variance Inflation Factors (VIFs)	Square Root of VIFs
Econ growth in agriculture$_{it-1}$	0.02	1.02	1.01
Econ growth in industry$_{it-1}$	0.04	1.04	1.02
Income inequality$_{it-1}$	0.08	1.09	1.04
State failure$_{it-1}$	0.13	1.15	1.07
Econ development$_{it-1}$	0.10	1.11	1.05
Population$_{it-1}$	0.07	1.08	1.04
Post–Cold War$_i$	0.06	1.06	1.03
Mean variance inflation factor		1.08	

	Eigenvalues	Condition Index
1	4.24	1.00
2	1.06	2.00
3	1.01	2.04
4	0.78	2.33
5	0.54	2.80
6	0.31	3.70
7	0.05	9.25
8	0.01	21.98
Condition number		21.98
Eigenvalues and condition index computed from the scaled raw sscp with an intercept		
Det(correlation matrix)		0.77

[a] A general rule of thumb: a serious multicollinearity problem is suspected if R^2 is greater than 0.80, if the mean of all the variance inflation factors is considerably larger than 10, or if condition number exceeds 1,000.

Table 5.A4
Growth and Terrorism, 1988–2007

Negative Binomial Regression

	Terrorism		Domestic Terrorism		International Terrorism		Suicide Terrorism	
	Model 1	Model 2	Model 3	Model 4	Model 5	Model 6	Model 7	Model 8
Econ growth$_{it-1}$	-0.021*		-0.020		-0.051***		0.035	
	(0.013)		(0.014)		(0.016)		(0.026)	
Econ growth in agriculture$_{it-1}$		-0.001		-0.002		-0.004		-0.003
		(0.007)		(0.008)		(0.008)		(0.015)
Econ growth in industry$_{it-1}$		-0.024***		-0.026***		-0.038***		0.019***
		(0.009)		(0.010)		(0.012)		(0.007)
Income inequality$_{it-1}$	-0.003	-0.003	-0.004	-0.004	-0.001	-0.001	0.004	0.005
	(0.012)	(0.012)	(0.013)	(0.013)	(0.015)	(0.012)	(0.021)	(0.007)
Democracy$_{it-1}$	0.020	0.018	0.020	0.017	0.002	-0.000	0.024	0.024
	(0.023)	(0.023)	(0.024)	(0.024)	(0.026)	(0.026)	(0.037)	(0.036)
State failure$_{it-1}$	0.343***	0.346***	0.355***	0.359***	0.290***	0.297***	0.271***	0.271***
	(0.053)	(0.053)	(0.054)	(0.054)	(0.056)	(0.057)	(0.067)	(0.065)
Population$_{it-1}$	0.580***	0.580***	0.603***	0.604***	0.536***	0.533***	0.734***	0.749***
	(0.063)	(0.063)	(0.065)	(0.064)	(0.068)	(0.068)	(0.084)	(0.081)
Constant	-4.558***	-4.525***	-4.938***	-4.905***	-6.082***	-6.093***	-10.759***	-10.872***
	(0.867)	(0.867)	(0.922)	(0.925)	(0.935)	(0.934)	(1.392)	(1.411)
Observations	1,787	1,787	1,787	1,787	1,787	1,787	1,787	1,787

Note: Robust standard errors are in parentheses.

* 0.10

** 0.05

*** 0.01

Table 5.A5
Growth and Terrorism: Three-Year Lag Effects

| | Negative Binomial Regression | | | | | | | |
| | Terrorism | | Domestic Terrorism | | International Terrorism | | Suicide Terrorism | |
	Model 1	Model 2	Model 3	Model 4	Model 5	Model 6	Model 7	Model 8
Econ growth$_{it-1}$	-0.002		-0.004		-0.002		0.041*	
	(0.008)		(0.009)		(0.008)		(0.025)	
Econ growth$_{it-2}$	-0.015**		-0.010		-0.017*		-0.020	
	(0.007)		(0.007)		(0.009)		(0.020)	
Econ growth$_{it-3}$	-0.013*		-0.011		-0.017**		-0.020	
	(0.007)		(0.008)		(0.008)		(0.028)	
Econ growth in agriculture$_{it-1}$		0.003		0.001		0.002		0.008
		(0.003)		(0.004)		(0.004)		(0.016)
Econ growth in agriculture$_{it-2}$		-0.002		-0.003		-0.006		0.025
		(0.004)		(0.004)		(0.005)		(0.018)
Econ growth in agriculture$_{it-3}$		-0.002		-0.001		-0.008*		0.005
		(0.004)		(0.004)		(0.005)		(0.016)
Econ growth in industry$_{it-1}$		-0.006		-0.006		-0.007		0.023**
		(0.005)		(0.006)		(0.006)		(0.009)
Econ growth in industry$_{it-2}$		-0.002		0.002		-0.002		-0.025**
		(0.004)		(0.004)		(0.006)		(0.012)
Econ growth in industry$_{it-3}$		-0.007*		-0.007		-0.007		-0.014

(Continued)

Table 5.A5
(Continued)

Negative Binomial Regression

	Terrorism		Domestic Terrorism		International Terrorism		Suicide Terrorism	
	Model 1	Model 2	Model 3	Model 4	Model 5	Model 6	Model 7	Model 8
		(0.004)		(0.005)		(0.006)		(0.021)
Income inequality$_{it-1}$	0.020***	0.020***	0.024***	0.025***	0.015*	0.016*	-0.006	-0.008
	(0.007)	(0.007)	(0.008)	(0.008)	(0.009)	(0.009)	(0.025)	(0.025)
Democracy$_{it-1}$	0.060***	0.060***	0.066***	0.066***	0.055***	0.054***	0.007	0.006
	(0.013)	(0.013)	(0.014)	(0.014)	(0.014)	(0.014)	(0.038)	(0.037)
State failure$_{it-1}$	0.263***	0.264***	0.275***	0.278***	0.239***	0.243***	0.265***	0.263***
	(0.037)	(0.036)	(0.040)	(0.040)	(0.034)	(0.034)	(0.067)	(0.066)
Population$_{it-1}$	0.369***	0.365***	0.402***	0.399***	0.343***	0.339***	0.776***	0.794***
	(0.046)	(0.046)	(0.048)	(0.048)	(0.051)	(0.052)	(0.093)	(0.092)
Post–Cold War$_i$	-0.437***	-0.434***	-0.345**	-0.345**	-0.610***	-0.609***		
	(0.140)	(0.138)	(0.154)	(0.153)	(0.144)	(0.143)		
Constant	-1.832***	-1.844***	-2.644***	-2.661***	-3.067***	-3.103***	-10.490***	-10.663***
	(0.592)	(0.592)	(0.650)	(0.648)	(0.632)	(0.639)	(1.486)	(1.522)
Observations	2,297	2,297	2,297	2,297	2,297	2,297	1,508	1,508

Note: Robust standard errors are in parentheses.

* 0.10

** 0.05

*** 0.01

NOTES

1. A slightly different version of this chapter appeared in Seung-Whan Choi. 2015. "Economic Growth and Terrorism: Domestic, International, and Suicide." *Oxford Economic Papers* 67(1): 157–181. Used by permission of Oxford University Press.

2. Sandler (2014) offers 11 reasons for distinguishing between domestic and international terrorism.

3. Table 5.A1 shows a list of sample countries.

4. For more detailed information on GTD, see http://www.start.umd.edu/gtd/. There are some problems with GTD; for example, the data for 1993 is missing (La Free and Dugan 2007). Note that the estimated results are virtually similar with or without the missing 1993 data.

5. Combining the Global Terrorism Database, the International *Terrorism*: Attributes of *Terrorist* Events, and the RAND Database of Worldwide Terrorism Incidents, Santifort-Jordan and Sandler (2014) collected a unique dataset of about 2,500 suicide terrorist incidents for the years 1998–2010. The time period of this data overlaps with only 10 years of this study, and the number of countries covers only 47 (excluding West Bank/Gaza) of the 127 sample countries of this study. When Santifort-Jordan and Sandler's data was merged with this study's, fewer than 300 observations were available for statistical runs, thereby making the estimated results offered by this data incompatible with those reported in the next section.

6. The agricultural sector consists of 2 percent of the total economic growth in dollars, and the industrial sector is 33 percent. The remaining 65 percent come from the services sector whose empirical implications are not explored in this study due to a lack of a theoretical explanation.

7. When those variables are included, they do not cause the main variables of interest to become insignificant, as shown in Table 5.A2.

8. The correlation between democracy and state failure is –0.18. The low correlation is not surprising given the fact that the former mainly measures political constraints on the chief executive (Gleditsch and Ward 1997), while the latter captures political instability (Piazza 2008).

9. It would be interesting to limit the total population to the share of youth to total population because young people may hold more extreme views and thus may be more likely to engage in terrorist activity (see Krueger 2008; Bloom 2012). Based on the U.N. Population Division data in http://esa.un.org/unpd/wpp/ASCII-Data/DISK_NAVIGATION_ASCII.htm, a ratio of young people, aged between 15 and 24, to population is calculated. The *ratio* variable turned out to be an insignificant predictor of terrorism, so I decided not to use it in place of the *population* variable that achieves statistical significance across models.

10. I conduct three sets of multicollinearity diagnostics: R^2 statistics, variance inflation factors, and condition index. As shown in Table 5.A3, there is no presence of severe multicollinearity among the predictors.

11. When the full years 1970–2007 are instead used for the suicide terrorism analysis, the results are very similar to those reported in Models 7 and 8. I also perform another robustness test by limiting domestic and international terrorism data to the years 1988–2007 so that all types of terrorism are during the same study period as suicide terrorism. As shown in Table 5.A4, the main findings of this study

still remain the same: industrial growth leads to decreases in domestic and international terrorism but not in suicide terrorism, where instead I find an increase.

12. When the two countries and the *post–Cold War* dummy are included, the main findings are virtually the same as those in Models 7 and 8.

13. The causal effect of growth-related variables is assumed to take one year in the statistical model. Yet there is a possibility that the process of tightening security followed by industrial growth may take more than one year. I test several different lag terms such as two, three, five, and eight because there is no existing theory about how many lags are appropriate. I find no consistent pattern for lag effect, as displayed in Table 5.A5—an example of a three-year lag effect analysis. I reason that because prevention of terrorist threats is one of the highest priorities for politicians and policy makers, adding enhanced security measures should not take more than one year as long as industrial economic growth continues. For example, the September 11 attacks prompted the Aviation and Transportation Security Act that required that all passenger screening must, by November 19, 2002, be conducted by federal employees.

14. Note that the average suicide attacks for the entire sample countries are 0.09.

15. The statistics literature also recommends that zero-inflated negative binomial regression be used for *cross-sectional* data with excessive zeros. A standard negative binomial regression model loses some of its effectiveness when the prevalence of zero counts in the data poses a statistical challenge by not being estimated appropriately (see Greene 2003; Hilbe 2007). However, zero-inflated negative binomial regression is not an appropriate estimation method for the cross-sectional, time-series terrorism data of this study in which the presence of excessive zeros, when estimated in Stata, is connected to individual *observations* with zero counts rather than to individual *countries* with no count events.

16. Keshk's (2003) two-stage probit least squares are a simultaneous equations model that can utilize the *converted* binary measure of terrorism and the continuous measure of economic growth. Adopted from Gaibulloev and Sandler's (2011, 358) baseline model, the first equation is constructed as *economic growth*$_{it}$ = α_0 + α_1*terrorism$_{it}$ + α_2*GDP per capita$_{it-1}$ + α_3*gross capital formation$_{it-1}$ + α_4*interstate war$_{it}$ + α_5*intrastate war$_{it}$ + ε_{3it}. The data is gathered from the World Banks' World Development Indicator 2013 and Gleditsch et al. (2002). The second equation is adopted from Model 1 of Table 5.2. The overall results appear to show that even when the mutual causality concerns are taken into consideration, the effect of industrial growth still remains as predicted. However, there is a serious problem with Keshk's simultaneous equations results because they are obtained under the unrealistic assumption that only industrial growth but not agricultural growth is endogenous to terrorism. Keshk's Stata syntax for the simultaneous equations model allows researchers to include only one endogenous variable in each parenthesis in the command line, making it impossible to accommodate two endogenous relationships at once. Put differently, the simultaneous equations model fails to account for the two endogenous relationships of industrial and agricultural growth at the same time, thereby yielding biased estimates. Therefore, a further exploration of mutual causality between different growth sectors and terrorism will have to await a subsequent methodology study.

REFERENCES

Abadie, A. 2006. "Poverty, Political Freedom and the Roots of Terrorism." *American Economic Review* 96(2): 159–177.

Achen, C. 2002. "Toward a New Political Methodology." *Annual Review of Political Science* 5: 423–450.

Berelson, B., P. Lazarsfeld, and W. McPhee. 1954. *Voting*. Chicago, IL: University of Chicago Press.

Berman, E. and D. D. Laitin. 2008. "Religion, Terrorism and Public Goods." *Journal of Public Economics* 92(10–11): 1942–1967.

Blomberg, S. B., G. D. Hess, and A. Weerapana. 2004. "Economic Conditions and Terrorism." *European Journal of Political Economy* 20(2): 463–478.

Bloom, D. 2012. "Youth in the Balance." *Finance & Development* 49(1): 7–11.

Caruso, R. and F. Schneider. 2011. "The Socio-Economic Determinants of Terrorism and Political Violence in Western Europe (1994–2007)." *European Journal of Political Economy* 27(S): 37–49.

Choi, S. 2010. "Fighting Terrorism through the Rule of Law?" *Journal of Conflict Resolution* 54(6): 940–966.

Choi, S. 2011. "Does U.S. Military Intervention Reduce or Increase Terrorism?" http://papers.ssrn.com/sol3/papers.cfm?abstract_id=1900375.

Choi, S. 2014. "Causes of Domestic Terrorism." *Korean Journal of International Studies* 12(1): 137–159.

Choi, S. and S. Luo. 2013. "Economic Sanctions, Poverty, and International Terrorism." *International Interactions* 39(2): 217–245.

Choi, S. and J. Piazza. 2015. "Internally-Displaced Populations and Suicide Terrorism." *Journal of Conflict Resolution* 60(6): 1008–1040.

Choi, S. and I. Salehyan. 2013. "No Good Deed Goes Unpunished." *Conflict Management and Peace Science* 30(1): 53–75.

Derin-Güre, P. 2009. "Does Terrorism Have Economic Roots?" Working Papers Series wp2009-01. Department of Economics, Boston University.

Drakos, K. and A. Gofas. 2006. "In Search of the Average Transnational Terrorist Attack Venue." *Defence and Peace Economics* 17(2): 73–93.

Enders, W. and T. Sandler. 1999. "Transnational Terrorism in the Post-Cold War Era." *International Studies Quarterly* 43(2): 145–167.

Enders, W. and T. Sandler. 2006. *The Political Economy of Terrorism*. New York: Cambridge University Press.

Enders, W., T. Sandler, and K. Gaibulloev. 2011. "Domestic versus Transnational Terrorism." *Journal of Peace Research* 48(3): 319–337.

Eubank, W. and L. Weinberg. 2001. "Terrorism and Democracy." *Terrorism and Political Violence* 13(1): 155–164.

Eyerman, J. 1998. "Terrorism and Democratic States." *International Interactions* 24(2): 151–170.

Fearon, J. D. and D. D. Laitin. 2003. "Ethnicity, Insurgency, and Civil War." *American Political Science Review* 97(1): 75–90.

Ferrara, P. 2014. "Why Economic Growth Is Exponentially More Important Than Income Inequality." January 14. *Forbes*. http://www.forbes.com/sites/peterferrara/2014/01/14/

why-economic-growth-is-exponentially-more-important-than-income-inequality/print/. Accessed September 1, 2014.

Freytag, A., J. J. Krüger, D. Meierrieks, and F. Schneider. 2011. "The Origins of Terrorism." *European Journal of Political Economy* 27(S): 5–16.

Gaibulloev, K. and T. Sandler. 2011. "The Adverse Effect of Transnational and Domestic Terrorism on Growth in Africa." *Journal of Peace Research* 48(3): 355–371.

Gaibulloev, K., T. Sandler, and D. Sul. 2014. "Dynamic Panel Analysis under Cross-Sectional Dependence." *Political Analysis* 22(2): 258–273.

Gleditsch, K. and M. Ward. 1997. "Double Take." *Journal of Conflict Resolution* 41(3): 361–383.

Gleditsch, N. P., P. Wallensteen, M. Eriksson, M. Sollenberg, and H. Strand. 2002. "Armed Conflict 1946–2001." *Journal of Peace Research* 39(5): 615–637.

Green, D., S. Y. Kim, and D. Yoon. 2001. "Dirty Pool." *International Organization* 55(2): 441–468.

Greene, W. 2003. *Econometric Analysis.* Upper Saddle River, NJ: Prentice Hall.

Gries, T., T. Krieger, and D. Meierrieks. 2011. "Causal Linkages between Domestic Terrorism and Economic Growth." *Defence and Peace Economics* 22(5): 493–508.

Hastings, J. V. and R. J. Chan. 2013. "Target Hardening and Terrorist Signaling." *Terrorism and Political Violence* 25(5): 777–797.

Hilbe, J. 2007. *Negative Binomial Regression.* Cambridge: Cambridge University Press.

Jain, S. and S. W. Mukand. 2004. "The Economics of High-Visibility Terrorism." *European Journal of Political Economy* 20(2): 479–494.

Keshk, O. 2003. "CDSIMEQ." *Stata Journal* 3(2): 157–167.

Krieger, T. and D. Meierrieks. 2011. "What Causes Terrorism?" *Public Choice* 147(1–2): 3–27.

Krueger, A. B. 2008. "What Makes a Homegrown Terrorist?" *Economic Letters* 101(3): 293–296.

Kurrild-Klitgaard, P., M. K. Justesen, and R. Klemmensen. 2006. "The Political Economy of Freedom, Democracy, and Transnational Terrorism." *Public Choice* 128(1–2): 289–315.

Kuznets, S. 1973. "Modern Economic Growth." *American Economic Review* 63(3): 247–258.

La Free, G. and L. Dugan. 2007. "Introducing the Global Terrorism Database." *Terrorism and Political Violence* 19(2): 181–204.

Lai, B. 2007. "'Draining the Swamp'." *Conflict Management and Peace Science* 24(4): 297–310.

Li, Q. 2005. "Does Democracy Promote or Reduce Transnational Terrorist Incidents?" *Journal of Conflict Resolution* 49(2): 278–297.

Lijphart, A. 1971. "Class Voting and Religious Voting in the European Democracies." *Acta Politica* 6(2): 158–171.

Lipset, S. M. and S. Rokkan. 1967. *Party Systems and Voter Alignments.* Toronto: Free Press.

Marshall, M. and K. Jaggers. 2007. "POLITY IV Project." http://www.systemic-peace.org/inscrdata.html.

Meierrieks, D. and T. Gries. 2013. "Causality between Terrorism and Economic Growth." *Journal of Peace Research* 50(1): 91–104.

Pape, R. A. and J. K. Feldman. 2010. *Cutting the Fuse*. Chicago, IL: University of Chicago Press.

Piazza, J. 2006. "Rooted in Poverty?" *Terrorism and Political Violence* 18(1): 159–177.

Piazza, J. 2008. "Incubators of Terror?" *International Studies Quarterly* 52(3): 469–488.

Political Instability Task Force. 2007. "Internal Wars and Failures of Governance, 1955–2006." http://www.gpanet.org/webfm_send/47

Rotberg, R. I. 2002. "Failed States in a World of Terror." *Foreign Affairs* 81(4): 127–140.

Sandler, T. 2014. "The Analytical Study of Terrorism." *Journal of Peace Research* 51(2): 257–271.

Sandler, T. and W. Enders. 2004. "An Economic Perspective on Transnational Terrorism." *European Journal of Political Economy* 20(2): 301–316.

Santifort-Jordan, C. and T. Sandler. 2014. "An Empirical Study of Suicide Terrorism." *Southern Economic Journal* 80(4): 981–1001.

Shahbaz, M. 2013. "Linkages between Inflation, Economic Growth and Terrorism in Pakistan." *Economic Modelling* 32(1): 496–506.

Solt, F. 2009. "Standardizing the World Income Inequality Database." *Social Science Quarterly* 90(2): 231–242.

Stewart, S. July 26, 2012. "The Persistent Threat to Soft Targets." http://www.stratfor.com/weekly/persistent-threat-soft-targets#axzz38geV10fl.

Tomz, M., G. King, and L. Zeng. 1999. "RELOGIT." http://gking.harvard.edu/.

U.S. Census Bureau, Population Division. 2008. "International Database (IDB)." http://www.census.gov/ipc/www/idb/summaries.html.

CHAPTER 6

New Findings on the Causes and Effects of Human Rights Violations

Scholars and pundits appreciate the collection of new data. David McCandless (2010), data journalist, once said, "Data is the new oil? No: Data is the new soil." In the area of international human rights, collecting and creating new and better data is particularly crucial as it allows us to draw more accurate inferences and conclusions, which can inform relevant policy recommendations. Indeed, Clark and Sikkink lament the use of two existing human rights datasets—the Political Terror Scale and the Cingranelli-Richards Human Rights Dataset: "Changes in quality and availability of information related to human rights violations raise questions about how best to use existing data to assess human rights change" (Clark and Sikkink 2013, 539). Similarly, Fariss asserts that existing human rights measures suffer from temporal bias resulting from improved information collection and increased scrutiny of human rights violations now as compared to the past (Fariss 2014). While human rights abuses appear to have increased over time according to old data collections, the reality is that researches have simply become better able to identify abuses now. As such, future research should take the temporal bias into account. By providing a new data collection on the protection of human rights that accounts for those changes over time, Fariss adequately addresses the temporal bias for future researchers.

With the advent of Fariss's new, unbiased measure, the next step in contributing to scientific discovery is to systematically investigate the impact of Farris's new measure on empirical findings that are reported in existing human rights studies. Will previously reported empirical patterns continue to hold up when the Fariss measure is introduced in place of old human rights indicators? This is a very critical question for scholars, policy makers, and activists as they seek to understand the determinants and consequences of human rights. Policy decisions regarding human rights protection should not be executed based on faulty empirical data. By replicating 18 previous studies informed by Fariss's recent data collection, this study offers new inferences and conclusions about the causes and effects of human rights violations. I first report replicated results from 18 original studies and then compare them with new estimates that are obtained after replacing the predictor or outcome variable of human rights in each of the studies with Fariss's new, unbiased measure.

My replications show that depending on how the Fariss measure is introduced in the model specification, many empirical patterns found in the previous studies may be directly challenged. When Fariss's human rights measure replaces the *outcome* variable of the previous studies, the significance and the sign of coefficients related to their main hypotheses hardly survives. In contrast, the replacement of the Fariss measure as the *predictor* rarely causes the validity of the main findings to disappear. These replications indicate that the existing literature requires revisions in regard to the determinants of human rights conditions, and related policy recommendations should be reformulated with this important new finding as well.

REPLICATING EIGHTEEN STUDIES OF HUMAN RIGHTS

Based on online accessibility and availability, I have collected replication materials from 18 previous studies pertaining to international human rights. Nine of the 18 studies aim to determine what factors influence the conditions of human rights. The other nine studies use a human rights measure as a predictor of various political phenomena. Taking the model construction of the 18 studies for granted, I replicate their main model one by one. Unlike previous human rights indicators such as the physical integrity index, Fariss's new data reveals that repressive practices have, on average, decreased over time. Because Fariss's measure has been discussed multiple times regarding its validity and reliability, this study does not go into lengthy detail on its construction (Fariss 2014, Forthcoming; Schnakenberg and Fariss 2014). Tables 6.1 and 6.2 provide an overview of the replication results for the 18 chosen studies. Due to the word limit, further details of replications and individual tables can be found in the Appendix.

Retesting the Determinants of Human Rights

Relying on the Fariss measure of human rights protection, I replicate each of nine previous studies in which a human rights index is used as the outcome variable. The replication strategy is simple: I replace the dependent variable of the nine human rights studies with the Fariss measure

Table 6.1
Human Rights as a Dependent Variable

Author Name(s)	Publication Year	Journal	Variable Names	Original Conclusion	Finding after Applying Farris Measure
Davenport and Armstrong	2004	AJPS	Vanhanen index; Vanhanen; Vanhanen interaction	The effect of democracy is nonlinear	When both Vanhanen (>0.693) and Vanhanen interaction are set at "0," the Vanhanen index exerts a linear, positive impact on the protection of human rights, in contrast to the original assertion
Bueno de Mesquita et al.	2005	ISQ	Participation competition; participation regulation; executive constraint; executive competition; openness of competition; election (executive competition threshold dummy); executive constraint threshold dummy; participation competition threshold dummy; openness of competition threshold dummy	Political participation is the most significant factor in reducing human rights abuses	The election and executive constraint threshold dummy lose significance while the openness of competition and openness of competition threshold dummy are statistically significant
Davenport	2007	JPR	Military; military-personalist; personalist; single-party (mil or pers); single-party; military-personalist-SP; Cold War (>89); military-personalist * Cold War; personalist * Cold War; single-party * Cold War; military-personalist-single party * Cold War	Single-party regimes are less repressive than other autocracies; the end of the Cold War has had a varied influence on repression	Single-party and Cold War are not significant predictors

(Continued)

Table 6.1
(Continued)

Author Name(s)	Publication Year	Journal	Variable Names	Original Conclusion	Finding after Applying Farris Measure
Spilker and Böhmelt	2013	RIO	PTA hard law	PTA hard law has little to do with human rights conditions	PTA hard law helps ameliorate human rights abuses
Neumayer	2005	JCR	Ratification; ratification * INGO p.c.; ratification * democracy; INGO p.c.; democracy	The beneficial effect of ratification of human rights treaties is typically conditional on the extent of democracy	Mature democracies alone help reduce the deterioration of human rights conditions
Hafner-Burton and Tsutsui	2007	JPR	CAT_{it-1}; $CCPR_{it-1}$; CAT_{it-1} * $Polity_{it-1}$; $CCPR_{it-1}$ * $Polity_{it-1}$; $Polity_{it-1}$	Human rights treaty effectiveness is conditional on democracy; civil society does not explain abusive governments	Commitment to International Convention against Torture and Other Cruel, Inhuman, or Degrading Treatment or Punishment may manifest in compliance, thereby improving the quality of human rights conditions even under rogue leaders

Murdie and Davis	2010	HRQ	Humanitarian purpose	Peacekeeping activities for humanitarian purposes are likely to encourage respect for human rights	The original conclusion holds
Peksen	2009	JPR	Human rights sanctions; nonhuman rights sanctions	Economic coercion worsens government respect for physical integrity rights	Human rights and nonhuman rights–related sanctions are insignificant; economic coercion neither improves nor deteriorates human rights conditions
Kim and Trumbore	2010	JPR	Cross-border mergers and acquisitions	Transnational mergers and acquisitions are positively associated with an increase in human rights conditions among developing countries	Transnational mergers and acquisitions are unlikely to contribute to the improvement of human rights

Table 6.2
Human Rights as an Independent Variable

Author Name(s)	Publication Year	Journal	Variable Names	Original Conclusion	Finding after Applying Farris Measure
Ramos, Ron, and Thoms	2007	JPR	Amnesty Political Terror Scale	Two media outlets studied cover human rights news more frequently when they occur in countries with higher levels of state repression	The original conclusion holds
Choi and James	2016	JCR	Human rights$_{t-1}$	When a country exhibits a high degree of human rights abuses, it is likely to be exposed to a greater risk of U.S. military intervention	The original conclusion holds
Bischof and Fink	2015	SPSR	Lagged repression$_{t-1}$; lagged repression$_{t-1}^2$	The relationship between repression and political violence is curvilinear	The curvilinear relationship persists but political violence decreases until human rights protection—not repression—reaches a threshold after which the level of the former arises
Daxecker and Hess	2013	BJPS	Repression; Polity; repression * Polity	The effect of repression on terrorist group termination is conditional on the country's regime type	Democracy and its interaction term with human rights protection lose significance
Barry, Clad, and Flynn	2013	ISQ	Physical integrity rights	INGO shaming reduces FDI inflows, while physical integrity rights exert no significant effect on foreign investment	The original conclusion holds

Murdie and Peksen	2014	JOP	Human rights abuses	The greater international exposure of human suffering through HRO naming and shaming activities puts increased pressure on the international community, and triggers humanitarian military intervention	The original conclusion holds
Murdie/Stapley	2014	II	CIRI physical integrity	While advocacy-based human rights NGOs make terrorism attacks against the whole NGO sector more likely, other types of NGOs, especially those that do not have an advocacy focus, are less likely to attract terrorism	The original conclusion holds
Choi and Piazza	2016	DPE	Physical integrity rights	Physical integrity rights have a dampening effect on domestic terrorism	The original conclusion holds
Uzonyi	2014	CMPS	Human rights abuse$_{t-1}$	Politicide leads to greater displacement of people	The original conclusion holds

and keep the original model specification as close as possible. Among the nine studies, the first three deal with the effect of democracy on human rights conditions, the next three address the impact of human rights laws, and the final three are related to a series of different issues.

Because the Fariss measure of human rights protection is continuous, I considered using a standard OLS regression as an estimation method; however, standard OLS regression is not ideal for cross-sectional, time-series data that suffers from serial correlation and heteroskedasticity. Thus, I perform the Wooldridge test for autocorrelation and a likelihood-ratio test for heteroskedasticity. The null hypothesis of the former test is no first-order correlation and that of the latter test is no heteroskedasticity (Wooldridge 2002; Drukker 2003). Because the test results lead me to reject the null hypotheses, I implement remedial measures for both panel heteroskedasticity and temporally correlated errors. To resolve the estimation issue, I choose Prais-Winsten regression (i.e., panel corrected standard errors (PCSEs) with ar(1)).[1] This statistical technique is frequently employed in political science studies, and it is also used in several of the 18 studies replicated here (Jensen 2003). For example, Davenport and Armstrong employ the same technique to evaluate the impact of democracy on human rights violations (Davenport and Armstrong 2004). I perform the significance tests at the 0.05, 0.01 and 0.001 levels.

I first replicate the three studies that looked at whether democratic institutions help reduce human rights abuses. Davenport and Armstrong postulate that the effect of democracy on the violation of human rights is nonlinear; there is a threshold below which democracy produces no dampening effect on repression but above which democracy is negatively and linearly associated with human rights violations (Davenport and Armstrong 2004). When I replace Davenport and Armstrong's dependent variable of human rights with Fariss's new, unbiased measure, all three Vanhanen-related variables become statistically significant.

Bueno de Mesquita et al. delve into the effects of several separate features of democratic institutions, asserting that "political participation at the level of multiparty competition appears more significant than other dimensions in reducing human rights abuses" (Bueno de Mesquita et al. 2005, 439). When Fariss's new measure replaces the dependent variable of human rights coming from the Political Terror Scale, *election (executive competition threshold dummy)* and *executive constraint threshold dummy* lose significance, while *openness of competition* and *openness of competition threshold dummy* become statistically significant.

Davenport finds evidence that "single-party regimes are generally less repressive than other autocracies . . . and the end of the Cold War has varied influences on repression" (Davenport 2007, 485). When the Fariss measure is introduced in the second column, neither *single-party* nor *Cold War* (>89) emerge as significant predictors.

The next group of three studies investigates how human rights treaties influence human rights conditions. Spilker and Böhmelt reexamine the impact of hard law PTAs on human rights compliance, demonstrating that PTA hard law has little to do with human rights conditions. When the Fariss measure is applied as the dependent variable instead of the political repression variable, PTA hard law does indeed help to ameliorate human rights abuses.

Neumayer examines whether PTA hard law ratification leads to improved respect for human rights in the ratifying country (Neumayer 2005). Neumayer finds that "a beneficial effect of ratification of human rights treaties is typically conditional on the extent of democracy" (Neumayer 2005, 926). When replacing Neumayer's human rights measure with Fariss's and employing Prais-Winsten regression, only mature democracies help reduce the deterioration of human rights conditions.

Hafner-Burton and Tsutsui assert that human rights commitments "mostly have no effects on the world's most terrible repressors . . . recent findings that treaty effectiveness is conditional on democracy and civil society do not explain the behavior of the world's most abusive governments" (Hafner-Burton and Tsutsui 2007, 407). Application of the Fariss measure indicates that the commitment to the International Convention against Torture and Other Cruel, Inhuman, or Degrading Treatment or Punishment may manifest in compliance, thereby improving the quality of human rights conditions even under rogue leaders.

The next three replications address new determinants of human rights conditions. Murdie and Davis present evidence that peacekeeping activities for humanitarian purposes are likely to encourage respect for human rights (Murdie and Davis 2010). Even when replacing Murdie and Davis's measure with the new Fariss measure, the significance of *humanitarian purpose* remains as before. This should be welcome good news for human rights advocates.

Peksen finds evidence that economic coercion worsens government respect for physical integrity rights (Peksen 2009). Peksen focuses on the effect of economic sanctions, particularly those implemented for the purpose of reducing human rights violations, on the infringement of human rights, using *human rights sanctions* and *nonhuman rights sanctions* as the main predictors. He reports the significance of the two sanction-related variables at the 0.05 level. When the Fariss measure is introduced as the dependent variable in place of the physical integrity index, the two sanction-related variables turn out to be insignificant. This implies that economic coercion has had little impact and neither improves nor leads to a deterioration in human rights conditions.

Kim and Trumbore show that transnational mergers and acquisitions are positively associated with an increase in human rights conditions among developing countries (Kim and Trumbore 2010). When I swap their physical integrity index with the Fariss measure, I find no significance of transnational mergers and acquisitions. Cross-border M&As (mergers and acquisitions) are not significantly different from zero, meaning that transnational mergers and acquisitions are unlikely to contribute to the improvement of human rights.

RETESTING THE EFFECT OF HUMAN RIGHTS

In this section, I discuss nine previous studies in which a human rights variable serves to predict diverse political outcomes of interest. The overall results suggest that the previous findings of human rights studies remain almost intact even after the use of the Farris measure.

Ramos, Ron, and Thoms investigate various causal factors that should affect the coverage of human rights abuses reported in *The Economist* and *Newsweek* (Ramos, Ron, and Thoms 2007). In particular, they find that the two media outlets cover human rights news more frequently when they occur in countries with higher levels of state repression. The replacement of their Political Terror Scale variable with Fariss's new, unbiased measure maintains the original finding.

Choi and James demonstrate that when a country exhibits a high degree of human rights abuses, it is likely to be exposed to a greater risk of U.S. military intervention (Choi and James 2016). When I replace Choi and James's independent variable of human rights with Fariss's new measure, the effect of human rights remains relevant.

Bischof and Fink contend that for the Middle Eastern and North African countries, the relationship between repression and political violence is curvilinear, meaning that the latter decreases until the former reaches a critical point after which it starts to increase (Bischof and Fink 2015). The insertion of Fariss's new measure demonstrates the curvilinear relationship still persists, but political violence decreases until human rights *protection*—not repression—reaches a threshold after which the level of the former arises.

Daxecker and Hess test the hypothesis that the effect of repression on terrorist group termination is conditional on the country's regime type (Daxecker and Hess 2013). When I introduce Fariss's new measure in place of Daxecker and Hess's repression measure—Political Terror Scale—both democracy and its interaction term with human rights protection lose significance; the conditional effect of regime type no longer sustains.

When investigating the relationship between naming and shaming activities by international nongovernmental organizations (NGOs) and foreign direct investment (FDI), Barry, Clay, and Flynn include *physical integrity rights* as an intervening variable in their model specification (Barry, Clay, and Flynn 2013). When the Fariss new measure replaces *physical integrity rights* as the independent variable, the result confirms the main finding of Barry, Clay, and Flynn: naming and shaming matter.

Murdie and Peksen contend that the greater international exposure of human suffering through HRO naming and shaming activities puts increased pressure on the international community, which consequently triggers humanitarian military intervention (Murdie and Peksen 2014). The replacement of Murdie and Peksen's human rights variable with Fariss's new measure does not cause the significance of naming and shaming and human rights abuses to disappear.

Murdie and Stapley assert that while advocacy-based human rights NGOs make terrorist attacks against the whole NGO sector more likely, other types of NGOs, especially those that do not have an advocacy focus, are less likely to attract terrorism (Murdie and Stapley 2014). When Fariss's new measure replaces the *physical integrity rights index,* the insignificance and the sign on the coefficient does not change.

Choi and Piazza examine whether the exclusion of ethnic groups from political power leads to increased domestic terrorist attacks (Choi and Piazza 2016). When the physical integrity rights measure—which relates to respect for physical integrity rights and is used as a control in the model—is dropped and Fariss's new measure is instead added in Model 2, I notice the persistence of the same positive effect of human rights protection.

When considering the connection between state-sponsored mass killing and forced migration, Uzonyi includes Cingranelli and Richards's *human rights abuses* as a control variable that turns out to be a significant and positive predictor (Cingranelli and Richards 2010; Uzonyi 2014). The introduction of Fariss's new measure does not alter the significant effect of the human rights variable in relation to forced migration.

CONCLUSION

International human rights is one of the most hotly debated subjects in the discipline of political science. In addition to the search for the causes and effects of human rights violations, the most accurate way to measure human rights conditions is another controversial issue among scholars and practitioners. Fariss's data collection is timely and relevant to the debate; however, he overlooks the important discussion of the implications of his new, unbiased measure with respect to previously published studies that arrive at a number of conclusions on the basis of old human rights datasets such as the Cingranelli-Richards Human Rights Dataset and the Political Terror Scale (Fariss 2014). As data journalist David McCandless (2010) wrote, "Data is the new soil"; as such, current scholarship needs to reevaluate the findings harvested from the old fields of human rights studies before we begin to plant new seeds. In doing so, we will improve our advancement of rigorous scientific endeavors and discoveries and provide the basis for accurate and relevant policy recommendations.

My replications indicate that existing human rights studies require re-visions to their findings that were discovered based on old datasets. It is indeed a poignant time for human rights researchers to look for a new direction for more accurate inferences and conclusions as well as policy recommendations. When the Fariss measure is introduced in place of the *outcome* variable of human rights in the previous studies, the significance and the sign of coefficients related to the main hypotheses hardly persist: only one out of the nine replications passes the robustness test (see also Choi and James 2017). In contrast, when the Fariss measure is used as the *predictor* in the other nine existing studies, the overall results do not devi-ate much from the previous empirical regularities. These new discover-ies are very important for our understanding of the causes and effects of human rights conditions. In many ways, previously reported studies may, due to incorrect inferences and conclusion from their empirical analyses, have misled scholars, policy makers, and activists who have had keen in-terests in learning how best to mitigate the violations of human rights. Such misunderstanding comes from previous studies that neglected to take into consideration the changing standard of accountability in human rights reports over time while relying on old datasets, as detailed in the Fariss (2014) study.

Why does the use of the Fariss measure as the dependent—but not independent—variable produce huge discrepancies? The simple answer is that the introduction of Fariss's new measure changes the variance-covariance of regression models in favor of much less biased estimation, which is not accounted for in the previous studies that employ old human rights data sources. This means that the change of statistical significance is much more salient when the Fariss measure is used as the outcome vari-able rather than the predictor. For example, the effect of regime type on human rights conditions matters but not the same way that previous stud-ies identify. Unlike Davenport's empirical claim, the type of autocratic po-litical systems is shown to neither improve nor deteriorate the condition of human rights (Davenport 2007). Among various human rights treaties, only those that contain a strong emphasis on condemnation and punish-ment of human rights abusers are likely to result in encouraging respect for human rights (e.g., PTA hard law or CAT). Other factors such as human rights sanctions and transnational mergers and acquisitions that have pro-jected as strong predictors in previous studies turn out to be ineffective in protecting human rights.

My replications have a significant implication for publication enter-prises. These days, reviewers tend to increasingly require the author to provide endless robustness tests using different indicators, control vari-ables, and estimators. After the publication of the Fariss work, reviewers began to demand more robustness tests using the Fariss measure in in-stances when the author relies on old human rights data collections. My replications suggest that when papers under review use human rights as a predictor, the main findings are less likely to change whichever human rights dataset is utilized. As a result, additional robustness tests with the Fariss measure should not be required in this case, which should save research time and energy. By contrast, when any papers examine the determinants of human rights conditions, it is reasonable for reviewers to ask for additional robustness tests using the Fariss measure if they do not employ the Fariss dataset as the primary source.

In addition, I believe that the public availability of the replication materials is very important to the advancement of our scientific knowledge of human rights. If the authors whose work is replicated in this study did not make their data and programs publicly available online, I would not have been able to discover new patterns in activities of human rights abusers. Without such access, researchers and activists would always face some distance from scientific truth. It should also be noted that replication materials should include all necessary materials such as data, programs, and a short note on how to replicate. If one of these items is missing, replication becomes increasingly difficult to perform and may lead to imprecise estimates despite well-intentioned efforts. If researchers are all on the same page, trying to move the area of human rights forward, then making replication materials publicly available should be made a priority on publication. This way, researchers could learn from possible errors and flaws. Put differently, replication should not aim to take down previous studies but rather to learn from them to advance our scientific knowledge. Along the same vein, my study is not, as Winston Churchill said, "the beginning of the end"—it is rather the "end of the beginning" (1942).

Details of Replications and Individual Tables

RETESTING THE DETERMINANTS
OF HUMAN RIGHTS

I first replicate three studies on whether democratic institutions help reduce human rights abuses. Davenport and Armstrong postulate that the
effect of democracy on the violation of human rights is nonlinear (Davenport and Armstrong 2004). Their data analysis supports the claim: there
is a threshold below which democracy produces no dampening effect on
repression but above which democracy is negatively and linearly associated with human rights violations. Davenport and Armstrong post the
replication data—but not the statistical programs—online.[2] I rebuild their
model in Table 2 on page 550 that utilizes Vanhanen's democracy data
(Vanhanen 2000).[3] I reproduce their coefficients and standard errors that
are displayed in the first column in Table 6.A1. Though the replicated estimates do not exactly match those reported by Davenport and Armstrong,
the overall effects of three Vanhanen-related variables are consistent with
their results. While the *Vanhanen index* is statistically insignificant, both
Vanhanen (>0.693) and *Vanhanen interaction* achieve significance. However,
when I replace Davenport and Armstrong's dependent variable of human
rights with Fariss's new, unbiased measure, all three Vanhanen-related
variables become statistically significant. This suggests that when both
Vanhanen (>0.693) and *Vanhanen interaction* are set at "0," the *Vanhanen
index* exerts a linear, positive impact on the protection of human rights, in
contrast to the original assertion.

By disaggregating Polity's composite index of democracy, Bueno de Mesquita et al. delve into the effects of several separate features of democratic

Table 6.A1
Effect of Democracy on Human Rights: Davenport and Armstrong 2004,
Table 2, p. 550

| | Replacement of Dependent Variable | |
| | Replicated | Fariss's Measure |
Independent Variable	Political Terror Scale	HR Protection
Lag repression	0.686***	0.954***
	(0.042)	(0.011)
Vanhanen index	−0.087	0.061*
	(0.062)	(0.025)
Vanhanen (>0.693)	1.417***	−0.323**
	(0.283)	(0.114)
Vanhanen interaction	−1.894***	0.421**
	(0.379)	(0.149)
International war	0.120*	0.002
	(0.060)	(0.017)
Civil war	0.491***	−0.081***
	(0.078)	(0.020)
Military control	0.087*	−0.021
	(0.037)	(0.014)
ln(*Population*)	0.063***	−0.011**
	(0.011)	(0.004)
ln(*GNP/capita*)	−0.035**	0.006
	(0.012)	(0.005)
Intercept	0.028	0.128**
	(0.131)	(0.047)
Wald chi^2	8,534.24	46,636.83
Probability > chi^2	0.001	0.001
R^2	0.75	0.97
N	2,315	2,315

Note: Robust and panel-corrected standard errors are in parentheses.

*$p < 0.05$ two-tailed tests

**$p < 0.01$ two-tailed tests

***$p < 0.001$ two-tailed tests

institutions. Their data analysis underscores that "political participation at the level of multiparty competition appears more significant than other dimensions in reducing human rights abuses" (Bueno de Mesquita et al. 2005, 439). I choose to replicate Model 4 in Table 2 on page 448 because

Table 6.A2
**Effects of Democratic Institutions on Human Rights: Bueno de Mesquita et al.
2005, Model 4, Table 2, p. 448**

Independent Variable	Replacement of Dependent Variable	
	Replicated	Fariss's Measure
	Political Terror Scale	HR Protection
Amnesty International ($t = 0$)	0.894***	0.625***
	(0.133)	(0.080)
War (civil or interstate)	1.162***	−0.039
	(0.338)	(0.046)
Population (log)	0.351***	−0.097***
	(0.070)	(0.023)
Per capita income residual	−0.047	0.137*
	(0.137)	(0.056)
Participation competition	1.479	−0.152
	(1.066)	(0.210)
Participation regulation	0.342	0.219
	(1.217)	(0.201)
Executive constraint	0.174	0.033
	(0.753)	(0.126)
Executive competition	−1.433	0.377
	(1.497)	(0.249)
Openness of competition	1.382	−0.389*
	(1.307)	(0.178)
Election (executive competition threshold dummy)	2.199*	−0.228
	(1.042)	(0.198)
Executive constraint threshold dummy	−1.836**	0.148
	(0.682)	(0.121)
Participation competition threshold dummy	−3.934**	0.411*
	(1.247)	(0.171)
Openness of competition threshold dummy	−1.396	0.384***
	(0.896)	(0.111)
Intercept		0.508*
		(0.218)

	Replacement of Dependent Variable	
	Replicated	Fariss's Measure
Independent Variable	Political Terror Scale	HR Protection
Log pseudolikelihood	−974.57	
Wald chi^2	294.02	106.97
Probability > chi^2	0.001	0.001
Pseudo R^2	0.24	
R^2		0.58
N	900	900

Note: Panel-corrected standard errors are in parentheses.

*$p < 0.05$ two-tailed tests

**$p < 0.01$ two-tailed tests

***$p < 0.001$ two-tailed tests

it contains the key features of democratic institutions. As shown in the first column in Table 6.A2, the replicated estimates are the same as what Bueno de Mesquita et al. produced 10 years ago.[4] However, when Fariss's new measure replaces the dependent variable of human rights coming from the Political Terror Scale, a different picture emerges in which *election (executive competition threshold dummy)* and *executive constraint threshold dummy* lose significance, while *openness of competition* and *openness of competition threshold dummy* become statistically significant.

By switching his analytical focus from democracy to autocracy, Davenport finds evidence that "single-party regimes are generally less repressive than other autocracies . . . and the end of the Cold War has varied influences on repression" (Davenport 2007, 485). The replicated estimates that are obtained from the reconstruction of his last, personal integrity ordered-logit model in Table 3 are not similar to his reported results,[5] as shown in the first column in Table 6.A3. Unlike Davenport's empirical claim, *single-party* turns out to have no bearing on the violation of human rights, though *Cold War (>89)* is statistically significant at the 0.001 level. When the Fariss measure is introduced in the second column, neither *single-party* nor *Cold War (>89)* emerges as significant predictors.

The next group of three studies investigate how human rights treaties impact human rights conditions. Spilker and Böhmelt reexamine the impact of hard law PTAs on human rights compliance that was previously studied by Hafner-Burton (Hafner-Burton 2005; Spilker and Böhmelt 2013). Using the replication data and programs posted online by Spilker

Table 6.A3
Effects of Autocratic Institutions on Human Rights: Davenport 2007, Model 6, Table 3, p. 499

Independent Variable	Replacement of Dependent Variable	
	Replicated	Fariss's Measure
	Political Terror Scale	**HR Protection**
Personal integrity$_{t-1}$ = 2	3.227***	
	(0.237)	
Personal integrity$_{t-1}$ = 3	5.263***	
	(0.275)	
Personal integrity$_{t-1}$ = 4	7.530***	
	(0.347)	
Personal integrity$_{t-1}$ = 5	9.119***	
	(0.503)	
Human rights protection$_{t-1}$		0.947***
		(0.010)
Log (GNP)	−0.238***	0.013*
	(0.050)	(0.006)
Log (Population)	0.202***	−0.010**
	(0.039)	(0.004)
Civil war	1.431***	−0.070***
	(0.235)	(0.020)
Interstate war	0.372	−0.004
	(0.290)	(0.016)
Violent dissent	0.449***	−0.030***
	(0.131)	(0.006)
Executive constraints	−0.210***	0.017***
	(0.032)	(0.003)
Leftist regime	0.141	0.008
	(0.191)	(0.024)
Military	0.280	−0.020
	(0.262)	(0.028)
Military-personalist	0.113	0.020
	(0.307)	(0.025)
Personalist	−0.269	−0.007
	(0.216)	(0.020)
Single-party (mil or pers)	−0.347	0.030
	(0.266)	(0.032)

	Replacement of Dependent Variable	
	Replicated	Fariss's Measure
Independent Variable	Political Terror Scale	HR Protection
Single-party	−0.129	0.011
	(0.199)	(0.015)
Military-personalist-SP	0.099	0.006
	(0.310)	(0.030)
Cold War (>89)	0.501***	0.017
	(0.126)	(0.009)
*Military * Cold War*	0.305	−0.093
	(0.437)	(0.061)
*Military-personalist * Cold War*	−0.230	0.009
	(0.529)	(0.045)
*Personalist * Cold War*	0.177	0.015
	(0.267)	(0.031)
Single-party-military or *personalist * Cold War*	0.279	−0.076
	(0.474)	(0.049)
*Single-party * Cold War*	−0.434	0.018
	(0.289)	(0.023)
*Military-personalist-single party * Cold War*	0.062	−0.041
	(0.297)	(0.049)
Intercept		0.027
		(0.051)
Log pseudolikelihood	−1,858.67	
Wald chi^2	1,364.16	59,961.63
Probability > chi^2	0.001	0.001
Pseudo R^2	0.47	
R^2		0.97
N	2,399	2,553

Note: Robust and panel-corrected standard errors are in parentheses.

*$p < 0.05$ two-tailed tests

**$p < 0.01$ two-tailed tests

***$p < 0.001$ two-tailed tests

and Böhmelt,[6] I successfully replicate Model 6[7] in Table 4 on page 357 and report the results in the first column of Table 6.A4. As expected, PTA hard law is shown to have little to do with human rights conditions. However, when I employ the Fariss measure as the dependent variable instead of the political repression variable, PTA hard law becomes statistically significant at the 0.001 level (see the second column). This result nullifies Spilker and Böhmelt's claim but corroborates what Hafner-Burton report 10 years ago: PTA hard law helps ameliorate human rights abuses.

Table 6.A4
Effect of Hard Law PTAs on Human Rights: Spilker and Böhmelt 2013, Model 6, Table 4, p. 357

	Replacement of Dependent Variable	
	Replicated	Fariss's Measure
Independent Variable	Political Terror Scale	HR Protection
PTA hard law	−0.041	0.162***
	(0.212)	(0.037)
Population density	0.001	−0.001**
	(0.001)	(0.000)
Political stability	−0.013*	0.008***
	(0.006)	(0.001)
Democracy	−0.088***	0.032***
	(0.016)	(0.003)
GDP per capita	−0.461***	0.305***
	(0.115)	(0.022)
Trade	−0.661**	0.294***
	(0.238)	(0.042)
Intercept		−3.464***
		(0.203)
Log pseudolikelihood	−3,408.57	
Wald chi^2	102.05	996.36
Probability > chi^2	0.001	0.001
Pseudo R^2		
R^2	0.75	0.33
N	2,754	2,096

Note: Robust and panel-corrected standard errors are in parentheses.
*$p < 0.05$ two-tailed tests
**$p < 0.01$ two-tailed tests
***$p < 0.001$ two-tailed tests

Neumayer addresses the question of whether PTA hard law ratification leads to improved respect for human rights in the ratifying country (Neumayer 2005). Neumayer finds that "a beneficial effect of ratification of human rights treaties is typically conditional on the extent of democracy" (Neumayer 2005, 926). Thanks to the replication materials having been made available and posted online,[8] my replication related to the International Covenant on Civil and Political Rights (ICCPR) comes out without any complications (see the first column in Table 6.A5). Because ICCPR is deemed as "the most ambitious human rights treaty" and because its empirical evidence is strong, I choose to replicate the ordered probit model under ICCPR in Table 2 on page 942 (Goldsmith 2000, 329). By replacing Neumayer's human rights measure with Fariss's and employing Prais-Winsten regression, I re-estimate the ICCPR equation without the year dummies.[9] The result does not coincide with what Neumayer reported 10 years ago. *Ratification* and *ratification * democracy* turn out to be statistically insignificant, while *democracy* achieves significance. It appears that mature democracies alone help reduce the deterioration of human rights conditions.

By focusing on the behavior of repressive states, Hafner-Burton and Tsutsui further discuss the issue of whether the commitments to human rights laws affect the conditions of human rights themselves. Their main findings suggest that "these commitments mostly have no effects on the world's most terrible repressors . . . recent findings that treaty effectiveness is conditional on democracy and civil society do not explain the behavior of the world's most abusive governments" (Hafner-Burton and Tsutsui 2007, 407). Because only the replication data—but not the programs—is publically available,[10] I am unable to produce the same estimates reported under the heading of Democracy, States repressive at the time of ratification in Table 1 on pages 416–417 by Hafner-Burton and Tsutsui eight years ago. The first column in Table 6.A6 displays the replicated results that are generally in line with their empirical claim: repressive regimes' commitments to human rights law do not matter. However, the replacement of their dependent variable of human rights with the Fariss new measure causes CAT_{it-1} to become statistically significant at the 0.01 level. This indicates that the commitment to the International Convention against Torture and Other Cruel, Inhuman, or Degrading Treatment or Punishment may manifest in compliance, thereby improving the quality of human rights conditions even under repressive rogue leaders.

The next three replications address new determinants of human rights conditions. Murdie and Davis present evidence that peacekeeping activities for humanitarian purposes are likely to encourage respect for human rights (Murdie and Davis 2010). I am able to reproduce their coefficients and standard errors reported under the heading of CIRI-Physical Integrity, Future Performance (+3 Years) in Table 2 on page 66. The first column in

Table 6.A5
Effect of ICCPR on Human Rights: Neumayer 2005, Model 6, Table 2, p. 942

Independent Variable	Replacement of Dependent Variable	
	Replicated	Fariss's Measure
	Political Terror Scale	HR Protection
Rights violation(t–1)	1.127***	0.928***
	(0.043)	(0.012)
Ratification	0.287**	−0.027
	(0.093)	(0.016)
*Ratification * INGO p.c.*	−0.001	0.000
	(0.001)	(0.000)
*Ratification * democracy*	−0.024**	0.002
	(0.008)	(0.001)
INGO p.c.	0.000	−0.000
	(0.001)	(0.000)
Democracy	0.001	0.003**
	(0.006)	(0.001)
External conflict	0.003	0.002
	(0.090)	(0.009)
Internal conflict	0.337***	−0.052***
	(0.032)	(0.007)
GDP p.c. (ln)	−0.147***	0.019***
	(0.024)	(0.005)
Population (ln)	0.055*	−0.014**
	(0.025)	(0.005)
Intercept		0.091
		(0.082)
Log pseudolikelihood	−2,002.63	
Wald chi^2	1,454.02	77,649.71
Probability > chi^2	0.001	0.001
Pseudo R^2		
R^2	0.75	0.96
N	2,193	2,891

Note: Robust and panel-corrected standard errors are in parentheses.

*$p < 0.05$ two-tailed tests

**$p < 0.01$ two-tailed tests

***$p < 0.001$ two-tailed tests

Table 6.A6

Effects of Human Rights Laws on Human Rights: Hafner-Burton and Tsutsui 2007, Table 1, pp. 416–417

Independent Variable	Replacement of Dependent Variable	
	Replicated	Fariss's Measure
	Political Terror Scale	HR Protection
CAT_{it-1}	0.116	0.073**
	(0.247)	(0.026)
$CCPR_{it-1}$	–0.218	0.014
	(0.277)	(0.026)
$CAT_{it-1} * Polity_{it-1}$	0.006	0.004
	(0.032)	(0.003)
$CCPR_{it-1} * Polity_{it-1}$	–0.084*	0.009**
	(0.033)	(0.003)
$GDPp.c._{it-1}$	–0.000	0.000***
	(0.000)	(0.000)
$Trade_{it-1}$	–0.015***	0.002***
	(0.004)	(0.000)
$Population_{it-1}$	0.000	–0.000***
	(0.000)	(0.000)
$Polity_{it-1}$	0.050	0.004
	(0.026)	(0.003)
$Regime\ durability_{it-1}$	0.008	0.002
	(0.012)	(0.001)
$Civil\ war_{it-1}$	1.766***	–0.119***
	(0.304)	(0.030)
War_{it-1}	–0.256	–0.067
	(0.864)	(0.099)
Intercept		–0.662***
		(0.059)
Log pseudolikelihood	–2,596.39	
Wald chi^2	Not reported	81.89
Probability > chi^2	Not reported	0.001
Pseudo R^2		
R^2	0.08	0.14
N	2,008	1,920

Note: Robust and panel-corrected standard errors are in parentheses.

*$p < 0.05$ two-tailed tests

**$p < 0.01$ two-tailed tests

***$p < 0.001$ two-tailed tests

Table 6.A7 displays the replicated results that precisely concur with Murdie and Davis's report. Even when the Fariss new measure is used instead of Murdie and Davis's, the significance of *humanitarian purpose* remains as before. This should be welcome news for human rights advocates.

Peksen finds evidence that economic coercion worsens government respect for physical integrity rights (Peksen 2009). Because he focuses on the effect of economic sanctions, particularly those implemented specifically

Table 6.A7
Effect of Peacekeeping Interventions on Human Rights: Murdie and Davis 2010, Table 2, p. 66

	Replacement of Dependent Variable	
	Replicated	Fariss's Measure
Independent Variable	Physical Integrity Rights	HR Protection
Humanitarian purpose	1.439*	0.391*
	(0.700)	(0.194)
GDP per cap (ln)	0.802***	0.305***
	(0.160)	(0.074)
Population (ln)	−0.708*	−0.395***
	(0.302)	(0.117)
Battle deaths (ln)	−0.371*	−0.182**
	(0.154)	(0.061)
Democracy	1.912***	0.302**
	(0.459)	(0.101)
Conflict duration	0.102	0.040
	(0.066)	(0.021)
Intercept	11.439*	4.880*
	(5.311)	(2.058)
F	15.11	
Probability > *F*	0.001	
Wald chi^2		87.78
Probability > chi^2		0.001
R^2		0.45
N	104	137

Note: Newey-West and panel-corrected standard errors are in parentheses.
*$p < 0.05$ two-tailed tests
**$p < 0.01$ two-tailed tests
***$p < 0.001$ two-tailed tests

for the purpose of reducing human rights violations, on the infringement of human rights, I choose to replicate Model 2 in Table 4 on page
72 in which *human rights sanctions* and *nonhuman rights sanctions* are the
main predictors. He reports the significance of the two sanction-related
variables at the 0.05 level. My replicated estimates in the first column in
Table 6.A8 are not the same as Peksen's because only the dataset—but not

Table 6.A8
**Effects of Human Rights Sanctions on Human Rights: Peksen 2009, Model 2,
Table 4, p. 72**

Independent Variable	Replacement of Dependent Variable	
	Replicated	Fariss's Measure
	Physical Integrity Rights	HR Protection
Human rights sanctions	0.164	0.022
	(0.086)	(0.015)
Nonhuman rights sanctions	0.155*	0.026
	(0.067)	(0.015)
GDP per capita	−0.122***	0.011
	(0.031)	(0.006)
Democracy	−0.020***	0.003**
	(0.006)	(0.001)
Civil war	0.638***	−0.049**
	(0.122)	(0.017)
Interstate war	0.054	−0.017
	(0.124)	(0.017)
Past practice	0.497***	0.955***
	(0.031)	(0.013)
Intercept		−0.072
		(0.049)
Log pseudolikelihood	−1,762.51	
Wald chi²	754.56	12,108.67
Probability > chi²	0.001	0.001
Pseudo R^2	0.27	
R^2		0.96
N	1,110	1,210

Note: Robust and panel-corrected standard errors are in parentheses.
*$p < 0.05$ two-tailed tests
**$p < 0.01$ two-tailed tests
***$p < 0.001$ two-tailed tests

the programs—is publically available[11] and because I am unable to figure out exactly how the model is built from the description of his research design. My best efforts show that *human rights sanctions* are not statistically significant, while *nonhuman rights sanctions* achieve significance. When the Fariss measure is introduced as the dependent variable in place of the physical integrity index, the two sanction-related variables turn out to be insignificant. This implies that economic coercion neither improves nor deteriorates human rights conditions.

Kim and Trumbore show that transnational mergers and acquisitions are positively associated with an increase in human rights conditions among developing countries (Kim and Trumbore 2010). Because Kim and Trumbore's replication materials include the data, programs, and codebook,[12] I am easily able to reproduce their results reported in Model 1.4 in Table 1 on page 728. The first column in Table 6.A9 displays the replicated estimates, which are identical to what Kim and Trumbore reported five years ago. However, when I swap their physical integrity index with the Fariss measure, I find no significance of transnational mergers and acquisitions. As shown in the second column, *cross-border M&As* are not significantly different from zero, meaning that transnational mergers and acquisitions are unlikely to contribute to the improvement of human rights.

Table 6.A9

Effects of Transnational Mergers and Acquisitions on Human Rights: Kim and Trumbore 2010, Model 1.4, Table 1, p. 728

	Replacement of Dependent Variable	
	Replicated	Fariss's Measure
Independent Variable	Physical Integrity Rights	HR Protection
Cross-border M&As	0.395*	0.014
	(0.191)	(0.016)
Manufacturing	0.023	0.011***
	(0.017)	(0.003)
Service	0.032	0.011**
	(0.020)	(0.003)
Government expenditure	−0.007	0.000
	(0.006)	(0.001)
GDP per capita (log)	0.125	0.128***
	(0.100)	(0.017)
Population (log)	−0.593***	−0.350***
	(0.082)	(0.016)

Independent Variable	Replacement of Dependent Variable	
	Replicated	Fariss's Measure
	Physical Integrity Rights	HR Protection
Trade	−0.054	0.019
	(0.070)	(0.012)
Human rights NGOs	−0.130	−0.043
	(0.095)	(0.023)
Conflict	−1.740***	−0.182***
	(0.170)	(0.028)
Intercept		4.263***
		(0.323)
Log pseudolikelihood	−2,886.29	
Wald chi^2	421.63	3,370.76
Probability > chi^2	0.001	0.001
Pseudo R^2	0.27	
R^2		0.44
N	1,597	1,857

Note: Robust and panel-corrected standard errors are in parentheses.

*$p < 0.05$ two-tailed tests

**$p < 0.01$ two-tailed tests

***$p < 0.001$ two-tailed tests

RE-RETESTING THE EFFECT OF HUMAN RIGHTS

In this section, I discuss nine previous studies in which a human rights variable serves to predict diverse political outcomes of interest. The overall results suggest that the previous findings of human rights studies remain mostly intact even after the use of the Farris measure.

Ramos, Ron, and Thoms investigate various causal factors that should affect the coverage of human rights abuses reported in *The Economist* and *Newsweek* (Ramos, Ron, and Thoms 2007). In particular, they find that the two media outlets cover human rights news more frequently when they occur in countries with higher levels of state repression. Based on their replication materials that are posted in the replication datasets website of the *Journal of Peace Research*,[13] I attempt to reproduce the estimated results under Model 1 in Table 3 on page 397. However, because the dataset is missing one of the control variables—*UIA number of NGOs*—my replicated results deviate somewhat from theirs, but the significance and the sign of the main predictor—Amnesty Political

Terror Scale—closely resemble the original values (see the first column in Table 6.A10). When the Political Terror Scale variable is replaced with Fariss's new, unbiased measure, the main finding still holds, as shown in the second column.

Table 6.A10
Factors Influencing the Northern Media's Human Rights Coverage: Ramos, Ron, and Thoms 2007, Model 1, Table 3, p. 397

Independent Variable	Replacement of Independent Variable	
	Replicated	Fariss's Measure
	Political Terror Scale	HR Protection
Lag term	0.219***	0.208***
	(0.050)	(0.047)
Amnesty Political Terror Scale	0.387***	−0.639***
	(0.074)	(0.081)
Polity IV	−0.020	−0.013
	(0.011)	(0.011)
Number of battle deaths	−0.000	−0.000
	(0.000)	(0.000)
ODA, $US millions (log)	0.028	−0.018
	(0.052)	(0.049)
U.S. military aid, $US millions (log)	0.011	−0.011
	(0.044)	(0.041)
GDP per capita, $US (log)	0.270**	0.349***
	(0.083)	(0.084)
Size of national military, thousands (log)	0.010	−0.014
	(0.127)	(0.125)
Population, millions (log)	0.397**	0.379**
	(0.137)	(0.130)
Amnesty press releases	0.094***	0.094***
	(0.010)	(0.010)
Constant	−6.126***	−5.363***
	(0.770)	(0.717)
Probability > chi^2	0.001	0.001
Wald chi^2	832.36	948.63

Note: Semi-robust standard errors are in parentheses.

*$p < 0.05$ two-tailed tests

**$p < 0.01$ two-tailed tests

***$p < 0.001$ two-tailed tests

Choi and James demonstrate that when a country exhibits a high degree of human rights abuses, it is likely to be exposed to a greater risk of U.S. military intervention (Choi and James 2016). Choi and James use a logit model to produce their empirical results. They have made the replication materials available, which include the data, do and log files, and the authors' note.[14] Accordingly, my replication went forward smoothly, and I show the results in the first column in Table 6.A11. I replicate Model 5, Table 1, page 12, because it represents their main findings. When I replace Choi and James's independent variable of human rights with Fariss's new measure in the second column, the effect of human rights remains relevant.

Table 6.A11
Determinants of U.S. Military Intervention: Choi and James 2016, Model 5, Table 1, p. 12

	Replacement of Independent Variable	
	Replicated	Fariss's Measure
Independent Variable	Reversed Physical Integrity Rights	HR Protection
$Democracy_{t-1}$	−0.021	−0.010
	(0.026)	(0.026)
$Human\ rights_{t-1}$	0.329***	−0.897***
	(0.077)	(0.191)
$Terrorism_{t-1}$	−0.001	−0.014
	(0.027)	(0.031)
$U.S.\ military\ intervention_{t-1}$	3.059***	2.989***
	(0.379)	(0.381)
$Alliance_{t-1}$	0.258	0.176
	(0.546)	(0.561)
$Oil\ exporter_{t-1}$	−0.035	−0.054
	(0.420)	(0.420)
$Economic\ development_{t-1}$	−0.040	0.101
	(0.195)	(0.206)
$Americas_{t-1}$	−0.040	−0.120
	(0.602)	(0.618)
$Europe_{t-1}$	−0.820	−0.688
	(0.621)	(0.622)
$Africa_{t-1}$	−0.856	−0.617
	(0.518)	(0.525)

(Continued)

Table 6.A11
(Continued)

	Replacement of Independent Variable	
	Replicated	Fariss's Measure
Independent Variable	Reversed Physical Integrity Rights	HR Protection
$Asia_{t-1}$	−0.399	−0.251
	(0.502)	(0.494)
Constant	−5.076**	−5.384**
	(1.935)	(1.970)
LR chi^2	110.22	115.28
Probability $>$ chi^2	0.001	0.001
Log likelihood	−221.76	−218.84
Pseudo R^2	0.20	0.21
N	3,375	3,375

Note: Standard errors are in parentheses.

*$p < 0.05$ two-tailed tests

**$p < 0.01$ two-tailed tests

***$p < 0.001$ two-tailed tests

Bischof and Fink contend that for the Middle Eastern and North African countries, the relationship between repression and political violence is curvilinear, meaning that the latter decreases until the former reaches a critical point after which it starts to increase (Bischof and Fink 2015). Their data analysis, based on OLS regression with a correction for Driscoll-Kraay standard errors, supports the curvilinear hypothesis. Thanks to their replication materials posted online,[15] my replication of their Model 2 in Table 1 on page 386 is successful with no difficulties, and the results are reported in the first column in Table 6.A12. Although their main findings remain the same, my replicated results are slightly different from theirs because 14 observations are dropped after I add Fariss's new measure in the dataset. The results in the second column are obtained after Bischof and Fink's repression variables are replaced with Fariss's measures. The curvilinear relationship still persists, but political violence decreases until human rights *protection*—not repression—reaches a threshold after which the level of the former arises.

Daxecker and Hess test the hypothesis that the effect of repression on terrorist group termination is conditional on the country's regime type (Daxecker and Hess 2013). Their Cox Proportional Hazards model shows that democracy and an interaction term between repression and democracy achieve significance with a positive sign, thus supporting their conjecture.

Table 6.A12

Curvilinear Effect of Repression on Political Violence: Bischof and Fink 2015, Model 2, Table 1, p. 386

Independent Variable	Replacement of Independent Variable	
	Replicated	Fariss's Measure
	Political Terror Scale	HR Protection
Monarchy dummy	−0.816	−0.136
	(0.742)	(0.611)
Lagged repression$_{t-1}$	−2.957***	−3.170**
	(0.675)	(0.882)
Lagged repression$_{t-1}^{2}$	0.600***	0.357**
	(0.105)	(0.112)
Total fuel income (log)	−0.212	−0.161
	(0.105)	(0.109)
Population (log)	0.850**	0.903***
	(0.248)	(0.225)
Area (log)	−0.133	−0.180
	(0.121)	(0.117)
Percentage of Muslims	−0.037	−0.058
	(0.038)	(0.035)
Ethnic fractionalization	1.149	0.338
	(1.740)	(1.502)
Per capita income (log)	0.170	0.441
	(0.268)	(0.306)
Persian Gulf dummy	0.050	0.158
	(0.382)	(0.417)
Democracy dummy	2.255*	2.239*
	(0.801)	(0.781)
Constant	−11.674*	−9.525*
	(4.094)	(3.679)
N	526	526
Number of countries	19	19
R^2	0.32	0.31

Note: Driscoll-Kraay standard errors are in parentheses.

*$p < 0.05$ two-tailed tests

**$p < 0.01$ two-tailed tests

***$p < 0.001$ two-tailed tests

Without any difficulties, I am able to replicate the Cox model with interaction in Table 2 on page 572, which is displayed in Table 6.A13.[16] However, when I introduce Fariss's new measure in place of Daxecker and Hess's repression measure—Political Terror Scale—both democracy and its interaction term with human rights protection lose significance; the conditional effect of regime type no longer sustains.

Table 6.A13
Determinants of Terrorist Group Termination: Daxecker and Hess 2013, Table 2, p. 572

Independent Variable	Replacement of Independent Variable	
	Replicated	Fariss's Measure
	Political Terror Scale	HR Protection
Repression	1.121	1.118
	(0.101)	(0.096)
Polity	1.074*	0.958
	(0.038)	(0.021)
Repression * Polity	0.976**	1.007
	(0.009)	(0.008)
GDP per capita (log)	0.951	0.924
	(0.074)	(0.076)
Population (log)	0.887***	0.899***
	(0.025)	(0.026)
Size	0.287***	0.293***
	(0.041)	(0.042)
Leftist	0.776	0.792
	(0.130)	(0.135)
Religious	0.708	0.708
	(0.183)	(0.187)
Nationalist	0.700*	0.721
	(0.122)	(0.127)
Goal breadth	0.915*	0.904**
	(0.035)	0.035
Foreign presence	0.775	(0.755)
	(0.149)	(0.148)
N	4,979	4,957
Wald chi^2	172.87	175.91

Note: Hazard ratios with robust standard errors in parentheses are reported.
*$p < 0.05$ two-tailed tests
**$p < 0.01$ two-tailed tests
***$p < 0.001$ two-tailed tests

When investigating the relationship between naming and shaming activities by international NGOs and FDI, Barry, Clay, and Flynn include *physical integrity rights* as an intervening variable in their model specification (Barry, Clay, and Flynn 2013). Because the dependent variable—*FDI inflows*—is continuous, Barry, Clay, and Flynn run a Prais-Winsten regression model. Thanks to their replication materials,[17] I successfully produce the same estimates reported in Model 3, Table 2, by Barry, Clay, and Flynn (see the first column in Table 6.A14) (Barry, Clay, and Flynn 2013, 540). The replicated results indicate that while *INGO shaming* reduces FDI inflows, *physical integrity rights* exert no significant effect on foreign investment. When the Fariss new measure replaces *physical integrity rights* as the independent variable, the protection of human rights still remains insignificant, while the effect of *INGO shaming* does not change. This result confirms the main finding of Barry, Clay, and Flynn: naming and shaming matter.

Table 6.A14
**Effects of INGO Shaming and Human Rights on FDI: Barry, Clad, and Flynn
2013, Model 2, Table 2, p. 540**

Independent Variable	Replacement of Independent Variable	
	Replicated	Fariss's Measure
	Physical Integrity Rights	HR Protection
INGO shaming	−0.118***	−0.120***
	(0.026)	(0.029)
Physical integrity rights	0.047	0.008
	(0.031)	(0.123)
Instability	−0.206	−0.198
	(0.120)	(0.135)
Property rights	0.159	0.182*
	(0.082)	(0.081)
Capital account openness	0.015	0.017
	(0.012)	(0.011)
GDP growth	0.073	0.075
	(0.050)	(0.051)
ln (Development)	0.475**	0.464**
	(0.176)	(0.178)
ln (Trade)	0.649***	0.611***
	(0.091)	(0.091)

(Continued)

Table 6.A14
(Continued)

Independent Variable	Replacement of Independent Variable	
	Replicated	Fariss's Measure
	Physical Integrity Rights	HR Protection
ln (Urban population)	0.001	0.001
	(0.003)	(0.003)
Resource exports	−0.029	−0.031
	(0.016)	(0.017)
Government consumption	0.030**	0.031***
	(0.009)	(0.009)
Female life expectancy	0.038**	0.038**
	(0.013)	(0.014)
Polity	0.008*	0.007
	(0.003)	(0.004)
Regime durability	0.037	0.038
	(0.043)	(0.045)
ln (FDI stock)	0.501***	0.503***
	(0.075)	(0.074)
World FDI flow	0.000	0.000
	(0.000)	(0.000)
Intercept	−13.876***	−13.193***
	(1.921)	(1.963)
Wald chi^2	1,293.66	1,346.71
Probability > chi^2	0.001	0.001
R^2	0.62	0.61
N	705	710

Note: Panel-corrected standard errors are in parentheses.

*$p < 0.05$ two-tailed tests

**$p < 0.01$ two-tailed tests

***$p < 0.001$ two-tailed tests

Murdie and Peksen contend that the greater international exposure of human suffering through HRO naming and shaming activities puts increased pressure on the international community and consequently triggers humanitarian military intervention (Murdie and Peksen 2014). They present supporting evidence for the contention, and they introduce human rights violations as a way to avoid omitted variable bias. They rely on rare event logit as their estimator, and their replication materials are publicly available online.[18] I replicate their main model that appears in the first column in Table 1 on page 223. The first column in Table 6.A15 displays my replicated coefficients and standard errors. The replacement of Murdie and Peksen's human rights variable with Fariss's new measure does not cause the significance of naming and shaming and human rights abuses to disappear, as shown in the second column.

Table 6.A15
Effects of HRO Shaming and Human Rights on Humanitarian Interventions: Murdie and Peksen 2014, Table 1, p. 223

	Replacement of Independent Variable	
	Replicated	Fariss's Measure
Independent Variable	Political Terror Scale	HR Protection
HRO shaming (count)	0.615***	0.571***
	(0.165)	(0.153)
Human rights abuses	0.860**	–1.579***
	(0.272)	(0.381)
Media exposure	0.458	0.355
	(0.235)	(0.259)
State capacity	–0.815***	–0.915***
	(0.237)	(0.248)
Democracy	–0.026	0.010
	(0.030)	(0.035)
Ethnic fractionalization	–9.271**	–8.229**
	(3.085)	(3.058)
Ethnic fractionalization squared	10.338**	9.265**
	(3.522)	(3.588)
Civil war	0.456	0.222
	(0.568)	(0.509)
Oil producer	–0.177	0.068
	(0.607)	(0.634)
Economic sanctions	0.356	0.292
	(0.266)	(0.272)
Genocide	0.559	–0.212
	(0.459)	(0.474)

(Continued)

Table 6.A15
(Continued)

	Replacement of Independent Variable	
	Replicated	Fariss's Measure
Independent Variable	Political Terror Scale	HR Protection
Past intervention	−0.026*	−0.025*
	(0.012)	(0.011)
Constant	−14.134***	−12.389***
	(2.634)	(2.902)
Region dummies	Yes	Yes
N	1,933	1,975

Note: Robust standard errors are in parentheses.

*$p < 0.05$ two-tailed tests

**$p < 0.01$ two-tailed tests

***$p < 0.001$ two-tailed tests

Murdie and Stapley assert that while advocacy-based human rights NGOs increase the likelihood of terrorist attacks against the whole NGO sector more likely, other types of NGOs, especially those that do not have an advocacy focus, are less likely to attract terrorism (Murdie and Stapley 2014). They offer supporting evidence for the assertion. My replication of Model 1 in Table 1 on page 95 does not encounter any complications, and the re-estimated results are displayed in Table 6.A16.[19] In the model, *CIRI physical integrity rights index* is used as a control. When Fariss's new measure replaces the *physical integrity rights index*, neither insignificance nor the sign on the coefficient changes.

Choi and Piazza examine whether the exclusion of ethnic groups from political power leads to increased domestic terrorist attacks (Choi and Piazza 2016). Their negative binomial regression estimation on 130 countries during the period 1981–2005 shows a positive relationship between the two factors. After having obtained the replication materials from the first author, I successfully reran Model 1 in Table 1 on page 12, as displayed in Model 1 in Table 6.A17. The measure of respect for physical integrity rights—the right not to be abused or harmed—is included as a control in the model. The results indicate a dampening effect of physical integrity rights on domestic terrorism. When the physical integrity rights measure is dropped and Fariss's new measure is instead added in Model 2, I notice the persistence of the same benevolent effect of human rights protection.

When considering the connection between state-sponsored mass killing and forced migration, Uzonyi include Cingranelli and Richards's *human*

Table 6.A16
Determinants of NGO-Targeted Terrorist Attacks: Murdie and Stapley 2014,
Model 1, Table 1, p. 95

Independent Variable	Replacement of Independent Variable	
	Replicated	Fariss's Measure
	Physical Integrity Rights	**HR Protection**
Human rights NGOs$_{t-1}$[a]	0.611**	0.569**
	(0.216)	(0.211)
Other NGOs$_{t-1}$[a]	–0.128*	–0.128*
	(0.050)	(0.050)
Polity	–0.025	–0.026
	(0.024)	(0.025)
Conflict	–0.006	–0.057
	(0.342)	(0.375)
Intervention	0.465	0.480
	(0.271)	(0.283)
Population (ln)	–0.088	–0.088
	(0.099)	(0.100)
GDP per capita (ln)	–0.276*	–0.271*
	(0.112)	(0.119)
CIRI physical integrity	0.094	0.170
	(0.065)	(0.260)
U.S. indicator	1.169*	1.153*
	(0.461)	(0.511)
Non-NGO attacks	0.664***	0.667***
	(0.098)	(0.121)
Constant	–1.804	–1.270
	(1.563)	(1.678)
N	1,777	1,777

Notes: Standard errors are in parentheses; GEE models with an AR1 correlation structure.
[a] NGO variables are capturing members/volunteers per county-year.
*p < 0.05 two-tailed tests
**p < 0.01 two-tailed tests
***p < 0.001 two-tailed tests

rights abuses as a control variable that turns out to be a significant and positive predictor (Cingranelli and Richards 2010; Uzonyi 2014). As reported in the first column of Table 6.A18, my replication is consistent with the finding of Uzonyi.[20] The introduction of Fariss's new measure does not

Table 6.A17

Effect of Political Exclusion on Domestic Terrorism: Choi and Piazza 2016, Model 1, Table 1, p. 12

Independent Variable	Replacement of Independent Variable	
	Replicated	Fariss's Measure
	Physical Integrity Rights	HR Protection
Political exclusion	0.189**	0.107
	(0.059)	(0.060)
Political rights	0.261***	0.316***
	(0.050)	(0.047)
Ethnic fractionalization	−0.956**	−0.658*
	(0.356)	(0.322)
State failure	0.224***	0.161***
	(0.051)	(0.046)
Physical integrity rights	−0.210***	−0.889***
	(0.035)	(0.104)
Independent judiciary	−0.431*	−0.037
	(0.175)	(0.178)
Economic development	0.073	0.317**
	(0.106)	(0.109)
Population	0.475***	0.384***
	(0.073)	(0.069)
Lagged terrorism	0.024***	0.019***
	(0.005)	(0.005)
Constant	−4.457***	−6.938***
	(0.951)	(0.885)
Wald chi^2	362.57	478.62
Probability > chi^2	0.001	0.001
Log pseudolikelihood	−5,730.67	−5,653.65
Dispersion = 1	3.41	3.09
Country and year fixed effects	No	No
Observations	2,794	2,794

Note: Robust standard errors are in parentheses.

*$p < 0.05$ two-tailed tests

**$p < 0.01$ two-tailed tests

***$p < 0.001$ two-tailed tests

Table 6.A18
Effects of Genocide and Politicide on Forced Migration: Uzonyi 2014, Table 2,
p. 237

Independent Variable	Replacement of Independent Variable	
	Replicated	Fariss's Measure
	Reversed Physical Integrity Rights	HR Protection
Genocide	−0.142	−0.434*
	(0.182)	(0.176)
Politicide	0.307**	0.044
	(0.099)	(0.089)
Human rights abuse$_{t-1}$	0.596***	−1.532***
	(0.068)	(0.133)
Civil war$_{t-1}$	0.749**	0.510*
	(0.261)	(0.229)
Democracy$_{t-1}$	0.015	0.008
	(0.027)	(0.023)
ln(GDP)$_{t-1}$	−0.280*	−0.171
	(0.130)	(0.129)
ln(Population)$t-1$	0.135	0.022
	(0.180)	(0.175)
ln(Area)$_{t-1}$	−0.592***	−0.554***
	(0.141)	(0.155)
ln(Borders)$_{t-1}$	1.024**	0.877**
	(0.352)	(0.322)
Neighborhood democracy$_{t-1}$	−0.046	−0.003
	(0.029)	(0.029)
Years since displacement	−0.984***	−1.027***
	(0.103)	(0.108)
Years since displacement^2	0.061***	0.063***
	(0.010)	(0.011)
Years since displacement^3	−0.001***	−0.001***
	(0.000)	(0.000)
Constant	13.195***	14.040***
	(1.833)	(1.670)
ö	7.278	6.575
N	3,021	3,128
Log pseudolikelihood	−7,742.307	−8,127.099

Note: Errors are clustered by country.
*$p < 0.05$ two-tailed tests
**$p < 0.01$ two-tailed tests
***$p < 0.001$ two-tailed tests

alter the significant effect of the human rights variable in relation to forced migration (see the second column).

NOTES

1. The Stata command is xtpcse with two options: pairwise and corr(ar1).

2. See http://quantoid.net/research.

3. I do not replicate the model with the *democracy trichotomy* variable because its functional form is not nonlinear, and thus, it is not ideal to assess the theoretical conjecture on the nonlinear relationship between democracy and repression.

4. See http://www.nyu.edu/gsas/dept/politics/data/insidethebox.shtml.

5. Davenport posts his replication data—but not the program files—at https://www.prio.org/JPR/Datasets/#2007.

6. See http://link.springer.com/article/10.1007/s11558-012-9155-8.

7. I do not replicate Model 7 with the Fariss measure because Beck, Katz, and Tucker's (1998) cubic splines are not applicable to Fariss's continuous measure.

8. See http://www.lse.ac.uk/geographyAndEnvironment/whosWho/profiles/neumayer/replicationdatasets2.aspx#DynamicJumpMenuManager_1_Anchor_12.

9. When I include the year dummies, I run into no estimates and the warning that the "variance matrix is nonsymmetric or highly singular." This statistical deadlock forces me to drop the year dummies out of the equation. If the same deadlock happens in other replication studies, I adopt the same approach.

10. See https://www.prio.org/JPR/Datasets/#2007.

11. See https://www.prio.org/JPR/Datasets/#2009.

12. See https://www.prio.org/JPR/Datasets/#2010.

13. See https://www.prio.org/JPR/Datasets/#2007.

14. See http://jcr.sagepub.com/content/early/recent.

15. See https://dataverse.harvard.edu/dataset.xhtml?persistentId=doi:10.7910/DVN/LIUJ4K.

16. The replication materials can be found at https://dataverse.harvard.edu/dataset.xhtml?persistentId=hdl:1902.1/22121.

17. See http://www.isanet.org/Publications/ISQ/Replication-Data.

18. See http://www.amandamurdie.org/research.html.

19. The replication is performed using the data and do-file obtained from https://dataverse.harvard.edu/dataset.xhtml?persistentId=doi:10.7910/DVN/25576.

20. The replication materials can be found at https://docs.google.com/file/d/0ByuZ-wd2lOa5UHAwSm5kSDBNd0E/edit?pli=1.

REFERENCES

Barry, Colin, Chad Clay, and Michael Flynn. 2013. "Avoiding the Spotlight." *International Studies Quarterly* 57(3): 532–544.

Beck, Neal, Jonathan Katz, and Robert Tucker. 1998. "Taking Time Seriously." *American Journal of Political Science* 42(4): 1260–1288.

Bischof, Daniel and Simon Fink. 2015. "Repression as a Double-Edged Sword." *Swiss Political Science Review* 21(3): 377–395.

Bueno de Mesquita, Bruce, George Downs, Alastair Smith, and Feryal Cherif. 2005. "Thinking Inside the Box." *International Studies Quarterly* 49(3): 439–457.

Cingranelli, David and David L. Richards, 2010. "The Cingranelli and Richards (CIRI) Human Rights Data Project." *Human Rights Quarterly* 32(20): 401–424.

Choi, Seung-Whan and Patrick James. 2016. "Why Does the U.S. Intervene Abroad?" *Journal of Conflict Resolution* 60(5): 899–926.

Choi, Seung-Whan and James Piazza. 2016. "Ethnic Groups, Political Exclusion and Domestic Terrorism." *Defence and Peace Economics* 27(1): 37–63.

Choi, Seung-Whan and Patrick James. 2017. "Are U.S. Foreign Policy Tools Effective in improving Human Rights Conditions?" *Chinese Journal of International Politics* 10(3): 331–356.

Churchill, Winston. 1942. "The End of the Beginning." The Lord Mayor's Luncheon, Mansion House. http://www.churchill-society-london.org.uk/EndoBegn.html

Clark, Ann and Kathryn Sikkink. 2013. "Information Effects and Human Rights Data." *Human Rights Quarterly* 35(3): 539–568.

Davenport, Christian. 2007. "State Repression and the Tyrannical Peace." *Journal of Peace Research* 44(4): 485–504.

Davenport, Christian and David Armstrong. 2004. "Democracy and the Violation of Human Rights." *American Journal of Political Science* 48(3): 538–554.

Daxecker, Ursula and Michael Hess. 2013. "Repression Hurts." *British Journal of Political Science* 43(3): 559–577.

Drukker, David. 2003. "Testing for Serial Correlation in Linear Panel-Data Models." *Stata Journal* 3(4): 168–177.

Fariss, Christopher. 2014. "Respect for Human Rights Has Improved over Time." *American Political Science Review* 108(2): 297–318.

Fariss, Christopher. Forthcoming. "The Changing Standard of Accountability and the Positive Relationship between Human Rights Treaty Ratification and Compliance." *British Journal of Political Science* 1–39.

Goldsmith, Jack. 2000. "Should International Human Rights Law Trump US Domestic Law?" *Chicago Journal of International Law* 1: 327–339.

Hafner-Burton, Emilie. 2005. "Trading Human Rights." *International Organization* 59(3): 593–629.

Hafner-Burton, Emilie and Kiyoteru Tsutsui. 2007. "Justice Lost!" *Journal of Peace Research* 44(4): 407–425.

Jensen, Nathan. 2003. "Democratic Governance and Multinational Corporations." *International Organization* 57(3): 587–616.

Kim, Dong-Hun and Peter Trumbore. 2010. "Transnational Mergers and Acquisitions." *Journal of Peace Research* 47(6): 723–734.

McCandless, David. 2010. "The Beauty of Data Visualization." TEDGlobal 2010. https://www.ted.com/talks/david_mccandless_the_beauty_of_data_visualization/transcript

Murdie, Amanda and David Davis. 2010. "Problematic Potential." *Human Rights Quarterly* 32(1): 49–72.

Murdie, Amanda and Dursun Peksen. 2014. "The Impact of Human Rights INGO Shaming on Humanitarian Interventions." *Journal of Politics* 76(1): 215–228.

Murdie, Amanda and Craig Stapley. 2014. "Why Target the 'Good Guys'?" *International Interactions* 40(1): 79–102.

Neumayer, Eric. 2005. "Do International Human Rights Treaties Improve Respect for Human Rights?" *Journal of Conflict Resolution* 49(6): 925–953.

Peksen, Dursun. 2009. "Better or Worse?" *Journal of Peace Research* 46(1): 59–77.

Ramos, Howard, James Ron, and Oskar Thoms. 2007. "Shaping the Northern Media's Human Rights Coverage, 1986–2000." *Journal of Peace Research* 44(4): 385–406.

Schnakenberg, Keith and Christopher Fariss. 2014. "Dynamic Patterns of Human Rights Practices." *Political Science Research and Methods* 2(1): 1–31.

Spilker, Gabriele and Tobias Böhmelt. 2013. "The Impact of Preferential Trade Agreements on Governmental Repression Revisited." *Review of International Organizations* 8(3): 343–361.

Uzonyi, Gary. 2014. "Unpacking the Effects of Genocide and Politicide on Forced Migration." *Conflict Management and Peace Science* 31(3): 225–243.

Vanhanen, Tatu. 2000. "A New Dataset for Measuring Democracy, 1810–1998." *Journal of Peace Research* 37(2): 251–265.

Wooldridge, Jeffrey. 2002. *Econometric Analysis of Cross Section and Panel Data*. Cambridge, MA: MIT Press.

CHAPTER 7

Demystifying the Impact of Naming and Shaming

Replication is a scientific ideal, but it also turns out to be good for scholars in practical, even career-oriented ways. (James 2003, 85)

Replication allows us as a discipline to probe the usefulness and robustness of previously published findings that may be sensitive to reasonable changes in research design strategy. (Park and Colaresi 2014, 8)

As scholars and policy makers become increasingly aware of activism by nongovernmental human rights organizations in domestic and international politics, they have developed a keen research interest in the relationship between these nongovernmental organizations (NGOs) and human rights themselves. In particular, several researchers have examined the effects of naming and shaming on political and economic outcomes, as well as its potential conditional effect on targeted-state repression during the past decade (e.g., Ron, Ramos, and Rodgers 2005; Franklin 2008; Hafner-Burton 2008; Murdie and Davis 2012; Murdie and Peksen 2014). The topic of naming and shaming has garnered such growing attention because they are popular strategies of nongovernmental organizations that publicize countries' violations of human rights and urge reform (Hafner-Burton 2008, 689). This growing literature, however, has offered inconsistent arguments and findings pertaining to the impact of naming and shaming.

Studies by Hafner-Burton (2008) and Franklin (2008) suggest that shaming can prompt the targeted governments to reduce repression but only in highly limited circumstances. Shaming produces little discernible effect over the long term, and it may actually be followed by a spike in repression. Murdie and Peksen (2014), however, indicate that shaming's real impact may be on foreign powers that can be motivated to undertake humanitarian intervention against the governments being shamed, though it is unclear whether that intervention would correlate with improved or worsened human rights. On the one hand, military interventions brought on by shaming—when they succeed—may stop internal conflicts, constrain violence, and otherwise improve the human rights situation inside countries. On the other hand, militarized humanitarian intervention may also cause a rise in human rights abuses.

In this study, I attempt to demystify this paradox within the shaming literature from an empirical standpoint because I find that existing model specifications drastically vary from one to another and because I suspect the paradoxical findings may be caused directly by the diverse model designs. For this purpose, I choose to replicate the recent work by Murdie and Peksen (2014), in that it appears to show strong empirical evidence that shaming by human rights organizations is an important factor in affecting realpolitik issues such as humanitarian intervention decisions. I argue, however, that Murdie and Peksen's finding is a statistical artifact, stemming from a model specification error as causal time order is incorrectly set in the statistical model. This violates the golden rule that cause must precede effect. I demonstrate that when Murdie and Peksen's statistical model is properly specified, it produces no significant and positive effect of human rights organizations on humanitarian interventions. Thus, it appears that naming and shaming does not produce significant impacts beyond the rhetorical statements of human rights organizations.

WHAT'S WRONG WITH THE GRANGER CAUSALITY TEST?

To justify their causal story, Murdie and Peksen (2014) offer the Granger causality tests in the article and in the online appendix. Without doubt, granger causality tests are known to be instrumental in determining whether one time series is useful in forecasting another. I decided to replicate the test results to verify their assertion. But I was unable to locate the command lines for the Granger causality tests using logit and OLS models in their Stata do-file. I made multiple attempts to obtain the commands by contacting the first author of the article by e-mail, but my attempts did not yield fruitful results. Thus, based on their model description, I re-created their command lines.

To evaluate the causal direction from shaming to intervention, Murdie and Peksen suggest the following two logit regression models:

$$Humanitarian\ Interventions_{it} = \gamma_1 + \gamma_2 HRO\ shaming_{it\text{-}1}$$
$$+ \gamma_3 Humanitarian\ Interventions_{it\text{-}1} + \varepsilon_3$$
$$Humanitarian\ Interventions_{it} = \delta_1 + \delta_2 HRO\ shaming_{it\text{-}1} + \delta_3 HRO\ shaming_{it\text{-}2}$$
$$+ \delta_4 Humanitarian\ Interventions_{it\text{-}1}$$
$$+ \delta_5 Humanitarian\ Interventions_{it\text{-}2} + \varepsilon_4$$

To assess the causal influence of intervention on shaming, the following two OLS regression models are built:

$$HRO\ shaming_{it} = \theta_1 + \theta_2 Humanitarian\ Interventions_{it\text{-}1} + \theta_3 HRO\ shaming_{it\text{-}1} + \varepsilon_3$$
$$HRO\ shaming_{it} = \varphi_1 + \varphi_2 Humanitarian\ Interventions_{it\text{-}1}$$
$$+ \varphi_3 Humanitarian\ Interventions_{it\text{-}2}$$
$$+ \varphi_4 HRO\ shaming_{it\text{-}1} + \varphi_5 HRO\ shaming_{it\text{-}2} + \varepsilon_4$$

After referring the reader back to a summary table of the Granger causality tests posted in their online appendix, Murdie and Peksen conclude in their main article that "the p-values of these tests clearly indicate that shaming Granger-causes humanitarian intervention but intervention does not Granger-cause shaming" (p. 225).

My Granger causality test replications, however, result in estimates that substantially deviate from what Murdie and Peksen report. Their online appendix on page 3 indicates that HRO shaming (count) Granger-causes intervention with p value of 0.00 and χ^2 of 38.39, and that HRO shaming (count) is Granger-caused by intervention with p value of 0.11 and χ^2 of 4.51.[1] I was unable to reproduce these statistics in my replication. As displayed in Table 7.1, my results indicate no significant relationship between shaming and intervention, regardless of the causal direction. Columns 2 and 3 test whether shaming Granger causes intervention using a χ^2-test; however, the p-value is either 0.614 or 0.523, indicating that I cannot reject the null hypothesis that shaming and intervention are unrelated. The insignificance of the Granger causality test is largely in line with the multivariate regression results reported in Table 7.3, where the shaming variable at time t-1 fails to emerge as a significant and positive predictor of humanitarian intervention at time t. Note also that when I test the reversed causal direction using an F-test as in columns 4 and 5 in Table 7.3, the p value is either 0.054 or 0.117. Simply put, the failed replication of my Granger causality tests seriously questions the validity of the causal relationship between shaming and intervention that are set at the same time t in the Murdie and Peksen model.

In the next section, I take one step back from the empirical investigation and provide a theoretical reason for establishing causal time order correctly.

Table 7.1
Granger Causality Tests

Independent Variables	Causal Direction			
	From Shaming to Intervention		From Intervention to Shaming	
HRO Shaming (count)$_{it-1}$	-0.140	-0.542	0.187***	0.114
	(0.278)	(0.508)	(0.049)	(0.063)
HRO Shaming (count)$_{it-2}$		0.034		0.074
		(0.067)		(0.045)
Humanitarian intervention$_{it-1}$	2.371***	2.077***	-0.245	-0.153
	(0.469)	(0.506)	(0.126)	(0.079)
Humanitarian intervention$_{it-2}$		2.131***		-0.092
		(0.551)		(0.073)
Constant	-3.919***	-4.123***	0.166***	0.152***
	(0.226)	(0.241)	(0.029)	(0.028)
χ^2	0.25	1.29		
Prob > χ^2	0.614	0.523		
F			3.80	2.18
Prob > F			0.054	0.117
N	1,829	1,722	1,829	1,722

Notes: Robust standard errors are in parentheses. *$p<0.05$; **$p<0.01$; ***$p<0.001$, two-tailed tests.

Source: Murdie and Peksen, 2014, Online Appendix, p. 3.

WHY CAUSAL TIME ORDER MATTERS

It is important to note that just because two variables are related, changes in one variable do not necessarily cause changes in the other variable. To establish cause and effect between the two variables, proper time order must be specified—whatever causes the outcome actually has to occur before the outcome because the connection between cause and effect takes place in time (Davis 1985; Büthe 2002). Thus, proper time order negates "the idea that an effect might *precede* [emphasis added] a cause in time" (Holland 1986, 950). For example, if researchers were interested in the impact of democracy (i.e., the explanatory variable) on the onset of international conflict (i.e., the outcome variable), they would expect that the explanatory variable came before the outcome variable, and not the other way around. Put differently, the onset of international conflict (i.e., the dependent variable) cannot influence the quality of democratic political institutions (i.e., the predictor). Instead, the democratic institutions should cause a change in the onset of international conflict. Simply put, cause always precedes effect.

Murdie and Peksen (2014) assert that shaming activities lead to the onset of humanitarian military intervention. This assertion assumes that shaming activities must happen before military actions. Note that if shaming activities are going to have an effect on intervention, the effect is likely going to develop over a period of time. Nongovernmental human rights organizations must publish their reports, taking some time to collect information and disseminate it. Simply putting up a report online or getting media sources to report on it is unlikely to draw large-scale immediate attention from either the targeted government or other actors. If shaming works at all by providing new information, creating coalitions, raising public awareness, and so on, it certainly does not do so instantaneously. All of those processes require time.[2]

More important, even though we assume that shaming activities are effective in inspiring foreign powers to take action, we must know that preparations for military operations and deployments also take a considerable amount of time. I illustrate this point by discussing how the UN makes the decision to undertake a new military operation, because the UN is responsible for a majority of humanitarian military interventions (see Table 7.2).[3] One must understand how much time the UN requires to deploy its troops on the ground and how many steps the UN needs to go through to form a new operation. The UN itself describes the process as follows:[4]

It takes considerable time to deploy troops and we are often asked why we do not have a standing reserve. The UN can only deploy military personnel when there is a UN Security Council resolution authorizing them to do so. The Security Council will say how many military personnel are required, and then UN Headquarters will liaise with the Member States to identify personnel and deploy them. *This can take time—perhaps more than six months from the date of the resolution.* (emphasis added)

The UN clearly states that even after the Security Council formally authorizes a new military operation by adopting a resolution, the deployment of troops on the ground would require at least six months because they have no standing reserve. It should be noted that before passing a resolution, a number of additional steps must happen before the decision to deploy is even reached. In order to respond to international crises, the UN seeks initial consultations to determine the best response by the international community. On completing the initial consultations, the Secretariat deploys a technical assessment mission to the crisis area. Based on the findings of the assessment mission, the UN secretary-general issues a report to the Security Council. Then, if it can reach a consensus among member countries, the Security Council issues a resolution; then the secretary general will appoint a head of mission to direct the peacekeeping

Table 7.2

Number of Shaming and 41 Onsets of Humanitarian Military Intervention out of 1,933 Total Observations: Murdie and Peksen 2014, Model 1, Table 1, p. 223

Country	Number of Shaming	Start Date of Intervention	End Date of Intervention	Brief Description
Haiti	0	01/09/1993	03/06/1996	UN in Haiti
Haiti	0	03/10/1994	31/03/1995	Multinational force attempts to restore elected government in Haiti, etc.
Haiti	0	01/07/1996	31/07/1997	UN in Haiti
Haiti	1	01/08/1997	30/11/1997	UN transition mission in Haiti
Haiti	0	1999	Unknown	Not included in the merged IMI data but appear in Murdie and Peksen's dataset
Guatemala	1	01/01/1997	31/05/1997	United States in Guatemala
El Salvador	2	01/07/1991	30/04/1995	UN in El Salvador
Albania	0	11/04/1999	01/09/1999	NATO gives humanitarian aid to Albania in Operation Allied Harbor
Macedonia	0	31/03/1995	28/02/1999	UN mission to Macedonia
Croatia	0	15/01/1996	15/01/1998	UN in Eastern Slavonia, Baranja, Western Sirmium
Croatia	0	1998	Unknown	Not included in the merged IMI data but appear in Murdie and Peksen's dataset
Bosnia	0	12/04/1993	20/12/1995	NATO air strikes against Bosnian Serbs as part of Operation Deny Flight
Bosnia	1	20/12/1995	31/12/2002	UN in Bosnia-Herzegovina, peacekeeping
Guinea-Bissau	0	28/12/1998	07/06/1999	ECOMOG peacekeepers intervene in Guinea-Bissau to end war

Country	Number of Shaming	Start Date of Intervention	End Date of Intervention	Brief Description
Ivory Coast	1	17/11/2002	05/04/2004	ECOMOG monitors ceasefire in Ivory Coast
Ivory Coast	0	05/04/2004	Unknown	UN peacekeeping operation in Ivory Coast
Liberia	0	22/09/1993	30/09/1997	UN established to give humanitarian aid to Liberia
Liberia	4	19/09/2003	Unknown	UN to ensure ceasefire in Liberia and provide humanitarian aid
Sierra Leone	1	13/07/1998	22/10/1999	UN monitors the military and security situation in Sierra Leone
Congo	1	30/07/1994	30/09/1994	U.S. troops provide humanitarian assistance in Zaire
Congo	0	31/08/1999	Unknown	UN to monitor ceasefire between the Democratic Republic of the Congo and neighboring states
Congo	1	06/06/2003	01/09/2003	EU sends peacekeeping force to DRC in Operation Artemis
Uganda	0	10/07/1991	01/11/1993	Organisation of African Unity sends border guards and peacekeepers to Uganda's border with Rwanda
Burundi	0	27/04/2003	01/06/2004	African Union deploys peacekeeping force to war-torn Burundi
Burundi	1	01/06/2004	Unknown	UN peacekeeping mission in Burundi following civil war
Rwanda	1	29/03/1991	05/10/1993	OAU sends peacekeeping force to Rwanda

(Continued)

Table 7.2
(Continued)

Country	Number of Shaming	Start Date of Intervention	End Date of Intervention	Brief Description
Rwanda	2	30/07/1994	30/09/1994	United States provides humanitarian relief in Rwanda
Somalia	0	24/04/1992	09/03/1993	UN mission to monitor ceasefire in Somalia
Somalia	0	31/03/1993	31/03/1995	UN mission to Somalia to provide humanitarian relief and security
Angola	0	20/04/1995	20/07/1995	British peacekeeping troops provide assistance in Angola
Angola	0	30/06/1997	26/02/1999	UN mission established to monitor peace and reconciliation in Angola
Sudan	1	16/12/2004	24/12/2004	Germany provides logistical support to Sudan
Sudan	1	27/04/2005	Unknown	UN peacekeepers in Sudan
Iraq	25	03/04/1991	30/09/2003	UN in Iraq for peacekeeping on Kuwaiti border
Iraq	0	1995	Unknown	Not included in the merged IMI data but appear in Murdie and Peksen's dataset
Iraq	10	20/03/2003	Unknown	U.K. troops launch attack on possible missile sites in Iraq
Afghanistan	6	07/10/2001	08/12/2001	U.S. forces attack Taliban positions in Afghanistan
Tajikistan	0	04/12/1994	15/05/2000	UN in Tajikistan after civil war
Cambodia	0	01/10/1991	31/03/1992	UN in Cambodia
Cambodia	1	01/02/1992	30/09/1993	UN in Cambodia
Papua New Guinea	0	08/10/1994	19/10/1994	South Pacific peacekeeping force in Papua New Guinea

operation; then planning begins for the political, military, operational lo-
gistics, and finally the deployment.[5]

It should be clear by now that shaming activities and troop deployments on humanitarian missions necessitate a number of critical steps
that must precede any real action on the ground, thereby requiring a
considerable amount of time. Murdie and Peksen (2014) claim, however, that the decision to undertake humanitarian intervention is a
very time-sensitive and quick decision, usually happening very soon
after publicity of human rights abuses by human rights organizations
(HROs). To test the theoretical claim, they construct a statistical model
that evaluates the impact of shaming activities at time t on the intervention onset at the same time period. This theoretical claim and model
construction fails to allow for the fact that a majority of humanitarian
missions require considerable time for preparation and development.
This is why setting a proper causal time order that allows a reasonable
time lapse between shaming and intervention becomes very important,
ensuring that the former serves as a cause of the latter in statistical
evaluations.

REPLICATING MURDIE AND PEKSEN'S (2014) STUDY

Murdie and Peksen (2014, 225) invoke Hafner-Burton (2008) and Drezner
(2009)[6] as a group of scholars who "doubt the ability of human rights organizations to actually matter on realpolitik issues, like the foreign policy
decision of humanitarian intervention." And then Murdie and Peksen contend that the greater international exposure of human suffering through
HRO naming and shaming activities puts increased pressure on the international community and, consequently, triggers humanitarian military interventions. To test this contention, Murdie and Peksen build a rare event
logit model as follows:

$$Humanitarian\ interventions_{it} = \beta_1 + \beta_2 HRO\ shaming_{it} + \beta_3 human\ rights$$
$$abuses_{it-1}{}^7 + \beta_4 media\ exposure_{it}$$
$$+ \beta_5 state\ capacity_{it-1} + \beta_6 democracy_{it-1}$$
$$+ \beta_7 ethnic\ fractionalization_{it}{}^*$$
$$+ \beta_8 ethnic\ fractionalization\ squared_{it}{}^*$$
$$+ \beta_9 civil\ war_{it-1} + \beta_{10} oil\ producer_{it-1}{}^*$$
$$+ \beta_{11} economic\ sanctions_{it-1} + \beta_{12} genocide_{it-1}$$
$$+ \beta_{13} past\ years\ of\ humanitarian\ interventions_{it}$$
$$+ \beta_{14+k} region\ dummies_{it}{}^* + \varepsilon_2$$

*where variables with * are time invariant.*

To justify the causal time order between the independent and dependent
variables in the humanitarian intervention model, Murdie and Peksen put
forward a caveat that "to reduce the possibility of simultaneity bias and

make sure that the independent variables precede the dependent variable, we lag the right-hand side-control variables one year, except for our variable of IDEA-based Media Exposure, which is not lagged in order to correspond to the year of the IDEA-based HRO shaming variable in all models" (222). This justification guarantees that HRO shaming activities at time t have the potential to cause the onset of humanitarian military intervention at the same time point t.

Since Murdie and Peksen declare that "the country-year is the unit of analysis" (219), their model assumes that HRO shaming targeted at Guatemala in year 1997, as shown in Table 7.2, helped incite UN humanitarian intervention in that country in the same year. This causal timeline assumption about the predictor and the dependent variable is unfeasible because no time interval existed for naming and shaming to occur before the military intervention in Guatemala. According to the historical description of the International Military Intervention dataset, the original source of the dependent variable in the Murdie and Peksen study, the Guatemalan intervention began on the first day of January 1997 and lasted till the last day of May in the same year (Pickering and Kisangani 2009). Thus, it is impossible to imagine that the naming and shaming took place on the morning on January 1 and then UN intervention ensued on the afternoon of the same day. As noted earlier, this impossibility stems from the simple fact that military mobilization and deploying soldiers on the ground takes time to prepare, let alone the time required for political leaders to make war decisions. Another example is the UN intervention in Croatia that took place on January 15, 1996, according to the Murdie and Peksen data collection. Again, it is impractical to trace a reasonable causal timeline between possible HRO shaming activities and UN intervention in Croatia that happened in the same year.[8]

The important question is how to correct the erroneous cause and effect order in the Murdie and Peksen model. A quick, easy, and simple solution is to replace *HRO shaming*$_{it}$ with its lagged term—*HRO shaming*$_{it-1}$—to ensure that shaming serves as a potential cause of humanitarian interventions. Obviously, this is not a new strategy for fixing the causal time order, as previous literature of naming and shaming has commonly implemented it. For example, Hafner-Burton's (2008) study, which is consulted in the construction of the Murdie and Peksen model, assumes that a lagged term for shaming affects the degree of political terror. Murdie and Davis's (2012) work that is referenced in the 2014 Murdie and Peksen study[9] makes use of a lagged term of *HRO shaming*$_{it}$ instead of its original term. Interestingly, when Murdie and Peksen (2013) explore the impact of the same measure—human rights INGO activities—on economic sanctions, they also employ the HRO shaming variable at time $t-1$ over time t.

After having replaced *HRO shaming*$_{it}$ with *HRO shaming*$_{it-1}$ in the Murdie and Peksen model, I reevaluated the results reported in their Table 1

Table 7.3
Effects of HRO Shaming on Humanitarian Military Interventions: Murdie and Peksen 2014, Table 1, p. 223

Variables	HRO Shaming (Count)				HRO Shaming (Intensity)			
	Replicated	At t-1	Replicated	At t-1	Replicated	At t-1	Replicated	At t-1
	1	2	3	4	5	6	7	8
HRO shaming (count)$_{it}$	0.615*** (0.165)		0.664* (0.270)					
HRO shaming (count)$_{it-1}$		-0.112 (0.330)		-0.157 (0.531)				
HRO shaming (intensity)$_{it}$					0.340*** (0.074)		0.273** (0.106)	
HRO shaming (intensity)$_{it-1}$						-0.097 (0.091)		0.022 (0.197)
Human rights abuses$_{it-1}$	0.860** (0.272)	0.846** (0.277)	0.919*** (0.220)	0.800*** (0.207)	0.941*** (0.241)	0.832** (0.284)	0.963*** (0.208)	0.774*** (0.210)
Media exposure$_{it}$	0.458 (0.235)	0.739** (0.245)			0.445 (0.245)	0.729** (0.248)		
Negative news media coverage$_{it-1}$			-0.013 (0.068)	-0.001 (0.073)			-0.016 (0.065)	0.006 (0.068)
State capacity$_{it-1}$	-0.815*** (0.237)	-0.788*** (0.230)	-0.847*** (0.223)	-0.625*** (0.180)	-0.814*** (0.235)	-0.773*** (0.233)	-0.764*** (0.190)	-0.636*** (0.181)

(Continued)

Table 7.3
(Continued)

Variables	HRO Shaming (Count)				HRO Shaming (Intensity)			
	Replicated	At t–1	Replicated	At t–1	Replicated	At t–1	Replicated	At t–1
	1	2	3	4	5	6	7	8
$Democracy_{it-1}$	-0.026	-0.042	-0.026	-0.032	-0.026	-0.041	-0.021	-0.033
	(0.030)	(0.028)	(0.035)	(0.033)	(0.029)	(0.028)	(0.033)	(0.034)
$Ethnic$ $fractionalization_{it-1}$	-9.271**	-6.774**	-9.222*	-7.581*	-8.495**	-6.828*	-9.119*	-7.382
	(3.085)	(2.949)	(4.014)	(3.748)	(3.159)	(2.997)	(3.923)	(3.791)
$Ethnic$ $fractionalization$ $squared_{it-1}$	10.338**	7.327*	9.804*	7.715	9.818**	7.289*	10.046*	7.307
	(3.522)	(3.372)	(4.643)	(4.354)	(3.562)	(3.448)	(4.548)	(4.473)
$Civil\ war_{it-1}$	0.456	0.481	0.741	1.008	0.352	0.509	0.607	1.073
	(0.568)	(0.604)	(0.658)	(0.656)	(0.506)	(0.619)	(0.615)	(0.674)
$Oil\ producer_{it-1}$	-0.177	-0.054	0.202	0.075	-0.002	-0.095	0.230	0.061
	(0.607)	(0.465)	(0.687)	(0.651)	(0.544)	(0.465)	(0.707)	(0.654)
$Economic\ sanctions_{it-1}$	0.356	0.047	0.422	0.293	0.301	0.094	0.414	0.350
	(0.266)	(0.282)	(0.344)	(0.320)	(0.263)	(0.279)	(0.332)	(0.311)
$Genocide_{it-1}$	0.559	0.757	0.386	0.860*	0.668	0.819*	0.470	0.934
	(0.459)	(0.408)	(0.428)	(0.422)	(0.449)	(0.403)	(0.449)	(0.481)
$Past\ intervention_{it}$	-0.026*	-0.029*	-0.026	-0.028	-0.027*	-0.030**	-0.027	-0.030
	(0.012)	(0.012)	(0.018)	(0.018)	(0.013)	(0.012)	(0.019)	(0.018)

Constant	-14.134***	-15.495***	-11.362***	-9.095***	-14.391***	-15.231***	-10.714***	-9.102***
	(2.634)	(2.815)	(2.196)	(1.715)	(2.699)	(2.835)	(1.824)	(1.643)
Region dummies	Yes	Yes	Yes	Yes	Yes	Yes	Yes	Yes
N	1,933	1,829[a]	1,430	1,325[a]	1,933	1,829[a]	1,430	1,325[a]

Note: Robust standard errors are in parentheses.

[a] The total observations are smaller than the replicated ones due to the inclusion of a lagged term for shaming.

*p < 0.05 two-tailed tests

**p < 0.01 two-tailed tests

***p < 0.001 two-tailed tests

on page 223. Using Murdie and Peksen's Stata data and do-files,[10] the replication and the re-estimation are completed without any complications. My re-estimated results are shown in Table 7.3 in which the replicated estimates of Murdie and Peksen's *HRO shaming (count)* at time *t* are presented in columns 1 and 3; those with *HRO shaming (count)* at time *t–1* are in columns 2 and 4; those with *HRO shaming (intensity)* at time *t* are in columns 5 and 7; and those with *HRO shaming* (intensity) at time *t–1* are in columns 6 and 8. Surprisingly, the revised model specification in columns 2, 4, 6, and 8 yields no supporting evidence for the significant and positive effect of naming and shaming on humanitarian intervention. These two shaming variables at *t–1* not only lose statistical significance but also change their signs from positive to negative. Put differently, the new evidence does not lend credence to Murdie and Peksen's claims that "HRO shaming makes humanitarian intervention more likely even after controlling for several other covariates of intervention decisions. HRO activities appear to have a significant impact on the likelihood of military missions by IGOs" (215). The overall results of my replication indeed refute the main findings of the Murdie and Peksen study in which the cause and effect variables are set at the same time point *t*.

By running the conditional mixed-process (CMP) recursive regression models that are reported in Table 2, Murdie and Peksen also assert that the causal time order between shaming and intervention should be at the same time *t*. However, when scrutinizing the CMP models, I find very serious flaws, which indicate no proper causal impact of shaming on intervention at time *t*. The serious flaws come from a gap between the theoretical justification the authors make for the choice of their CMP model and what they reported in Table 2 on page 224 (i.e., how they actually executed their model in Stata to obtain the estimates). While the estimation problems related to Murdie and Peksen's CMP system are too serious to fix, I lay out three issues for the purposes of this study.

First, in footnote 13 of their article, Murdie and Peksen assert that "the CMP fits the equations with clearly defined stages: X [e.g., Human rights abuses, Media exposure, etc.] can be a modeled determinant of Z [i.e., HRO Shaming at time *t*] in the first equation, and Z [i.e., HRO Shaming at time *t*] can be a determinant of Y [i.e., Humanitarian Intervention at time *t*] in the second equation. But Y cannot be a modeled determinant of X or Z." According to the Stata do-file posted on the first author's website, they issue the following command lines to produce the results of CMP Model 1 in Table 2:

```
cmp (shamingcountDV = lagPTStarget lnreportcount hrfilled lagpolity2
lagpoplog lagtradelog lagincidence lamerica ssafrica eeurop nafrme)
(humonset2 = humanrightsNGO2govnoposmgold2 lagPTStarget
lnreportcount laglncinc lagpolity2 ethfrac ethfracsq lagincidence lagoil
```

laghumsanction laggenocidepresence humonsetyears lamerica ssafrica eeurop nafrme) if western==0, nolr ind ($cmp_cont $cmp_probit) cluster(ccode)

Note that in Murdie and Peksen's Stata *data* file, I find that shamingcountDV is a one-year lagged term for humanrightsNGO2govnoposmgold2.

When closely analyzing Murdie and Peksen's Stata data and do-file, I find that the first model in the first parentheses is constructed as follows:

shamingcountDV at time *t*–1 = f (lagPTStarget at time *t*–1, **lnreportcount at time *t*, hrfilled at time *t*,** *etc.)*

And the second model is built as follows:

humonset2 at time t = f (humanrightsNGO2govnoposmgold2 at time t, lagPTStarget at time t–1, etc.)

In the first model, Murdie and Peksen let the second and third predictors at time *t* determine the outcome variable, **shamingcountDV at time *t*–1.** This means that **lnreportcount at time *t*** (i.e., media exposure) that will take place in the future, say 2001, serves as a predictor of **shamingcountDV at time *t*–1** (i.e., HRO shaming) that occurs in the present time, say 2000. Simply put, the next year events cause the current year events—effect occurs before cause. Because this model construction is not consistent with what they theoretically claim in footnote 13 and because the causal time order does not make sense at all, the results that they reported in Table 2 are erroneous.

Murdie and Peksen assert that the construction of the first model "[followed] the earlier research on the determinants of HRO shaming (Hafner-Burton and Ron 2013; Hill, Moore, and Mukherjee 2013; Ron, Ramos, and Rodgers 2005)" (225). However, I find that none of these three previous studies theoretically or empirically justifies the setting of predictors at time *t* and the outcome variable at time *t*–1. Despite the fact that researchers understand that cause always precedes effect, Murdie and Peksen let effect precede cause in their first model.

Second, according to Murdie and Peksen's theoretical claim, the dependent variable from the first equation in their CMP system, *HRO shaming at time t*, serves as the main predictor of the dependent variable, *humanitarian intervention at time t*, in the second equation. This theoretical claim can be expressed as follows:

First equation: **HRO shaming at time *t*** = f (predictors)
Second equation: *Humanitarian intervention at time t* = f (**HRO shaming at time *t*** and control variables)

But, when carefully examining Murdie and Peksen's Stata do-file, they build their model differently as follows:

First equation: **shamingcountDV at time *t*–1** = f (predictors)
Second equation: humonset2 at time *t* = f (**humanrightsNGO2 govnoposmgold2 at time *t*** and control variables)

Note that the dependent variable, **shamingcountDV at time *t*–1**, in the first equation is not the same as the main predictor, **humanrightsNGO2govnoposmgold2 at time *t*,** in the second equation. Note also that the two dependent variables are not set at the same time period *t*; instead, they put the first dependent variable at time *t*–1 and the second one at time *t*. (In Murdie and Peksen's Stata *data* file, I find that **shamingcountDV** is a one-year lagged term for **humanrightsNGO2govnoposmgold2.**) The Stata do-file clearly reveals that Murdie and Peksen's data analysis went wrong so that their results reported in Table 2 cannot be valid.

What would happen if I, as Murdie and Peksen theoretically claimed, include **humanrightsNGO2govnoposmgold2 at time *t*** as the dependent variable in the first equation in place of **shamingcountDV at time *t*–1**? The revised CMP system should be as follows:

First equation: **humanrightsNGO2govnoposmgold2 at time *t*** = f (predictors)
First equation: humonset2 at time *t* = f (**humanrightsNGO2govnoposm gold2 at time *t*** and control variables)

My result shows that the replacement causes the significance of their main variable—*human rights abuses* denoted as lagPTStarget in the Stata do-file—in the first equation to disappear (coefficient: 0.026, standard error: 0.022, and *p* value: 0.228). This means that there is no justification for the CMP modeling due to the breakdown of the first equation.

What would happen if I set **lnreportcount at time *t*–1** (i.e., media exposure) and **hrfilled at time *t*–1** (i.e., human rights INGOs) in the first equation, and **humanrightsNGO2govnoposmgold2 at time *t*–1** (which is the same as **shamingcountDV at time *t*–1**) in the second equation? These adjustments yield to the following equations:

First equation: shamingcountDV at time *t*–1 = f (lagPTStarget at time *t*–1, **lnreportcount at time *t*–1, hrfilled at time *t*–1,** etc.)
Second equation: humonset2 at time *t* = f (**humanrightsNGO2gov noposmgold2 at time *t*–1** and control variables)

These adjustments lead to no significance on the main variable—*human rights abuses*—in the first equation, thereby nullifying the rationale for introducing the CMP system as an additional diagnostic test on causality.

When I set all predictors at time *t*–2 in the first equation and the first predictor at time *t*–1 in the second equation, its main variable—*human rights abuses*—in the first equation again emerges as no significant and positive predictor. The revised CMP system that is used for this estimation is as follows:

First equation: shamingcountDV at time t–1 = f (**lagPTStarget at time t–2, lnreportcount at time t–2, hrfilled at time t–2, etc.**)
Second equation: humonset2 at time t = f (**humanrightsNGO2gov noposmgold2 at time t–1** and control variables)

Table 7.4 displays the full estimated results that are obtained from the preceding equations.

Third, it is important to note that the CMP works only with models built on the normal distribution, because that distribution has a natural multidimensional generalization, which makes it suited for multi-equation

Table 7.4
Conditional Mixed-Process Recursive Regression: Murdie and Peksen 2014, Table 2, p. 224

Variables	HRO Shaming (Count)	
	Replicated	Further Lagged
DV: Humanitarian intervention$_{it}$		
HRO shaming (count)$_{it}$	0.353***	
	(0.081)	
HRO shaming (count)$_{it-1}$		0.004
		(0.035)
Human rights abuses$_{it-1}$	0.448***	0.447***
	(0.112)	(0.117)
Media exposure$_{it}$	0.233*	0.354***
	(0.105)	(0.105)
State capacity$_{it-1}$	−0.455***	−0.450***
	(0.104)	(0.100)
Democracy$_{it-1}$	−0.008	−0.012
	(0.013)	(0.012)
Ethnic fractionalization$_{it-1}$	−4.440**	−3.497**
	(1.351)	(1.283)
Ethnic fractionalization squared$_{it-1}$	4.945**	3.757**
	(1.535)	(1.444)
Civil war$_{it-1}$	0.252	0.232
	(0.236)	(0.250)
Oil producer$_{it-1}$	−0.082	−0.100
	(0.238)	(0.201)

(Continued)

Table 7.4
(Continued)

Variables	HRO Shaming (Count)	
	Replicated	Further Lagged
Economic sanctions$_{it-1}$	0.184	0.046
	(0.130)	(0.135)
Genocide$_{it-1}$	0.246	0.415*
	(0.220)	(0.196)
Past intervention$_{it}$	−0.013*	−0.014**
	(0.005)	(0.005)
Constant	−7.711***	−8.313***
	(1.205)	(1.231)
Region dummies	Yes	Yes
DV: HRO shaming$_{it-1}$		
Human rights abuses$_{it-1}$	0.049*	
	(0.023)	
Human rights abuses$_{it-2}$		0.024
		(0.021)
Media exposure$_{it}$	0.092***	
	(0.024)	
Media exposure$_{it-2}$		0.087***
		(0.018)
Human rights INGOs$_{it}$	−0.002	
	(0.002)	
Human rights INGOs$_{it-2}$		−0.003*
		(0.002)
Democracy$_{it-1}$	−0.005	
	(0.007)	
Democracy$_{it-2}$		−0.005
		(0.006)
Population$_{it-1}$	0.050	
	(0.029)	
Population$_{it-2}$		0.052*
		(0.024)
Economic openness$_{it-1}$	0.076*	
	(0.033)	
Economic openness$_{it-2}$		0.045
		(0.030)

	HRO Shaming (Count)	
Variables	Replicated	Further Lagged
Civil war$_{it-1}$	0.030	
	(0.092)	
Civil war$_{it-2}$		0.076
		(0.065)
Constant	−1.504***	−1.337***
	(0.404)	(0.369)
Region dummies	Yes	Yes
N	1,933	1,829[a]

Note: Robust standard errors are in parentheses.

[a] The total observations are smaller than the replicated ones due to the inclusion of further lagged terms.

*$p < 0.05$ two-tailed tests

**$p < 0.01$ two-tailed tests

***$p < 0.001$ two-tailed tests

models (Roodman 2011). To quote from Help CMP in Stata, "The choices, all generalized linear models with a Gaussian error distribution, are: continuous and unbounded (the classical linear regression model), tobit (left-, right-, or bi-censored), interval-censored, probit, ordered probit, multinomial probit, and rank-ordered probit." However, one of Murdie and Peksen's dependent variables is a count measure (i.e., the total number of shaming events), so it does not take the normal distribution but rather the negative binomial distribution. When I closely examine Murdie and Peksen's do-file, I notice that they ran the CMP model by treating the count measure as if it had the normal distribution (their Stata command was $cmp_cont). As is well known, there is a huge estimation difference between OLS (ordinary least squares) and negative binomial regression. The underlying probability density function of an OLS regression model is the Gaussian or normal distribution, with a variance of 1 and an identity link—the mean and linear predictor are the same. Yet, because the variance of count data varies with the value of the mean, a negative binomial regression model produces the coefficients and standard errors that are very different from OLS estimates. Accordingly, the choice of an estimation technique likely yields very different estimates and thus inferences (see Hardin and Hilbe 2012; Hilbe 2013). Murdie and Peksen's incorrect estimation strategy gave them the biased results that they reported in Table 2. In addition, I notice even though the Stata log-file issued several error messages after the executions of their CMP command lines, Murdie and Peksen ignored them and reported the results anyway. An example of this error message is, "Warning: regressor matrix for humonset2 equation appears ill-conditioned. (Condition number = 857.02814.)"

In short, the CMP estimated results that Murdie and Peksen reported in their article cannot be valid due to the incorrect model specifications, and thus they fail to support their claim that shaming and intervention should be set at the same time point t.

CONCLUSION

When researchers confront contradictory findings in empirical studies, it becomes exceedingly difficult to draw conclusions that will help both further study and inform policy decision-making. The existing studies of naming and shaming have bewildered scholars and policy makers for an obvious reason. While some studies show no effectiveness of naming and shaming by human rights organizations, others appear to uphold the usefulness of human rights advocacy organizations. By dissecting the estimated results in Tables 1 and 2 in Murdie and Peksen's (2014) study, I have attempted to trace the origin of the inconsistent findings. I note that Murdie and Peksen's model contains a critical error related to causal time order between the predictor (shaming) and the outcome variable (intervention). Murdie and Peksen's causal timeline is incorrectly specified in their model: the onset of humanitarian intervention in January 1991 was, for instance, assumed to be caused by shaming activities that would happen later in that year, say November—11 months later. For causality to be supported, this ordering is problematic. After I rectify Murdie and Peksen's model specification, I produce results that move away from Murdie and Peksen's main findings. Simply put, my study provides new evidence to add to the skepticism regarding the human rights–related consequences of shaming on the foreign governments that might intervene in an effort to help.

This study underlines the importance of replication projects. Consistent with the epigraphs from James (2003) and Park and Colaresi (2014), this study makes a meaningful contribution to the literature on naming and shaming. The replication emphasizes that the accurate analysis of empirical research—including a proper causal timeline—is a critical step in conducting rigorous empirical work and, therefore, in avoiding incorrect inferences and conclusions. In doing so, this research zeroes in on the cause of contradicting empirical findings in existing studies and uncovers no effective role of human rights organizations in influencing the likelihood of an international response to human rights atrocities. If replication was not encouraged in the discipline, the relationship between shaming and intervention would remain muddled. I hope that my study gives scholars and students the incentive to take replication projects seriously as a way to advance scientific progress.

NOTES

1. χ^2 is an incorrect statistic for the HRO shaming OLS regression model. It should have been denoted as an F-test in their Granger Causality Test table.

2. I am grateful to an anonymous reviewer who helped me better understand the complexity of NGOs activities.

3. Murdie and Peksen's Model 1 in Table 1 on page 223 uses 1,933 observations, of which 41 country-years (2.12%) are recorded as the onsets of humanitarian military intervention. (Among the 41 country-years, 18 (44%) show a record of shaming activities). Re-creating the 41 cases based on the Merged International Military Intervention (IMI) dataset is challenging for two reasons (see https://www.k-state.edu/polsci/intervention/, accessed on October 1). First, there are three cases that appear in Murdie and Peksen's dataset that I am unable to locate in the IMI dataset. Second, there are multiple events per case in the IMI dataset, so I have to use my best guess on which event is represented in the Murdie and Peksen dataset. The monthly frequency of the 41 intervention onsets is as follows: 2 in January, 1 in February, 4 in March, 8 in April, 3 in June, 6 in July, 2 in August, 3 in September, 4 in October, 1 in November, 4 in December, and 3 for unknown. Because the dates of the shaming events are not available to the public, I am unable to determine how many of the 41 interventions occurred prior to the shaming activities.

4. See http://www.un.org/en/peacekeeping/issues/military.shtml.

5. See http://www.un.org/en/peacekeeping/operations/newoperation.shtml.

6. Hafner-Burton (2008) designs three original indicators of naming and shaming (i.e., NGOs, the news media, and the UN) and creates a global index by combining all the three sources. My replication of Hafner-Burton yields findings consistent with the original study: the shaming activities by NGOs are positively, not negatively, associated with an increase of political terror in countries in the spotlight; the media and the UN, as well as the global index, have no bearing on discouraging human rights violations. Although Drezner (2009) is introduced as one of the two counter examples by Murdie and Peksen, I did not replicate it because it mainly takes a qualitative approach and because it did not focus on NGOs shaming. In fact, Drezner (2009) only mentions shaming in passing.

7. When Murdie and Peksen's human rights abuse variable is replaced with Fariss's (2014) measure, the latter achieves significance, which is consistent with the effect of the former. The replacement does not substantively alter the effect of Murdie and Peksen's shaming variable (for more information on human rights abuse, see Kim and Sikkink 2010; Kim and Sharman 2014).

8. There were actually no shaming activities that took place before the January intervention in Croatia, which is inconsistent with Murdie and Peksen's claim that HRO shaming is associated with an increased risk of intervention.

9. The exact wording was that "to assess the impact of HRO shaming on the likelihood of humanitarian interventions, we use two different measures, HRO Shaming (count) and HRO Shaming (intensity)" (Murdie and Davis 2012; 2014, 220).

10. Available through the website of Amanda Murdie at http://www.amandamurdie.org/research.html.

REFERENCES

Büthe, Tim. 2002. "Taking Temporality Seriously." *American Political Science Review* 96(3): 481–493.

Davis, James. 1985. *The Logic of Causal Order*. Thousand Oaks, CA: Sage.

Drezner, Daniel W. 2009. *All Politics Is Global*. Princeton, NJ: Princeton University Press.

Fariss, Christopher. 2014. "Respect for Human Rights Has Improved over Time." *American Political Science Review* 108(2): 297–318.

Franklin, James. 2008. "Shame on You." *International Studies Quarterly* 52(1): 187–211.

Hafner-Burton, Emilie. 2008. "Sticks and Stones." *International Organization* 62(4): 689–716.

Hafner-Burton, Emilie, and James Ron. 2013. "The Latin Bias: Regions, the Anglo-American Media, and Human Rights." *International Studies Quarterly.* 57(3): 474-91.

Hardin, James and Joseph Hilbe. 2012. *Generalized Linear Models and Extensions.* College Station, TX: Stata Press.

Hilbe, Joseph. 2013. *Modeling Count Data*. New York: Cambridge University Press.

Hill, Daniel, Will H. Moore, and Bumba Mukherjee. 2013. "Information Politics Versus Organizational Incentives: When Are Amnesty International's "Naming and Shaming" reports biased?" *International Studies Quarterly* 57(2): 219–232.

Holland, Paul. 1986. "Statistics and Causal Inference." *Journal of the American Statistical Association* 81(396): 945–960.

James, Patrick. 2003. "Replication Policies and Practices at International Studies Quarterly." *International Studies Perspectives* 4(1): 85–88.

Kim, Hun Joon and Jason Sharman. 2014. "Account and Accountability: Corruption, Human Rights, and the Individual Accountability Norm." *International Organization* 68(2): 417–448.

Kim, Hun Joon and Kathryn Sikkink. 2010. "Explaining the Deterrence Effect of Human Rights Prosecutions for Transitional Countries." *International Studies Quarterly* 54(4): 939–963.

Murdie, Amanda and David Davis. 2012. "Shaming and Blaming: Using Events Data to Assess the Impact of Human Rights INGOs." *International Studies Quarterly* 56(1): 1–16.

Murdie, Amanda and Dursun Peksen. 2013. "The Impact of Human Rights INGO Activities on Economic Sanctions." *Review of International Organizations* 8(1): 33–53.

Murdie, Amanda and Dursun Peksen. 2014. "The Impact of Human Rights INGO Shaming on Humanitarian Interventions." *Journal of Politics* 76(1): 215–228.

Park, Johann and Michael Colaresi. 2014. "Safe across the Border." *International Studies Quarterly* 58(1): 118–125.

Pickering, Jeffrey and Emizet Kisangani. 2009. "The International Military Intervention Data Set." *Journal of Peace Research* 46(4): 589–600.

Ron, James, Howard Ramos, and Kathleen Rodgers. 2005. "Transnational Information Politics." *International Studies Quarterly* 49(3): 557–587.

Roodman, David. 2011. "Fitting Fully Observed Recursive Mixed-Process Models with cmp." *Stata Journal* 11(2): 159–206.

CHAPTER 8

Preferential Trade Agreements and Human Rights Abusers

Whether human rights treaties provide the international community with an effective enforcement mechanism for penalizing human rights abusers is a controversial issue.[1] More than 10 years ago, scholars began to assert that preferential trade agreements (PTAs) that contain clauses allowing for a reduction of economic benefits to human rights abusers can, in some important instances, help improve the human rights conditions in beneficiary countries. For example, Hafner-Burton (2005) argued for the beneficial effect of PTAs with hard human rights standards on improvement of human rights conditions. However, by introducing genetic matching techniques, Spilker and Böhmelt (2013) dispute the claims of scholars, arguing that enforceable trade conditionality can help reduce government repression. Spilker and Böhmelt point out the potentially critical failure of the statistical modeling in previous studies, which ignore the fact that countries tend to agree on hard human rights standards in PTAs only when they are already willing to show their respect for human rights. To take this point into account, Spilker and Böhmelt (2013) employ a new methodological approach—genetic matching techniques—that fits their new data on PTAs and political repression for the years 1976/1977–2009. Spilker and Böhmelt's statistical analysis shows that PTA hard law has little to do with human rights violations, thus discrediting the claim of beneficial effects resulting from PTAs.

By reexamining Spilker and Böhmelt's matched sample data and results, this comment contributes to the ongoing debate. I argue that the repression variable in the Spilker and Böhmelt dataset does not accurately capture the degree of human rights violations across countries and times. Their operationalization of the repression variable relies on two data sources: Poe and Tate's (1994) physical integrity rights and Gibney,

Cornett, and Wood's (2005, 2011) Political Terror Scale. Combined, these two sources suggest a misleading and inaccurate trend that human rights practices, despite the global promotion of improved human rights, have been essentially constant since the mid-1970s. This inaccuracy is due mainly to the failure to account for the changing standard of accountability in human rights reports over time, as explained in detail in recent studies (see Fariss 2014, forthcoming; Schnakenberg and Fariss 2014). Clark and Sikkink (2013, 543) express a similar reservation and concern: "Recognizing how information effects accrue due to variation in the availability and precision of country-specific information should lead researchers to interpret study results with care." I argue that the use of this imprecise repression measure leads Spilker and Böhmelt to produce the erroneous inference and conclusion regarding the relationship between PTA hard law and the frequency of human rights violations. Of course, in their defense, Spilker and Böhmelt are not alone. They stand alongside a generation of other human rights scholars who have depended on those same sources of imperfect data because they were the best quantifiable series available at the time of their writing.

In sum, the use of the inaccurate measure of human rights leads to measurement error in Spilker and Böhmelt's dependent variable. After properly addressing the measurement error related to existing human rights data sources, Fariss (2014) provides a new dataset, which is a collection of unbiased estimates of political repression. Fariss's new data indicates that state repression practices have, on average, declined over time. Fariss's criticism of previous human rights measures rests on the grounds that they suffer from temporal bias as a result of improved information collection and more heightened scrutiny of human rights violations over time. After incorporating information from 13 different data sources, Fariss uses a Bayesian measurement model to account for this temporal bias.[2] When I replace Spilker and Böhmelt's repression variable with Fariss's new, unbiased measure, my replication indicates that PTA hard law is statistically significant at the 0.001 level, thereby corroborating what Hafner-Burton (2005) reported 10 years ago.

REPLICATING SPILKER AND BÖHMELT'S (2013) MODEL WITH MATCHED SAMPLE

After following Hafner-Burton's (2005) research design as closely as possible, Spilker and Böhmelt (2013) created their own dataset for 174 countries during the period 1976–2009. The total number of observations in this dataset comes to 4,117 when 249 PTAs are gathered and operationalized. These 249 PTAs were collected by examining the content of all formal PTA contracts which include treaties, protocols, and other forms of amendments. Based on Hafner-Burton's (2005, 618) definition, Spilker and

Böhmelt count PTA hard laws in cases where a PTA contract includes "the explicit adoption of human rights language and principles, and whether the benefits accorded by the contract formally depend on those principles (benefits can be withheld for violation)." In contrast, when a PTA contract does not contain such a specific human rights clause, it is classified as PTA soft law.

Despite some discrepancies between their data and Hafner-Burton's original collection, Spilker and Böhmelt successfully replicate Hafner-Burton's Table 2 on page 619 with respect to the significance and the causal sign of the main two variables of interest—PTA hard and soft law. Spilker and Böhmelt's Table 3 on page 354 displays the replicated results, demonstrating that PTA hard law is negatively associated with the violation of human rights, while PTA soft law is positively correlated. Thanks to their replication data and programs posted online,[3] my replication of Spilker and Böhmelt's Table 3 comes out without any complications, which is not reported in this comment because it is not my primary results of interest.

After completing the necessary groundwork to produce the replicated estimates of Hafner-Burton's study, Spilker and Böhmelt test their main theoretical contention that "countries that agree to include hard human rights standards in their PTAs should differ in important and predictable ways from those countries that do not want to include these standards in their PTAs" (353). Their two illustrative examples are the European Union's treaty with Chile in 2003 that added hard human rights standards compared with Egypt in the same year that did not include any reference to human rights at all. In the former case, any (major) human rights violations are unlikely to emerge as a major issue because both the EU and Chile are committed to democratic values. Yet, in the latter case, due to its poor track record on human rights, Egypt's PTA was not contingent on human rights commitments in order to avoid losing any gains from trade or begetting any reputational costs. To translate this theoretical contention into statistical modeling, Spilker and Böhmelt introduce genetic one-to-one matching with replacement, a method borrowed from Diamond and Sekhon (2013). The matching approach narrows Spilker and Böhmelt's sample size to 2,754 from their 4,117 total observations. After performing an analysis of ordered logit models that rely on the matched sample data in which the dependent variable—human rights violations—is ordinal on a scale of 1 to 5, Spilker and Böhmelt summarize their results in Table 4 on page 357.[4]

Using the same matching technique that Spilker and Böhmelt described in their article and statistical code, I am successfully able to reproduce results that mirror theirs. I report my replicated estimates in Models 1–3 in Table 8.1, which is identical to those in Models 4–6 of Spilker and Böhmelt's Table 4. I do not replicate Spilker and Böhmelt's Model 7 for a statistical reason that I will return to momentarily. For more precise

Table 8.1 Hard Law PTAs and Human Rights: Matched Sample Spilker and Böhmelt 2013, Models 4–6, Table 4, p. 357

Variable	Spilker and Böhmelt's Political Repression Scores						Fariss's Latent Human Rights Protection Scores		
	Ordered Logit (ologit)						Prais-Winsten Regression (xtpcse with ar(1))		
	Model 1	Model 2	Model 3	Model 4	Model 5	Model 6	Model 7	Model 8	Model 9
PTA hard law	-0.058	-0.123	-0.041	-0.221	-0.225	-0.113	0.142***	0.164***	0.162***
	(0.250)	(0.214)	(0.212)	(0.242)	(0.215)	(0.213)	(0.041)	(0.037)	(0.037)
Human rights ratification		0.734***			0.720***			-0.010	
		(0.156)			(0.143)			(0.017)	
Population density		0.001	0.001		0.001	0.001		-0.001***	-0.001***
		(0.001)	(0.001)		(0.001)	(0.001)		(0.000)	(0.000)
Political stability		-0.013**	-0.013**		-0.012**	-0.012**		0.008***	0.008***
		(0.006)	(0.006)		(0.006)	(0.006)		(0.001)	(0.001)
Democracy		-0.124***	-0.088***		-0.128***	-0.093***		0.032***	0.032***
		(0.016)	(0.016)		(0.016)	(0.016)		(0.003)	(0.003)
GDP per capita		-0.472***	-0.461***		-0.503***	-0.492***		0.305***	0.305***
		(0.111)	(0.115)		(0.104)	(0.108)		(0.022)	(0.022)
Trade		-0.761***	-0.661***		-0.977***	-0.875***		0.296***	0.294***
		(0.236)	(0.238)		(0.227)	(0.218)		(0.042)	(0.042)
Constant							0.208***	-3.462***	-3.464***
							(0.051)	(0.203)	(0.203)
Observations	2,754	2,754	2,754	2,094	2,094	2,094	2,096	2,096	2,096
Log pseudolikelihood	-4,094.484	-3,328.300	-3,408.573	-3,125.285	-2,486.026	-2,546.255	n/a	n/a	n/a
Wald chi^2	0.05	160.41***	102.05***	0.83	211.01***	173.38***	12.31***	1,031.88***	996.36***

Notes: Robust and panel-corrected standard errors are in parentheses. n/a: not applicable.

*p < .10 two-tailed tests

**p < .05 two-tailed tests

***p < .01 two-tailed tests

analysis, Models 4–6 in my table replicate the previous three models (i.e., Models 1–3) after dropping 660 duplicated observations that I found in Spilker and Böhmelt's dataset. The exclusion of the duplicated observations does not alter the main finding of Spilker and Böhmelt: PTA hard law is an insignificant predictor.

I now introduce Fariss's new, unbiased measure in order to replicate Models 4–6 of Spilker and Böhmelt's table. The use of the Fariss measure as the dependent variable requires a change of the estimation method from ordered logit to a Prais-Winsten regression model. The change is due to the fact that Fariss variable is a continuous, rather than an ordinal, measure. Numerous political science studies prescribe the Prais-Winsten regression as an appropriate estimation method, when their dependent variable is continuous and when the data structure is cross-national, time-series (e.g., Jensen 2003; Barry, Clay, and Flynn 2013). I choose the same approach to complete my replication.[5] Because the unit of analysis is the country-year, the matched sample data requires correction for serial correlation and heteroskedasticity.[6] The Prais-Winsten regression (i.e., panel-corrected standard errors (PCSEs) with AR(1)) remedies the two statistical issues.[7]

After replacing Spilker and Böhmelt's political repression variable with the new measure provided by Fariss, I replicate Models 4–6 in Table 8.1 and report coefficients and standard errors in Models 7–9. I find compelling new evidence that PTA hard law is significantly different from zero across models: it is statistically significant at the 0.001 level with a positive sign. This result unarguably corroborates the finding of other researchers, including Hafner-Burton (2005, 607), who contend that "state commitment to PTAs supplying hard human rights standards does systematically produce improvement in human rights behaviors after commitment." In contrast, this result calls into question Spilker and Böhmelt's empirical claim that PTA hard law does not help ameliorate human rights abuses.

CONCLUSION

This comment contributes to the ongoing debate regarding the effect of human rights treaties on government repression. I replicate Spilker and Böhmelt's (2013) empirical claim on the ineffectiveness of PTA hard law and provide evidence that their main finding does not hold when their repression variable is replaced with Fariss's new, unbiased measure. As previously shown in other studies examining the relationship between human rights treaties and repression, PTA hard law indeed produces a dampening effect on the infringement of human rights because it provides human rights abusers with an economic incentive to better observe and comport to international norms. It is evident that the arrival of the Fariss measure advances our scientific knowledge on human rights politics. It is time for scholars, policy makers, and activists to update the information on the powerful determinant—PTA hard law—of human rights violations.

NOTES

1. The controversial issue regarding human rights treaties stems from a large and ongoing debate related to how economic globalization impacts human rights. Existing studies look at various aspects of globalization such as trade, foreign direct investment flows, economic institutions, and international organizations. Yet their empirical findings are mixed partly due to a different sample of countries and years (see Hafner-Burton 2005).

2. Because Fariss's measure has been discussed numerous times with regard to validity and reliability (e.g., Fariss 2014, forthcoming; Schnakenberg and Fariss 2014), I do not discuss it in detail to save space.

3. See http://link.springer.com/article/10.1007/s11558-012-9155-8.

4. Following Spilker and Böhmelt's step, I use the significance tests at the 0.10, 0.05, and 0.05 levels. However, the use of higher significance levels does not change the main findings.

5. The change of the estimation method makes it unnecessary to replicate Spilker and Böhmelt's Model 7 in Table 4 in which Beck, Katz, and Tucker's (1998) cubic splines are controlled for as an additional robustness check. Note that Beck et al.'s cubic splines are not applicable to Fariss's continuous measure. When the cubic splines are removed from Model 7, the estimates become the same as those in Model 5.

6. I perform a likelihood-ratio test for heteroskedasticity and the Wooldridge test for autocorrelation. The null hypothesis of the former test is no heteroskedasticity and that of the latter test is no first-order correlation (Wooldridge 2002; Drukker 2003). The test results lead me to reject the null hypotheses and thus require correction for both panel heteroskedasticity and temporally correlated errors.

7. The Stata command is xtpcse with two options: pairwise and corr(ar1).

REFERENCES

Barry, Colin, Chad Clay, and Michael Flynn. 2013. "Avoiding the Spotlight." *International Studies Quarterly* 57(3): 532–544.

Beck, Nathaniel, Jonathan N. Katz, and Richard Tucker. 1998. "Taking Time Seriously: Time-Series-Cross-Section Analysis with a Binary Dependent Variable." *American Journal of Political Science.* 42(4): 1260–1288

Clark, Ann and Kathryn Sikkink. 2013. "Information Effects and Human Rights Data." *Human Rights Quarterly* 35(3): 539–568.

Diamond, Alexis and Jasjeet Sekhon. 2013. "Genetic Matching for Estimating Causal Effects." *Review of Economics and Statistics* 95(3): 932–945.

Drukker, David. 2003. "Testing for Serial Correlation in Linear Panel-Data Models." *Stata Journal* 3(2): 168–177.

Fariss, Christopher. 2014. "Respect for Human Rights Has Improved over Time." *American Political Science Review* 108(2): 297–318.

Fariss, Christopher. 2018. "The Changing Standard of Accountability and the Positive Relationship between Human Rights Treaty Ratification and Compliance." *British Journal of Political Science* 48(1): 239–271.

Gibney, Marl, Linda Cornett, and Reed Wood. 2005. "Political Terror Scale, 1976–2002." http://www.politicalterrorscale.org/.

Gibney, Marl, Linda Cornett, and Reed Wood. 2011. "Political Terror Scale, 1976–2009." http://www.politicalterrorscale.org/.

Hafner-Burton, Emilie. 2005. "Trading Human Rights." *International Organization* 59(3): 593–629.

Jensen, Nathan. 2003. "Democratic Governance and Multinational Corporations." *International Organization* 57(3): 587–616.

Poe, Steven and Neal Tate. 1994. "Repression of Human Rights to Personal Integrity in the 1980s." *American Political Science Review* 88(4): 853–872.

Schnakenberg, Keith and Christopher Fariss. 2014. "Dynamic Patterns of Human Rights Practices." *Political Science Research and Methods* 2(1): 1–31.

Spilker, Gabriele and Tobias Böhmelt. 2013. "The Impact of Preferential Trade Agreements on Governmental Repression Revisited." *Review of International Organizations* 8(3): 343–361.

Wooldridge, Jeffrey. 2002. *Econometric Analysis of Cross Section and Panel Data*. Cambridge, MA: MIT Press.

CHAPTER 9

Leaders' Education, Democracy, and Use of Torture

Education shall be directed to the full development of the human personality and to the strengthening of respect for human rights and fundamental freedoms. (Universal Declaration of Human Rights, 1948, Article 26)

No one shall be subjected to torture or to cruel, inhuman or degrading treatment or punishment. (Universal Declaration of Human Rights, 1948, Article 5)

Torture has been a serious political issue throughout human history, and it generally "refers to the purposeful inflicting of extreme pain, whether mental or physical, by government officials or by private individuals at the instigation of government officials" (Cingranelli and Richards 1999, 408).[1] It is an unfortunate reality that the use of torture persists in most countries despite legal prohibitions enumerated in many national constitutions and in their stated commitment to the tenets of the United Nations Convention against Torture. Nonetheless, we have observed that some countries, such as Spain and Malaysia, have managed to bring an end to the political use of torture, while the majority of other countries have not. Why does the cessation of political torture differ so widely between countries? Under what conditions are countries willing to terminate the use of torture? To answer these questions, existing literature focuses heavily on the role of democratic institutions that are conceived as providing a better prevention mechanism against the inhumanity of torture practices (see Rejali 2007; Conrad and Moore 2010; P. Miller 2011; Conrad et al. Forthcoming).

This study contributes to the growing empirical literature on torture by examining how the involvement in higher education might decrease the likelihood of a government leader engaging in the practice of torture. In doing so, I argue that higher education plays an effective role in stopping the use of torture by governments. In an attempt to offer a causal framework as to how best to end the practice of torture, I begin with the theoretical debate about individuals versus institutions. I then proceed by underlining the significance of highly educated leaders capable of stopping torture practices, under the assumption that political institutions are being held constant. Results from statistical models show evidence that leaders with a college or graduate degree are, in the absence of violent dissent, more likely to stop the torture than those with less than a college education. When I examine the substantive effects of educated leaders and political institutions such as democracy and freedom of expression, I find evidence that the likelihood of terminating the use of torture becomes largest when leaders with a graduate education are responsible for national security. More specifically, leaders with a college degree, compared to with less than college education, have a 668,360 percent greater probability of terminating the use of torture. When the level of democracy increases by one unit, a country is approximately 2 percent more likely to stop the torture.

In the next section, I offer a theoretical explanation as to why more educated leaders are better equipped to enact policies that lead to terminating torture practices. The research design then follows to explain how to test the theoretical claim. I present empirical results after the research design and consequently provide concluding remarks.

WHY DO MORE EDUCATED LEADERS END THE PRACTICE OF TORTURE?

Torture is uncivilized, often favors the guilty, and is an immoral practice for a civilized government (Beccaria 2009). For these reasons, many nation-states show no hesitation in publicly denouncing the inhumane nature of torture. Even as it applies to suspected criminals and terrorists, it is still generally regarded as an illegitimate practice. It is, nonetheless, true that the brutality of torture is found in almost every corner of the contemporary world (Kearns 2015). What explains this apparent paradox between the strong public condemnation of torture and its prevalence worldwide? Existing studies seek to find an answer from an institutional perspective. For example, borrowing from a principal-agent model, Conrad and Moore (2010) reason that democratic institutions are effective in constraining the abusive power of government officials at detention centers, police stations, and prisons. In their empirical analysis, they successfully demonstrate that three key institutional features of democracy (universal suffrage, veto points, and freedom of speech) are highly associated with the prohibition of torture in the context of an absence of violent dissent.

Although existing studies offer insightful empirical findings, their institutional approaches do little to explain the unlawful practice of torture by most democratic countries despite the existence of several institutional constraints, in the absence of violent dissent. Accordingly, the question related to the undemocratic use of torture in democratic nation-states remains only partially resolved in the institutional literature. In this study, I attempt to complement the institutional approaches by arguing that consideration should be made for the competency of the decision-making of the individual leaders who design and govern political institutions. It is not unreasonable to imagine that, because torture is a highly contentious issue among the public, politicians, and journalists (e.g., the Abu Ghraib Torture and Prisoner Abuse), it is left to presidents and prime ministers to make crucial policy decisions pertaining to the incidents of illegal torture that occur during the interrogation process or to the reinforcement of a policy to bring an end to torture. It is political leaders who possess political power to either enforce or reinforce the termination of torture in response to the outcry from the international community of human rights or leave the prohibition of torture embedded in the constitution as a mere façade. It is also political leaders who may have incentives to respect the constitutional rights of suspects and thus stop torture by addressing the abrasive behavior of jailers or interrogators.

My conjecture, with an emphasis on the role of individual leaders, comes from the debates regarding the relative influence of individuals and institutions (Peters 1996). Though most of the literature in this debate focuses on the primacy either of individuals or of institutions, my study surmises that individuals and institutions operate together to affect the likelihood of terminating the use of torture. Because previous studies have elegantly presented the positive impact of democratic institutions in regard to torture termination, my theoretical argument attends to the function of individual leaders. The question asks what attributes of leaders incline them to stop the use of torture, as stipulated in their national constitution and the Convention against Torture. All other things being equal (e.g., the quality of democratic institutions), I argue that the educational attainment of leaders plays a major role in their decision-making in regard to national security policy, including torture. This argument is bolstered by the findings of previous studies that education level is strongly associated with public spiritedness, suggesting that education should be a useful indicator of a leader's civic-mindedness (see Tarrow 1987; Nie, Junn, and Stehlik-Barry 1996; Besley and Reynal-Querol 2011).

More generally, as the public becomes more educated, an understanding of ethical dilemmas should become more lucid. Those with advanced educations should be able to better predict negative consequences of wrong decisions or illegal actions and may be less likely to engage in behaviors that are not legally or morally justifiable. In this regard, Nie, Junn, and Stehlik-Barry (1996) provide evidence that the absolute years of formal education are positively correlated with the development of prodemocratic principles and tolerance for minority groups. In addition, as Article 26 of the Universal Declaration of Human Rights (1948) puts it, "Education shall be directed to the full development of the human personality and to the strengthening of respect for human rights and fundamental freedoms." When future leaders are educated and trained, they should be well aware of their rights, the law, and their responsibilities toward the national and international audiences.

Highly educated leaders should also be better informed of the relevant knowledge, skills, and resources necessary for the establishment of programs and institutions that are useful in stopping torture as a political practice. For example, before many lawyers join the realm of politics in a democratic society, they learn principles of justice and fairness as part of their study and practice of law (Dee 2004; Milligan, Moretti, and Oreopoulos 2004). This type of legal knowledge should better provide politicians with legal skills that can be used to run security and interrogation programs consistent with the principle of human dignity.

When Costas Simitis served as prime minister of Greece from 1996 to 2004, his civil law background as a former professor at the University of Giessen and at the Panteion University of Athens made him more likely to govern Greece as a torture-free country whenever his regime was not threatened by violent dissent.[2] Interestingly, although Mahathir Mohamad, who practiced medicine before politics, is known for curbing civil liberties during his premiership in Malaysia from 1981 to 2003, torture was not one of his repression tactics except for those times that his governance was under serious threat from political oppositions. Indeed, since he left the government, Mahathir Mohamad has become a human rights advocate. Mahathir Mohamad charged the International Criminal Court in The Hague for bias in its selection of cases to cover and then established the Kuala Lumpur War Crimes Tribunal in 2007—a Malaysian organization that aims to investigate war crimes.

Before turning themselves into politicians, Costas Simitis and Mahathir Mohamad were highly educated and trained in their respective disciplines, and their previous backgrounds were likely an influence on the way they, as prime ministers, chose to run their country in a manner where people could live without fear of torture in the absence of the constant eruption of violent riots. This line of reasoning is consistent with Hambrick and Mason's (1984) study that views demographic characteristics to be acceptable proxies to capture differences in the thinking of individuals. Therefore, I argue that education is an important characteristic for leaders when they contribute in establishing the rule of law, social order, and the internal peace works against the prevalence of cruel torture tactics.

Inglehart and Welzel's (2005) work is relevant here because it makes a persuasive argument that when the public and leaders are well informed and well educated in the process of economic development, a set of changes in value orientations should occur. When relating their work on value change to torture, Inglehart and Welzel make the comparison that "genital mutilation of women is still practiced in a number of societies, but it is becoming viewed as unacceptable in most societies, including a majority of Islamic societies. The use of torture is on a similar trajectory" (293). Though confined to U.S. respondents, public opinion surveys by Flavin and Nickerson (2010) and Mayer and Armor (2012) find that Americans with low levels of education are most likely to support the use of torture (see also Lightcap and Pfiffne 2014). I also note that some previous studies suggest that better educated and trained politicians tend to be more open to ideas enforcing good governance and that poorly educated politicians are more likely to transgress the principles and practices of good governance (e.g., Potůček 2003; Rocamora 2004). Terminating the practice of torture should be part of a leader's good governance program, in that it is an attempt to restore fundamental human rights as well as to curtail crimes against humanity and civilization. Better educated leaders should be better equipped to combat the prevalence of abusive jailers and interrogators.

I argue that linking the educational attainment of leaders to the termination of torture provides additional clue to the puzzle of why most democratic countries fail to stop the practice of torture. When political leaders have no ethical incentive for abolishing illegal torture practices—providing no leadership, the commitment (not necessarily compliance) to democratic political institutions to the Convention against Torture—these structures are unlikely to activate as self-enforcing mechanisms. By contrast, even when democracy functions as a loose institutional bulwark, stopping the practice of torture should become possible under the proper direction of political leaders who are, no matter the costs, determined and willing to enforce and reinforce a zero-tolerance policy on torture at the law enforcement and government levels. The force of change is the political will of individual leaders. When leaders have a strong political will to make progress in regard to societal issues, they can either send a powerful message of "no more torture" to those who are prone to employ unlawful torture tactics or enact strict policies that prohibit jailers and interrogators from relying on torture for intelligence gathering. Leaders can make it clear that interrogation officials will not be pressured to gather security-sensitive information through torture; if intelligence gathering is accomplished by torture, then it will not be used as a legitimate source under any circumstance; and torturers will be sanctioned or even fired rather than rewarded with promotions and raises. By contrast, when leaders lack political will due mainly to national security concerns, they can either neglect to oversee the abusive powers of their subordinates engaging in torture or turn a blind eye to evidence of illegal torture practices during their tenure. Who then can provide the effective leadership of stopping the practice of torture? I argue that when leaders are better educated and trained, they are more prone to assume the role of leadership as well as show their determination to end illegal activities of torture in the name of "freedom." Simply put, it is the right thing to do for more educated leaders. As such, my hypothesis is as follows:

H_1: More educated leaders are more likely to terminate torture practices.

By looking at the profiles of contemporary U.S. presidents who have post-college degrees from the most prestigious universities, one may raise a question about the validity of the preceding hypothesis. It is true that better-educated leaders in the United States have failed to stop the use of torture. In particular, although the United States is one of the most democratic countries in the contemporary world that signed and ratified the international human rights treaty in 1988 and 1994, respectively, it has been running harsh enhanced interrogation programs. This includes torture for the sake of protecting national security interests since 9/11 (Risen July 10, 2015). Yet the United States is a unique case, in that it is a hegemon that constantly encounters threats from all fronts. To continuously govern the world in the presence of constant security threats, U.S. leaders have been unable to terminate the practice of torture, regardless of their educational level. Furthermore, my conceptualization is probabilistic, meaning that I am not trying to predict all torture events, just those that are most likely to occur, as explained later.

RESEARCH DESIGN

Previous studies point out that when faced with the threat of violent dissent, it is highly unlikely that incumbent governments will terminate the political use of torture (see Davenport, Moore, and Armstrong 2007; Conrad and Moore 2010). This means that statistical models are, when a threat factor is conditioned in estimation, incapable of producing a meaningful result due to a lack of variation in the torture data. Put it another way, the research question of whether more educated leaders are predisposed to end the use of torture should be examined under a specific condition—when the threat of violent dissent has dissipated. For this reason, I build a survival model in which the dependent variable is related to torture spells:[3] the start of torture spells is coded for a scenario in which a country that used torture at time $t-1$ under the threat of violent dissent has the potential to resort back to torture at time t even in the absence of violent dissent.

The construction of the torture spells leads a country to three possible options: (1) the continuation of torture despite no threat of violent dissent, (2) the termination of torture in the absence of violent dissent, and (3) the continuation of torture due to the reemergence of violent dissent. I use these three choices of a country as a way to finalize the operation of the dependent variable: "0" denotes the occurrence of torture in the absence of violent dissent per country-year; "1" is recorded for a country that is completely free from any torture practices according to the Cingranelli-Richards Human Rights Dataset; and "2" indicates the presence of torture under the threat of violent dissent that is measured as at least one act of guerrilla war according to Banks's (2001) Cross-National Time-Series Data Archive or the presence of a civil war according to the Correlates of War (COW) project.

The main independent variable measures the educational attainment of leaders. I categorize it into three levels for the purposes of parsimony. The first level encompasses leaders with at least high/finishing/secondary education or trade school; the second level refers to college-educated leaders; and the third level corresponds to leaders who have qualifications from a graduate or professional school (e.g., master's degree) or who earn a doctoral degree. For empirical estimation, these three levels are converted into three dummy variables, representing each level of a leader's educational attainment: *below college, college,* and *graduate.* The names of effective leaders are identified using the Archigos data collection,[4] and the classification of a leader's educational attainment follows Ludwig's (2002) scheme.

A leader's educational attainment may be correlated with his or her occupation before assuming top leadership. For example, many democratic leaders practiced law before becoming politicians, thus meaning a higher level of education—possibly graduate training. When describing the British Labour Party, Cuperus (2006, 79) asserts that "[Labour Party representatives] are professional, highly-educated politicians with a public sector background" rather than originating from a working-class background. Accordingly, a more educated leader may serve as a proxy for leaders from specific occupational groups, as democracies tend to have more leaders with law backgrounds. To consider this possibility, I classify leaders into four categories according to their former profession: lawyer, professor/scientist, military professional, and others. Each profession is dichotomous, "1" if a leader was in the military, a lawyer, a professor/scientist, or in another profession, immediately before holding office. Besley and Reynal-Querol's (2011) study provides a detailed discussion of the occupational background of leaders.

To measure the notion that democratic institutions provide a thwarting effect on use of torture, I rely on the Polity IV data collection (Marshall and Jaggers 2007). Based on an 11-point additive score, Polity records democracies and autocracies, ranging from "0" to "10." Subtracting the autocracy score from the democracy score gives an overall Polity score that goes from full autocracy (−10) to full democracy. The correlation between leader education and democracy is −0.19 (*below college*), −0.29 (*college*), and 0.41 (*graduate*).

To avoid omitted variable bias and thus produce spurious results, I include four control variables: *media coverage, threat to leader tenure, GDP growth,* and *national capabilities*. When a country's torture practices are exposed by international media outlets, that country may be inclined to terminate unlawful interrogation programs to save face. I take this possibility into consideration by counting the total number of country reports appearing in Reuters Global News Service. To correct the positive skew of the data, I take the natural log of this variable (Bell, Clay, and Murdie 2012).

When a leader approaches the end of his or her tenure, he or she may be less inclined to end the use of torture due to no prospect of reelection. To control for this alternative explanation, I use Young's (2008) *threat to leader tenure* that evaluates the risk of an executive's removal from office on the basis of the length of the term served, economic growth rate, and the past turnover rate for executives.

When the national economy is growing well, a country may be less likely to stir economic grievances and thus to have less incentives to use repressive measures such as torture (P. Miller 2011; Choi 2015). This possibility is operationalized with annual GDP growth rate, garnered from the Penn World Tables.

When countries possess ample material capabilities such as iron and steel production so that the population can enjoy a life of material and even spiritual abundance, they may be more likely to terminate torture practices. To account for the impact of national capabilities, I include the Composite Index of National Capability score collected from the COW's national material capabilities dataset (Singer, Bremer, and Stuckey 1972).

After having created the torture spells and cleaning the data for independent variables, I am left with a small sample size that includes 44 countries during the period 1991–2000.[5] The primary reason for such a small number of sample countries is that many torture spells were excluded due to no varying values: many countries either were always experiencing the threat of violent dissent or did not experience any violent dissent at all. My sample size is similar to Conrad and Moore's that was used for their main statistical analysis: 39 countries for the years 1986–1999. As additional robustness check, I will further test my main variable—the educational attainment of leaders—using Conrad and Moore's data and model specification. This test purports to alleviate the concern that my main findings reported later may be subjected to sample selection bias.

The dependent variable is nominal because the three categories (0 for torture, 1 for no torture, and 2 for threat) are assumed to be unordered. For this reason, I employ a multinomial logic model as an estimation method. I add Carter and Signorino's (2006) third-order polynomial time counter t, t^2, and t^3 into the model as an attempt to control for time dependence in the torture data.

EMPIRICAL RESULTS

Table 9.1 presents results from the multinomial logit estimation. I utilize two-tailed tests by setting the significance levels at 0.05, 0.01, and 0.001. While odd models (Torture Terminates) display coefficients and robust standard errors of predictors when countries terminate their use of torture given the absence of violent dissent, even models (Threat Returns) provide estimates when countries reencounter the threat of violent dissent. Because the main research question is whether more educated leaders are predisposed to end torture when their country no longer confronts violent dissent, my discussion is confined to interpretations of odd models.

In Model 1, leaders with less than a college education are used as the base category. As hypothesized, the two leader education-related variables (*college* and *graduate*) are significantly different from zero and the institution-related variable (*democracy*) is also significant. This implies that, as compared to leaders with below-college education, those with college or graduate training display a greater tendency to terminate the inhumane practice of torture in the absence of violent dissent. Simply put, more educated leaders are more willing to implement the prohibition of torture when a hostile political environment has dissolved. Unsurprisingly, democratic institutions appear to be better equipped for eliminating torture practices than their nondemocratic counterparts, which corroborates the main finding of previous studies. Among the four control variables, only *threat to leader tenure* achieves significance with a negative sign. This suggests that when leaders are near the completion of their terms, the ending of inhumane torture practices is unlikely to remain as one of their top policy priorities.

The discussion on the estimated results has so far focused on the significance and sign of coefficients given that they provide key information related to the hypothesis testing. Another way to discuss the results is to examine the magnitude of coefficients. Yet the coefficients are multinomial log-odds (logits), which are not easy to interpret or comprehend. For easy interpretation, I convert log-odds to the relative risk ratios. The relative risk ratios are 668,360.100 for *college*, 1,618,262.000 for *graduate*, and 1.566 for *democracy*. These are exceptionally large ratios of two odds for the leader education-related variables. Considering that the other variables, including *democracy*, in the model are held constant, I note that leaders

Table 9.1
Do More Educated Leaders Stop the Torture?

	Multinomial Logit					
	Reference Category: Torture Continues (0)					
	Torture Terminates (1)	Threat Returns (2)	Torture Terminates (1)	Threat Returns (2)	Torture Terminates (1)	Threat Returns (2)
Variable	Model 1	Model 2	Model 3	Model 4	Model 5	Model 6
Individual leaders						
$College_t$	13.413***	−1.514			14.954***	−2.292*
	(1.084)	(0.899)			(1.601)	(0.991)
$Graduate_t$	14.297***	−1.835			15.833***	−2.839*
	(1.068)	(0.977)			(1.500)	(1.170)
$Lawyer_t$			0.343	−0.553	0.282	0.166
			(0.860)	(1.101)	(1.075)	(1.149)
$Professor/scientist_t$			0.311	0.639	−0.118	1.240
			(1.126)	(0.829)	(1.078)	(0.921)
$Military professional_t$			−13.157***	0.381	−12.577***	−0.658
			(1.380)	(1.249)	(1.396)	(0.731)
Political institutions						
$Democracy_t$	0.448*	−0.024	0.470	0.010	0.404*	−0.031
	(0.191)	(0.070)	(0.302)	(0.073)	(0.187)	(0.078)

Controls

	(1)	(2)	(3)	(4)	(5)	(6)
Media coverage$_{t-1}$	-0.537	0.265	-0.437	0.124	-0.528	0.499
	(0.429)	(0.234)	(0.575)	(0.205)	(0.401)	(0.266)
Threat to leader tenure$_t$	-0.271***	-0.005	-0.252**	-0.017	-0.276**	0.036
	(0.064)	(0.056)	(0.083)	(0.053)	(0.102)	(0.060)
GDP growth$_t$	5.692	2.931	2.457	2.964	4.978	2.614
	(5.479)	(5.196)	(4.754)	(4.566)	(6.354)	(5.266)
National capabilities$_t$	42.453	6.215	28.059	6.213	41.722	-6.707
	(33.921)	(14.520)	(51.404)	(14.944)	(33.740)	(15.488)
Log pseudolikelihood	-72.41		-75.36		-70.58	
Observations	267		267		267	

Notes: Robust standard errors are in parentheses. Results from t, t^2, and t^3 and a constant are not reported.

*$p < .05$ two-tailed tests

**$p < .01$ two-tailed tests

***$p < .001$ two-tailed tests

with a college degree have a 668,360 percent greater probability of terminating the use of torture than those with less than a college education. Leaders with graduate training are also much more likely to stop the torture than those with below-college education. When the level of democracy increases by one unit, a country is approximately 2 percent more likely to terminate the use of torture.

A visual presentation may be more helpful in understanding the magnitude of coefficients than the description of the relative risk ratios. For this purpose, I use a graph that displays how a unit increase in each variable affects the probability of terminating the use of torture (which is denoted as "1" in the graph), compared to continuing to use torture (which is denoted as "0").[6] Figure 9.1 shows discrete changes of three variables of interest—the effects of a one-unit change in *college* or *graduate* and a standard deviation change in *democracy*. After inspecting the magnitude of the effects by measuring the physical distance between "0" and "1" for each variable, I find that the effect of leaders with a graduate degree is the largest and that the effect of democratic institutions is the smallest.

While a graph of discrete changes provides useful information, it is also useful to plot odds ratios (also known as factor change coefficients). In Figure 9.2, *college, graduate,* and *democracy* are represented on a separate row, and the horizontal axis indicates the relative magnitude of the β coefficients associated with each outcome ("1" and "2") compared to the base outcome of "0." By gauging the distance between "0" and "1" for each

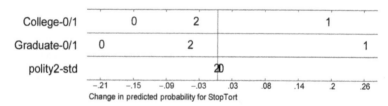

Figure 9.1 Educated leaders, democracy, and torture: discrete changes.

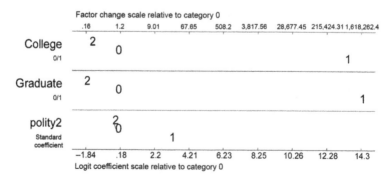

Figure 9.2 Educated leaders, democracy, and torture: odds ratios.

variable in each row, I find that the effect of *graduate* is the largest among the three variables, that of *college* is the next, and *democracy* has the smallest effect, which coincides with the analysis of the relative risk ratios.

Because the results thus far indicate that individual leaders and political institutions each exert a preventive effect on use of torture, it is worth investigating the relationship between leader education and democracy. In Figure 9.3, I plot the predicted probabilities of ending the practice of torture by leaders with a college or graduate degree, as a level of democracy changes from –10 to 10. The figure provides clear information that, as the quality of democratic institutions improves, leaders with graduate training are more likely to stop the use of torture than those with college education. Thus, the figure shows that both leaders' education and institutional mechanisms are beneficial factors in regaining humanity once the threat of violent dissent has dissolved. This finding is, to an extent, consistent with Besley and Reynal-Querol's (2011) work, reporting that democracies are more likely than autocracies to select highly educated leaders. Note that when interaction terms between *college* and *democracy*, as well as between *graduate* and *democracy*, are added in Model 1, I encounter no estimated results and also the warning of "variance matrix is nonsymmetric or highly singular." For these reasons, I perform no further investigation on the interaction effects of leaders and institutions.

Moving back to the remaining results in Table 9.1, I examine the effect of leaders' occupational background in Model 3 that is introduced as a proxy indicator for leader education. Among the three occupation-related variables, only *military professional* passes the standard significance test. It appears that when leaders developed their career in the military before they assume the top leadership, they are less likely to end the use of torture. This finding is not

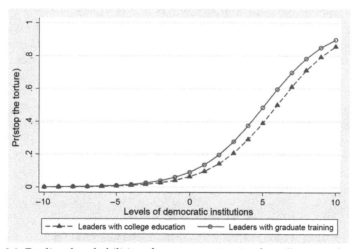

Figure 9.3 Predicted probabilities of torture termination for college, graduate, and democracy

surprising given S. Miller's (2011) observation that "the practice of torture is endemic in many, perhaps most, military, police, and correctional institutions in the world today." Conrad et al.'s empirical study also provides a similar insight, as it shows military agents engaging in a high degree of torture when responding to international terrorist plots. Unfortunately, the institution-related variable—*democracy*—fails to exhibit the expected effect: the inclusion of the occupation-related variables may have caused the significance of *democracy* to be weakened. The overall results in Model 3 undoubtedly confirm the importance of individual leaders in explaining and understanding the likelihood of terminating torture practices in the absence of violent dissent.

Model 5 pits both leader education and occupation against democracy along with the four control variables. I present this model specification as an effort to assuage a concern that education and occupation may exert slightly different impacts on torture termination, and thus, they can be included in the same model for estimation. The estimates in Model 5 are virtually identical to those in Models 1 and 3 combined: *college* and *graduate* are positively associated with torture termination, while *military professional* shows a negative association. In this model construction, *democracy* is also correlated with higher risks of ending the practice of torture. In general, Model 5 displays the estimated results, verifying that individual leaders are as important as political institutions when addressing the question of how best to stop the use of torture.

It is worth noting that in their seminal article "What Stops the Torture?" Conrad and Moore (2010) adeptly demonstrate that democratic institutions provide a bulwark to stop the torture. One of the main advantages of their study is that the model building and hypothesis testing have endured the rigorous peer review process at one of the most prestigious publication outlets in the discipline. In turn, this means that their research design has proven to be highly reliable, and thus, the possibility of coding errors or faulty model building in my replication followed should be at a minimal level. A further advantage of their study is that it introduces three unique qualities of democratic institutions, which is different from my model specification that relies on an aggregated, composite measure of democracy. The three institutional features are (1) *voice* that records "1" for a country with free elections, (2) *freedom of expression* that measures the degree of free speech on a scale of "0" to "3," and (3) *veto* that captures constraints on the executive, ranging from 0 to 1. Does the difference in the research designs between Conrad and Moore's study and mine lead to different empirical findings? This question is worth investigating.

I present replicated results from Conrad and Moore's torture model as a baseline model. The baseline model is below compared with my torture model with educated leaders. In doing so, I evaluate the effects of individual leaders versus political institutions one last time. Models 1 and 2 in Table 9.2 display the results from the baseline model, which is the replication of Conrad and Moore's (2010, 469) Table 1. The replicated estimates

Table 9.2

Who Stops the Torture? or What Stops the Torture?: Conrad and Moore 2010, *American Journal of Political Science*, Table 1, p. 469

Multinomial Logit

Reference Category: Torture Continues (0)

Variable	Torture Terminates (1) Model 1	Threat Returns (2) Model 2	Torture Terminates (1) Model 3	Threat Returns (2) Model 4	Torture Terminates (1) Model 5	Threat Returns (2) Model 6	Torture Terminates (1) Model 7	Threat Returns (2) Model 8
Individual leaders								
$College_t$			17.619***	-0.457			19.145**	-1.103
			(3.779)	(1.959)			(6.856)	(2.618)
$Graduate_t$			19.023***	1.290			20.649**	-0.012
			(4.320)	(2.261)			(7.150)	(2.737)
$Lawyer_t$					0.451	-0.202	1.391	-0.248
					(0.991)	(1.307)	(0.955)	(1.492)
$Professor/scientist_t$					2.422	-1.150	0.955	-0.686
					(1.734)	(1.870)	(2.189)	(2.065)
$Military$ $professional_t$					-15.334***	-19.377***	-15.644***	-19.266***
					(2.799)	(1.672)	(3.256)	(1.610)

(Continued)

Table 9.2
(Continued)

	Multinomial Logit							
	Reference Category: Torture Continues (0)							
	Torture Terminates (1)	Threat Returns (2)	Torture Terminates (1)	Threat Returns (2)	Torture Terminates (1)	Threat Returns (2)	Torture Terminates (1)	Threat Returns (2)
Variable	Model 1	Model 2	Model 3	Model 4	Model 5	Model 6	Model 7	Model 8
Political institutions								
$Voice_t$	3.939*	1.001	4.485**	1.370	3.354	−0.341	3.183*	0.327
	(1.965)	(1.161)	(1.444)	(1.594)	(1.817)	(1.258)	(1.562)	(1.213)
$Veto_t$	−5.468	−0.677	−7.181*	−1.534	−5.834	−0.040	−8.377*	−1.050
	(2.989)	(1.460)	(3.298)	(1.573)	(3.220)	(1.598)	(4.058)	(1.652)
$Freedom\ of\ expression_t$	4.559**	0.799	4.514***	0.657	5.425**	1.487*	5.329***	1.292
	(1.407)	(0.675)	(1.260)	(0.735)	(1.734)	(0.752)	(1.594)	(0.802)
Controls								
$Naming\ and\ shaming_{t-1}$	−0.380	0.968	−0.903	0.953	−0.175	1.115	−0.708	0.991
	(0.587)	(0.689)	(0.778)	(0.686)	(0.573)	(0.627)	(0.848)	(0.598)
$NGOs\ per\ capita_t$	0.227	0.011	0.204	−0.011	0.278	0.045	0.258	−0.027
	(0.236)	(0.065)	(0.219)	(0.068)	(0.202)	(0.088)	(0.137)	(0.127)
$Threat\ to\ leader\ tenure_t$	−0.534**	−0.019	−0.790*	0.014	−0.468***	−0.026	−0.649*	0.002

	(0.173)	(0.049)	(0.313)	(0.050)	(0.120)	(0.060)	(0.269)	(0.070)
Civil law$_t$	-3.274**	-0.388	-3.641**	-0.063	-4.648**	-0.478	-4.184*	-0.286
	(1.173)	(1.339)	(1.340)	(1.698)	(1.624)	(2.148)	(1.676)	(2.411)
GDP$_t$	-0.151	-1.982*	0.274	-2.498**	0.688	-2.327*	0.797	-2.262**
	(1.206)	(0.866)	(1.508)	(0.879)	(1.330)	(0.952)	(1.761)	(0.827)
Population$_t$	0.312	-0.900	-0.100	-1.020	1.029	-0.334	1.157	-0.716
	(1.238)	(0.824)	(1.818)	(1.115)	(1.664)	(0.903)	(1.045)	(1.182)
GDP growth$_t$	25.972***	3.551	45.861**	5.616	42.587*	-6.222	59.057*	-4.233
	(6.003)	(6.749)	(15.401)	(6.274)	(17.577)	(8.641)	(29.700)	(7.620)
Military personnel$_t$	0.514	1.035*	0.581	1.264*	0.097	0.764	-0.259	1.036
	(0.644)	(0.514)	(0.871)	(0.644)	(0.989)	(0.608)	(0.470)	(0.911)
Log pseudolikeli-hood	-48.49		-45.20		-43.00		-41.06	
Observations	252		252		252		252	

Notes: Robust standard errors are in parentheses. Results from t, t^2, and t^3 and a constant are not reported.

*$p < .05$ two-tailed tests

**$p < .01$ two-tailed tests

***$p < .001$ two-tailed tests

are consistent with what Conrad and Moore reported five years ago, despite the fact that the significance levels are set at 0.05, 0.01, and 0.001 for more strict tests.[7] Among the three institutional variables, *voice* and *freedom of expression* appear to provide institutional mechanisms to terminate torture practices, according to Model 1.

I now add leader education variables in the baseline model. The results are shown in Models 3 and 4. As expected, *college* and *graduate* are significantly different from zero in Model 3. This suggests that leaders with a college or graduate degree are more likely to stop the torture than those with less than a college education. These results confirm those reported in Table 9.1 that national leaders with higher education play a central role in preventing violations of human rights through the use of torture. Not surprisingly, Conrad and Moore's three institutional factors successfully predict the likelihood of torture events. *Voice* and *freedom of expression* show an increased chance of terminating the torture, while *veto* serves as a hindrance to abolishing torture practices. Model 5 shows evidence that leaders with a military background are less inclined to stop torture, which is in line with that reported in Table 9.1. In Model 7, I include both leader education and occupation along with Conrad and Moore's institutional variables. The results once again confirm those reported in Table 9.1: the educational attainment of leaders as well as democratic institutions matters.

CONCLUSION

The causes of ending torture are an understudied area of research in political science. While only a few previous studies examine the topic, their research revolves around institutional features of democratic political systems but overlooks the role of political leaders who design and deal with the daily operations of political institutions. In this study, I have probed the question of whether more educated leaders are more likely to stop torture when their country becomes free of threat from violent dissent. The empirical tests produce evidence that, all other causal factors, such as political institutions, being equal, the educational attainment of leaders does indeed matter: highly educated leaders are predisposed to terminate the use of torture. This finding is revealing when considering that national leaders are the central figures, capable of either exercising their political will to enforce or reinforce a strict policy of "no more torture" in the absence of violent dissent or permitting the practice of torture for national security exigency.

With a special focus on the role of individual leaders, I have also provided an additional important clue to the puzzling question of why many democracies engage in torture even in the absence of violent dissent though it is not a democratic norm. The answer should be clear by now: it is because democratic institutions are often improperly governed by political leaders who have no strong political resolve to stop torture for various reasons, including national security. All in all, it is apparent that the political will of leaders in ending illegal torture practices is an important causal factor when political leaders become better educated and trained and when there is no immediate threat of violent dissent in the near-future.

The starting point of my study was that previous studies focused on the institutionalist argument (democracies are less likely to torture and more likely to end torture), and their explanations are incomplete as to why there are many cases in which democracies torture. I believe that by looking into the educational attainment of leaders, my empirical study complements the institutional studies of torture. Yet it should be noted that my study also points out the possibility that there are highly educated leaders who still torture when confronted with the potential loss of power. This is why my empirical tests are confined to those sample countries that have the potential to stop or resume the use of torture once violent dissent no longer exists.

NOTES

1. A more complete definition of torture can be found in the United Nations' Convention against Torture and Other Cruel, Inhuman or Degrading Treatment or Punishment at http://legal.un.org/avl/ha/catcidtp/catcidtp.html

2. See http://www.britannica.com/biography/Konstantinos-Simitis.

3. Torture spells are a sequence of years in which countries have a record of committing at least one reported act of torture. Conrad and Moore (2010, 468–470) provide detailed operational procedures about how to record torture spells when the threat of violent dissent has stopped.

4. See http://www.rochester.edu/college/faculty/hgoemans/data.htm.

5. The study period ends one year before 9/11, which probably led to numerous countries feeling forced, including the United States, to deem torture as an effective interrogation method (Risen July 10, 2015). If I included the years since 9/11, I would end up with biased estimates and thus erroneous inferences.

6. The return of threats is denoted as "2," which is not the main focus of this study. The interpretations follow the instructions of Long and Freese (2006) on multinomial logit.

7. Conrad and Moore instead used 0.10, 0.05, and 0.01, which were probably conventional significance levels at the time of their publication.

REFERENCES

Banks, Arthur. 2001. Cross-national Time Series Data Archive. Databanks International. Jerusalem, Israel. https://www.cntsdata.com/

Beccaria, Cesara. 2009. *On Crimes and Punishments*. New Brunswick, NJ: Transaction Publishers.

Bell, Sam, Chad Clay, and Amanda Murdie. 2012. "Neighborhood Watch." *Journal of Politics* 74(2): 354–368.

Besley, Timothy and Marta Reynal-Querol. 2011. "Do Democracies Select More Educated Leaders?" *American Political Science Review* 105(3): 552–566.

Carter, David B. and Curtis S. Signorino. 2006. "Data Separation and the Statistical Exploration of Wars." Unpublished Manuscript, University of Rochester.

Choi, Seung-Whan. 2015. "Economic Growth and Terrorism." *Oxford Economic Papers* 67(1): 157–181.

Cingranelli, David and David Richards. 1999. "Measuring the Level, Pattern, and Sequence of Government Respect for Physical Integrity Rights." *International Studies Quarterly* 43(2): 407–417.

Conrad, Courtenay, Justin Conrad, James Walsh, and James Piazza. 2017. "Who Tortures the Terrorist?" *Foreign Policy Analysis* 13(4): 761–786.

Conrad, Courtenay and Will Moore. 2010. "What Stops the Torture?" *American Journal of Political Science* 54(2): 459–476.

Cuperus, René. 2006. "European Social Unease?" *Internationale Politik und Gesellschaft* 1: 65–90.

Davenport, Christian, Will Moore, and David Armstrong. 2007. "The Puzzle of Abu Ghraib." Paper Presented at the Annual Meeting of the International Studies Association. Chicago, IL.

Dee, Thomas. 2004. "Are There Civic Returns to Education?" *Journal of Public Economics* 88(9–10): 1697–1720.

Flavin, Patrick and David, Nickerson. 2010. "Reciprocity and Public Opinion on Torture." Unpublished paper. http://files.campus.edublogs.org/blogs.baylor.edu/dist/2/1297/files/2010/09/Torture_Reciprocity-2bdmo3i.pdf.

Hambrick, Donald and Phyllis Mason. 1984. "Upper Echelons." *Academy of Management Review* 9(2): 193–206.

Inglehart, Ronald and Christian Welzel. 2005. *Modernization, Cultural Change and Democracy*. New York: Cambridge University Press.

Kearns, Erin. 2015. "The Study of Torture." *Laws* 4(1): 1–15.

Lightcap, Tracy and James Pfiffne, eds. 2014. *Examining Torture*. New York: Palgrave MacMillan.

Long, J. Scott and Jeremy Freese. 2006. *Regression Models for Categorical Dependent Variables using Stata*. College Station, TX: StataCorp.

Ludwig, Arnold. 2002. *King of the Mountain*. Lexington: University Press of Kentucky.

Marshall, Monty and Keith Jaggers. 2007. "POLITY IV Project." Dataset Users' Manual.

Mayer, Jeremy and David Armor. 2012. "Support for Torture over Time." *Social Science Journal* 49(4): 439–446.

Miller, Peter. 2011. "Torture Approval in Comparative Perspective." *Human Rights Review* 12(4): 441–463.

Miller, Seumas. 2011. "Torture." The Stanford Encyclopedia of Philosophy Archive. http://plato.stanford.edu/archives/sum2015/entries/torture/.

Milligan, Kevin, Enrico Moretti, and Philip Oreopoulos. 2004. "Does Education Improve Citizenship?" *Journal of Public Economics* 88(9–10): 1667–1695.

Nie, Norman, Jane Junn, and Kenneth Stehlik-Barry. 1996. *Education and Democratic Citizenship in America*. Chicago, IL: University of Chicago Press.

Peters, Guy. 1996. "Political Institutions, Old and New." In Robert Goodin and Hans-Dieter Klingemann, eds., *A New Handbook of Political Science*. Oxford: Oxford University Press. 205–220.

Potůček, Martin. 2003. "The Capacities of Governance in Central and Eastern Europe." Unpublished paper. Center for Social and Economic Strategies, Charles University, Prague.

Rejali, Darius. 2007. *Torture and Democracy*. Princeton, NJ: Princeton University Press.

Risen, James. July 10, 2015. "Psychologists Shielded U.S. Torture Program, Report Finds." *New York Times*. http://www.nytimes.com/2015/07/11/us/psychologists-shielded-us-torture-program-report-finds.html?_r=0.

Rocamora, Joel. 2004. "Party Building and Local Governance in the Philippines." In John Harriss, Kristian Stokke, and Olle Tornquist, eds., *Politicising Democracy*. New York: Palgrave Macmillan. 148–170.

Singer, David, Stuart Bremer, and John Stuckey. "Capability Distribution, Uncertainty, and Major Power War, 1820–1965." In Bruce Russett, ed., *Peace, War, and Numbers*. Beverly Hills, CA: Sage. 19–48.

Tarrow, Norma. 1987. *Human Rights and Education*. New York: Pergamon.

CHAPTER 10

Civil War and Rule of Law

Most research on economic development agrees that a high-quality law and order not only cultivates the economic growth and development of a state but may also have positive spillover effects such as a reduction in violence (Barro 1999a). The potential benefits of this tradition are also manifest in Aristotle's declaration, more than two centuries ago, that "the rule of law is better than the rule of any one individual." In fact, the land dispute between Māori[1] and European New Zealanders did not erupt into a devastating civil war due to a long tradition of the rule of law. For more than a century New Zealand has continued to recognize the minority rights of the Māori. For example, the Māori were given permanent seats to fill in the New Zealand parliament, and a special court was established to hear land dispute cases (Fleras 1985). Māori protest movements grew significantly in the 1960s and 1970s seeking redress for past grievances, particularly in regard to land rights; however, they did not develop into civil conflict because there was another legal avenue that the indigenous Maori could access that the European settlers were accountable to (Bourassa and Strong 2002; O'Sullivan 2008). Unfortunately, the potential relationship between rule of law and civil conflict has not yet been tested with longitudinal data. This study attempts to fill that gap by examining whether or not the rule of law has a statistically ameliorating effect on the onset of civil war.

This study conceives a strong rule of law tradition as one in which an impartial judicial system is present and in which populations recognize the law as legitimate. Specifically, this study argues that when a minority group (defined in terms of ethnicity, religion, and/or political ideology) has the opportunity to resolve its grievances nonviolently by way of an impartial justice system, members of the group are less likely to develop feelings of hopelessness and bitterness which, ultimately, cause some individuals to resort to political violence as a challenge to the government. Therefore, a rule of law system that is perceived as legitimate by those it serves may help prevent minority groups from turning to violent rebellion; presumably, such a state is less likely to experience civil war. On the other hand, where we do not see the rule of law, we should not expect to see civil peace. A country that has instituted discriminatory laws against ethnic minorities is unlikely to offer impartial judges and security forces. In this case, citizens lack trust in the protective force of law because there exists no objective legal process to ameliorate the concerns of ethnic minorities. In Sri Lanka, for example, the adoption of Sinhalese as the dominant language and the promotion of Sinhalese communities in Tamil lands no doubt contributed to the onset of civil war. This case illustrates how legal actions were taken by a government to purposefully obstruct the ability of ethnic minorities such as the Tamils to seek legal redress, indicating that, in contrast to this example, we may consider the maintenance of the rule of law to be a formidable bulwark against the anti-government activities of rebel forces.

Built on logit regression models of 132 countries during the period 1984–2007, this study finds evidence that, all other things being equal, countries with a strong rule of law tradition are much less likely to experience civil war than are those with a weak rule of law tradition. Moreover, the strength of this effect increases when we correct for the possibility of reverse causation from civil war onset to the rule of law.

The study is organized as follows: the next section presents the causal linkage between the rule of law and the onset of civil war; then a discussion of the research design with variable operationalization and model building is offered, followed by a discussion of the empirical results. A variety of steps are then implemented to verify the robustness of the rule of law variable. First, we test alternate measures of the rule of law and civil conflict. Second, we employ several statistical estimation techniques including multiplicative interaction logit. Then, with simultaneous equations models, we investigate the possibility of reverse causality between the rule of law and civil war onset. Finally, this study concludes by summing up its main findings and putting forward some policy implications.

THE LINKAGE BETWEEN THE RULE OF LAW AND CIVIL WAR

This study considers the rule of law as a possible root cause of civil war by conceptualizing it as the establishment of a fair and impartial judicial system in conjunction with a people's recognition of the law as a legitimate means to redress their grievances.[2] As legal scholar Joseph Raz (1977,

198–201) notes, a fair and impartial judicial system refers to having—at least—an independent judiciary branch with fair-minded judges, prosecutors, and lawyers, as well as a strong and stable law enforcement community.[3] When an independent judiciary is firmly in place, it indicates a strong governmental commitment to the following basic principles: (1) that all citizens are equal before the law and (2) that all citizens deserve the opportunity to have grievances heard and disputes settled in court.

The theory of the rule of law assumes that it brings to a society a high level of trust in the legal institutions of the state and, consequently, a greater degree of order in political and social relations (Hardin 2001; O'Donnell 2004). Once it is established, citizens are supposed to be more trusting of legal norms, courts, and procedures and so would be inclined to consult them first in their efforts to reconcile political and personal differences, rather than resorting to physical violence as a primary means of conflict resolution. If not widely presumed that a legal ruling will be fair and impartial, citizens will hesitate to trust their judicial system to settle claims or challenge government policies.

The Dampening Effect of the Rule of Law on the Outbreak of Civil War

The preceding discussion indicates that the incentive to use political violence against a government is increased when legitimate channels of conflict resolution are absent or ineffective. Such a situation breeds feelings of hopelessness and bitterness, which can lead to acts of last resort, namely, political violence. This line of reasoning presumes that as long as citizens have access to peaceful legal mechanisms in order to redress their grievances, they are less likely to seriously consider violence as an option. As it employs this hypothesis as a causal explanation for civil war, this study pays close attention to the role of minority groups under two assumptions: (1) that the grievances brought by members of minority groups are related to unequal or unfair treatment based on their ethnicity, religion, and/or political ideology and (2) that the outbreak of a civil war often results from a conflict between one or more minority groups and the government (Gellner 1983; Horowitz 1985; Huntington 1996; Fearon and Laitin 2003; James 2010). Based on these assumptions, this study reasons that when minority groups have the opportunity to address issues of discrimination through an impartial judicial system, they are less inclined to use physical violence as a challenge to the existing regime; in other words, they are less inclined to become rebellious against the government. Therefore, it is fair to argue that, because it guarantees a trusted and effective mechanism for resolving conflicts between minority groups and the government, a country that implements a high-quality judiciary based on the rule of law is less likely to experience domestic insurgency or civil war.

It is important to note that a well-established justice system "serves to protect people against anarchy as well as from [the] arbitrary exercise of power by public officials" (Wilson 2006, 153). If a government establishes laws that serve to protect equally the rights of minority and majority groups and that ensure the independent adjudication of legal rules regardless of ethnicity, religion, and ideology, then it increases the likelihood that the interests at stake will be impartially heard in efficient legal outlets. Eyerman (1998, 154) makes a similar observation, claiming that when countries "increase the expected return of legal activity and offer multiple channels of non-violent expression without the threat of government retaliation," they assuage the dormant bitterness and dissatisfaction that could potentially make rebels out of ethnically and religiously disadvantaged individuals. Again we see that in societies with legitimate, independent judicial systems, minority groups are less prone to resort to violence to work out their grievances.

On the other hand, the rights of minority groups living in countries lacking sound judicial systems are likely to go unrecognized and unprotected. They will face serious obstacles with respect to matters of property, education rights, employment, wealth, political power, and so on. These governments are not committed to reviewing discriminatory laws because it is in their interest to entertain the policy preferences of majority groups in an effort to maintain power (see Adam 1971; Lustick 1980). Under such circumstances, minority groups are unable to obtain just and adequate reparation for damages they have endured; furthermore, minority groups have more grievances that go unaddressed because they suffer a greater number of rights violations in general. Worse still, ethnic and religious minority groups that publicly demand those same civil liberties and political rights enjoyed by the dominant group tend to be harshly repressed. Likewise, when such a group seeks to establish its own autonomously governed region, or insists on the right to receive an education in its mother tongue (e.g., Irish Republican Army vs. the British and PKK [Kurdistan Workers' Party] vs. Turkey), the government, in the absence of legitimate channels of communication, is not compelled to respond to their demands; thus, the government offers a nonresponse, likely for fear of losing territorial sovereignty or from the desire to maintain a hegemonic cultural identity. Sometimes governments use their domestic justice systems to actively persecute minority groups, seeking to advance or impose their own political ideology on the majority group. In cases like this, governments are more likely to suppress the demand for political freedom than to offer rights to ideological, zealous minorities. In response to oppressive measures taken by a government, however, minority groups may choose to embrace the principle of retributive justice; that is, they may, seeing this as the only course of action left open to them by which to obtain full political, economic, and religious rights, choose to launch a violent counteroffense.

On the other hand, a state possessing an impartial judicial system provides channels for the fair and peaceful resolution of grievances and can socialize minority groups to utilize these channels. Institutions, including legal systems, are agents of socialization whereby individuals internalize norms and learn to function as members of a particular society. Once socialized, political violence appears to a citizen as a less-attractive option than is legal redress. Therefore, to better understand minority politics, we must also look at socialization. If minority groups are socialized to trust in the fairness and impartiality of established laws, they are more likely to turn to the judicial system as a means of settling political grievances.[4] The socialization of trust depends on the internalization by minority groups of social norms relating to justice and the proper execution of justice. From this perspective, political violence is self-defeating, ultimately undermining legal institutions that are considered essential for the advancement of minority rights. When minority groups perceive these institutions as both legitimate and fair, they will subscribe to the established order as a whole, even when they disagree with individual legal statutes and rulings; that is, they will trust that legal adjudication produces a right and fair result, even when it is not the result they envisioned.[5]

To review, minority groups in states where the rule of law is perceived to be legitimate are less likely to engage in political violence than are groups in countries with weak or nonexistent rule of law traditions. In countries with weak or nonexistent traditions, the legal system is characterized by the arbitrary creation of laws and by unfair legal practices catering to the interests of dominant and powerful groups. If minority groups living in non-rule of law countries perceive their governments and systems of justice as illegitimate, they will also see public policy decisions as arbitrary and likely consider peaceful participation to be ineffective. As a result, they will be more inclined to pursue violent means of political redress. The socialization of minority groups to respect the legal establishment as a legitimate means of addressing political grievances is, however, no less important to the prevention of civil conflict than the presence of an impartial justice system with fair-minded judges and law enforcement officials. As we have seen, institutions alone cannot sustain a high-quality rule of law society. Other factors, especially ideological socialization, must be present. In order to maintain civil peace, all citizens must believe in and feel committed to the legitimacy of their judicial order (Hogg and Brown 1998; Hardin 2001). In sum, this study argues that countries with high-quality rule of law traditions, which provide minority groups with legitimate legal channels for the rectification of discrimination, are less likely to experience rebellion and civil war. This conceptualization leads to the following hypothesis:

H_1: As the level of the rule of law increases, the risk of the onset of civil war decreases.

RESEARCH DESIGN

This study tests the rule of law hypothesis using a statistical model that is standard in civil war studies, with a sample of 132 countries during the period 1984–2007.[6] Because Fearon and Laitin's (2003) civil war model has "[become] the standard formation for most cross-country work" (Blattman and Miguel 2009, 31), it provides consultation for the collection of a new dataset.

To increase the robustness of the findings reported, this study employs five distinct dependent variables. The first is the *onset of civil war* variable, the operationalization of which is based on the criteria and data of Fearon and Laitin (2003) and Fearon (2010). The second measure is *ethnic war*. The third through the fifth variables are operationalized using the Uppsala/PRIO's (Peace Research Institute Oslo's) armed conflict dataset (Harbom and Wallensteen 2010). A civil war is defined in this study as an armed conflict between agents of (or claimants to) a state and one or more organized, subnational groups who have resorted to political violence as a challenge to the government; it must have caused more than 1,000 deaths in total with an annual average of at least 100, and with more than 100 deaths on both sides (including civilians attacked by rebels). The nature of civil war can be ethnic, nationalist, or insurgent,[7] an ethnic war being a subset of civil war. Sambanis's (2001) study notes that, because it is supposed that they arise in response to racial discrimination rather than from a lack of economic opportunity, ethnic wars are important political events to study. These two civil war measures are dichotomous, coded as "1" for the onset of each war and as "0" otherwise. As Hegre and Sambanis (2006, 523) observe, "Depending on which data set we use, we can have twice as many civil war starts and country-years at war"; thus, the civil war literature tends to produce fragile results that depend entirely on a specific definition of the dependent variable. To account for such a concern, this study considers an alternative civil war definition, that is, that of the leading dataset offered by the Uppsala and PRIO groups (Harbom and Wallensteen 2010), which has the advantage of going below the 1,000 battle death threshold used by Fearon and Laitin. Hence, the third dependent variable refers to a civil war that has caused more than 25 annual battle deaths. It is coded as "1" for the case of a new civil war, or when two years have elapsed since the previous observation, and as "0" otherwise. The fourth dependent variable is a dichotomous measure of the incidence of conflict with a value of 1 for all country-years. The fifth dependent variable is the *onset of civil wars* that accumulate more than 1,000 battle-related deaths during the course of the entire conflict. As it is possible for a country enduring an ongoing armed conflict to experience the outbreak of a new and distinct conflict, the operationalizations of the third through fifth dependent variables include all country-year observations, which follow the year of onset and use all conflict onsets in the Uppsala/PRIO dataset for estimation.

The *rule of law* variable measures the conjunction of the two features conceptualized in the previous section: (1) the strength and impartiality of the legal system and (2) the degree of its popularly perceived legitimacy. The source for this variable is the International Country Risk Guide (ICRG), compiled by the Political Risk Services (PRS) Group, at http://www.prsgroup.com. The PRS measure is chosen for three reasons. First, it closely captures the theoretical argument developed in this study. Second, it has been widely used across disciplines due to its validity; for example, Robert Barro (1999b, S173), professor of economics at Harvard University, points out that the data "have the virtue of being prepared contemporaneously by local experts. Moreover, the willingness of customers to pay substantial amounts for this information is perhaps some testament to their validity." Third, previous studies used the PRS measure though most of them considered it to be a marker for an aspect of governance or state capacity (see Englehart 2009; Choi 2010; Fearon 2010; Taydas, Peksen, and James 2010).

The PRS first assesses each of the law and order components on a scale from 0 to 3. A single country might enjoy a high rating of 3 in terms of its judicial system but receive a low rating of 1 if the law is routinely ignored without effective sanction (e.g., by widespread rioting or looting) or if the crime rate is very high. The PRS then combines the scores from each feature to produce a seven-point scale, with 0 indicating a weak law and order tradition, where physical force or illegal means is relatively often an avenue of redress, and with 6 denoting a strong law and order tradition, where the established law enforcement and judicial channels are effectively utilized to settle disputes. We can see by looking at average scores during the study period for sample countries such as Iraq (1.7), Somalia (1.9), North Korea (2.1), the United States (5.8), and Australia (6.0) that the rule of law measure is quite accurate (see Table 10.A1). For estimation, the *rule of law* variable is lagged one year to ensure that it causes changes in the dependent variable rather than the other way around. According to the rule of law hypothesis, a high rating on this scale should produce a dampening effect on the onset of internal conflict, while a low score would indicate a much higher risk of the onset of civil war. It should be noted that the ICRG releases only the aggregated measure for public use[8] but that this data is ideal for testing a rule of law hypothesis, which predicts the dampening effect of the two combined features relevant for internal political conflict.[9]

To check the robustness of findings, this study employs four additional indicators that tap into concepts similar to those addressed by the PRS rule of law measure, the first two relating to the institutional aspect of the rule of law concept and the latter two relating to its social order aspect. If these four indicators exert a dampening effect on the onset of civil war, this will lend further support to the validity of the PRS rule of law measure. The first indicator is the rule of law garnered from the World Bank's (2011b) Worldwide Governance Indicators, the coverage of which starts in 1996. The second is a measure of judicial independence collected from Henisz's (2000) Political Constraint Index Dataset. The first two indicators are expected to show an ameliorating effect on the outbreak of civil war. The third indicator is Banks's (1996) count variable of the number of government crises per country-year which captures situations that threaten to remove the incumbent regime from power, thereby leading to disorder and anarchy, in other words, to the collapse of orderly rule of law societies. The fourth indicator is the Political Instability Task Force's (2007) state failure index. The fact that failed states exercise only a limited sovereignty over their territories and populations tends to engender chaotic political situations, including illegal strikes and riots. To facilitate easy interpretation of the estimated coefficients, the original values of government crises and state failure index are reversed so that low numbers correspond to disorderly situations and high numbers correspond to orderly situations; this implies that sociopolitical order should be associated with a lower risk of civil war.

To avoid the risk of omitted variable bias, this study includes nine control variables: *ethnic fractionalization, religious fractionalization, per capita income, population, mountainous terrain, noncontiguous state, oil exporter, political instability,* and *prior civil war.*[10] It is widely presumed that ethnic or religious tensions incite civil war (Horowitz 1985; James 2010). The *ethnic fractionalization* variable is constructed using data from *Atlas Narodov Mira* (1964), which reports the probability that two randomly drawn individuals in a country are from different ethnolinguistic groups. *Religious fractionalization* is based on the CIA Factbook and other related sources.

Per capita income is introduced to measure some financial and bureaucratic aspects of state capacity. Countries with fragile financial, military, or political institutions are more likely to experience internal conflict due to weak local policing and corrupt counterinsurgency practices. Per capita GDP is measured in thousands of 1985 U.S. dollars collected from Penn World Tables and the World Bank's (2011a) Economic Development Indicator; it is lagged one year to ensure that it affects the likelihood of the onset of internal war and not the other way around. We also control for population size, as internal warfare is more likely to occur in more populous countries. It is a logged term of the total population, in thousands, gathered from World Bank figures and lagged one year. It has been argued that mountainous countries have a higher risk of internal war onset than other countries because they provide rebels with natural sanctuaries such as swamps, caverns, and jungles. We have, therefore, included a logged term of an estimated percent of mountainous terrain according to the coding of geographer A. J. Gerard.

Civil war is more likely to occur when a potential rebel group resides in a territorial base separated from the country's center by either water or distance (e.g., Angola from Portugal); this variable is coded as "1" for noncontiguous countries and as "0" otherwise. Oil-exporting countries provide rebels with the material incentive to compete for control of state power; using World Bank data, a country is coded as "1" if it gets at least one-third of its export revenues from fossil fuels and as "0" otherwise. *Political instability* at the center reveals a country's weak and disorganized institutions, suggesting that it is more vulnerable to a separatist or center-seeking rebellion; this is operationalized as a dummy variable to indicate whether the country had a three-or-greater change on the Polity IV regime index in any of the three years prior to the country-year in question (Marshall and Jaggers 2007). *Prior civil war* is a variable that accounts for the effects of a country's having experienced a distinct internal conflict the prior year. Previous conflicts could indicate the continuation of a war or otherwise potentially influence the onset of subsequent conflicts. This is coded as "1" if a civil war was ongoing in the previous year and as "0" otherwise.

EMPIRICAL RESULTS

The first dependent variable of civil conflict is included in all models in Table 10.1; the models are tested with logit regression while controlling for the cluster effect. As shown in Model 1,[11] the *rule of law* variable is statistically significant at the 0.001 level and in the hypothesized direction. This result indicates that countries with high levels of the rule of law are associated with lower risks of the onset of civil war. Accordingly, the rule of law appears to serve as a mechanism for the nonviolent settlement of minority grievances and, consequently, reduces the likelihood of the onset of civil war. To put it another way, countries such as Congo (0.9 on a scale of 0 to 6), Haiti (1.7), and Sri Lanka (2.2) are less likely to sustain civil peace due to their lack of institutionalized rule of law systems. While the hypotheses regarding *per capita income, population size, political instability,* and *prior civil war* are supported, those regarding the other control variables are not. Models 2–5 introduce four additional measures of the rule of law, as discussed in the previous section. Models 2 and 3 show results of the *rule of law* and *judicial independence* variables, respectively; Models 4 and 5 report results of sociopolitical order.[12] Not surprisingly, these four additional indicators are negatively associated with the onset of civil war in a consistent manner, just as there is a negative association between the PRS rule of law measure and civil war onset. These results confirm that the rule of law matters.

Since statistical significance does not necessarily ensure a meaningful finding in a practical sense, the substantive effects of the variables should

Table 10.1
Effect of the Rule of Law on Civil War Onset

Variable	Model 1	Model 2	Model 3	Model 4	Model 5	Model 6	Model 7	Model 8
Rule of law	-0.607***	-2.169***				-0.513***	-1.008***	-1.799*
	(0.147)	(0.571)				(0.164)	(0.315)	(0.823)
Law: judicial independence			-1.125*					
			(0.630)					
Order: no government crises				-1.213***				
				(0.215)				
Order: no state failure					-0.673***			
					(0.157)			
Ethnic fractionalization	1.087	6.627**	1.145	0.932	1.734*	0.972	1.142	0.753
	(0.837)	(2.579)	(0.790)	(0.868)	(0.914)	(0.765)	(0.857)	(1.229)
Religious fractionalization	-0.437	-5.110*	-0.270	0.180	-2.409*	-0.794	-0.456	-1.336
	(1.090)	(2.603)	(0.978)	(0.999)	(1.151)	(1.079)	(1.179)	(1.691)
Per capita income	-0.203*	0.237*	-0.267**	-0.389***	-0.248**	-0.169*	-0.211*	-0.211
	(0.097)	(0.109)	(0.101)	(0.120)	(0.097)	(0.089)	(0.105)	(0.135)
Population	0.368**	0.760	0.337**	0.236	0.556***	0.409**	0.327*	0.565**
	(0.146)	(0.694)	(0.129)	(0.146)	(0.154)	(0.146)	(0.143)	(0.242)
Mountainous terrain	0.041	-0.154	0.067	-0.049	-0.070	0.059	-0.019	0.076
	(0.168)	(0.260)	(0.157)	(0.159)	(0.180)	(0.176)	(0.160)	(0.255)
Noncontiguous state	1.348	-1.080	1.323*	1.128	1.201	1.109	1.798*	1.894*
	(0.828)	(2.073)	(0.723)	(0.689)	(1.140)	(0.836)	(0.894)	(0.923)
Oil exporter	0.225	-1.173	0.273	0.543	-0.575	0.237	0.228	0.744
	(0.492)	(1.755)	(0.478)	(0.431)	(0.702)	(0.510)	(0.501)	(0.520)
Political instability	0.727*	1.371*	0.877*	0.714*	0.265	0.738*	0.566	0.595
	(0.420)	(0.663)	(0.401)	(0.389)	(0.437)	(0.417)	(0.482)	(0.556)

Prior civil war	−1.398*	−0.763	−1.142*	−1.009*	−4.626**	−1.451*	−1.789*	−2.639**
	(0.728)	(0.692)	(0.672)	(0.593)	(1.677)	(0.736)	(0.931)	(1.053)
Rule of law * ethnic fractionalization								
Ethnic polarization						−0.480		
						(0.877)		
Rule of law * ethnic polarization						−0.193		
						(0.314)		
Economic discrimination							−0.246	
							(0.224)	
Rule of law * economic discrimination							0.145	
							(0.096)	
Excluded population								−1.619
								(1.464)
Rule of law * excluded population								0.994
								(0.845)
Constant	−6.400***	−16.483*	−7.585***	−0.697	−0.186	−6.494***	−5.012***	−5.650**
	(1.730)	(7.386)	(1.583)	(1.986)	(2.718)	(1.714)	(1.590)	(2.405)
Wald chi²	84.51	82.94	71.78	72.13	129.02	94.63	68.55	34.70
Probability > chi²	0.001	0.001	0.001	0.001	0.001	0.001	0.001	0.001
Log pseudolikelihood	−126.94	−37.26	−130.38	−123.97	−111.88	−124.61	−118.66	−75.61
Pseudo R^2	0.18	0.30	0.16	0.20	0.28	0.19	0.19	0.25
Observations	2,568	1,192	2,561	2,564	2,568	2,568	2,231	1,776

Note: Numbers in parentheses are robust standard errors adjusted for clustering on country.

*p < .05 one-tailed tests

**p < .01 one-tailed tests

***p < .001 one-tailed tests

be reported for empirical verification. To calculate a baseline probability for civil war onset against which to make comparisons, this study sets the continuous variables at their means and the dichotomous variables at 0; it then adjusts the variables of greatest interest, one at a time, to observe the change in predicted probability of an internal war. Table 10.2 reports the substantive effects of the five variables that achieved significance in Model 1. The substantive analysis supports the main argument of this study, finding that the synthesis between a well-functioning legal system and minority group recognition of judicial legitimacy has a significantly ameliorating effect on the likelihood of civil war. As shown in the shaded rows, the risk that a country will experience internal conflict decreases by 61 percent when the quality of its rule of law increases by one standard deviation (i.e., 1.5). The likelihood of a civil war decreases by 84 percent if the rule of law quality increases by two standard deviations (i.e., 3.0). It is worth noting that, given the high human and financial costs associated with a civil war, even small changes in the predicted probability of political violence should not be dismissed. The benefit of the rule of law is a function of the cost of political violence and the probability of its occurrence. Reducing the annual probability of a civil war by 61 or 84 percent is hardly trivial when one recognizes that even a single incidence of civil

Table 10.2
Substantive Effects[a]

Variable	In Model 1 in Table 10.1
Rule of law	
1 standard deviation	−61%
2 standard deviations	−84%
Per capita income	
1 standard deviation	−72%
2 standard deviations	−92%
Population	
1 standard deviation	69%
2 standard deviations	186%
Political instability	
From 0 to 1	106%
Prior civil war	
From 0 to 1	−75%

[a]The baseline values are as follows: mean for continuous variables and 0 for dummy variables.

war might easily cost thousands of human lives and result in millions of dollars of damage.

This study has utilized the *rule of law* variable to measure the presence of legitimate legal channels of dispute resolution through which minority groups can effectively resolve their grievances before they erupt into political violence. However, one might assert that there is a disconnect between conceptualization and empirical testing on the grounds that the rule of law measure is too far removed to directly capture the domestic politics of minority groups. One way to account for this concern is to interact the PRS rule of law measure with some measure of potential minority grievances, although of course "[the concept of] grievances are difficult to measure" (Fearon and Laitin 2003, 79). This study relies on three proxy measures for minority grievances: ethnic polarization, economic discrimination, and excluded population.

Model 6 in Table 10.1 tests an interaction effect between the *rule of law* and *minority grievances* variables by introducing ethnic polarization as a proxy for the existence of minority grievances. In ethnically polarized countries, minority grievances are pervasive, and the most severe ethnic conflicts occur in countries where a substantial ethnic minority confronts an ethnic majority (Horowitz 1985). *Ethnic polarization* is a dichotomous variable marking those countries with 50 percent or greater ethnic majority and at least an 8 percent ethnic minority; the data is taken from Fearon and Laitin's (2003) study. Model 6 shows that while the rule of law is significantly different from zero, neither ethnic polarization nor the interaction is significantly different. This result confirms that when ethnic minority groups have access to a fair and independent judiciary, they are inclined to peacefully redress grievances and are, in turn, less likely to resort to violence. On the contrary, the other two factors appear to have no direct bearing on the outbreak of civil war.[13]

Model 7 is another multiplicative interaction logit model in which minority economic discrimination is used as a proxy for the existence of minority grievances. Minority *economic discrimination* is a dichotomous variable using the "ECDIS/Economic Discrimination Index" from the Minorities at Risk Project (2009). Following Lai's (2007) operational procedures, it is dichotomous, noting 1 for country-years indicating the presence of at least one Minority at Risk group and where ECDIS has a value of 2, 3, or 4. Model 7 also shows supporting evidence that a high-quality rule of law decreases the likelihood of the onset of civil war; however, neither economic discrimination nor its interaction term is related to the occurrence of civil war onset.

Model 8 is another multiplicative interaction logit model in which excluded population is introduced to capture the grievances of ethnic minorities. As the political exclusion of ethnic groups within a state becomes more acute, it generates resentment and increases the number of individuals who, lacking access to the executive power via orderly and nonviolent means, support civil violence as a means of redress (e.g., Catholics in Northern Ireland, see Wimmer, Cederman, and Min 2009). The *excluded population* variable measures the share of the excluded population that is ethnopolitically relevant within the total population. Wimmer, Cederman, and Min (2009) define an ethnic group as politically excluded if its members are excluded from service or representation in the executive branch of government—this includes the political executive, such as presidential cabinet and executive offices, as well as the top ranks of the national military organizations and bureaucracies. The excluded population measure may merit closer examination in regard to the possibility that relatively minor grievances are not likely to provoke civil violence. To correct the positive skew of the data, this study uses its logged transformation. This is consistent with the assumption that increases in the share of the excluded population have a greater effect on the likelihood of civil war outbreak at lower levels of exclusion than at higher levels. Model 8 shows no significance for the interaction term between the *rule of law* and *excluded population*, although the *rule of law* variable itself does appear to be statistically significant.

Using the four additional measures of the dependent variable of civil conflict, Table 10.3 delves further into the effects of a strong rule of law tradition on the propensity of domestic minority groups to initiate civil conflict. While Model 1 uses the onset of ethnic war, Models 2–4 rely on the Uppsala/PRIO's armed conflict variables. With the exception of the

Table 10.3
Ethnic War and Uppsala/PRIO Civil War

Variable	Ethnic War	Uppsala/PRIO Civil War		
	Model 1	Model 2	Model 3	Model 4
Rule of law	−0.367*	−0.207**	−0.327***	−0.467**
	(0.174)	(0.086)	(0.084)	(0.180)
Ethnic fractionalization	2.472***	1.607**	0.857*	1.814*
	(0.781)	(0.576)	(0.393)	(0.964)
Religious fractionalization	−1.291	−1.302*	−0.567	3.931*
	(0.970)	(0.674)	(0.480)	(1.991)
Per capita income	−0.161	−0.055	−0.024	−0.016
	(0.118)	(0.048)	(0.040)	(0.069)
Population	0.327**	0.325***	0.257***	0.798***
	(0.131)	(0.089)	(0.082)	(0.218)
Mountainous terrain	−0.054	0.005	0.059	−0.016
	(0.184)	(0.138)	(0.086)	(0.296)

Variable	Ethnic War	Uppsala/PRIO Civil War		
	Model 1	Model 2	Model 3	Model 4
Noncontiguous state	0.417	0.561	0.694*	1.977**
	(0.650)	(0.387)	(0.390)	(0.701)
Oil exporter	0.467	0.616*	0.131	0.504
	(0.401)	(0.353)	(0.272)	(0.549)
Political instability	0.450	0.055	−0.071	0.204
	(0.505)	(0.291)	(0.291)	(0.741)
Prior war	−0.359	0.502	4.749***	0.110
	(0.592)	(0.612)	(0.413)	(0.430)
Constant	−6.994***	−6.261***	−5.041***	−15.660***
	(1.506)	(1.057)	(0.855)	(3.662)
Wald chi^2	65.45	106.83	379.51	115.00
Probability > chi^2	0.001	0.001	0.001	0.001
Log pseudolikelihood	−136.56	−327.95	−426.85	−65.49
Pseudo R^2	0.16	0.13	0.64	0.33
Observations	2,568	2,538	2,538	2,538

Note: Numbers in parentheses are robust standard errors adjusted for clustering on country.

*$p < .05$ one-tailed tests

**$p < .01$ one-tailed tests

***$p < .001$ one-tailed tests

replacement of the dependent variable, Model 1 in Table 10.3, which is built to explain the variation of ethnic war, follows the same model specification as Model 1 in Table 10.1. Given that ethnic wars are the direct result of political grievances, or of discrimination against minority groups (Sambanis 2001), the following empirical results, if supported, will offer compelling evidence for the hypothesis concerning the rule of law and minority groups. In Model 1, the *rule of law* variable is significantly different from zero and its sign is in the theoretically predicted direction. This implies that the presence of an impartial judicial system, in conjunction with the perceived legitimacy of the legal system, provides an institutionalized channel for the resolution of disputes and grievances brought by ethnic minorities. Based on the Uppsala/PRIO's civil war onset with more than 25 battle deaths, incidence, and onset with more than 1,000 battle deaths, respectively, Models 2–4 provide another set of robustness tests, and their estimated results lend further support to the rule of law argument. All in all, Table 10.3 indicates that, regardless of the measure of the dependent variable, the mitigating effect of the rule of law on civil conflict remains.[14]

EXAMINING REVERSE CAUSALITY BETWEEN THE
RULE OF LAW AND CIVIL WAR ONSET

The main purpose of this study is to introduce the *rule of law* variable, a novel "grievance" predictor of the onset of civil war, into the literature on intrastate warfare and to examine whether or not it decreases the likelihood of the onset of civil war. To do so, it has relied on a single equation model; however, one might speculate that the causal arrow also points in the opposite direction, on the grounds that the onset of a civil/ethnic war may also cause a destabilization of the rule of law. The speculation is plausible insofar as we know that civil/ethnic violence may cause a state to abandon its constitutional principles in the midst of rebellion or internal strife by imposing martial law or by waiving the basic rights of its citizens. To account for the issue of mutual causality (i.e., endogeneity bias), this study employs the simultaneous equations model developed by Keshk (2003).[15]

Building a simultaneous equations model remains one of the most challenging tasks in civil war studies; most existing literature chooses to ignore the issue of endogeneity bias. For instance, as Hegre and Sambanis (2006, 513–514) state,

A concern with our approach as well as with all studies of civil war onset is that some of the variables included in civil war models may be endogenous . . . we assume exogeneity for all variables (as do almost all the studies that we surveyed in this literature). . . . Since very few of the papers in the literature on civil war deal with the issue of endogeneity, we also ignore it and simply try to reduce the risk by lagging independent variables.

This study encounters similar difficulties in dealing with endogeneity bias because the determinants of the rule of law are underexplored in the existing literature; that is, previous studies rarely treat the *rule of law* as an outcome variable. As a first attempt to account for mutual causality, this study models the rule of law as a function of the onset of civil/ethnic war, *terrorism, political conflict index, civil liberties,* and *per capita income* to obtain the predicted values of the rule of law. Next, the likelihood of the onset of civil/ethnic war is estimated as a function of the predicted values of the rule of law along with the control variables that appeared in the previous models. In this two-stage modeling, *terrorism, political conflict index,* and *civil liberties* are included as instrumental variables.[16]

The theoretical rationale for these instrumental variables is as follows: terrorist activity is likely to disrupt the institutionalization of the rule of law, specifically in cases where it prompts political leaders to compromise civil liberties and political rights in response to potential terrorist threats (e.g., the United States after September 11, the United Kingdom in the 1970s, and Russia after the mid-1990s; see Ramraj, Hor, and Roach 2005; Smith August 11, 2007). The *terrorism* variable is a log transformation of the annual total number of domestic and international terrorist events that occur within a country, as collected from the Global Terrorism Database Explorer (Lee 2008; see also LaFree and Dugan 2007). Frequent political conflict is another factor that may hinder the development of a rule of law tradition as institutions require time without major disturbance to take root within the political imaginary (Feng 1997). To measure political conflict, this study turns to Banks's (1996) event counts such as assassinations, general strikes, and purges; these counts are summed into an index of political conflict, which is then log transformed to address a skewed distribution. Previous studies have argued that the protection of civil liberties is essential to the establishment of a high-quality rule of law tradition (O'Donnell 2004; Carothers 2009), therefore, this study uses the data on civil liberties compiled by Freedom House (2009), which is considered the best set available due to its scope and quality (Keech 2009, 9).

Table 10.4, then, reports the simultaneous equations results. Model 1 shows the results when the dependent variable is the onset of civil war;

Table 10.4
Simultaneous Analysis of the Rule of Law and Civil War Onset

	Civil War		Ethnic War	Uppsala/PRIO Civil War	
Variable	Model 1	Model 2	Model 3	Model 4	Model 5
Rule of law equation					
Civil war onset	0.350***	0.057	0.112	–0.167***	0.012
	(0.113)	(0.067)	(0.080)	(0.027)	(0.033)
Terrorism	–0.081***	–0.060***	–0.068***	0.011	–0.060***
	(0.023)	(0.014)	(0.016)	(0.018)	(0.016)
Political conflict index	–0.068***	–0.059***	–0.061***	–0.044***	–0.057***
	(0.0116)	(0.008)	(0.008)	(0.007)	(0.007)
Civil liberties	0.209***	0.187***	0.195***	0.146***	0.182***
	(0.027)	(0.015)	(0.017)	(0.015)	(0.014)
Per capita income	0.163***	0.127***	0.124***	0.115***	0.122***
	(0.020)	(0.007)	(0.005)	(0.005)	(0.004)
Constant	3.128***	2.539***	2.615***	2.200***	2.463***
	(0.246)	(0.153)	(0.151)	(0.071)	(0.126)
F statistic	492.04	480.99	481.18	494.98	480.44
Probability > F statistic	0.001	0.001	0.001	0.001	0.001
R^2	0.48	0.48	0.48	0.49	0.48
Observations	2,627	2,627	2,594	2,594	2,594

(Continued)

Table 10.4
(Continued)

Variable	Civil War Model 1	Ethnic War Model 2	Uppsala/PRIO Civil War Model 3	Model 4	Model 5
Civil war onset equation					
Rule of law	−0.689**	−0.796**	−0.553***	−0.965***	−0.825*
	(0.288)	(0.295)	(0.139)	(0.179)	(0.361)
Ethnic fractionalization	0.351	0.998**	0.718***	0.475*	0.693
	(0.325)	(0.377)	(0.228)	(0.206)	(0.577)
Religious fractionalization	−0.333	−0.592	−0.627*	−0.521*	1.059
	(0.425)	(0.441)	(0.287)	(0.260)	(0.803)
Per capita income	−0.042	0.037	0.050*	0.097***	0.103
	(0.062)	(0.061)	(0.026)	(0.028)	(0.068)
Population	0.170**	0.191**	0.160***	0.173***	0.345***
	(0.063)	(0.068)	(0.043)	(0.042)	(0.102)
Mountainous terrain	0.029	−0.035	−0.022	0.012	−0.076
	(0.071)	(0.071)	(0.047)	(0.041)	(0.130)
Noncontiguous state	0.657**	0.239	0.241*	0.511***	0.649*
	(0.262)	(0.243)	(0.146)	(0.156)	(0.287)
Oil exporter	−0.109	0.001	0.098	−0.224	−0.017
	(0.231)	(0.213)	(0.132)	(0.142)	(0.311)
Political instability	0.212	0.031	−0.162	−0.255*	−0.197
	(0.194)	(0.201)	(0.149)	(0.142)	(0.335)
Prior war	−0.973**	−0.666**	0.232	2.034***	0.182
	(0.322)	(0.281)	(0.203)	(0.168)	(0.537)
Constant	−1.707*	−1.901*	−1.926***	−0.610	−4.803***
	(0.875)	(0.889)	(0.535)	(0.569)	(1.242)
LR chi^2	51.41	59.77	109.78	1,624.47	62.30
Probability > chi^2	0.001	0.001	0.001	0.001	0.001
Log likelihood	−138.30	−142.97	−332.70	−428.69	−66.21
Pseudo R^2	0.16	0.17	0.14	0.65	0.32
Observations	2,627	2,627	2,594	2,594	2,594

Note: Robust standard errors are in parentheses.

*$p < .05$ one-tailed tests

**$p < .01$ one-tailed tests

***$p < .001$ one-tailed tests

Model 2 displays the results for the onset of ethnic war; Models 3–5 report the results based on the Uppsala/PRIO's three civil conflict variables. The first stage equation of the rule of law in Model 1 shows that all the variables except *civil war onset* are statistically significant and in the theoretically predicted directions. The *onset of civil war* variable achieves significance, but it does not point in the hypothesized direction. This implies that the *onset of civil war* contributes to an increase in the quality of the rule of law. One might speculate that when confronted with the possibility of civil violence, the ruling class is more willing to accommodate the grievances or enhance the rights of minority groups in order to assuage it. Assuming that ruling class would prefer to avoid the outbreak of civil war by accommodating at least some minority grievances, this empirical finding seems right on. In fact, human history shows us that minority rights have continually been improved as a result of violent civil conflict. Several previous studies also provide evidence of a positive relationship between civil/ethnic violence and institution-building in East Africa and Southeast Asia (e.g., Weinstein 2005; Slater 2010).

The first-stage results in Models 2–5 are similar to those in Model 1 except for the *civil war onset* variable which turns out to be insignificant in Models 2, 3, and 5 but which is significant in Model 4. The second-stage equation for the *onset of civil war* in Models 1–5 once again confirms that countries with a high-quality rule of law experience a lower risk of the onset of civil or ethnic war (see the *rule of law* variable of the second stage in the shaded rows). It should also be noted that when the endogeneity bias is properly corrected, the magnitude of the rule of law coefficient becomes larger than that reported in Model 1 in Table 10.1 and in Models 1–4 in Table 10.3.

CONCLUSION

In the effort to explain the prevalence of civil conflict around the world, scholars have pointed primarily to matters of greed and economic disparity.[17] However, this study argues that many of the relevant statistical models that have supported these conclusions have not only neglected to consider some crucial justice-seeking variables but also suffered from potential endogeneity bias. This study has filled those gaps by introducing the *rule of law* as a critical "grievance" variable and by taking reverse causality into consideration. The introduction of the *rule of law* variable is justified by Carothers (1998, 95), who proclaimed that "one cannot get through a foreign policy debate these days without someone proposing the rule of law as the solution to the world's trouble."

Specifically, this study investigates whether or not adherence to the rule of law tends to reduce incidence of civil war outbreak. It puts forward a causal explanation, arguing that because well-established rule of law systems provide minority groups with a nonviolent means of conflict resolution, their members are less likely to be spurred to political violence by feelings of bitterness and resentment. Furthermore, this study hypothesizes that the presence of an impartial judicial system along with the widespread acceptance of its legitimacy is, in fact, what undermines the opportunity and willingness for minority groups to take up arms against the government. Just as gasoline is as necessary as an engine for the operation of an automobile, a public that has been socialized to the rule of law is the necessary adjunct to an independent judiciary in the effort to decrease the likelihood of civil war.[18] The empirical results of this study indeed show that a strong rule of law tradition corresponds to a decrease in the likelihood of civil conflict, implying that the lack of a stable rule of law tradition may be the root cause of rebellion.

Despite the fact that almost all existing studies on the onset of civil war ignore the issue of endogeneity bias, not for theoretical reasons but due to statistical estimation problems, this study has taken the first step toward uncovering a complex reciprocal relationship; it has indeed found that the rule of law and the onset of civil war reinforce one another. This study believes that the discussion of endogeneity bias is not damaging but complementary to the main hypothesis of this study. Empirical results of simultaneous equations models confirm this line of reasoning because the rule of law continues to emerge as a factor contributing to the reduction of the likelihood of civil war onset; furthermore, this study finds that the effect actually increases when the reciprocal relationship is taken into account. Simply put, the empirical analysis of this study consistently demonstrates that effective legal institutions provide for aggrieved ethnic groups a viable alternative to armed insurrection.

The empirical findings of this study offer important implications for American foreign policy. Characteristically, America has focused on the spread of democracy in the form of free elections; however, if we find that democratization can lead to an increase in violence (see Mansfield and Snyder 2005), promotion of democracy may not be in the best interest of the United States when its goal is to lower the risk of civil war. Fortunately, the results reported here provide strong evidence that the cultivation of a rule of law tradition is a more crucial factor in helping to reduce the incidence of internal warfare than democratization alone (as reported in footnote 9, the *democracy* variable does not achieve significance). In the absence of a strong rule of law tradition, ethnic groups compete to establish their own preferred rules of conduct, which, likely, conflict with one another. In the absence of an agreed-upon system of adjudication, entire societies can be plunged into chaos, precipitating the outbreak of civil war. Accordingly, political leaders and policy makers should emphasize judicial and legal training as well as civic education and socialization. In fact, the findings indicate that the role of the

U.S. Agency for International Development (USAID) and similar agencies in the European Union is significant, as one of their primary missions is to fund independent judiciaries in developing countries (see USAID 2008). Such agencies should, then, work together to channel more financial resources toward the establishment of sound rule of law traditions in insurgency-prone countries.

Table 10.A1
Average Scores of the Rule of Law by Country, 1984–2007

Albania	3.1	Greece	3.9	Norway	6.0
Algeria	2.2	Guatemala	1.9	Oman	4.5
Angola	1.9	Guinea	2.9	Pakistan	2.6
Argentina	3.7	Guinea-Bissau	1.1	Panama	2.7
Australia	6.0	Guyana	2.4	Papua New Guinea	3.0
Austria	6.0	Haiti	1.7	Paraguay	2.7
Azerbaijan	4.0	Honduras	2.3	Peru	2.3
Bahrain	4.8	Hungary	4.9	Philippines	2.3
Bangladesh	1.8	India	3.3	Poland	4.6
Belarus	4.0	Indonesia	2.8	Portugal	5.1
Belgium	5.5	Iran	3.5	Romania	3.7
Bolivia	2.3	Iraq	1.7	Russia	3.5
Botswana	4.5	Ireland	5.4	Saudi Arabia	4.7
Brazil	3.0	Israel	4.1	Senegal	2.6
Bulgaria	4.5	Italy	5.0	Sierra Leone	2.6
Burkina Faso	3.6	Ivory Coast	3.2	Singapore	5.4
Burma	2.9	Jamaica	2.2	Slovak Republic	4.6
Cameroon	2.5	Japan	5.3	Slovenia	4.8
Canada	6.0	Jordan	3.6	Somalia	1.9
Chile	4.6	Kazakhstan	4.0	South Africa	2.4
China	4.2	Kenya	3.0	Spain	4.7
Colombia	1.3	Korea North	2.1	Sri Lanka	2.2
Democratic Republic of the Congo	0.9	Korea South	3.5	Sudan	2.0
Congo Republic	2.1	Kuwait	4.4	Sweden	6.0
Costa Rica	4.0	Latvia	5.0	Switzerland	5.7
Croatia	5.0	Lebanon	1.8	Syria	2.9
Cuba	4.6	Liberia	1.6	Taiwan	4.8
Cyprus	4.5	Libya	2.0	Tanzania	4.4
Czechoslovakia	5.0	Lithuania	4.0	Thailand	4.1
Czech Republic	5.3	Madagascar	2.9	Togo	2.6

(Continued)

**Table 10.A1
(Continued)**

Denmark	6.0	Malawi	2.9	Trinidad and Tobago	3.7
Dominican Republic	3.1	Malaysia	4.0	Tunisia	3.9
Ecuador	3.6	Mali	2.7	Turkey	3.7
Egypt	3.4	Mexico	2.7	United Arab Emirates	3.7
El Salvador	2.3	Moldova	5.0	Uganda	2.7
Estonia	4.0	Mongolia	3.4	Ukraine	4.0
Ethiopia	2.1	Morocco	4.4	United Kingdom	5.5
Finland	6.0	Mozambique	2.6	United States	5.8
France	5.2	Namibia	5.6	Uruguay	3.0
Gabon	2.8	Netherlands	6.0	Venezuela	3.6
Gambia	4.2	New Zealand	6.0	People's Democratic Republic of Yemen	1.0
Germany East	5.0	Nicaragua	3.2	Yugoslavia	2.0
Germany West	5.4	Niger	2.4	Zambia	3.2
Ghana	2.3	Nigeria	2.2	Zimbabwe	2.5

**Table 10.A2
Multicollinearity Diagnostics[a]**

	R^2	Variance Inflation Factors (VIFs)	Square Root of VIFs
Rule of law	0.48	1.91	1.38
Ethnic fractionalization	0.33	1.49	1.22
Religious fractionalization	0.21	1.26	1.12
Per capita income	0.52	2.10	1.45
Population	0.27	1.37	1.17
Mountainous terrain	0.17	1.21	1.10
Noncontiguous state	0.27	1.36	1.17
Oil exporter	0.05	1.05	1.02
Political instability	0.09	1.10	1.05
Prior civil war	0.27	1.37	1.17
Mean variance inflation factors		1.42	

	Eigenvalues	Condition Index
1	6.36	1.00
2	1.22	2.28
3	0.95	2.59
4	0.77	2.88
5	0.63	3.18
6	0.41	3.95
7	0.34	4.34
8	0.15	6.56
9	0.12	7.21
10	0.05	11.17
11	0.01	26.98
Condition number		26.98
Eigenvalues and condition index computed from the scaled raw sscp with an intercept.		
Det(correlation matrix)		0.16

[a] A general rule of thumb: A serious multicollinearity problem is suspected if R^2 is greater than 0.80, if the mean of all the variance inflation factors is considerably larger than 10, or if condition number exceeds 1,000.

NOTES

1. The Māori are the indigenous Polynesian people of New Zealand. They make up roughly 15 percent of the national population, making them the second-largest ethnic group after European New Zealanders.

2. A comprehensive legal definition of the rule of law can be found in Schmid and Boland (2001, xi).

3. For a similar view, see Fuller (1969).

4. Given that norms of peaceful resolution of political disputes would make it difficult to mobilize resources for violent offenses, it may be useful to explore the role of socialization in light of Charles Tilly's (1978) resource-mobilization theory of political violence. This conceptualization goes beyond the scope of this study, so it is left for future research.

5. It should be noted that the rule of law cannot simply mean the legal coercion of citizens but must also imply some public understanding and acknowledgment of the legitimacy inherent in the tendency of the law's operations. For the purposes of this study, it is argued that this is achieved when the coercive element of the law is somehow linked up with, and justified by, a notion of public autonomy relevant to our political intuitions. In this sense, an effective and legitimate rule of law is obtained when there is a middle ground between, or coexistence of, pure voluntary adherence to law and pure submission to legal coercion. In this middle

ground, insofar as they are produced in some nonarbitrary fashion, and are adjudicated and processed by fair and impartial judicial systems, laws are seen as legitimate, entailing a recognition of, if not a voluntary subscription to, their sovereignty in political and social proceedings (see Rawls 1971/1999; Hobbes 1985). In short, the rule of law means that people, including minority groups, voluntarily subscribe to the legal system, even when being coerced to act in accordance with individual laws.

6. The starting year of this study is based on the data collection relative to the rule of law, which is available only as far back as 1984.

7. Fearon and Laitin (2003, 79) state that "if many post-1945 civil wars have been 'ethnic' or 'nationalist' as these terms are usually understood, then even more have been fought as *insurgencies*."

8. Put differently, there is no way to disaggregate the aggregated measure of the rule of law because the ICRG provides no information at all on its individual component.

9. The rule of law compiled by the PRS has no bearing on the presence of civil war because it captures only whether the law is routinely ignored without effective sanction (e.g., widespread illegal strikes). In fact, in order to avoid the empirical overlap between the rule of law and internal conflict, the ICRG provides a separate measure of internal conflict rather than combining the two concepts. The ICRG makes clear that the lowest rating for the internal conflict variable is given to a country embroiled in an ongoing civil war. It is also worth noting that the ICRG includes a separate measure for external conflict in the proprietary dataset; this measure is an assessment of the risk to the incumbent government from foreign action, ranging from nonviolent external pressure (diplomatic pressures, withholding of aid, trade restrictions, territorial disputes, sanctions, etc.) to violent external pressure (cross-border conflicts to all-out war). As is with the case of the internal conflict variable, the *rule of law* variable has, by construction, little to do with the external conflict variable.

10. *Democracy* and *civil liberties* are excluded from the model specification because they may be conceptually related to the rule of law. When they are included, one at a time, they fail to achieve significance and they do not cause the rule of law to become insignificant.

11. Three of the most widely used diagnostic tests on multicollinearity are performed: R^2 statistics, variance inflation factors, and condition index (see Greene 2003; Gujarati 2003). Table 10.A2 shows no indication of severe multicollinearity problems among independent variables.

12. The correlation between the PRS *rule of law* variable and the four measures is 0.78 (Henisz's judicial independence), 0.75 (the World Banks's rule of law), 0.05 (Banks's government crises), and 0.37 (the Political Instability Task Force's state failure).

13. By comparing the overall fit of two competing models (i.e., one with the interaction term and the other without it), one can offer a justification for the insignificance of the interaction effect. This study determines whether the interaction term included in Model 6 contributes enough additional information to assist in explaining the onset of civil war. This study implements two commonly used comparative statistics, namely, an information criterion (AIC) test and Bayesian

information criterion (BIC) test. The AIC value is 275.88 for the no-interaction model (not shown in Table 10.1 to save space) and 277.83 for the interaction Model 6. The smaller value for the no-interaction model indicates that the model specification without the interaction term does a better job than the model specification with the term in explaining the causes of civil war onset. The BIC value is 340.24 for the no-interaction model and 348.04 for the interaction Model 6. Since the model with the lower BIC value indicates the better result, the no-interaction model is again shown to be superior to the interaction model.

14. When country fixed effects are considered for Model 1 in Table 10.1 and Models 1–4 in Table 10.3, the rule of law is still statistically significant across models except for Model 2 of Table 10.3. The results are not reported in order to save space, as well as to avoid misleading the reader with the estimated coefficients. As Schneider, Barbieri, and Gleditsch (2003, 22) warn, fixed-effects logit "does not seem ideal for binary dependent variables whose one outcome represents a rare event." Because of this shortcoming, the fixed-effects logit leads to a dramatic loss of observations, resulting in a biased logit analysis. For example, more than 83 percent of the total observations are, by definition, dropped in the estimation process of Model 1 of Table 10.1, though the rule of law still surpasses the conventional significance levels.

This study has also conducted other types of robustness tests with alternative estimation methods (e.g., generalized estimating equations, rare event logit, and peace splines) and found no substantive differences between the results reported in Tables 10.1 and 10.3 and those from the robustness tests. To save space, the results are not reported in this study.

15. Keshk (2003) provides technical details of two-stage probit least squares, which is designed to address the endogeneity problem after properly adjusting standard errors, when one endogenous variable is continuous and the other is dichotomous.

16. This study tests for the validity of these three instrumental variables to make sure that they are uncorrelated with the error term, an essential condition for the validity of the instruments; it finds that they are useful instrumental variables because they are not correlated with the error term.

17. Exceptions include Wimmer, Cederman, and Min (2009).

18. The automobile example is analogous to Berger's (1998, 11–12) insight that "institutions and culture exist in an interdependent relationship, each relying upon the other in an ongoing way."

REFERENCES

Adam, Heribert. 1971. *Modernizing Racial Domination*. Berkeley: University of California Press.

Atlas Narodov Mira. 1964. Moscow: Glavnoe Upravlenie Geodezii Ikartografii.

Banks, Arthur S. 1996. *Political Handbook of the World*. New York: CSA Publications.

Barro, Robert J. 1999a. *Determinants of Economic Growth*. 2nd ed. Cambridge, MA: MIT Press.

Barro, Robert J. 1999b. "Determinants of Democracy." *Journal of Political Economy* 107(6): S158–S183.

Berger, Thomas U. 1998. *Cultures of Antimilitarism*. Baltimore, MD: Johns Hopkins University Press.

Blattman, Christopher and Edward Miguel. 2009. "Civil War." Working paper number 166, Center for Global Development.

Bourassa, Steven C. and Ann Louise Strong. 2002. "Restitution of Land to New Zealand Maori: The Role of Social Structure." *Pacific Affairs* 75(2): 227–260.

Carothers, Thomas. 1998. "The Rule of Law Revival." *Foreign Affairs* 77(2): 95–106.

Carothers, Thomas. 2009. "Rule of Law Temptations." *The Fletcher Forum of World Affairs* 33(1): 49–61.

Choi, Seung-Whan. 2010. "Fighting Terrorism through the Rule of Law?" *Journal of Conflict Resolution* 54(6): 940–966.

Englehart, Neil A. 2009. "State Capacity, State Failure, and Human Rights." *Journal of Peace Research* 46(2): 163–180.

Eyerman, Joe. 1998. "Terrorism and Democratic States: Soft Targets or Accessible Systems." *International Interactions* 24(2): 151–170.

Fearon, James D. 2010. "Governance and Civil War Onset." World Development Report 2011: Background Paper. http://siteresources.worldbank.org/EXT-WDR2011/Resources/6406082-1283882418764/WDR_Background_Paper_Fearon.pdf.

Fearon, James D. and David D. Laitin. 2003. "Ethnicity, Insurgency, and Civil War." *American Political Science Review* 97(1): 75–90.

Feng, Yi. 1997. "Democracy, Political Stability, and Economic Growth." *British Journal of Political Science* 27(3): 391–418.

Fleras, Augie. 1985. "From Social Control towards Political Self-Determination? Maori Seats and the Politics of Separate Representation in New Zealand." *Canadian Journal of Political Science* 18(3): 551–576.

Freedom House. 2009. *Freedom in the World 2009: Setbacks and Resilience*. New York: Rowman and Littlefield.

Fuller, Lon L. 1969. *The Morality of Law*. New Haven, CT: Yale University Press.

Gellner, Ernest. 1983. *Nations and Nationalism*. Ithaca, NY: Cornell University Press.

Greene, William H. 2003. *Econometric Analysis*. 5th ed. Upper Saddle River, NJ: Prentice Hall.

Gujarati, Damodar N. 2003. *Basic Econometrics*. 4th ed. New York: McGraw-Hill, Inc.

Harbom, Lotta and Peter Wallensteen. 2010. "Armed Conflicts, 1946–2009." *Journal of Peace Research* 47(4): 501–509.

Hardin, Russell. 2001. "Law and Social Order." *Philosophical Issues* 11: 61–85.

Hegre, Håvard and Nicholas Sambanis. 2006. "Sensitivity Analysis of Empirical Results on Civil War Onset." *Journal of Conflict Resolution* 50(4): 508–535.

Henisz, Witold J. 2000. "The Institutional Environment for Economic Growth." *Economics and Politics* 12(1): 1–43.

Hobbes, Thomas. 1985. *Leviathan*. London: Penguin Books.

Hogg, Russell and David Brown. 1998. *Rethinking Law & Order*. Annandale, NSW: Pluto Press.

Horowitz, Donald L. 1985. *Ethnic Groups in Conflict*. Berkeley: University of California Press.

Huntington, Samuel P. 1996. *The Clash of Civilizations and the Remaking of World Order*. New York: Simon & Schuster.

James, Patrick, ed. 2010. *Religion, Identity and Global Governance*. Toronto: University of Toronto Press.

Keech, William. 2009. "A Scientifically Superior Conception of Democracy." Presented at the Midwest Political Science Association Conference, Chicago, Illinois, April 16–19.

Keshk, Omar M. G. 2003. "CDSIMEQ: A Program to Implement Two-Stage Probit Least Squares." *Stata Journal* 3(2): 157–167.

LaFree, Gary and Laura Dugan. 2007. "Introducing the Global Terrorism Database." *Terrorism and Political Violence* 19(2): 181–204.

Lai, Brian. 2007. "Draining the Swamp." *Conflict Management and Peace Science* 24(4): 297–310.

Lee, Joonghoon. 2008. "Exploring Global Terrorism Data." *ACM Crossroads* 15(2): 7–16.

Lustick, Ian. 1980. *Arabs in the Jewish State*. Austin: University of Texas Press.

Mansfield, Edward D. and Jack Snyder. 2005. *Electing to Fight*. Cambridge, MA: MIT Press.

Marshall, Monty and Keith Jaggers. 2007. "POLITY IV Project: Political Regime Characteristics and Transitions, 1800–2006." Dataset Users' Manual. http://www.systemicpeace.org/inscr/p4manualv2015.pdf

Minorities at Risk Project. 2009. *Minorities at Risk Database*. College Park, MD: Center for International Development and Conflict Management.

O'Donnell, Guillermo. 2004. "Why the Rule of Law Matters." *Journal of Democracy* 15(4): 32–46.

O'Sullivan, Dominic. 2008. "Needs, Rights and 'One Law for All': Contemporary Debates in New Zealand Maori Politics." *Canadian Journal of Political Science* 41(4): 973–986.

Political Instability Task Force. 2007. "Internal Wars and Failures of Governance, 1955–2006." http://www.worldcat.org/title/state-failure-internal-wars-and-failures-of-governance-1955-2006/oclc/613998227.

Ramraj, Victor V., Michael Hor, and Kent Roach, eds. 2005. *Global Anti-Terrorism Law and Policy*. New York: Cambridge University Press.

Rawls, John. 1971/1999. *A Theory of Justice, Revised Edition*. Cambridge, MA: Harvard University Press.

Raz, Joseph. 1977. "The Rule of Law and Its Virtue." *Law Quarterly Review* 93: 195–211.

Sambanis, Nicholas. 2001. "Do Ethnic and Nonethnic Civil Wars Have the Same Causes? A Theoretical and Empirical Inquiry (Part 1)." *Journal of Conflict Resolution* 45(3): 259–282.

Schmid, Alex P. and Etihne Boland, eds. 2001. *The Rule of Law in the Global Village: Issues of Sovereignty and Universality*. Milan: ISPAC.

Schneider, Gerald, Katherine Barbieri, and Nils Petter Gleditsch. 2003. "Does Globalization Contribute to Peace?" In Gerald Schneider, Katherine Barbieri, and Nils Petter Gleditsch, eds., *Globalization and Armed Conflict*. Lanham, MD: Rowman & Littlefield Publishers, Inc. 3–29.

Slater, Dan. 2010. *Ordering Power: Contentious Politics and Authoritarian Leviathans in Southeast Asia*. New York: Cambridge University Press.

Smith, Andreas Whittam. August 11, 2007. "I'd Rather Risk Terrorism Than Destroy the Rule of Law." *The Independent*. http://www.independent.co.uk/

voices/commentators/andreas-whittam-smith/id-rather-risk-terrorism-than-destroy-the-rule-of-law-488957.html

Taydas, Zeynep, Dursun Peksen, and Patrick James. 2010. "Why Do Civil Wars Occur? Understanding the Importance of Institutional Quality." *Civil Wars* 12(3): 195–217.

Tilly, Charles. 1978. *From Mobilization to Revolution*. Reading, MA: Addison-Wesley.

USAID. 2008. "This Is USAID." http://www.usaid.gov/about_usaid/.

Weinstein, Jeremy M. 2005. "Autonomous Recovery and International Intervention in Comparative Perspective." Working paper number 57. 1–35, Center for Global Development.

Wilson, Jeremy M. 2006. "Law and Order in an Emerging Democracy." *Annals of the American Academy of Political and Social Science* 605(1): 152–177.

Wimmer, Andreas, Lars-Erik Cederman, and Brian Min. 2009. "Ethnic Politics and Armed Conflict." *American Sociological Review* 74(2): 316–337.

World Bank. 2011a. "World Development Indicators 2011." http://documents.worldbank.org/curated/en/245401468331253857/World-development-indicators-2011.

World Bank. 2011b. "Worldwide Governance Indicators, 1996–2007." https://papers.ssrn.com/sol3/papers.cfm?abstract_id=1148386.

CHAPTER 11

Civil War, Volunteer Soldiers, and the Military

In 1865, Friedrich Engels wrote that "universal conscription is the necessary and natural corollary of universal suffrage; it puts the voters in the position of being able to enforce their decisions gun in hand against any attempt at a coup d'état."[1] Although it appears that Engels values conscription as the most democratic approach to military recruitment, the existing literature has neglected to investigate this claim with empirical data. However, Peter D. Feaver (1999), a leading scholar in civil-military relations, has urged scholars and policy makers to explore possible linkages between patterns of civil-military relations and the propensity of a government to use force. He puts forward a key question for the next generation of researchers, asking, "Is a country more prone to use force if it has an all-volunteer army, which can be deployed almost as mercenary force?" (235).[2] So far, researchers have failed to address this question adequately in the context of *civil* conflict. While looking at political and economic conditions such as grievances, opportunity costs, and institutional quality (e.g., Tayda, Peksen, and James 2010), previous studies have neglected to incorporate the character of a state's military—specifically, whether its soldiers are volunteers or conscripts—into their causal explanations. In particular, there is very little systematic cross-sectional, time-series research exploring how the choice of military manpower system influences the vulnerability of a state to the experience of civil war; this is, of course, unfortunate considering that the eruption of civil conflict is all too common in the contemporary world and that the overwhelming response of incumbent regimes to popular uprisings is the deployment of military force.

It should be noted that previous studies of civil war have conceptualized the presence of an officially sanctioned armed force within a state as a possible deterrent to internal conflict. This conceptualization is based on the unrealistic assumption that a national military is a unified force employed absolutely at the discretion of civilian leadership, thus serving as a tool of governmental repression against dissident groups. For example, when considering the possibility that a state's military capacity may contribute to internal stability and peace, these studies have underlined the use by civilian regimes of the armed forces to put down popular uprisings prior to their having developed into civil war (see Fearon and Laitin 2003). However, the claim that the state maintains an exclusive control of all decisions to use military force against a rebellion is contrary to the observation of Robert Dahl (1971, 49) that "the capacity of a government to use violence or sanctions against an opposition" is contingent not only on the size of military and police forces but also on such resources being "so widely dispersed that no unified group . . . has a monopoly over them." Consistent with Dahl's observation, this study argues that a military may, during a period of internal crisis, fail to respect the commands of the state; it is suspected that this failure may depend upon the internal organization of the forces themselves.[3]

This study reconceptualizes the military as two distinct forms of organization—one composed of volunteer soldiers and the other composed of conscripted soldiers. This study then postulates that a state's choice between these two military manpower systems affects its vulnerability to civil violence. The postulation is based on the argument that, compared to conscripted soldiers, volunteer soldiers are more likely to regard themselves as guardians of a sacred nation and are, therefore, more inclined to perceive episodes of social unrest as opportunities to defend certain moral positions in defiance of sitting governments.[4] Consider, for example, the 1999 military intervention laid out by Pakistani general Pervez Musharraf, who was at that time the army chief. His rationale epitomizes the perspective of a volunteer soldier as this study conceives it: he reasoned that it was because the nation was in a state of political turmoil and economic collapse that the "[the military intervened] with all sincerity, loyalty and selfless devotion to the country" (quoted in Dugger October 13, 1999). From this perspective, the volunteer military sees itself as acting extrapolitically, if you will, in order to safeguard the unity and security of the nation.

In order to empirically test the prediction that states possessing a volunteer military force are at a higher risk for the occurrence of civil war than are those countries that rely on conscription, this study collects a new dataset of military manpower systems and civil war onset variables for 156 countries covering 1946 to 1999. The results show that, all other things being equal, countries with volunteer militaries are more likely to experience outbreaks of civil war than are countries with conscripted militaries; a review of three historical cases—Nigeria, Pakistan, and Senegal—points in the same direction. These findings indicate that, in order to prevent the proliferation of civil warfare overseas, the United States should encourage conflict-prone countries to adopt and maintain mass-based conscription as the main recruitment method for their militaries.

The rest of this study is divided into five sections. The following section lays out the conceptual linkages between a volunteer military and the onset of civil war; next, the research design is defined in terms of statistical model building, operationalization, and data sources; this is followed by a discussion of the empirical results, as well as several additional tests for robustness; then, three cases of civil war (in Nigeria, Pakistan, and Senegal) are presented as a historical complement to the statistical analysis; the final section, then, sums up the study's main findings and discusses future policy implications.

VOLUNTEER SOLDIERS, CONSCRIPTED SOLDIERS, AND CIVIL WAR ONSET

The military recruitment type of many modern countries is an inheritance from their respective colonial periods. For example, the volunteer manpower systems of Pakistan and Nigeria resemble that of Britain, their former colonial power, and Senegal's system of conscription is modeled after the French army. The category of volunteer soldiers includes voluntarily enlisted men in uniform at all ranks, while the category of conscripted soldiers includes draftees who may be privates, corporals, sergeants, or officers. Because the officer corps in many countries with conscripted forces also includes volunteers, attention to the recruitment of nonofficer groups is important for the differentiation of these two types of military systems. Certainly it is the case that the officer corps is the most politically active group, regardless of system; however, we also note that a military revolt cannot be accomplished without the successful mobilization of rank-and-file troops and noncommissioned officers (NCOs). After all, when push comes to shove, the nonofficer groups are responsible for carrying out orders on the ground. If rank-and-file troops do not agree that the use of military force is the only solution to ongoing political chaos, officers will have a hard time convincing them to take up arms against the incumbent government (Finer 1962; Luttwak 1969).

In theory, the officer corps is a unified force under civilian control (Huntington 1957; Feaver 1999; Desch 1998, 2001); in practice, the officer corps is a heterogeneous group of persons manifesting the conventional wisdom that "where you stand depends on where you sit" (Gray 1975, 86; see also Allison 1971). Ideological unity cannot be presumed across the board because soldiers are likely to take dissimilar stances on questions regarding military response to internal crises, such as riots. Some soldiers may be more inclined than others to squash social disorder by wielding military muscle. More importantly, the choice of military manpower system tends to affect the socioeconomic diversity of the armed forces. That is, while a volunteer military, insofar as it provides avenues for social advancement, attracts soldiers mostly from the lower socioeconomic strata of any given society, the obligatory nature of conscription facilitates recruitment from all socioeconomic strata (Choi and James 2003; Pickering 2011). As Vasquez (2005, 852) notes, "Militaries that rely on conscription are more likely to have in their ranks citizens from high status or wealthy social groups with access to political power when compared to militaries that depend on voluntary enlistment." The implication is that the choice of military recruitment format determines the quality and the disposition of soldiers, which, in turn, affects policy decisions regarding whether, when, and where to deploy military force.

As Janowitz (1971) correctly points out, a soldier's perspective is significantly shaped by his or her social background. In comparison to conscripted militaries, the privates, corporals, sergeants, and officers of a volunteer military are more likely to come from underprivileged classes and to share certain socioeconomic characteristics such as a relatively low level of educational achievement. For instance, the majority of volunteer Nigerian soldiers serving in the army prior to the first military intervention in January 1966 had only obtained an elementary school diploma; they had, however, received further schooling through the Army Education Corps and "a number of them [had] risen from the ranks in this way to get commissioned as officers" (Jemibewon 1998, 6). This study postulates that, given their socioeconomic background, volunteer soldiers have a greater aspiration than conscripted soldiers for achieving political and social advancement through the military (a claim that will receive further support later in the chapter). For this reason, as officers deliberate on whether or not to employ military force in the effort to engage in a military intervention, they will anticipate more eager participation from their voluntarily enlisted soldiers than from their conscripts. In other words, the officer corps is less likely to carry out anti-incumbent military action when their conscripted soldiers—who may have been drafted from upper-class and ruling elite families—have less incentive to oppose the civilian leadership hierarchy. On the other hand, an all-volunteer military, because its recruitment format attracts soldiers looking for social and political advancement, is predisposed to see in a popular uprising a legitimate opportunity to forcefully intervene into a domestic political dispute and, thus, to challenge an existing government.[5]

The key point is that volunteer militaries tend more often than conscripted militaries to take an interventionist posture. Because a volunteer recruitment system attracts more politically motivated soldiers at all ranks, one may reasonably suspect that these individuals are eager to prove their ambition by engaging in military action, thereby fulfilling their perceived responsibilities to the nation as well as advancing their own careers. Furthermore, volunteer militaries tend to generate a greater number of militant officer types because they receive more enthusiastic support and inspire greater loyalty from their privates, corporals, and sergeants than the officers of conscripted forces. Conscripted soldiers, in contrast, are recruited by compulsion rather than conviction, making them less willing to take on combat missions and more likely to fall into the military manager type. Also unlike volunteer soldiers, draftees expect to be able to leave the barracks immediately after having completed their military duty; therefore they prefer to stay out of conflict and are less interested in acquiring high-level martial and combat skills. Accordingly, the officer corps of conscripted armies will have reservations about sending their men on combat missions. They will focus more time on developing military technology rather than promoting combat strategy or developing individual skills. What follows is a more detailed discussion of the differences between conscripted and all-volunteer militaries.

Because conscripted militaries rely on a constitutional obligation to arm all eligible citizens, they are likely to recruit talented individuals from across all socio-educational levels of a society; retention rates are low, however, because there is little incentive for a conscripted soldier to pursue a military career when he or she has better opportunities to achieve individual and social freedoms in the civilian sector.[6] Moreover, we see that because some of these drafted soldiers are the sons and daughters of the ruling elites, military officers have a more difficult time justifying the deployment of troops against the establishment during times of internal crisis (see Kester 1986; Halfbinger and Holmes March 30, 2003; Vasquez 2005; Pickering 2011). For these reasons, mass-based conscription contributes to the decreased likelihood of civil war onset. For example, Tanzania, Brazil, and Senegal are three nations that require compulsory military service, and their soldiers have yet to serve as main actors in the outbreak of civil warfare; while neither Tanzania nor Brazil has experienced a civil war since their independence, Senegal has seen only a low level of civil war since 1982's Casamance conflict, an incident in which the Senegalese conscripts did not oppose civilian leadership, but put down a separatist movement in order to preserve national integrity (Evans 2004).

Volunteer enlistment, on the other hand, does not depend upon a constitutional obligation or upon the consideration of national security needs, but upon market forces and the individual freedom to choose. Volunteers usually come from the lower socioeconomic classes (a phenomenon that is unlikely to change, as the system simply does not encourage the recruitment or retention of military personnel with high levels of education or who come from politically influential families) (Arlinghaus 1981; Kennedy 1982). The consensus is that volunteer soldiers join the military because it is the best economic opportunity available to them given their lower socio-educational background. That is, less privileged youth seek upward mobility by way of the military because it is often the *only* career prospect they have. It should come as no surprise that many poor but ambitious young people will seek careers in the armed forces, considering the fact that the military is often one of the most well-established and modernized institutions in a developing country. Naturally, acquisition is a more influential motive for volunteer soldiers who often enlist in pursuit of personal enrichment (as is the case in many economically deprived countries such as Nigeria, Pakistan, Nicaragua, Uganda, Ghana, and Congo), than it is for conscripted soldiers who do not wish to pursue a career in the military (Geddes 1999, 126).

This recognizable pattern of difference between the behavior of volunteer and conscripted recruits is especially apparent when looking at the early stages of nation-building. After gaining independence, nascent countries tend to rely on a small, regular army comprised of volunteer soldiers. The volunteer army of Nigeria, a nation that gained its independence on October 1, 1960, exemplified this trend. Although some have contended that a numerically smaller force precludes military intervention into domestic affairs (e.g., Gutteridge 1964), this argument overlooks the fact that, as compared to the weakly equipped civil institutions they confront, volunteer soldiers are better trained and constitute a relatively cohesive group with the coercive capacity of a modern army. As Hilaire Belloc observes in reference to the colonial period during which a small number of European soldiers were able to maintain control over a large number of natives, "we have got the Maxim gun and they have not" (quoted in Luckham 1970, 59). Similarly, we must understand that a volunteer military, even one of a relatively small size, can always become a formidable actor in domestic politics because, if necessary, they retain the sole capacity to rattle the saber.

In pursuit of a military career, a volunteer soldier risks developing an unwarrantedly grandiose idea about his role in civilian politics; especially in a newly formed national military, soldiers are more likely to have an inflated sense of elite privilege (Finer 1962). The armed forces of Burma and Indonesia since the late 1950s and those of Thailand since 1932 have, for example, acted as much politically as militarily, seeing themselves as creator-guardians of their respective nations (Yawnghwe 1997). As noted, volunteer soldiers of all ranks very often lack prominent family backgrounds and have few political connections; however, many of them, especially those in the officer corps, are talented and ambitious. They view themselves as modernizers and feel deeply affected by political and economic struggles, as they themselves have come from underprivileged social groups (Needler 1975). Some of the earlier literature concerning civil-military relations puts forward a similar argument—namely, that militaries in developing countries act as vanguards of modernization, reform, and change (e.g., Johnson 1962). In a later study, Londregan and

Poole (1990) show that economic backwardness and poverty drive military leaders to become modernizers and to engage in domestic politics (see also Finer 1962; Luttwak 1969). Volunteer soldiers can be characterized by a strong sense of obligation, a confidence in their own talents relative to what they perceive to be a corrupt civilian leadership, and a dedication to the betterment of their society. Unfortunately, the qualities of ambition and sympathy—which in and of themselves are commendable attributes—may compel these soldiers to abandon their barracks and to intervene in domestic politics.

All in all, these disparities between military manpower systems seem to indicate that volunteer soldiers are more likely than conscripts to project themselves as protectors of national integrity. In so doing, they develop romanticized expectations about the leadership role of the military within the civilian sector; for example, they may have convinced themselves that only they can safeguard the nation from social disorder and corruption. Such a politicization of the military encourages volunteer soldiers to perceive themselves as agents of social justice who have to intervene in domestic political crises, especially those involving questions of governmental accountability (see Luckham 1970; Ferguson 1987; Arif 2001; Hussain 2003; Ejiogu 2011). Therefore, one may reasonably argue that a state with an all-volunteer force is exposed to a greater risk of civil violence than is a country whose armed forces are predominantly conscripted.

H_1: Countries with volunteer militaries are more vulnerable to the onset of civil war than are countries with conscripted militaries.

It should be noted that civilian control of the military is an alien concept for volunteer soldiers during the early stages of the development of military institutions in newly independent countries (Huntington 1957; Luckham 1970; Desch 1998, 2001). A lack of military professionalism restricts the soldiers' internalization of the notion of civilian supremacy, a notion that saturates the hearts and minds of soldiers in mature democratic countries. In fact, in nations like the United States or the United Kingdom it is taken for granted that "regardless of how strong the military is, civilians are supposed to remain the political masters"; that is, "the military may be best able to identify the threat and the opportunity responses to that threat for a given level of risk, but only the civilian can set the level of acceptable risk for society" (Feaver 1999, 215). However, when soldiers collectively exploit the use of military force in an effort to realize their personal political ambitions, they drastically weaken the hierarchy, discipline, and cohesion of the institution itself. This generalization is truer for volunteer forces than it is for those composed of conscripted soldiers, who do not view their participation in the military as a way to advance their career goals. When politicization runs rampant, volunteer soldiers become intoxicated by the idea that the armed forces alone are qualified to solve the political and social problems caused by incompetent and corrupt civilian rulers. Such a perception can quickly lead to the outbreak of a civil war.

RESEARCH DESIGN

This study tests the volunteer soldier hypothesis using the standard statistical model of civil war studies. Fearon and Laitin's (2003, 84) civil war study, particularly Model 1 in Table 11.1, is used as a frame of reference as it has become the standard formation for most cross-country work. In order to facilitate a straightforward comparison of the findings, the dataset for this study consists of the same 156 countries during the same span of years (from 1946 to 1999) as that used in Fearon and Laitin's analysis.[7] The data structure necessitates that the unit of analysis in this study is the country-year.

The dependent variable, civil war onset, captures the civil violence associated with dissident groups. It is defined as an armed conflict between agents of (or claimants to) a state and organized, subnational groups who resort to political violence as a challenge to the sitting government. To qualify for inclusion in this study, the civil war must have caused more than 1,000 deaths in total, with a yearly average of at least 100, and more than 100 deaths on each of both sides of the struggle. The onset of civil war data is collected from Fearon and Laitin's (2003, 76 and 79) study and is represented by a dichotomous variable that is coded as "1" for all country-years in which a civil war started and as "0" otherwise. In addition to the civil war variable, this study includes ethnic war and the Uppsala and PRIO groups' civil war as robustness checks.

The main independent variable, volunteer soldier, is also a dichotomous measure. It is coded as "1" if a state adopts a volunteer recruitment system for active duty military personnel, and as "0" if its forces are conscripted. This operationalization reflects the theoretical logic of this study, which underscores the politicization of volunteer, as compared to conscripted, soldiers. No publicly available data on military manpower systems exists over an extended spatial and temporal domain; therefore, this study relies on an original data collection of the military recruitment format variable. This study has consulted the following two sources, which are the most comprehensive and representative with respect to each state's military manpower system: Horeman and Stolwijk (1998) and Prasad and Smythe (1968).[8]

To avoid the risk of omitted variable bias, this study includes the same 11 control variables that appear in Fearon and Laitin's (2003) study. The inclusion of control variables such as ethnic and religious fractionalization is necessary to control for the possibility of a spurious relationship between military format and civil war onset. Each control variable is explained briefly below in order to expedite the following section's discussion of the empirical results.

To begin, prior war is a variable that takes into account the effect of whether or not a country, in the previous year, has experienced a distinct internal war. Preceding conflicts could serve as indicators for the continuation of an ongoing civil war or could potentially influence the onset of subsequent engagements of a similar nature. It is coded as "1" if internal war was ongoing in the previous year and as "0" if conflict was absent. Second, the per capita income variable measures the financial and bureaucratic aspects of a state's capacity as a way to capture the likelihood of conflict. Countries that have fragile financial, military, and political institutions are more likely to experience internal conflict due to weak local police forces and corrupt counterinsurgency practices. The data is collected from Penn World Tables and World Bank data, and is measured in thousands of 1985 U.S. dollars. To make certain that per capita income affects the likelihood of internal war onset rather than vice versa, this variable is lagged one year.

Third, the analysis must control for population size because some countries are more difficult to police than others. That is, civil violence is more prevalent in highly populated countries because it is less likely that a large and effective local police force exists in proportion to the population. This variable is a logged term of the total population in thousands for the previous country year and is gathered from World Bank figures. Fourth, it has been argued that the terrain of a country can significantly impact the emergence of internal conflict. For example, countries with swamps, caverns, and jungles can provide rebels with natural hideouts, thereby increasing the risk of the onset of internal war relative to countries with a more mild terrain. This variable is drawn from the coding of geographer A. J. Gerard and represents a logged term of an estimated percentage of mountainous terrain. Fifth, potential rebels who reside in a territorial base separated from the country's center by water or by great distance (e.g., Angola from Portugal) tend to be beyond the reach of the central government, which, consequently, increases the likelihood of the onset of civil war. This noncontiguity variable is coded as "1" for noncontiguous countries and as "0" otherwise.

Sixth, it is common for rebels to compete for control of state power within oil-exporting countries because this resource provides substantial material benefits. The oil-exporting variable is drawn from World Bank data and is coded as "1" if a country is a major producer of oil, making a minimum of one-third of its export revenues from fossil fuels, and as "0" otherwise. Seventh, a new state is often associated with a higher risk of the onset of civil war within its first two years of independence due to the fact that it is no longer under the security umbrella of its former imperial power and is, therefore, in the process of readjustment. Eighth, political instability at the center, which indicates a country's disorganization and institutional weakness, allows for a separatist or center-seeking rebellion to develop relatively easily. This dummy variable indicates whether a country experienced a three-point or greater change on the Polity IV composite democracy score in any of the three years prior to the country-year in question (Marshall and Jaggers 2007).

Ninth, democracy is a variable that is expected to capture lower risks of internal war onset. Along with institutional frameworks to decrease discrimination, democratic features like contested and competitive elections should decrease the risk of civil war. The Polity IV dataset provides the basis for this variable, as it captures the general quality of democratic institutions. Polity evaluates countries on an 11-point scale, ranging from 0 to 10. An overall polity score from full autocracy (–10) to full democracy (+10) is calculated by subtracting the autocracy score from the democracy score (see Marshall and Jaggers 2007). Tenth and eleventh, ethnic and religious tensions, respectively, are believed to contribute to the onset of internal warfare. Ethnic fractionalization can be interpreted as the probability that two randomly drawn individuals in a country are from different ethnolinguistic groups; religious fractionalization can be interpreted similarly with respect to different religious groups. Whereas ethnic fractionalization is based on estimates of ethnic group population from *Atlas Narodov Mira* (1964) and updated for the inclusion of newer countries by Fearon and Laitin (2003), religious fractionalization is based mainly on information from the CIA Factbook.

EMPIRICAL RESULTS

Table 11.1 shows the statistical results produced by three different estimation techniques. The first technique is Fearon and Laitin's (2003) standard logit model, but the second and third techniques are, as robustness tests, generalized estimating equations and logit with a cubic polynomial of time. A one-tailed test at the 0.05, 0.01, and 0.001 levels is utilized because the hypotheses are directional. The following discussion is limited only to the theoretically interesting variables in this study; to save space, the results of the other control variables are addressed only minimally. To test the main hypothesis, Model 1 employs a standard logit regression model after having accounted for a cluster effect produced by the fact that the observations are independent across, but not necessarily within, countries. Fearon's (2010) recent study on governance and civil war onset employs the same estimation technique—logit with clustering—for his basic models. The volunteer soldier variable is statistically significant at the 0.05 level and in the hypothesized direction. This implies that countries with volunteer soldiers are more prone to experience the onset of civil war, as the soldiers are more likely to attempt to oust existing regimes

Table 11.1
Effect of Volunteer Soldiers on Civil War Onset

	Clustering	GEEs	Time Dependence
Variable	Model 1	Model 2	Model 3
Volunteer soldier	0.367*	0.368*	0.368*
	(0.216)	(0.217)	(0.216)
Prior war	−0.917***	−0.952***	−0.877***
	(0.257)	(0.260)	(0.271)
Per capita income	−0.290***	−0.291***	−0.293***
	(0.069)	(0.069)	(0.075)
log (population)	0.265***	0.267***	0.264***
	(0.065)	(0.065)	(0.066)
log (% mountainous)	0.210**	0.210**	0.211**
	(0.090)	(0.090)	(0.091)
Noncontiguous state	0.235	0.241	0.240
	(0.284)	(0.285)	(0.294)
Oil exporter	0.815**	0.818**	0.826**
	(0.309)	(0.310)	(0.318)
New state	1.855***	1.853***	1.954***
	(0.367)	(0.367)	(0.484)
Instability	0.684***	0.681***	0.690***
	(0.216)	(0.216)	(0.210)
Democracy	0.008	0.009	0.009
	(0.019)	(0.019)	(0.019)
Ethnic fractionalization	0.314	0.316	0.304
	(0.393)	(0.394)	(0.390)
Religious fractionalization	0.188	0.186	0.190
	(0.565)	(0.567)	(0.576)
Constant	−7.006***	−7.014***	−7.114***
	(0.690)	(0.691)	(0.764)
Wald chi^2	90.75	91.25	95.15
Prob > chi^2	0.001	0.001	0.001
Log pseudolikelihood	−437.89		−437.83
Pseudo R^2	0.11		0.11
Observations	5,730	5,730	5,730

Note: Robust standard errors are in parentheses in Models 1 and 3, and semirobust standard errors in Model 2. The estimated coefficients of cubic polynomial of time in Model 3 are not reported to save space.

*p < .05

**p < .01

***p < .001, one-tailed tests

either on their own or in conjunction with civilian elites. The effects of the 11 control variables corroborate the findings of Fearon and Laitin's (2003) study: civil wars are more likely to occur in countries that are poor, are highly populated, have rough terrain, and so on. However, democracy, ethnic fractionalization, and religious fractionalization turn out to have no relation to the onset of civil war, as reported in Fearon and Laitin's (2003) study.[9]

It is possible that alternative statistical estimation methods may cause the significance of the volunteer soldier variable to disappear if it is not robust; for this reason, Models 2 and 3 evaluate the robustness of the results reported in Model 1 by employing two additional estimators: generalized estimating equations (GEEs) and logit with a cubic polynomial of time. The Wooldridge test for autocorrelation and a likelihood-ratio test for heteroskedasticity indicate that correction for both panel heteroskedasticity and temporally correlated errors is needed in order to obtain unbiased estimates (Wooldridge 2002; Drukker 2003). As discussed in Zorn's (2001) study, GEEs are a suitable estimator to correct for first-order autocorrelation as well as heteroskedasticity. Model 2 reports the results of GEEs, which are virtually identical to those in Model 1 with respect to coefficient signs and significance levels. These findings reconfirm the main hypothesis of this study that countries with volunteer militaries are more likely to experience the onset of civil war than are countries with conscripted militaries.

The estimated results from logit with clustering and GEEs could be biased insofar as they are obtained without consideration for temporal dependence in the dichotomous dependent variable, civil war onset. For instance, when a country has had civil peace for eight years before a civil war erupts, the onset of civil war variable is recoded as eight zeros during the peace years, followed by a one in the year when the civil war erupted. The presence of temporal dependence may, then, require special attention. Students of political methodology have suggested at least two estimation methods. The first one is Beck, Katz, and Tucker's (1998) logit splines. The second is Carter and Signorino's (2010) cubic polynomial of time. In both of these methods the data is assumed to have an underlying temporal dimension, and the binary observations are assumed to represent grouped duration data. This study takes advantage of Carter and Signorino's recent methodological improvement and reports those results in Model 3.[10] These estimated results once again verify the positive relationship between volunteer soldier and the onset of internal war.

There is a possibility that volunteer soldiers are, as noted earlier, even more likely to become politicized in the presence of ethnic cleavages or under poor economic conditions. This possibility warrants the inclusion of a multiplicative interaction model to test a three-way interaction effect among the variables for volunteer soldier, ethnic fractionalization, and per

capita income, along with their constitutive terms.[11] Conventionally researchers must determine, by comparing the overall fit of two competing
models, whether the interaction variable included in a new model contributes enough additional information to assist in explaining the onset
of civil war.

This study implements the Bayesian information criterion (BIC) test, one
of the most commonly used comparative statistics (see Schwarz 1978; Burnham and Anderson 1998). The BIC value is 988.27 for Model 1 in Table 11.1
and 1006.23 for a multiplicative interaction model. The larger value in the
latter model indicates that the multiplicative specification fails to perform
better than the additive specification in explaining the relationship among
volunteer soldier, ethnic fractionalization, and per capita income. This
study also builds a two-way interaction model in which volunteer soldier
and ethnic fractionalization interact to cause the onset of civil war. The
BIC value is 988.27 for Model 1 and 992.76 for the new model. The model
with the lower BIC value indicates the better result; therefore Model 1 is
once again preferable to the multiplicative model. Because these two comparative statistics point consistently to the superiority of nonmultiplica-
tive interaction modeling (i.e., Model 1), the results of the multiplicative
interaction models are not reported in order to save space. Moreover, the
results of these comparative statistics are in line with the comparison of
the three historical examples that will be reviewed in the next section. In
these cases, it is neither ethnic cleavages nor economic development that
is identified as the main cause of military intervention in domestic politics;
rather, it is the difference in military recruitment systems.

Since statistical significance does not necessarily ensure a meaningful
finding in a practical sense, the substantive effects of the variables should
be reported for empirical verification (see Greene 2003; Gujarati 2003).
To calculate a baseline probability of internal war against which to make
comparisons, this study sets the continuous variables at their means and
the dichotomized variables at "0"; it then adjusts the variables of greatest interest one at a time to see the change in the predicted probability of
civil war. Table 11.2 reports the substantive effects of the volunteer soldier variable that appear in Models 1 through 3 of Table 11.1. It is evident
that volunteer soldiers are a contributing factor to the increased likelihood
of civil war. As shown in the shaded row under Model 1, the risk that a
country with a volunteer military will experience a civil war is 44 percent
higher than that for a country with a conscripted military. It is worth noting, given the high human and financial costs associated with an internal
conflict, that even small changes in the predicted probability of political
violence should not be dismissed. Increasing the annual probability of a
civil war by 44 percent is substantial when it is recognized that a single
incidence of civil war might result in a tremendous loss of human life and
great financial cost.

Table 11.2
Substantive Effect of Volunteer Soldiers[a]

Variable	Logit with Clustering	GEEs	Logit with Cubic Polynomial of Time
	Model 1	Model 2	Model 3
Volunteer soldier	44%	44%	44%

[a]The baseline values are as follows: mean for continuous variables and 0 for dummy variables.

As noted in Sambanis' (2001) study, ethnic wars are a subset of civil wars and have important implications of their own. Ethnic warfare is generally considered to arise not from a lack of economic opportunities, but from discrimination against minority groups. If that argument is correct, this study should find some compelling evidence for the democracy, ethnicity, and religion variables if it were to look exclusively at ethnic warfare. Additionally, it is crucial to determine whether or not the positive and significant relationship between volunteer soldiers and the onset of civil war will hold up under conditions of ethnic conflict. Models 1 through 3 in Table 11.3 display the estimated results from the three different estimation methods. Although democracy, ethnicity, and religion do not emerge as causal factors, volunteer soldier remains an important causal factor across all the models.

Hegre and Sambanis (2006, 523) contend that "depending on which data set we use, we can have twice as many civil war starts and country-years at war." This means that the civil war literature tends to produce fragile results that are contingent upon a precise definition of the dependent variable. To account for such a concern, this study considers an alternative definition of civil war—that is, a leading dataset offered by the Uppsala and PRIO groups, which has the advantage of allowing for fewer than the 1,000 battle deaths threshold used by Fearon and Laitin. More specifically, civil war is operationalized as an internal conflict causing more than 25 annual battle deaths. It is coded as "1" for either a new civil war or for a case in which two years have elapsed since the last observation of an ongoing civil war, and as "0" otherwise. The results from Models 4 through 6 do not deviate from those in previous models: volunteer soldiers remain a motivator of civil war even when the concept is operationalized differently.

The empirical models, so far, have been built on the hypothesis that the volunteer soldier variable exerts a direct effect on the onset of civil war. However, there remains an alternative possibility that will not damage, but which may in fact complement, the hypothesis. That is, it may be the case that volunteer militaries lead to an increase in military coups,

Table 11.3
Effect of Volunteer Soldiers on Ethnic and Uppsala/PRIO War Onset

Variable	Ethnic War			Uppsala/PRIO Civil War		
	Clustering	GEEs	Time	Clustering	GEEs	Time
	Model 1	Model 2	Model 3	Model 4	Model 5	Model 6
Volunteer soldier	0.663*	0.660*	0.688**	0.479**	0.463**	0.467**
	(0.288)	(0.287)	(0.292)	(0.190)	(0.184)	(0.183)
Prior war	-0.876**	-0.831**	-0.723*	0.257	0.710***	-0.057
	(0.360)	(0.356)	(0.390)	(0.287)	(0.219)	(0.248)
Per capita income	-0.340***	-0.338***	-0.365***	-0.140***	-0.136***	-0.132***
	(0.099)	(0.099)	(0.106)	(0.035)	(0.035)	(0.039)
log (population)	0.315**	0.313**	0.305**	0.263***	0.252***	0.254***
	(0.107)	(0.106)	(0.110)	(0.057)	(0.056)	(0.055)
log (% mountainous)	0.097	0.097	0.107	0.161*	0.157*	0.158*
	(0.109)	(0.109)	(0.112)	(0.074)	(0.071)	(0.070)
Noncontiguous state	0.549	0.540	0.617	0.005	-0.009	-0.011
	(0.467)	(0.464)	(0.510)	(0.232)	(0.223)	(0.225)
Oil exporter	0.722*	0.719*	0.774*	0.696**	0.680**	0.667**
	(0.357)	(0.356)	(0.394)	(0.315)	(0.306)	(0.305)
New state	1.976***	1.977***	2.406***	0.566	0.506	0.320
	(0.434)	(0.433)	(0.524)	(0.633)	(0.642)	(0.650)
Instability	0.414	0.417	0.417	0.413*	0.406*	0.392*
	(0.263)	(0.262)	(0.258)	(0.185)	(0.180)	(0.184)

(Continued)

Table 11.3
(Continued)

Variable	Ethnic War			Uppsala/PRIO Civil War		
	Clustering	GEEs	Time	Clustering	GEEs	Time
	Model 1	Model 2	Model 3	Model 4	Model 5	Model 6
Democracy	−0.001	−0.001	0.002	0.010	0.010	0.010
	(0.022)	(0.022)	(0.024)	(0.012)	(0.012)	(0.012)
Ethnic fractionalization	0.044	0.047	0.015	0.946**	0.918**	0.910**
	(0.676)	(0.674)	(0.707)	(0.319)	(0.311)	(0.318)
Religious fractionalization	1.232	1.236	1.224	−0.284	−0.268	−0.286
	(0.860)	(0.858)	(0.912)	(0.532)	(0.515)	(0.511)
Constant	−7.910***	−7.899***	−8.333***	−6.549***	−6.444***	−6.007***
	(1.099)	(1.096)	(1.081)	(0.582)	(0.566)	(0.671)
Wald chi^2	72.12	72.51	75.38	155.88	191.03	184.53
Prob > chi^2	0.001	0.001	0.001	0.001	0.001	0.001
Log pseudolikelihood	−286.81		−285.71	−775.07		−773.64
Pseudo R^2	0.13		0.13	0.09		0.1
Observations	4,667	4,667	4,667	5,563	5,563	5,563

Note: Robust standard errors are in parentheses in odd models, and semirobust standard errors in even models. The estimated coefficients of cubic polynomial of time are not reported to save space.

*p < .05

**p < .01

***p < .001, one-tailed tests

which, in turn, lead to the onset of civil war (as shown in the causal chain in Table 11.A3). This speculation introduces military coups as an intervening variable between volunteer militaries and the onset of civil war. An intervening variable acts as a mediator, thereby calling for a distinct type of statistical modeling, commonly known as mediation analysis. This model would require its own full-length statistical analysis and so, without going into detail, only the preliminary results are reported later in the chapter. To test for mediation, this study relies on Baron and Kenny's (1986) four-step approach in which four regression analyses are conducted and the significance of the coefficients is examined at each step (Table 11.A3 displays estimated coefficients and standard errors in four steps). Step one shows the significant and positive effect of the volunteer military variable on civil war onset; step two indicates that the volunteer soldier variable is positively associated with military coups;[12] step three confirms the positive relationship between military coups and civil war onset; and step four demonstrates that both volunteer militaries and military coups are predictors of civil war onset. Because both volunteer militaries and military coups are significant predictors for the outbreak of civil war, the mediation analysis offers evidence for partial mediation of the military coup variable and also reaffirms the link between volunteer soldiers and civil war onset.

THREE HISTORICAL ILLUSTRATIONS: NIGERIA, PAKISTAN, AND SENEGAL

This study briefly presents three historical examples as a complement to the main task of the work, the longitudinal statistical analysis. The three cases trace public assertions made by volunteer and conscripted soldiers during times of crisis in an effort to capture and compare the psychological motivations for their initiation of civil conflict. To reduce sample selection bias, the cases pertain to three countries whose political institutions are similarly disorganized (thus leveling the playing field for comparison) but which are located on two different continents (sub-Saharan Africa and Asia, respectively). The total number of active soldiers does differ, however, in each of the three cases (from a small number in Senegal, to medium in Nigeria, and large in Pakistan).

The Pakistani and the Nigerian Civil War cases illustrate the connection between an all-volunteer force and the likelihood of the onset of civil war, while the Senegalese case allows us to look at the relationship between conscription and civil conflict. The first civil war case in each country's history is the object of discussion, which should mitigate the concern that the choice between volunteer or compulsory military service might result from previous internal and/or external conflicts.[13] On the contrary, in each of the three countries military recruitment type was inherited from their respective colonial periods (the volunteer manpower systems of Pakistan and Nigeria resembling that of Britain, their former colonial power, and Senegal's system of conscription being modeled after the French army).

Pakistani Civil War

Today the armed forces of Pakistan is the seventh largest in the world in terms of active forces with its 617,000 personnel (army 550,000, navy 22,000, and air force 45,000) (Hacket 2010). Many young people volunteer for service as a means of upward social and economic mobility (Nawaz 2008). The Pakistani military establishment has been involved frequently in domestic politics since the nation's inception in 1947. Having already experienced a post-seizure monopolization of power at the hands of their former military colleagues, volunteer soldiers are open to the idea that they should negotiate detailed rules about consultation and succession prior to the launch of any military campaigns (Geddes 2009).

When the Pakistani volunteer military first came into existence, the organization was peculiar in the sense that 85 percent of the force was originally from the Punjab, a single province of West Pakistan, while East Pakistan almost completely lacked representation (i.e., less than 7%) despite their making up 56 percent of the country's population. This absurd disparity resulted from a conviction held by West Pakistanis that the East Pakistanis, who were Bengalis, did not belong to a martial race (Khan 1983). Hussain's (2003, 21) study describes how most Pakistani volunteer soldiers considered themselves to be archetypal combative soldiers as opposed to military managers.

Some officers really believed that they were holy warriors and compared themselves to old Muslim military leaders. Some adopted the code names after these generals like Tariq. Others were commissioning their portraits in the likeness of Napolean, Rommel and the Duke of Wellington.

Such grandiose ideas accompanied the soldiers' characterization of civil society as backward, corrupt, and inefficient. They felt, therefore, that intervention against civilian rulers was inevitable.

At the same time, East Pakistanis were resentful for several reasons: First, their native language, Bangla, had not been introduced as an official national language; second, they felt they were receiving an unjust allocation of national resources; and third, they resented that there was such a blatant underrepresentation of Bengalis in the civil service. Given their political and economic disadvantages, the East Pakistanis had tried initially to accommodate the needs of the ruling class; however, when the leader of the military, Yahya Khan, refused to transfer power to Bengali nationalist politician Sheikh Mujib-ur-Rehmand and the Awami League (which was the majority party in the National Assembly following a Bengali win in the country's first general election in December 1970), the nation was thrown into turmoil as the East Pakistanis sought political rights. Huge demonstrations and general strikes paralyzed life in the city of Dhaka where banks, government offices, and other official business were completely shut down (Khan 1983; Nawaz 2008; Lieven 2011a, 2011b).

Upon the realization that this nonviolent movement was having no effect, East Pakistani civilians, students, and intelligentsia began to demand separation from West Pakistan so that they could establish a government from and for their own region; Bengalis took down Pakistani flags and flew their own. Yahya Khan and his military, operating under the conviction that they were the only ones who could guarantee the survival of the state, tried to prevent the breakup of Pakistan. As Khan (1983, 21) points out, General Yahya Khan himself was a firm believer that "the solution of the country's political, constitutional and regional problems required a military government." Yahya Khan's military, which was composed of all-volunteer soldiers swept up in his grandiose expectations, viewed the East Pakistani uprisings as an opportunity to intervene in domestic political affairs by removing the incumbent government. On March 25, 1969, Yahya Khan became the de facto head of the government and immediately imposed a brutal military rule, claiming emphatically that "my sole aim in imposing martial law is to protect life, liberty and the property of the people and put the administration back on the rails. . . . I have no ambition other than the creation of conditions conducive to the establishment of a constitutional government."[14] Yahya Khan had convinced himself that his all-volunteer military was the only force capable of maintaining social order and cleaning up political corruption in the absence of democratic governance. Siddiqi (2004) outlines the state of mind of the initiators of the coup: "[The Army] was the national savior when Ayub Khan was toppled from power" (see also Siddiqi 1996). From this we can see that the outbreak of the Pakistani Civil War—which lasted from March 26 to December 16, 1971—was imminent once volunteer military forces stepped into the domain of domestic politics (Khan 1983; Lieven 2011a, 2011b).

Nigerian-Biafran War

The military of Nigeria has been an all-volunteer force since its inception, and as of 2010 was comprised of about 80,000 active-duty personnel (army 62,000, n8,000, and air force 10,000) (Hacket 2010). In July 1966, General Yakubu Jack Dan-Yumma Gowon came to power as head of the Federal Military Government following a military intervention that overthrew the previous president, General Johnson Aguiyi-Ironsi, who had himself seized power by force only five months prior. At the time of the first intervention, in January 1966, the military had no more than 10,500 soldiers, of whom only 330 were officers with combat status. Many of these officers considered themselves to be heroic national leaders who were, at a relatively early age, in the process of rapid promotion over their military manager peers; to a growing extent they shared a delusion about the role of the military in domestic politics (Luckham 1970; Ejiogu 2011). An interview with Major Nzeogwu, a spokesman for the perpetrators of the first coup, provides evidence of their wishful thinking: "We had a short list of people who were undesirable for the future progress of the country or who by their positions at the time had to be sacrificed for peace and stability" (quoted in Odetola 1978, 10).[15] First's (1970, 300) study confirms the motivation for revolt: "The [January] coup grew out of the angry . . . political purposes of young officers, who shared the disgust of their generation at the iniquity of the politicians, not least their use of the army to further their purposes."

Although these remarks originated from the officers, there is little doubt that the same logic was used to mobilize the rank-and-file soldiers and the NCOs. For instance, when Major Nzeogwu addressed his force with the full details of the military revolt, he was well aware that "any man had the chance to drop out. More than that, they had bullets. They had been issued with bullets but [he] was unarmed. If they disagreed they could have shot [him]" (quoted in Luckham 1971, 31). However, because these volunteer soldiers came from the socially marginalized class and were led to believe that the revolt would provide them personally with career opportunities, they readily served as *hit men* against the presumably corrupt and nepotistic government. On the other hand, if this military had been composed of conscripted soldiers, who do not depend upon their service in the military for career advancement, the revolt would likely have been more difficult to accomplish at each stage, from its inception to the firing of guns. It seems fair to say that the January uprising was made possible by the presence of volunteer soldiers who felt themselves to be national defenders against social and political disorder.

Although it is unlikely that they were the root cause, political cleavages between Ibos and non-Ibos, as well as a regional antagonism between the North and the South/East, did play some role in the genesis of the 1966 coup (Luckham 1970). As Ibo soldiers became more aware of political and regional differences, they became more personally invested in domestic politics, many of them taking an interest in Ibo politicians as well as certain radical figures in the United Progressive Grand Alliance, a political party known for its rhetoric in support of the South (Dent 1970, 1997). By the time social unrest finally broke out along these tribal and regional cleavages, the interest of these volunteer soldiers in the issues at stake had been greatly intensified, raising their expectations to unwarranted heights. They became increasingly intolerant of the political disorder that had led to incidents of looting, killings, and arson, effectively destabilizing the entire country. As Luckham (1970, 76–77) observes, "Unfavorable environmental conditions were superimposed, from the civil violence in the Western Region set off by the Regional Election of October 1965, which provided the immediate stimulus for the January 1966 coup, onwards." The soldiers felt compelled to do something to save their country, which had been thrown into chaos by a corrupt incumbent government.

More importantly, they believed that they were the only force capable of rectifying a situation in which electoral fraud had been committed by the civilian government of President Benjamin Nnamdi Azikiwe, who was the first president of Nigeria after its having gained independence from the British Empire on October 1, 1960. President Azikiwe and his civilian colleagues were removed from power during the first military coup of January 15, 1966. The Ibo, one of three prominent Nigerian ethnic groups, blamed the non-Ibo of the Eastern region for the corruption of the government and, therefore, for the civil unrest. Following the coup, Ibo soldiers wiped out non-Ibo soldiers in retaliation. However, one must be cautious about characterizing the military action as merely an ethnic conflict between Ibo and non-Ibo soldiers. Though such a characterization might be correct if Ibo soldiers had been the minority group in despair, according to Ejiogu (2011) more than 85 percent of the senior officers were Ibo at the time of the coup. It was these Ibo soldiers who were captivated with the grandiose idea of using military force to restore social order and democracy, regardless of the fact that they were already the privileged ethnic group in the barracks. First (1970, 300) agrees with Ejiogu's analysis, stating that "it was a coup inspired by widespread political grievances" rather than by an attempt to acquire political power over another tribe.

The second military intervention of July 29, 1966, was largely a reaction to the killing of non-Ibo soldiers following the first intervention in January. This uprising put into power Lieutenant Colonel Yakubu Jack Dan-Yumma Gowon as head of the Federal Military Government; his government was then blamed for the (presumably retaliatory) murders of Ibo officers and civilians alike. The 4th Battalion in the North, for example, was accused of engaging in indiscriminate military violence in late September 1966, when they not only looted extensively but also brutally raped and even executed Ibo civilians over the span of several days. The soldiers responsible for the second coup—also part of a volunteer force—maintained the same conviction as their Ibo predecessors had: that only they were capable of cleansing the nation of the sins committed by the previous regime and its supporters; that social disorder can be rectified only by the sword. Ultimately though, this vindictive violence only plunged their society further into chaos. Any former unity that had been enjoyed by the Nigerian military quickly evaporated and was replaced by an ideologically zealous volunteer force. It was the ideological zealotry, or politicization, of these soldiers, who in their own minds were volunteering so that they might become heroic leaders in their own terms, that catalyzed the Civil War which lasted from July 6, 1967, to January 15, 1970 (Dent 1970, 1997; Luckham 1970, 1971; Panter-Brick 1970).

Senegalese Civil War

If these illustrations are to speak to the research question at hand, we must determine whether or not conscripted soldiers respond to mounting ethnic tensions and internal disorder in the same way that the volunteer soldiers did in the preceding examples. Senegal is a useful case for comparison because its armed forces are currently maintained by conscription, yielding it a combined force of 13,620 personnel in the army, air force, and navy, and also because its social and economic environment has been roughly similar to that of Nigeria and Pakistan throughout its postcolonial period (Hacket 2010). Per capita income is a commonly used proxy for a state's overall financial, administrative, police, and military capabilities (see Fearon and Laitin 2003, 80). Senegal has one of the lowest per capita income rates in Africa; in fact, Senegal's per capita income is ranked 190th worldwide, which is 14 states behind Pakistan and 15 states behind Nigeria.[16] Although Senegal's overall financial resources are less than those of Pakistan and Nigeria, its military, which is composed of conscripted forces, has not initiated a civil war since it gained independence in 1960.

Although ethnic cleavages and internal disorder have just as frequently emerged as serious threats to the Senegalese government, the military has yet to take advantage of these conditions as an opportunity to depose the sitting government; instead they have remained loyal to the civilian leadership. Of course, ethnic issues are not a trivial matter in Senegal. The nation incorporates a wide variety of ethnic groups, and several distinct languages are spoken among its people. Rioting and unrest was prevalent to such an extent that the military establishment could have easily—as they did in the cases of Nigeria and Pakistan—used them as pretexts for seizing power. The army did in fact intervene in December 1963 after the police force had been overwhelmed by demonstrations on the scale of an insurrection, but it was in order to rescue the civilian regime, not to overthrow it. Other major social crises including the student revolt of May 1968 and the general social troubles of the 1970s were similarly not enough to provoke conscripted soldiers to turn on the civilian regime (Diop and Paye 1998). On the contrary, since gaining its independence in 1960, the state has employed its conscripted force as a means of managing a domestic balance of power along ethnic lines. It is easy to imagine how the frequent deployment of the military may have given this ethnically and economically heterogeneous force the impression that the survival of their nation rests solely on its shoulders. So how do we explain the politically indifferent behavior of Senegal's military?

One plausible explanation is that the soldiers of its officer corps were less psychologically fixated on the desire to seize political power by force because they understood *a priori* that rank-and-file conscripted soldiers were unlikely to follow any orders to forcibly depose the government. As discussed earlier, draftees have no particular incentive to sacrifice their own lives to enable the realization of their military officers' political ambitions. That is, a conscripted force is not wholly composed of soldiers from the lower socioeconomic strata; there is also a good number from the privileged classes who are less interested in pursuing social advancement through a military career. Furthermore, because a conscripted military is apt to broadly reflect the larger community, soldiers are not likely to want to participate in the militarized destruction of their own civil society.[17]

The preceding example demonstrates that, when controlling for the country's domestic problems such as ethnic antagonism and political disorder (which have been at least as bad if not worse as that in Nigeria and Pakistan), Senegal can be distinguished from the other two cases insofar as its military is not primarily responsible for the onset of civil war; in fact, the Senegalese military actually serves as the government's instrument of repression against the Movement of Democratic Forces of Casamance. This example strongly suggests that, all other things being equal—ethnic tensions included—the onset of civil war is more likely within a state possessing an all-volunteer army than it is within a state possessing a conscripted force. This observation is consistent with previous empirical findings in the literature on civil war. The quantitative research by Fearon and Laitin (2003) and Collier and Hoeffler (2004), for example, shows that in countries with more ethnically or religiously diverse populations, discrimination against these diverse groups has no bearing on civil war onset.[18] However, before the widely cited studies by Fearon and Laitin and Collier and Hoeffler came out, many scholars and journalists had taken for granted that ethnicity, religion, and political discrimination were the main causes of civil war (e.g., Gellner 1983; Huntington 1996).

CONCLUSION

Existing studies on civil war have thus far conceptualized the military as a unified force acting at the sole discretion of the leaders of the state. They presume that the military plays a significant role in the suppression of popular uprisings prior to a nation's deterioration into civil war. This study has problematized such a conceptualization on account of its failure to consider the fact that soldiers may be more or less sympathetic to opposition causes depending on their socioeconomic background. The work presented here has reconceptualized the military into two different categories: volunteer forces and conscripted forces. This study has reasoned and has provided the historical cases of the Pakistani and Nigerian civil wars as illustration that, given their socioeconomic background, volunteer soldiers are more likely to identify the role of the military as guardian of the nation's values. They are, therefore, more likely to exploit a social uprising in order to further their own career interests, thereby increasing the risk of the onset of civil war. This dynamic is absent for those states that rely on conscripted armies.

The reason that a volunteer military can act as a predictor of civil war is that, as a major political actor, it has both the power and opportunity to initiate a military revolt against the wishes of a sitting government. The officers of a volunteer military manpower system are more likely than those of a conscripted force to take action against an incumbent government because they can be more confident that their troops will follow their lead due to the fact that they share a similar socioeconomic background as well as a certain psychological grandiosity. Therefore, this study projects that volunteer soldiers are more likely than conscripted soldiers to engage in civil warfare as a result of their personal political ambitions but also as a result of their conviction that the military occupies a special role as leader and protector of civil society.

In order to test the relationship between the volunteer soldier variable and the dependent civil war onset variable, this study employed three different estimation methods (i.e., logit with clustering, GEEs, and logit with a cubic polynomial of time) and three different measures of the dependent variable (i.e., civil war onset, ethnic war onset, and the Uppsala and PRIO groups' civil war onset). The empirical results have consistently confirmed the aggravating effect of the volunteer soldier variable on the onset of civil war, irrespective of estimators and civil violence variables. The conceptualization and empirical findings of this study shed new light on the role of the military in the civil war literature. For those who accept the argument that the enemy within is far more dangerous than the enemy without, this study further demonstrates the urgency of the ongoing war against the enemy *inside* the incumbent government. This study demonstrates that one type of insider enemy is a volunteer military force which, instead of suppressing dissident groups and protecting the existing regime, may work secretly from within to pose a much more immediate threat to a ruler's grip on power.

This study has significant implications for American foreign policy. In order to prevent the proliferation of civil war, the United States should encourage conflict-prone countries to adopt and maintain mass-based conscription. It is important to note that in most countries a military service obligation for every eligible citizen is justified as a necessary condition for national security. Furthermore, the constitutional obligation to serve is consistent with the principles of democracy to the extent that it emphasizes egalitarianism and rejects notions of privilege (Beukema 1982;

Friedman 2002).[19] Therefore, the adoption of a mass-based conscription system as the dominant military manpower system would be to the benefit of states prone to internal conflict on two fronts: First, it will promote a reduction in the probability of the outbreak of civil war, and second, it will promote an egalitarian sentiment among democratic citizens who prefer political order to internal violence. This policy recommendation may sound somewhat hypocritical as the United States currently maintains a volunteer system, but it should be noted that this policy recommendation is appropriate only for those foreign countries in which civilian supremacy in civil-military relations has yet to take root and where volunteer soldiers have the tendency to possess "the military conviction that they can rule better than incompetent or corrupt civilians" (Feaver 1999, 229). Compared to such countries, we see that the United States has institutionalized and maintained a volunteer system firmly within the tradition of the rule of law, where the civilian state is in control of the military; this tradition has prevented America's volunteer soldiers from becoming politicized to the point of triggering civil violence. This tradition should be promoted only after soldiers have learned the proper role of a military in a nation where the ultimate rule is the rule of law.

Table 11.A1
A List of Sample Countries

Afghanistan	Costa Rica	India	Moldova	Spain
Albania	Cuba	Indonesia	Mongolia	Sri Lanka
Algeria	Cyprus	Iran	Morocco	Sudan
Angola	Czechoslovakia	Iraq	Mozambique	Swaziland
Argentina	Czech Republic	Ireland	Namibia	Sweden
Armenia	Democratic Republic of Congo	Israel	Nepal	Switzerland
Australia	Denmark	Italy	Netherlands	Syria
Austria	Djibouti	Ivory Coast	New Zealand	Taiwan
Azerbaijan	Dominican Rep.	Jamaica	Nicaragua	Tajikistan
Bahrain	Ecuador	Japan	Niger	Tanzania
Bangladesh	Egypt	Jordan	Nigeria	Thailand
Belarus	El Salvador	Kazakhstan	Norway	Togo
Belgium	Estonia	Kenya	Oman	Trinidad and Tobago
Benin	Ethiopia	Korea, North	Pakistan	Tunisia
Bhutan	Fiji	Korea, South	Panama	Turkey
Bolivia	Finland	Kuwait	Papua New Guinea	Turkmenistan
Botswana	France	Kyrgyzstan	Paraguay	United Arab Emirates
Brazil	Gabon	Laos	Peru	Uganda
Bulgaria	Gambia	Latvia	Philippines	United Kingdom
Burkina Faso	Georgia	Lebanon	Poland	Ukraine
Burma	German Democratic Republic	Lesotho	Portugal	Uruguay
Burundi	German Federal Republic	Liberia	Romania	United States
Cambodia	Ghana	Libya	Russia	Uzbekistan
Cameroon	Greece	Lithuania	Rwanda	Venezuela
Canada	Guatemala	Madagascar	Saudi Arabia	Vietnam
Central African Republic	Guinea	Malawi	Senegal	Vietnam, South
Chad	Guinea Bissau	Malaysia	Sierra Leone	Yemen
Chile	Guyana	Mali	Singapore	Yemen Arab Republic.
China	Haiti	Mauritania	Slovakia	Yemen People Republic
Colombia	Honduras	Mauritius	Somalia	Yugoslavia
Congo	Hungary	Mexico	South Africa	Zambia
				Zimbabwe

Table 11.A2
Muliticollinearity Diagnostics[a]

	R^2	Variance Inflation Factors	Square Root of VIFs
Volunteer soldier	0.08	1.09	1.04
Prior war	0.15	1.17	1.08
Per capita income	0.32	1.47	1.21
log (population)	0.25	1.34	1.16
log (% mountainous)	0.13	1.14	1.07
Noncontiguous state	0.25	1.34	1.16
Oil exporter	0.14	1.16	1.08
New state	0.02	1.02	1.01
Instability	0.06	1.06	1.03
Democracy	0.26	1.35	1.16
Ethnic fractionalization	0.24	1.32	1.15
Religious fractionalization	0.18	1.23	1.11
Mean variance inflation factors		1.22	

	Eigenvalues	Condition Index
1	5.91	1.00
2	1.40	2.05
3	1.09	2.33
4	0.98	2.46
5	0.77	2.76
6	0.75	2.81
7	0.59	3.16
8	0.51	3.40
9	0.36	4.07
10	0.35	4.10
11	0.17	5.90
12	0.11	7.27
13	0.01	24.72
Condition number		24.72

Eigenvalues and condition Index computed from the scaled raw sscp with an intercept.

Det(correlation matrix)	0.30

[a] A general rule of thumb: A serious multicollinearity problem is suspected if R^2 is greater than 0.80, if the mean of all the variance inflation factors is considerably larger than 10, or if condition number exceeds 1000.

Table 11.A3
Causal Chain

| Volunteer Soldiers | → | Military Coups | → | Civil War Onset |

Step 1: Dependent Variable Is Civil War Onset

Variable	Clustering Model 1
Volunteer soldier	0.602**
	(0.237)
Constant	−4.352***
	(0.164)
Observations	5,730

Note: *p < .05, **p < .01, ***p < .001, one-tailed tests.

Step 2: Dependent Variable Is Military Coups

Variable	Clustering Model 2
Volunteer soldier	0.398*
	(0.234)
Constant	−2.896***
	(0.175)
Observations	5,730

Step 3: Dependent Variable Is Civil War Onset

Variable	Clustering Model 3
Military coup	1.642***
	(0.264)
Constant	−4.254***
	(0.144)
Observations	5,730

Step 4: Dependent Variable Is Civil War Onset

Variable	Clustering Model 4
Volunteer soldier	0.598**
	(0.232)
Military coup	1.638***
	(0.269)
Constant	−4.541***
	(0.172)
Observations	5,730

NOTES

1. Marx/Engels Collected Works at http://www.marxists.org/archive/marx/works/1865/02/12.htm.

2. Existing studies disagree on the nature of the relationship between recruitment type and the decision to use force in times of *international* crisis. Some consider volunteer soldiers to be combat-ready forces due to the fact that they are drawn from a smaller, less privileged, less politically important segment of society (e.g., Califano 1982). Other studies, however, assert that because the draft is capable of maintaining a large combat-ready supply of manpower, it is easier for political leaders to quickly launch foreign military operations than if they relied upon a smaller volunteer force (e.g., Pickering 2011).

3. Note that Desch's studies (1998, 2001) ascribe the weakening of civilian supremacy in the post–Cold War era to structural changes in society and the international system.

4. In states with volunteer forces, the officer corps may be dominated by men with loyalties to socioeconomically privileged groups (economic classes, ethnic groups, etc.). This may serve as a means of maintaining a politically loyal military. In this situation, volunteer soldiers may be inclined to intervene into domestic politics in undemocratic ways when they believe that their ethnic group interests are being threatened. This possibility will be discussed in the context of multiplicative interaction models in the Empirical Results section.

5. The relationship outlined earlier between military recruitment format and the socioeconomic basis of troop attitudes may appear nongeneralizable if one does not classify the U.S. all-volunteer military as an organization with a heavy lower-class bias; however, Kriner and Shen (2010) find that the U.S. military has in fact over time come to disproportionately rely on soldiers from the lower socioeconomic classes in the years since the end of the draft.

6. Milton Friedman (2002), a recipient of the 1976 Nobel Memorial Prize in Economic Sciences, maintains that because conscription is inequitable and arbitrary, preventing young men from shaping their lives as they see fit, it is inconsistent with a free society.

7. Table 11.A1 provides a list of sample countries.

8. The following sources also have been used for either cross-checking or complementing military manpower data with respect to reliability and validity: International Institute for Strategic Studies (1970 through 2000), Anderson (1976), Keegan (1979, 1983), Stockholm International Peace Research Institute (1985), Pope (1987) and Schumacher, Sevrens, O'Donnell, Torrence, and Carney (1989).

9. Some regions may be more conflict-prone than other regions in which conscription-based armies are the norm. When regional dummies are included in Model 1, the estimated results are not substantively different from those reported. It is conceivable that there is multicollinearity among the independent variables; thus, this study has conducted three sets of rigorous diagnostic tests for multicollinearity: R^2 statistics, variance inflation factors (VIFs), eigenvalues and condition index (see Belsley, Kuh, and Welsch 1980; Gujarati 2003). The test results are found in Table 11.A2, and none indicate severe multicollinearity among the predictors. For instance, when the VIFs test is employed to determine whether multicollinearity is a problem in the estimation, this study finds no concerns as none of the variable's VIFs exceeds the threshold of 10.

10. The estimated results obtained from logit splines do not substantively deviate from those using a cubic polynomial of time. To save space, the results are not reported here.

11. It should be noted that while ethnic fractionalization is not associated with an increase of the onset of civil war across standard logit models in Table 11.1, per capita income exerts a dampening effect.

12. For the operationalization of military coups, see Powell and Thyne (2011).

13. Desch (1998) argues that militaries become more involved in domestic politics as external threats to the state decline; Cohen (1985) maintains that states often opt for conscription when they face mounting external threats.

14. http://pakistanspace.tripod.com/archives/69yahya26.htm.

15. The same motive for the military action is also expressed in Major Nzeogwu's January radio address: "Our enemies are the political profiteers, swindlers . . . those that seek to keep the country divided permanently so that they can remain in office as ministers and VIPs . . . those that have corrupted our society and put the Nigerian political calendar back by their words and deeds" (Kirk-Greene 1971, 126).

16. The World Factbook 2011 at https://www.cia.gov/library/publications/the-world-factbook/geos/sg.html.

17. It should be noted that the main players in the ongoing Senegalese civil war against the government since 1989 are the Movement of Democratic Forces of Casamance (MFDC), a southern separatist group in the Casamance region. The dominant ethnic group in the Casamance is the Jola. Although this group represents only 4 percent of the total population of Senegal, its sense of economic disenfranchisement as compared to the Wolof, the dominant ethnic group, contributed to the founding of the MFDC in 1982 (Diop and Paye 1998; Evans 2004; Humphreys and Mohamed 2005).

18. The empirical section of this study also reveals no evidence for ethnic fragmentation as a root cause of the onset of civil war.

19. See Janowitz (1982) and Simmons (2001, 43–64) on political fairness, and Segal (1989, 1–16) and Cohen (1985, 117–133) on citizen-soldiers in particular.

REFERENCES

Allison, Graham T. 1971. *Essence of Decision*. Boston: Little Brown.

Anderson, Martin. 1976. *Conscription*. Stanford, CA: Hoover Institution Press.

Arif, Khalid Mahmud. 2001. *Khaki Shadows*. Karachi: Oxford University Press.

Arlinghaus, Bruce E. 1981. "'Dumb' Soldiers and 'Smart' Bombs." In William J. Taylor, Jr., Eric T. Olson, and Richard A. Schrader, eds., *Defense Manpower Planning*. New York: Pergamon. 80–87.

Atlas Narodov Mira. 1964. Moscow: Glavnoe Upravlenie Geodezii Ikartografii.

Baron, R. M. and D. A. Kenny. 1986. "The Moderator-Mediator Variable Distinction in Social Psychological Research." *Journal of Personality and Social Psychology* 51(6): 1173–1182.

Beck, Nathaniel, Jonathan N. Katz, and Richard Tucker. 1998. "Taking Time Seriously in Binary Time-Series, Cross-Section Analysis." *American Journal of Political Science* 42(4): 1260–1288.

Belsley, D. A., E. Kuh, and R. E. Welsch. 1980. *Regression Diagnostics*. New York: John Wiley & Sons.

Beukema, Herman. 1982, "The Social and Political Aspects of Conscription." In Martin Anderson with Barbara Honegger, eds., *The Military Draft*. Stanford, CA: Hoover Institution Press. 479–491.

Burnham, Kenneth P. and David R. Anderson. 1998. *Model Selection and Inference*. New York: Springer-Verlag.

Califano, Joseph A. Jr. 1982. "Doubts about an All-Volunteer Army." In Martin Anderson with Barbara Honegger, eds., *The Military Draft*. Stanford, CA: Hoover Institution Press. 536–539.

Carter, David B. and Curtis S. Signorino. 2010. "Back to the Future." *Political Analysis* 18(3): 271–292.

Choi, Seung-Whan and Patrick James. 2003. "No Professional Soldiers, No Militarized Interstate Disputes?" *Journal of Conflict Resolution* 47(6): 796–816.

Cohen, Eliot A. 1985. *Citizens and Soldiers*. Ithaca, NY: Cornell University Press.

Collier, Paul and Anke Hoeffler. 2004. "Greed and Grievance in Civil Wars." *Oxford Economic Papers* 56(4): 563–595.

Dahl, Robert A. 1971. *Polyarchy*. New Haven, CT; London: Yale University Press.

Dent, M. J. 1970. "The Military and the Politicians." In Simone K. Panter-Brick, ed., *Nigerian Politics and Military Rule*. London: Athlone Press. 78–93.

Dent, M. J. 1997. *Nigeria*. London: Frank Cass.

Desch, Michael C. 1998. "Soldiers, States, and Structures." *Armed Forces & Society* 24(3): 389–405.

Desch, Michael C. 2001. *Civilian Control of the Military*. Baltimore: Johns Hopkins University Press.

Diop, Momar Coumba and Moussa Paye. 1998. "The Army and Political Power in Senegal." In Eboe Hutchful and Abdoulaye Bathily, eds., *The Military and Militarism in Africa*. Dakar, Senegal: Codesria. 315–353.

Drukker, David M. 2003. "Testing for Serial Correlation in Linear Panel-Data Models. *Stata Journal* (3)2: 168–177.

Dugger, Celia W. October 13, 1999. "Coup in Pakistan." *New York Times*. http://www.nytimes.com/1999/10/13/world/coup-pakistan-overview-pakistan-army-seizes-power-hours-after-prime-minister.html.

Ejiogu, E. C. 2011. *The Roots of Political Instability in Nigeria*. Burlington, VT: Ashgate.

Evans, Martin. 2004. "Senegal: Mouvement des Forces Démocratiques de la Casamance (MFDC)." Briefing Paper. Downloaded from https://www.chathamhouse.org/sites/default/files/public/Research/Africa/bpmedec04.pdf.

Fearon, James D. 2010. "Governance and Civil War Onset." *World Development Report 2011*.

Fearon, James D. and David D. Laitin. 2003. "Ethnicity, Insurgency, and Civil War." *American Political Science Review* 97(1): 75–90.

Feaver, Peter D. 1999. "Civil-Military Relations." *Annual Review of Political Science* 2: 211–241.

Ferguson, Gregor. 1987. *Coup d'état*. Dorset, UK: Arms and Armour.

Finer, Samuel E. 1962. *The Man on Horseback*. New York: Praeger.

First, Ruth. 1970. *The Barrel of a Gun*. London: Allen Lane.

Friedman, Milton. 2002. *Capitalism and Freedom*. Chicago, IL: University of Chicago Press.

Geddes, Barbara. 1999. "What Do We Know about Democratization after Twenty Years?" *Annual Review of Political Science* 2: 115–144.

Geddes, Barbara. 2009. "How Autocrats Defend Themselves against Armed Rivals." Paper presented to the American Political Science Association annual meeting, Toronto, Canada.

Gellner, Ernest. 1983. *Nations and Nationalism*. Ithaca, NY: Cornell University Press.

Gray, Colin S. 1975. "Hawks and Doves." *Journal of Political and Military Sociology* 3(1): 85–94.

Greene, William H. 2003. *Econometric Analysis*. 5th ed. Upper Saddle River, NJ: Prentice Hall.

Gujarati, Damodar N. 2003. *Basic Econometrics*. 4th ed. New York: McGraw-Hill, Inc.

Gutteridge, W. F. 1964. *Military Institutions and Power in the New States*. London: Pall Mall.

Hackett, James. Ed. 2010. *The Military Balance 2010*. London: International Institute for Strategic Studies.

Halfbinger, David M. and Steven A. Holmes. March 30, 2003. "Military mirrors Working-Class America." *New York Times*. http://www.nytimes.com/2003/03/30/us/a-nation-at-war-the-troops-military-mirrors-a-working-class-america.html.

Hegre, Håvard and Nicholas Sambanis. 2006. "Sensitivity Analysis of Empirical Results on Civil War Onset." *Journal of Conflict Resolution* 50(4): 508–535.

Horeman, Bart and Marc Stolwijk. Eds. 1998. *Refusing to Bear Arms*. London: War Resister's International.

Humphreys, Macartan and Habaye Ag Mohamed. 2005. "Senegal and Mali." In Paul Collier and Nicholas Sambanis, eds., *Understanding Civil War*. Washington: World Bank. 247–302.

Huntington, Samuel P. 1957. *The Soldier and the State*. Cambridge, MA: Belknap Press of Harvard University Press.

Huntington, Samuel P. 1996. *The Clash of Civilizations and the Remaking of World Order*. New York: Simon & Schuster.

Hussain, Hamid. 2003. "Professionalism and Discipline of Armed Forces in a Society with Repeated Military Interventions." *Defence Journal* 6(6): 20–31.

International Institute for Strategic Studies. 1970 through 2000. *The Military Balance 1970–1971* through *2000/01*. London: Oxford University Press.

Janowitz, Morris. 1971. *The Professional Soldier*. New York: Macmillan.

Janowitz, Morris. 1982. "The Logic of National Service." In Martin Anderson with Barbara Honegger, eds., *The Military Draft*. Stanford, CA: Hoover Institution Press. 403–443.

Jemibewon, D.M. 1998. *The Military, Law and Society*. Ibadan, Nigeria: Spectrum Books.

Johnson, John J. Ed. 1962. *The Role of the Military in Underdeveloped Countries*. Princeton, NJ: Princeton University Press.

Keegan, John. 1979. 1st ed. *World Armies*. New York: Facts on File.

Keegan, John. 1983. *World Armies*. 2nd ed. Detroit, MI: Gale Research Company.

Kennedy, Edward M. 1982. "Inequities in the Draft." In Martin Anderson with Barbara Honegger, eds., *The Military Draft*. Stanford, CA: Hoover Institution Press. 527–529.

Kester, John G. 1986. "The Reasons to Draft." In William Bowman, Roger Little, and G. Thomas Sicillia, eds., *The All-Volunteer Force after a Decade*, Washington: Pergamon-Brassey. 286–315.

Khan, Mohammad Asghar. 1983. *Generals in Politics*. New Delhi: Vikas.

Kirk-Greene, A.H.M. 1971. *Crisis and Conflict in Nigeria*. London: Oxford University Press.

Kriner, Douglas L. and Francis X. Shen. 2010. *The Casualty Gap: The Causes and Consequences of American Wartime Inequalities*. New York: Oxford University Press.

Lieven, Anatol. 2011a. "Military Exceptionalism in Pakistan." *Survival* 53(4): 53–68.

Lieven, Anatol. 2011b. *Pakistan*. New York: Public Affairs.

Londregan, John B. and Keith T. Poole. 1990. "The Coup Trap, and the Seizure of Executive Power." *World Politics* 42(2): 151–183.

Luckham, A.R. 1970. "The Nigerian Military." In Simone K. Panter-Brick, ed., *Nigerian Politics and Military Rule*. London: Athlone Press. 58–77.

Luckham. Robin. 1971. *The Nigerian Military*. New York: Cambridge University Press.

Luttwak, Edward. 1969. *Coup d'etat*. New York: Alfred A. Knopf.

Marshall, Monty, and Keith Jaggers. 2007. POLITY IV Project. Dataset Users' Manual.

Nawaz, Shuja. 2008. *Crossed Swords*. Karachi: Oxford University Press.

Needler, Martin C. 1975. "Military Motivations in the Seizure of Power." *Latin American Research Review* 10(3): 63–79.

Odetola, Theophilus Olatunde. 1978. *Military Politics in Nigeria*. New Brunswick, NJ: Transaction Books.

Panter-Brick, Simone K., ed. 1970. *Nigerian Politics and Military Rule*. London: Athlone Press.

Pickering, Jeffrey. 2011. "Dangerous Drafts? A Time-Series, Cross-National Analysis of Conscription and the Use of Military Force, 1946–2001." *Armed Forces & Society* 37(1): 119–140.

Pope, Barbara H., ed. 1987. *World Defense Forces*, 1st ed. Santa Barbara, CA: ABC-CLIO.

Powell, Jonathan and Clayton Thyne. 2011. "Global Instances of Coups from 1950 to 2010: A New Dataset." *Journal of Peace Research* 48(2): 249–259.

Prasad, Devi and Tony Smythe, eds. 1968. *Conscription*. London: War Resisters' International.

Sambanis, Nicholas. 2001. "Do Ethnic and Nonethnic Civil Wars Have the Same Causes?" *Journal of Conflict Resolution* 45(3): 259–282.

Schumacher, Rose, Gail K. Sevrens, Timothy S. O'Donnell, Lee Torrence, and Kate Carney, eds. 1989. *World Defense Forces*. 2nd ed. Santa Barbara, CA: ABC-CLIO.

Schwarz, Gideon E. 1978. "Estimating the Dimension of a Model." *Annals of Statistics* 6(2): 461–464.

Segal, David R. 1989. *Recruiting for Uncle Sam*. Lawrence: University Press of Kansas.

Siddiqi, A. R. 1996. *The Military in Pakistan*. Lahore: Vanguard.

Siddiqi, A. R. 2004. *East Pakistan*. Karachi: Oxford University Press.

Simmons, A. John. 2001. *Justification and Legitimacy*. Cambridge: Cambridge University Press.

Stockholm International Peace Research Institute. 1985. *World Armaments and Disarmament: SIPRI Yearbook 1985*. London: Taylor & Francis.

Tayda, Zeynep, Dursun Peksen, and Patrick James. 2010. "Why Do Civil Wars Occur?" *Civil Wars* 12(3): 195–217.

Vasquez, Joseph Paul III. 2005. "Shouldering the Soldiers" *Journal of Conflict Resolution* 49(6): 849–873.

Wooldridge, Jeffrey M. 2002. *Econometric Analysis of Cross Section and Panel Data*. Cambridge: MIT Press.

Yawnghwe, Chao-Tzang. 1997. The Politics of Authoritarianism. Ph.D. thesis. University of British Columbia.

Zorn, Christopher. 2001. "Generalized Estimating Equation Models for Correlated Data." *American Journal of Political Science* 45(2): 470–490.

Conclusion

The demise of the bipolar world order and the emergence of a new security environment have changed the domestic and international politics so profoundly that many have deemed the old ways of thinking about security problems to be no longer relevant. The arrival of the changed political environment means that security implications stemming from subnational actors such as terrorist and insurgent groups overshadow international threats. Naturally, scholars and policy makers have begun to demonstrate more research interest in internal crisis than interstate crisis. With a special focus on four critical issue areas, this book analyzes newly emerged security challenges surrounding internal crisis: (1) American jihad, (2) terrorism, (3) civil wars, and (4) human rights violations. Although each of these issues has gained considerable scholarly and journalistic attention during the past two decades, no extant, solo-authored publications have thus far provided a comprehensive and statistical analysis on all the four security matters accompanied with relevant policy recommendations. This book fills the gap in the security literature.

The empirical analyses of this book uncover four important findings for students of security studies. First, America's homegrown terrorism has developed into a real security threat on both American soil and the international stage. The rise of American homegrown terrorism appears to be closely related to worsening socioeconomic conditions that many recent studies dismiss as a potential cause. This book presents findings that Americans are more likely to engage in jihadist war at home or abroad when America is hit by economic hardship such as the housing bubble or when more immigrants from terrorism-prone countries are admitted. Accordingly, the American security community should devote more time to designing counterterrorism measures by weighing in on the socioeconomic factors such as poverty and ethnic ties that Chapters 1 and 2 identify.

Second, Chapters 3–5 show how best to deal with terrorism that threatens a nation-state's stability and security. Given the high human and financial costs associated with terrorism, the question of how best to discourage terrorist activities within a nation-state's territory is a crucial security issue. One of the effective ways to deter acts of terrorism appears to push for a high level of economic growth in underdeveloped countries. This policy recommendation becomes clearer when taking into account the effect of poverty on America's homegrown terrorism, which is identified in Chapter 1. Improving poor economic conditions may be the best counterterrorism measure that does not require to compromise democratic qualities in the name of national security. It is true that to reduce the risk of terrorism, national leaders often curtail average citizens' civil liberties and privacy rights. Emphasis on economic growth as a counterterrorism measure should relieve the burden of national leaders, who must make difficult political choices in response to growing terrorist threats. Put differently, as economic growth produces a more secure environment against terrorism, national leaders are more likely to balance their concerns about security exigency with respect for democratic values.

Third, Chapters 6–9 tell us that improvement in the quality of human rights is not an easy undertaking—there is no simple solution for addressing it effectively. The main reason is that the issue of human rights is directly related to national sovereignty. Human rights abusers do not accept the protection of human rights as justification for intervention by foreign powers. Some scholars contend, however, that naming and shaming by human rights organizations compels humanitarian intervention in those countries where human rights violations are rampant. Chapter 7 cast serious doubts on the human rights–related consequences of naming and shaming on the foreign powers that deploy their soldiers in the name of humanity. Perhaps, the improvement of human rights should not come from the outside but from the inside. For example, it appears that countries that are governed by leaders with high levels of education are more effective in addressing problems with human rights abuses, especially the reduction of torture practices.

Fourth, because the frequent outbreaks of civil conflict have emerged as a far greater security threat than the intermittent incidence of interstate conflict in the post–Cold War world, scholars and policy makers have become increasingly interested in the question of how to reduce the risk of the former. Chapters 10 and 11 suggest two institutional features that should help decrease the likelihood of civil war. When national leaders live by the rule of law or when they mandate the military service of young men and women for the national defense, their country is less likely to experience civil conflict. The reduced internal security risk associated with the rule of law and with conscripted military service allows national leaders to redirect their time and energy to other political problems to secure their legacy.

It should be noted that this book takes a unique approach in the sense that the scope goes beyond a single security concern; the methodological approach brings in advanced statistical techniques to identify a certain set of empirical patterns followed by the presentations of causal explanations; and each chapter offers potentially effective policy recommendations. The following detailed summary of each chapter contains all the three unique features that this book has underlined.

Based on an original dataset of individual terrorists, Chapter 1 explores the origins of America's homegrown terrorism. This chapter presents 12 hypotheses of interest, compiles data from 235 American jihadists since 9/11, and compares them with Muslim Americans and the general public surveyed by the Pew Research Center. A battery of weighted logistic regression analyses supplemented by six case studies of homegrown terrorism show three distinctive characteristics of American jihadists. First, they are more likely to be young, male, and economically disadvantaged. Second, they are more likely to hold citizenship than average Muslim Americans. Finally, they are better educated when compared to those Muslim Americans who expressed a favorable opinion of al-Qaeda in a 2011 phone interview. These findings help the counterterrorism community identify the mechanisms and motives of radicalization, so it can develop new optimal strategies for preventing the proliferation of homegrown terrorism on American soil.

Chapter 2 addresses why America's homegrown jihadists choose to fight abroad rather than at home. This chapter draws 11 hypotheses related to ethnic ties to the target country, 8 personal characteristics of perpetrators, counterterrorism capabilities of the target country, and legitimacy of foreign fighting over domestic fighting. This chapter then presents a set of logistical regression analyses on a sample of 235 American jihadists who were active during the past two decades. These analyses show the significance of ethnic ties between the perpetrator and the target country and the counterterrorism capabilities of the target country in the jihadist's decision to fight overseas. Furthermore, the results suggest that younger jihadists and those who act alone are more likely to strike abroad than domestically. Of these four findings, ethnic terrorism emerges as one of the most compelling determinants of American jihadists.

Do democratic countries compromise civil liberties in their attempts to deter terrorist activity? Chapter 3 looks into the question from the viewpoint of the selectorate theory. The hypothesis states that countries with large winning coalitions (i.e., democracies) are likely to restrict civil liberties when confronted with the threat of terrorism. However, a cross-sectional, longitudinal data analysis indicates that despite growing terrorist threats, democratic countries are less likely to constrain civil liberties than nondemocratic countries where such liberties are less profuse.

Chapter 4 investigates a gap between the theory of terrorist outbidding and empirical findings. Established theoretical literature maintains that domestic competition among terrorist organizations is positively associated with the prevalence of political violence as each organization tries to distinguish itself with increasingly violent acts. However, previous empirical studies fail to provide concrete supporting evidence for this theory. This chapter argues that when a causal time order is properly set in the model specification, the theory of outbidding garners robust empirical support across countries and across time. To test the argument, a new statistical model is proposed in which the dependent variable is measured in multiple ways: domestic, international, and then with a particular look at suicide terrorism. The estimated results support the theoretical prediction that regardless of the specific type of terrorist tactic, terror group competition leads to increased activities of political violence, thus damaging the stability and security of a nation-state.

Whether or not economic growth exerts a beneficial effect on reducing terrorism is a controversial issue. Unlike previous studies, Chapter 5 conceptualizes economic growth into two sectors—agricultural and industrial—and categorizes terrorism into three forms—domestic, international, and suicide. It offers a modified theory of hard targets. A cross-national, time-series data analysis of 127 countries for the years 1970–2007 shows evidence that when countries enjoy high levels of industrial growth, they become less vulnerable to domestic and international terrorist events; however, they are more likely to experience suicide attacks. These findings indicate that economic growth is not a cure-all for terrorism because it may be associated, in some select instances, with more terrorist incidents. Nonetheless, we can conclude that healthy economic conditions are, without a doubt, beneficial to the war on terrorism since most suicide attacks are densely concentrated in a few countries.

By relying on newly constructed data regarding human rights, Chapter 6 draws new inferences and conclusions about the causes and effects of human rights violations. This chapter first reexamines 18 original studies and then compares them with new analyses that are performed after replacing the predictor or outcome variable of human rights in each of the 18 studies with the new measure. Introducing the newly constructed measure as the dependent variable makes most of the empirical patterns that are found in the previous studies untenable. In contrast, when the new measure is used as the independent variable, the significance of coefficients related to the hypotheses rarely disappears. These reexaminations indicate that the existing literature requires revision as to the determinants of human rights conditions, and thus, related policy recommendations should be reformulated.

Does the naming and shaming of alleged human rights violators influence the political behavior of rogue nations? Some scholars argue that shaming leads to the improvement of human rights and brings about humanitarian intervention in crisis situations. Others are more skeptical, arguing that shaming is not usually followed by real improvements in human rights except in rare conditions and may sometimes even be followed by deteriorating protections for rights (Franklin 2008; Hafner-Burton 2008). Chapter 7 revisits a published work by Murdie and Peksen (2014) in which shaming by human rights organizations (HROs) is projected to influence realpolitik issues such as military intervention decisions. This chapter asserts that the previous finding contains an error as causal time order is incorrectly set in the statistical model. This chapter demonstrates that when the previous statistical model is properly specified, it produces no significant and positive impact of HROs on humanitarian interventions. In doing so, this chapter provides new evidence to suggest real skepticism about the human rights–related consequences of naming and shaming on the foreign governments that might intervene in an effort to help.

Chapter 8 looks into the controversy of whether human rights treaties exert a dampening effect on the frequency of human rights violations. More than 10 years ago, scholars began to assert that preferential trade agreements containing clauses allowing the reduction of economic benefits to human rights abusers can, in some important instances, help improve human rights conditions in beneficiary countries. However, by introducing genetic matching techniques, Spilker and Böhmelt (2013) dispute the claims of scholars who argue that enforceable trade conditionalities help reduce government repression. This chapter reevaluates Spilker and Böhmelt's matched sample data using a new—and more accurate—indicator of human rights violations. The replacement of Spilker and Böhmelt's repression variable with the new measure reveals new evidence that membership in trade agreements with enforceable human rights conditions is indeed a significant and positive predictor of improvements in human rights.

Why do some countries stop torture while others do not? Chapter 9 contends that, aside from democratic institutional constraints, education levels among leaders play a critical role in ending the political practice of torture. Results from statistical analysis show supporting evidence: leaders with a college or graduate degree are less likely to use torture than those without a college education. After examining the substantive effects of educated leaders and institutional features such as democracy and freedom of expression, this chapter finds that the likelihood of terminating torture as a political practice increases when leaders with graduate-level training are in charge of statecraft. More specifically, leaders with a college degree, compared to leaders with less than college education, have a 668,360 percent greater probability of terminating the use of torture. By contrast, when the level of democracy increases by one unit, a country is approximately 2 percent more likely to stop the torture.

The question of what explains the prevalence of civil war is one of today's most highly debated topics among scholars and policy makers. Chapter 10 explores the causes of civil war outbreaks from a rule of law perspective, positing that a high-quality rule of law is instrumental to reducing the likelihood of civil war because it diminishes the opportunity and willingness of minority groups to engage in political violence as a challenge to the government. A cross-national, time-series data analysis of 132 countries during the period from 1984 to 2007 shows evidence that, ceteris paribus, upholding a strong rule of law tradition significantly decreases the likelihood of civil war. Moreover, the strength of this effect increases when accounting for the possibility of reverse causation from civil war onset to the rule of law. These findings suggest that by promoting a strong rule of law tradition, countries can significantly reduce the risk of civil conflict.

Existing studies neglect to examine whether a country's method of military recruitment (i.e., volunteer vs. conscripted) has an effect on outbreaks of internal civil conflicts in a country. Chapter 11 argues that because volunteer soldiers have the tendency to envision themselves as protectors of their nation's values, they are likely to perceive social disorder as an opportunity to intervene in domestic politics and to challenge the sitting government. A cross-national, time-series data analysis shows evidence that, ceteris paribus, countries with volunteer militaries are more likely to experience civil violence than countries with conscripted militaries. A review of three historical examples—Nigeria, Pakistan, and Senegal—comes to the same conclusion. These findings indicate that the United States, insofar as it is attempting to prevent the proliferation of civil war overseas, should encourage conflict-prone countries to adopt and maintain largely conscription-based recruitment as their primary source for military manpower.

REFERENCES

Franklin, James. 2008. "Shame on You." *International Studies Quarterly* 52(1): 187–211.

Hafner-Burton, Emilie. 2008. "Sticks and Stones." *International Organization* 62(4): 689–716.

Murdie, Amanda and Dursun Peksen. 2014. "The Impact of Human Rights INGO Shaming on Humanitarian Interventions." *Journal of Politics* 76(1): 215–228.

Spilker, Gabriele and Tobias Böhmelt. 2013. "The Impact of Preferential Trade Agreements on Governmental Repression Revisited." *Review of International Organizations* 8(3): 343–361.

Index

About the Author

Seung-Whan Choi is professor in the Department of Political Science at the University of Illinois at Chicago. His research interests include terrorism, human rights, conflict studies, and research methods. His work has been published in such major journals as the *American Journal of Political Science, British Journal of Political Science, International Studies Quarterly, Journal of Conflict Resolution, Journal of Peace Research,* and *Oxford Economic Papers*. He is the author of *New Explorations into International Relations: Democracy, Foreign Investment, Terrorism and Conflict* (2016) and coauthor (with Patrick James) of *Civil-Military Dynamics, Democracy, and International Conflict: A New Quest for International Peace* (2005).